John Phillips

D1712420

Photographs provided courtesy of Rossignol Inc., Atomic Ski Inc., Massanutten Resort, Timberline Resort, Wintergreen Resort, Ski Liberty, Big Boulders/Jack Frost Mountains, Seven Springs, Ski Denton, Elk River Touring Center, Sugar Mountain, Blue Mountain, Camelback, Hidden Valley, Whitetail, Snowshoe, Shawnee Mountain, and The Inn at Starlight Lake. A special thanks to Chip Chase at White Grass Touring Center for photographs and helpful information. Photographs also by John Phillips, Charles Samuels.

Printed in the United States of America by Automated Graphic Systems Inc.

Published by Beachway Press
9201 Beachway Lane
Springfield, VA 22153-1441

10 9 8 7 6 5 4 3 2 1

ISBN 1-882997-08-5

Library of Congress Cataloguing-in-Publication Data
    Phillips, John
    Mid-Atlantic Winter Sports Guide:
    1st ed. Springfield, VA: Beachway Press ©1997.
272 pages: Illustrations, Photographs, Maps, Graphics
1. Skiing, Snowboarding–Mid-Atlantic–Guidebooks.
Mid-Atlantic–Guidebooks

MID-ATLANTIC
winter sports
GUIDE

BEACHWAY PRESS
The Finest in Outdoor Adventure and Travel Guidebooks

TABLE OF CONTENTS

TABLE OF CONTENTS

Introduction 1
First, A Disclaimer... 1
Inside The Mid-Atlantic 1
Skiing: Past to Present 2
Snowboarding 3
Inside the Mid-Atlantic Winter Sports Guide 4
Information Sections 5
Cross-Country Skiing Destinations 7

Alpine Resorts 8
Mid-Atlantic Region Area Map 9
Resorts at a glance 10
Mileage Chart 12

Alpine Resorts: PENNSYLVANIA 14
Introduction and State Map 15
Major Alpine Resorts
1. Alpine Mountain 16
2. Big Boulder/Jack Frost 20
3. Blue Knob 26
4. Blue Mountain 31
5. Camelback 35
6. Doe Mountain 40
7. Elk Mountain 43
8. Hidden Valley Resort 48
9. Montage Mountain 52
10. Seven Springs 57
11. Shawnee Mountain 62
12. Ski Denton 66
13. Ski Liberty 71
14. Ski Roundtop 75
15. Whitetail 79

Other Alpine Ski Areas 85
16. Blue Marsh 86
17. Boyce Park 88
18. Mount Tone 90
19. Mystic Mountain 92
20. Mountain View at Edinboro 94
21. Ski Sawmill 96
In Addition: Laurel Mountain 98
22. Spring Mountain 99
23. Tanglwood 101
24. Tussey Mountain 103

Alpine Resorts: MARYLAND/WEST VIRGINIA 106
Introduction and State Map 107
Maryland:
25. Wisp 109
West Virginia:
26. Alpine Lake 114
27. Canaan Valley 116
28. New Winterplace 122
29. Snowshoe/Silver Creek 126
30. Timberline 135

Alpine Resorts: VIRGINIA 140
Introduction and State Map 141
31. Bryce 142
32. Massanutten 145
33. The Homestead 150
34. Wintergreen 153

Alpine Resorts: NORTH CAROLINA 158
Introduction and State Map 159
Major Alpine Resorts
35. Beech Mountain 160
36. Sugar Mountain 165

Other Alpine Ski Areas 170
37. Appalachian Ski Mountain 171
38. Cataloochee 174
39. Sapphire Valley 177
40. Scaly Mountain 179
41. Ski Hawksnest 181
42. Wolf Laurel 185

Cross-Country Skiing 190
Mid-Atlantic Area Map 191
Cross-Country Skiing: PENNSYLVANIA 192
Introduction and State Map 193
Pocono Mountain Lodging At A Glance 194
Cross-Country Ski Touring Centers
1. Evergreen Park at Penn Hills Resort 196
2. Laurel Ridge State Park 196
3. Hidden Valley 197
4. The Inn at Starlight Lake 198
5. Hanley's Happy Hill 199
6. Sterling Inn 201
7. Stone Valley Recreation Area 202
8. Callender's Windy Acre Farms 203

9. Crystal Lake Ski Center 204
10. Skytop Lodge 206
11. Camp Spears Eljabar/YMCA 207
12. Elk Valley Cross-Country Center 207

State Parks and Forests
Introduction 209
Southwest Pennsylvania:
13. Blue Knob State Park 209
14. Forbes State Forest 210
15. Kooser State Park 211
16. Ohiopyle State Park 212
In Addition: Pennsylvania's Laurel Highlands Region 212
South-Central Pennsylvania:
17. Caledonia State Park 213
18. Cowans Gap State Park 214
19. Gifford Pinchot State Park 214
Southeast Pennsylvania:
20. Delaware Canal State Park 215
Northeast Pennsylvania:
21. Lackawanna State Forest 216
North-Central Pennsylvania:
22. Elk State Forest 217
Northwest Pennsylvania:
23. Cook Forest State Park 218
24. Oil Creek State Park 218
Allegheney National Forest:
25. Laurel Mill Cross-country Ski Center/Hiking Area 219
26. Brush Hollow Cross-country Ski Center/Hiking Area 220
27. Westline Cross-country Ski Center/Hiking Area 221
In Addition: Pennsylvania's Northern Alleghenies 221

Cross-Country Skiing: MARYLAND/WEST VIRGINIA 222
Introduction and State Map 223
Maryland:
28. New Germany State Park 224
29. Herrington Manor State Park 225
Other State Parks and Forests
30. Cunningham Falls State Park 226
31. Patapsco Valley State Park 226
32. Greenbrier State Park 226
In Addition: Maryland's Ice Fishing 226
33. Gunpowder Falls State Park 227
West Virginia:
Cross-Country Ski Touring Centers
34. Alpine Lake Resort Nordic Center 227
35. Elk River Touring Center 228
36. White Grass Ski Touring Center 229

37. Canaan Valley Resort State Park 231
State Parks and Forests
38. Cathedral State Park 232
In Addition: Canaan Valley—Winter Paradise of the Allegheny 233
39. Blackwater Falls State Park 234
40. Babcock State Park 235
41. Pipestem Resort State Park 236
42. Watoga State Park 237
43. Coopers Rock State Forest 238
In Addition: Snowshoeing Can Be Fun 239

Cross-Country Skiing: VIRGINIA 240
Introduction and State Map 241
44. Shenandoah National Park: Skyline Drive 242
45. Mount Rogers National Recreation Area 243
46. Grayson Highlands State Park 244
47. Hungry Mother State Park 245
48. New River Trail State Park 246

Cross-Country Skiing: NORTH CAROLINA 248
Introduction and State Map 249
49. Blue Ridge Parkway, NC 250
50. Great Smoky Mountains National Park 251
51. Pisgah National Forest 252
52. Mount Mitchell State Park 252

Other Useful Stuff:
Glossary of Terms 255
Mid-Atlantic Ski Clubs 258

Index 260

About the Author 271

Special thanks to the following: *Chris Dennis for his editorial help, Dan Hartinger and Brian Moran for their photography and assistance, Keith Murlless for his insight into North Carolina skiing, Ned West for his expertise on Pennsylvania's Laurel Highlands region, Jeff Wright for his knowledge of the Pocono Mountain region, Alex Torres, Carl Ohlke, Vay McNeil, Marco DiPaul, Rich Lucera, Simon Webb, Scott Adams,*

ACKNOWLEDGEMENT

Chuck Samuels, Chip Chase at White Grass, Gil Willis at Elk River, Joe Stevens at Snowshoe, Steve McKnight at Blue Knob, Tim Tishner at Elk Mountain, Hank Montz at Montage, Gina Bertucci at Camelback, Missy Merrill at Ski Liberty, Rachel Nichols at Whitetail, Jerry Geisler at Wisp, Dave Zunker at Wintergreen, Bob McKinney at Mount Rogers, Terry Seyden at Pisgah National Forest, John Sharp at Mount Mitchell State Park, the Malinowski family for their computer support, my family, and my wife, Mary, for her patience.

INTRODUCTION

INTRODUCTION

First, A Disclaimer...

Relative to western and northeastern mountains, remaining ski regions just can't compare—the topography and natural conditions of the Rockies, Sierras, Cascades, and Vermont's Green Mountains offer unparalleled skiing. The Mid-Atlantic area, for one, has been cast aside from the U.S. ski scene with barely a hint of recognition. New England skiers derisively refer to the Mid-Atlantic as the "Banana Belt," loosely known by northerners as any ski resort located south of New York.

Although sporadic snowfall, washout rains, and severe fluctuations in temperatures and conditions riddle many mountains here in the "Banana Belt" numerous other Mid-Atlantic ski areas lie in higher-elevation, major snow-belt regions. West Virginia, for example, has an arctic micro-climate within its expansive Monongahela National Forest that allows four ski areas to operate with a primarily natural snow base. Snowfall here averages an amazing 150 to 180 inches per year. The same Great Lakes snow belt runs through Pennsylvania's Blue Knob, Seven Springs, and Hidden Valley, as well as Maryland's Wisp Resort. Little-known Ski Denton in northcentral Pennsylvania also averages over 100 inches of yearly snowfall. Even North Carolina gets its share—neighboring Beech and Sugar Mountain both average 70 to 80 inches per year at their 5,000-foot elevations (though snow stashes tend to be short-lived because of the warm Gulf Coast effect). *(See U.S. snowfall map on page 4).*

Inside The Mid-Atlantic

Most Mid-Atlantic ski areas, however, rely on advanced snowmaking systems in order to keep their lift tickets moving. Because weather patterns are so unpredictable, skiers and snowboarders are wise to bring goggles, hats, and scarves along for the trip. Snow guns may be firing just at the moment you hit the slopes, and it's often hard to predict when a sudden cold snap will hit a mountain or lingering winds will affect normal comfort zones.

Granted, the majority of these ski areas have vertical drops (the distance in altitude between the base of the ski area and its highest point) that are less than half of the New England giants—and an even further cry from Rocky Mountain, Sierra, and Cascade resorts. The one factor the region has in its favor is numbers. With so many resorts in easy reach of numerous urban centers, Mid-Atlantic skiers can pick and choose as they wish.

Though most "mountains" here are technically considered plateaus, plenty of steep trails exist for upper intermediate and advanced skiers, albeit mostly short-lived. Pennsylvania's Blue Knob, in the heart of the state's Laurel Highlands region, offers a spate of steeps that wind through glades, drop over headwalls, and skirt rocky, mountainous obstacles. West Virginia's Timberline is also expertly designed with numerous steep, tree-lined trails in the high country of Canaan Valley. And Pennsylvania's Elk and Montage Mountains host plenty of heavily pitched black diamond trails on their networks.

Experts who ski the Mid-Atlantic also know that the region is home to formidable mogul areas, which pro-

1

vide difficult bumpy track that's left ungroomed for advanced skiers to negotiate. The region's mogul terrain is further complicated by notorious "eastern ice," which tends to develop when the sun goes down and freezing temperatures set in.

It's the voluminous beginner terrain, though, for which the Mid-Atlantic is widely regarded. Advanced skiers may find a half-day is more than enough to satisfy them at many local resorts, but novices and intermediates have an overwhelming degree of smoothly groomed terrain available for learning and developing. Over 40 percent of skiers and snowboarders in the Mid-Atlantic rank their skills as beginner to intermediate, and the region serves as ideal training grounds for this crowd.

According to the National Ski Areas Association, over 700 ski areas existed in the U.S. during the mid-1980s. That number shrunk to just over 500 by the early 1990s. While other ski areas have faded over the years, over 50 Mid-Atlantic facilities have battled the barriers to make homes here, including the country's most recent major ski resort to open up shop—southern Pennsylvania's Whitetail Resort began selling lift tickets just seven years ago, attracting strong visitor bases in both Baltimore and Washington, DC.

Skiing: Past to Present

Origins

The original form of skiing is known as cross-country, or Nordic, which was crafted thousands of years ago in Scandinavia. Several 3,000-year-old models with leather bindings were uncovered here, and skis dating as far back to 2500 B.C. have been discovered in Siberia.

Over 1,500 years ago, inhabitants of Scandinavia, northern Russia, and Central Asia required an efficient means of transport during their long, snow-filled winters. Further evolution of the ski occurred as militaries in winter combat used them during the thirteenth and seventeenth centuries in Scandinavian regions, giving them a more efficient means of movement. In Norway, the first ski troopers began operating in 1747, using long, wooden ski boards and a pole for basic transportation through snow-covered mountains. From centuries of practical applications, skiing as sport was born.

Skiing As A Sport

Skiing was brought to America by Scandinavians in the early 1800s. It is believed to have taken hold when gold miners in California's Sierra Nevada mountains strapped on 12-foot skis made of solid oak—one long ski and one short—with a heavy pole used for push-off. Farther north in the Rockies, Idaho's Sun Valley holds the distinction as being the country's first ski area, opening in 1936 and having been inspired by Union Pacific Railroad president W. Averell Harriman.

The Mid-Atlantic was not without its own pioneers, as Pennsylvania's Big Boulder, the now-defunct Laurel Mountain, and Ski Roundtop did something few other resorts could offer. Each opened its mountain to skiing within reasonable drives of major metropolitan areas. And it's only fitting that a region plagued by fickle winter conditions is credited with helping to develop and refine an innovative artificial snowmaking system that would be used by ski areas throughout the country. Big Boulder was the first resort to commercially apply the system, devised by local inventor John Garish, who used a garden hose and varying water pressures to create one of the country's first snow guns.

Cross-Country Skiing

With the emergence of alpine skiing as a popular sport, Nordic skiing had become nearly a forgotten pastime from its humble Scandinavian origins. But lately its re-emergence is growing beyond its faithful coterie of followers. The physical benefits that cross-country offers far outweigh those of alpine skiing, requiring considerable stamina and strength over longer distances. The sport combines a full cardiovascular workout with a discovery of the great outdoors. When a strong natural snow base develops in their areas, Nordic skiers traverse woodland trails at designated touring centers, state parks and forests, and national recreation areas. Here they can encounter rugged topography, varied wildlife, and scenic vistas. But perhaps the most appealing aspect of Nordic skiing is that one can roam on just about any open surface with enough of a powder base. In fact, many skiers simply use parking lots, campgrounds, road shoulders, golf courses, or open fields.

This variation of skiing has generated substantial interest and become a major facet of the U.S. ski industry. Ski Fest—an annual celebration of cross-country skiing to be held at selected sites throughout the U.S. and Canada—will be featured at two Mid-Atlantic locations during the 1997-1998 season: Pennsylvania's Hidden Valley and West Virginia's White Grass Ski Touring Center. Ski Fest offers free lessons for first-time cross-country skiers, ski equipment and product demonstrations, and numerous events. You can find dates and further information on the World Wide Web at: **http://www.cross-countryski.org/skifest.html.**

As far as equipment is concerned, the difference between an alpine and Nordic ski is size, width and binding. Nordic skis are thinner and usually longer than alpine skis; and Nordic boots are attached to the skis only at the toe, allowing the heel to lift off, similar to a person's walking motion. A sticky wax coats the Nordic ski's base so that skiers can push off the ski and turn.

Telemark Skiing

While alpine skis have themselves undergone serious changes in design ("shaped" skis, also known as hourglass or parabolic skis, are designed to ease novice skiers into carving turns —a skill that most agree is more difficult to learn on standard skis), Nordic skis also have some interesting variations. Over a decade ago, ski skating was developed—a faster technique that involves using steps similar to ice-skating. In addition, Telemark skiing—its name derived from the Telemark district of Norway—is a variation of downhill skiing, but on Nordic skis. The "tele" turn is its distinguishing component: The outside ski is advanced ahead of the other, then turned inward at a continually widening angle through the carve. To facilitate this propulsive motion, Telemarkers use specially designed skis that are usually lighter and thinner than alpine skis. The sport's hybrid nature allows Telemark skiers to hit both backcountry trails and commercial downhill slopes.

This versatility has brought a wider range of skiers out to test their mettle on the slopes of Mid-Atlantic resorts, many of which permit Telemarking (though you're not likely to spot an abundance of Tele skiers on any alpine mountain).

Snowboarding

Snowboarding has not only taken the ski industry by storm—it's practically taken over as the number-one pastime among the ranks of young snow-sport enthusiasts. The American-bred sport was created in the 1960s by inventor Sherman Poppen, whose "Snurfer" was a popular toy-store item that sold over one million sets. Snurfers were made of wood, and steered by a rope attached to the front tip. The modern snowboard would be pioneered in the late 1970s when surfer Jake Burton teamed with champion skateboarders Tom Sims and Chuck Barfoot to design a single, metal-edged board that would run faster than skis and be able to carve mountains with ease. Burton picked up the idea when he jokingly participated in a ski resort Snurfer event, and later realized that a foot-retention device would allow more stability on the wooden board. He took his concept to Vermont's Stratton Mountain, incorporating into his designs steel edges and high-back foot bindings more familiar to skiers.

It took awhile for the U.S. ski industry to accept the alternative snowboard into its tradition-laced sport. As recently as 1985, only 7 percent of ski areas in the country permitted snowboards on their trail networks. Today just a small number of resorts still restrict boarding, and they're hard-pressed to ignore its economic potential. Like skis, modern snowboards come in varying sizes and weights, but differ depending on the style of rider, offering varying shapes and flex patterns. Boards are generally broken down into four types: race, alpine, free-riding, and freestyle, and nearly all are made of a wood core, fiberglass, and p-tex. Not surprisingly, the world's largest manufacturer and seller of snowboards is Jake Burton.

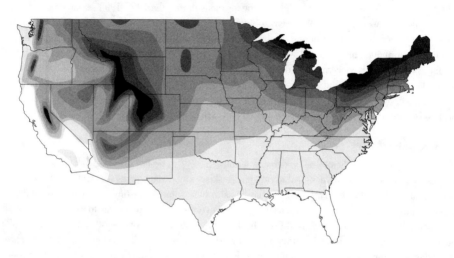

Average annual regional snowfall for the continental U.S.
(darker areas indicate heavier coverages)

Amazingly, snowboarding's growth shows no visible sign of slowing. It's estimated that more than 12 percent of the country's lift tickets sold during the 1996-97 season were to snowboarders, and the rate is growing each year. Boarders can either shred downhill slopes cutting giant-slalom turns, or roam "freestyle" in designated snowboard parks filled with obstacles made of hard-packed snow—or just about any "hits" the ski area will allow. Since ski areas generally prohibit dangerous jumping on their trails, snowboard parks allow freestylers the opportunity to catch air on obstacles such as gap jumps, spines, tabletops, slides, quarterpipes, ramps, and wales. While snowboard parks are more prevalent and easier to maintain, some resorts construct cylindrical trenches of hard-packed snow known as halfpipes—an idea taken from skateboard parks and ramps. Halfpipes are difficult to maintain, requiring an expensive grooming apparatus or the constant work of employees to keep them operating. A fair number of Mid-Atlantic ski areas offer halfpipes, though natural conditions often limit their availability.

Inside the Mid-Atlantic Winter Sports Guide:
Alpine Resorts

The major portion of this book comprises alpine (or downhill) ski areas. Each of the following 42 Mid-Atlantic ski area listings adopt the same format, with resorts in Pennsylvania, Maryland, West Virginia, Virginia, and North Carolina listed in alphabetical order. Because of the relatively large number of ski areas in Pennsylvania, the state is broken down into two categories: *Major Alpine Resorts* and *Other Alpine Ski Areas*. North Carolina, with eight ski areas, is classified similarly.

First, the ski area's address and all relevant phone numbers are listed, including any toll-free and direct ski reports, and numbers for information, lodging, or reservations. Credit cards accepted at the ski area are also identified, typically used for lift tickets, rentals, instruction, dining, and ski shop items. Next, Internet and E-mail addresses are provided by participating resorts. Skiers may use a resort's Internet address to find up-to-the-hour trail conditions, number of operating slopes and lifts, and other basic information about the ski area. E-mail is generally used to offer suggestions, complaints, or ask questions, and can be accessed via a separate address or inside the resort's Internet site.

The guide then provides the resort's daily operating hours, excluding holiday times, and the normal open and close dates during its ski seasons. Since weather patterns vary dramatically, open and close dates are based on the resort's average season.

Quick-reference mountain and resort statistics are also listed for each ski area; their definitions appear in the *Glossary of Terms* appendix. Readers can use these statistics to get a glimpse of the mountain's offerings, including elevation, vertical drop, breakdown of slopes and trails, longest run, average annual snowfall, percentage of snowmaking on the trail system, percentage of trails equipped for night skiing, number and type of lifts, and uphill capacity.

Information Sections

- **Getting There** displays full directions from regional metropolitan centers to the ski area.

- **Lift Tickets** provides the times and rates of daily lift passes, and indicates any reduced rates for children, seniors, group rates, midweek specials, and any other discount packages. Lift rates are generally priced relative to the size of the ski area's trail network and proximity to metropolitan areas. Though many Mid-Atlantic resorts seem pricey, there are some good ways to save money on lift tickets. Be sure to inquire about any discounts, special days, and group-skier discounts; and watch for ski coupons at supermarkets, ski shops, and in local newspapers. You can also cash in on reduced rates by joining a large group with a local ski club. Consult your local ski shop for a list of ski clubs in your area. Those who are trying skiing for the first time may wish to choose a smaller ski area, where lift tickets are more affordable, slopes are less crowded, and instruction may be more personalized.

- **Ski School** shows the number of full- or part-time instructors employed by the ski area. Most Mid-Atlantic instructors are PSIA certified (Professional Ski Instructors of America) and use the American Teaching System (ATS), which is among the most respected teaching systems in the world. The section goes on to display private and group instruction rates, and lists all adult and childrens' programs offered, with times and rates included. Many resorts offer learn-to-ski packages that include rental, lesson, and lift ticket, while others offer complementary group instruction for first-time skiers who rent skis or snowboards. Offered at selected resorts, SKIwee and MINIrider are *SKI* magazine-sponsored national programs aimed at introducing young children, generally aged four to 11, to skiing and snowboarding, and include instruction and supervision, optional lunch, and play time.

- **Adaptive Skier Program** indicates any available programs for physically disabled skiers.

- **Racing** lists any junior or adult programs offered for slalom racing. NASTAR (National Association of Standardized Racing) is a national racing program employed by many ski areas, which provides a designated trail with slalom gates for time-trial runs. Racing programs are displayed by the trail on which they are typically held, and include rates and times (often weekends only).

- **Calendar of Events** displays races, competitions, programs, festivals, demo days, or other events held annually.

- **Base/Summit Lodge Facilities** is a list of amenities offered at a ski area's lodge(s), typically including ski and rental shops, cafeterias/restaurants/lounges, specialty shops, lockers, and any other lodge features.

- **Day Care** lists operating child supervision hours and rates, if offered. This is an important consideration for parents whose children are too small for the slopes, or just don't care to ski. Day care is usually offered on weekends, with weekday hours at many larger resorts.

- **Other Winter Sports** lists any other recreation offered either at the resort or nearby, (excluding snowboarding, which warrants its own section). The list includes snow tubing, cross-country skiing, Telemark skiing, snowshoeing, snow skating, snowmobiling, ice fishing, ice-skating, horse-drawn sleigh rides, and sledding.

  For resorts with snow tubing parks, the book identifies the length of the tubing area, number of lanes, vertical drop (when available), type of uphill transport, ticket rates, and hours. For cross-country skiing, any on-site or nearby destinations are listed and cross-referenced to the second half of the book where readers will find full information on touring centers, state parks and forests, and national recreation areas. Telemark skiing, snowshoeing, and snow skating are listed if they are permitted on the resort's trail network, with rental and instruction rates provided when available. Snowmobiling, ice fishing, ice skating, horse-drawn sleigh rides, and sledding are featured with location and rental and instruction rates.

- **Lodging** displays all on-site and numerous nearby overnight accommodations, with locations and phone numbers provided. Lodging usually includes houses, townhouses, condominiums, chalets, inns, cabins, hotels/motels, and bed & breakfasts. Most on-site and nearby accommodations offer affordable ski-and-stay packages, some of which include meals and/or free lodging for children.

- **Dining/Après-ski** is a list of on-site and nearby eateries, lounges, and nightspots with locations and phone numbers listed.

  The text throughout each alpine skiing section offers a broad dissection of each ski area, including an analysis of slopes and trails relative to different skier abilities, average natural conditions, mountain topography, snowmaking capability, and typical resort crowds. It also offers historical tidbits, recommendations, and other pertinent information. Within most alpine-resort sections is a separate snowboarding segment, which examines the scope and details of available snowboarding terrain, including parks, terrain gardens, and halfpipes. It also features information on events, races, instructional programs, and equipment rentals.

Cross-Country Skiing Destinations

Immediately following the book's Alpine Resorts section is a second section on cross-country (Nordic) skiing. When natural snowfall is sufficient, cross-country skiing is available at designated touring centers, national and state parks and forests, and national recreation areas. Addresses and all relevant phone numbers are provided, as well as any Internet or E-mail addresses. Additionally, average annual snowfall and elevation are detailed for each area. Where applicable, cross-country ski touring centers are listed first, followed by state parks and forests; with states listed in the same order as in the alpine resorts section. Cross-country ski touring centers provide marked, groomed (track-set) trail systems for skiers, and generally offer rental equipment and/or instruction. Trails are groomed by tracking snowfall with snowmobiles, machines, or skis. Pennsylvania and West Virginia are the only states herein that offer touring centers.

State and national parks, forests, and recreation areas make up the remaining cross-country trail systems provided in the book. Multi-use hiking and skiing trails are available here, and often there is a park office on-site wherein guests can check in, obtain trail maps, and get necessary information. Office hours are generally from 8:30 a.m. to 4:00 p.m. Readers should remember that the addresses listed often identify the location of park headquarters, and not necessarily the site of the ski trails. While many headquarters are in the same general area as the trail systems, others are miles away, sometimes in more urban settings.

Pennsylvania's Laurel Ridge and several other state parks in West Virginia are equipped with their own cross-country touring centers, and as a result is listed under that section. A limited number of other state parks and forests in Pennsylvania, West Virginia and Maryland offer on-site concessions with rentals and/or instruction, as well as year-round cabin lodging, either fully equipped or primitive (without running water/bathrooms). The book also mentions, when available, nearby lodging options and phone numbers, including bed and breakfasts, resorts, inns, and hotels/motels. To a limited degree, restaurants and eateries are provided, with phone numbers.

Be sure to call touring center and park offices before departing to learn current snow conditions on the trail networks and on the roads leading to them. Their employees should also provide important trail information, such as any obstacles or barriers. Likewise, phone ahead to alpine ski areas for current conditions—or just to make sure they're open.

Happy trails!

ALPINE RESORTS

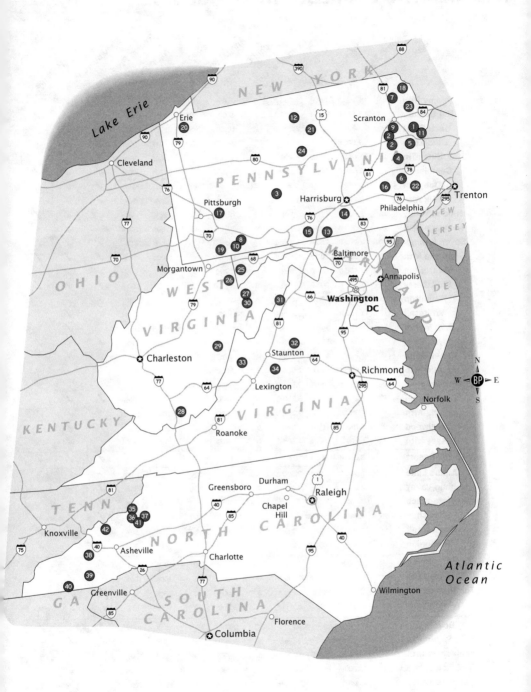

MID-ATLANTIC SKI RESORTS AT A GLANCE

	Slopes & Trails	Summit Elevation	Vertical Drop	Longest Run	Number of Lifts	Uphill Capacity	Avg Annual Snowfall	Snowmaking	Night Skiing	Racing Programs	Snowboard Park	Halfpipe
Alpine Mtn	18	1,150 ft	550 ft	3,500 ft	3	5,800	55"	100%	✗	✓	✓	✗
Big Boulder	13	2,175 ft	475 ft	2,900 ft	7	9,600	60"	100%	100%	✗	✓	✓
Jack Frost	20	2,000 ft	600 ft	3,200 ft	7	10,800	55"	100%	✗	✗	✓	✓
Blue Knob	34	3,172 ft	1,072 ft	9,200 ft	7	5,200	120"	72%	20%	✓	✗	✗
Blue Mtn	20	1,645 ft	1,082 ft	6,400 ft	7	8,400	25"	100%	100%	✓	✗	✗
Camelback	33	2,050 ft	800 ft	1 mi	12	18,600	40"	100%	80%	✓	✓	✓
Doe Mtn	15	1,100 ft	500 ft	1.5 mi	7	7,000	40"	100%	93%	✓	✓	✓
Elk Mtn	26	2,693 ft	1,000 ft	1.75 mi	6	5,400	50"	98%	30%	✓	✓	✗
Hidden Valley	17	3,000 ft	610 ft	1 mi	8	12,000	150"	98%	93%	✓	✓	✓
Montage Mtn	21	1,960 ft	1,000 ft	6,300 ft	7	8,300	45"	100%	100%	✓	✓	✗
Seven Springs	30	2,990 ft	750 ft	1.25 mi	18	24,600	100"	95%	75%	✓	✓	✓
Shawnee Mtn	23	1,350 ft	700 ft	5,100 ft	9	12,600	50"	100%	95%	✓	✓	✓
Ski Denton	20	2,400 ft	650 ft	1 mi	5	4,200	100"	95%	85%	✗	✗	✗
Ski Liberty	16	1,186 ft	606 ft	1 mi	8	10,920	28"	100%	100%	✓	✓	✓
Ski Roundtop	15	1,355 ft	600 ft	4,100 ft	10	11,000	30-40"	100%	93%	✓	✓	✓
Whitetail	17	1,800 ft	935 ft	1 mi	6	11,200	38"	100%	70%	✓	✓	✓
Blue Marsh	12	590 ft	300 ft	3,500 ft	5	5,400	35	100%	100%	✗	✓	✗
Boyce Park	9	1,232 ft	160 ft	1,300 ft	5	2,000	70"	100%	78%	✓	✗	✓
Mount Tone	9	n/a	450 ft	1,300 ft	4	n/a	65"	90%	55%	✗	✓	✗
Mystic Mtn	5	2,030 ft	300 ft	2,600 ft	2	2,000	100"	100%	100%	✗	✗	✗
Mountain View	9	1,550 ft	350 ft	2,800 ft	3	2,400	120"	60%	100%	✗	✗	✗
Ski Sawmill	8	2,215 ft	515 ft	3,250 ft	3	3,200	45"	100%	100%	✓	✓	✗
Spring Mtn	8	528 ft	420 ft	2,200 ft	4	8,000	35"	100%	100%	✗	✓	✓
Tanglwood	9	1,750 ft	415 ft	1 mi	5	4,300	65"	100%	100%	✗	✓	✗
Tussey Mtn	8	1,810 ft	500 ft	4,100 ft	4	4,800	48"	85%	85%	✓	✓	✓
Wisp Ski Resort	23	3,080 ft	610 ft	1.5 mi	7	9,120	91"	90%	90%	✓	✓	✓
Alpine Lake	6	3,000 ft	400 ft	3,300 ft	3	900	120"	90%	100%	✗	✗	✗
Canaan Valley	34	4,280 ft	850 ft	1.25 mi	3	6,100	155"	85%	30%	✓	✗	✗
New Winterplace	27	3,600 ft	603 ft	1.25 mi	9	13,000	100"	100%	90%	✓	✓	✗
Snowshoe	35	4,848 ft	1,500 ft	1.5 mi	7	12,200	180"	100%	✗	✓	✓	✗
Silvercreek	18	4,818 ft	670 ft	1 mi	5	7,000	180"	100%	40%	✓	✓	✓
Timberline	35	4,268 ft	1,000 ft	2 mi	3	4,000	150"	94%	30%	✓	✗	✓
Bryce	8	1,750 ft	500 ft	3,55- ft	5	2,500	30"	100%	90%	✓	✗	✗
Massanutten	14	2,880 ft	1,110 ft	4,100 ft	5	6,350	30"	100%	100%	✓	✓	✗
The Homestead	10	3,200 ft	700 ft	4,200 ft	5	3,000	50"	100%	70%	✓	✓	✓
Wintergreen	17	3,515 ft	1,003 ft	1.4 mi	5	8,200	40"	100%	70%	✓	✓	✗
Beech Mtn	14	5,505 ft	830 ft	5,000 ft	9	8,400	62"	100%	100%	✓	✗	✗
Sugar Mtn	18	5,300 ft	1,200 ft	1.5 mi	8	8,800	78"	100%	90%	✓	✗	✗
Appalachian Mtn	9	4,000 ft	400 ft	2,700 ft	5	n/a	60"	100%	100%	✗	✗	✗
Cataloochee	9	5,400 ft	740 ft	4,000 ft	3	2,200	55"	100%	100%	✓	✗	✗
Sapphire Valley	4	4,800 ft	425 ft	2,400 ft	2	n/a	n/a	100%	100%	✗	✗	✗
Scaly Mtn	3	4,025 ft	225 ft	1,080 ft	2	1,500	25"	100%	100%	✗	✗	✗
Ski Hawksnest	13	4,819 ft	619 ft	2,600 ft	4	3,200	80"	100%	100%	✓	✓	✗
Wolf Laurel	14	4,650 ft	700 ft	1 mi	3	2,200	60"	100%	100%	✓	✓	✓

PENNSYLVANIA RESORTS

MD

W. VIRGINIA

VIRGINIA

NORTH CAROLINA

Sledding	Snow Tubing	Snowmobile Trails	XC Ski Trails	XC Rentals	XC Lessons	SKIwee Program	Adaptive Ski Prgm	Day Care	On-site Lodging	On-site Restaurant	On-site Lounge/Pub	Hiking Trails	Mtn Biking	Golf Course
✗	✓	✓	nearby	✗	✗	✗	✓	✓	✓	✓	✓	✗	✗	nearby
✗	✓	✗	✓	✓	✓	✗	✗	✓	✓	✓	✓	✓	✗	✗
✗	✓	✓	✓	✓	✓	✗	✗	✓	✓	✓	✓	✓	✓	✗
✗	✗	✗	✓	✓	✗	✗	✗	✓	✓	✓	✓	✓	✓	✓
✗	✓	✗	✗	✗	✗	✓	✓	✓	✗	✓	✓	✓	✗	✗
✗	✓	✗	nearby	✗	✗	✗	✗	✓	✗	✓	✓	✓	✓	✓
✗	✓	✗	✗	✗	✗	✗	✗	✓	✗	✓	✓	✗	✗	✗
✗	✗	✗	nearby	✗	✗	✓	✗	✓	✗	✓	✓	✓	✗	✗
✗	✓	✗	✓	✓	✓	✗	✗	✓	✓	✓	✓	✓	✓	✓
✗	✗	✗	nearby	✗	✗	✓	✗	✗	✗	✓	✓	✓	✗	✗
✓	✓	✗	nearby	✗	✗	✗	✗	✓	✓	✓	✓	✓	✗	✗
✗	✓	✗	nearby	✗	✗	✓	✓	✓	✓	✓	✓	✗	✗	✗
✗	✓	✗	✓	✓	✗	✓	✓	✓	✗	✓	✓	✗	✗	✗
✗	✗	✗	✗	✗	✗	✗	✓	✓	✓	✓	✓	✗	✗	✗
✗	✓	✗	nearby	✗	✗	✗	✗	✓	✓	✗	✓	✗	✗	✗
✗	✗	✗	✗	✗	✗	✗	✓	✓	✓	✓	✓	✗	✓	✗
✗	✓	✗	✗	✗	✗	✓	✗	✗	✗	✓	✓	✗	✗	✗
✗	✗	✗	nearby	✗	✗	✗	✗	✗	✗	✓	✓	✗	✗	✗
✓	✗	✗	✓	✓	✗	✗	✗	✗	✗	✓	✗	✗	✗	✗
✗	✓	✗	✓	✓	✗	✗	✗	✗	✓	✓	✗	✗	✗	✗
✗	✗	✗	✓	✓	✗	✗	✗	✗	✓	✓	✓	✓	✓	✓
✗	✗	✗	nearby	✗	✗	✗	✗	✗	✗	✓	✗	✗	✗	✗
✗	✗	✗	✗	✗	✗	✗	✗	✓	✓	✓	✓	✗	✗	✗
✗	✗	✗	✗	✗	✗	✗	✗	✗	✗	✓	✗	✗	✗	✗
nearby	✗	nearby	nearby	✗	✗	✓	✗	✗	✓	✓	✓	✗	✗	✗
✗	✓	✗	nearby	✗	✗	✗	✗	✗	✗	✓	✓	✗	✗	✓
nearby	✗	nearby	nearby	✗	✗	✓	✗	✓	✓	✓	✓	✓	✓	nearby
✓	✗	✗	✓	✓	✓	✗	✗	✗	✓	✓	✓	✗	✗	✗
✗	✗	✗	✓	✓	✓	✓	✗	✓	✓	✓	✓	✓	✓	✗
✗	✓	✗	nearby	✗	✗	✓	✗	✓	✓	✓	✓	✗	✗	✗
✗	✗	✗	nearby	✗	✗	✗	✗	✓	✓	✓	✓	✓	✓	✗
✗	✗	✗	nearby	✗	✗	✗	✓	✓	✓	✓	✓	✗	✗	✗
nearby	✗	✗	✓	✓	✓	✓	✗	✓	✓	✓	✓	✓	✗	nearby
✗	✗	✗	✗	✗	✗	✓	✗	✓	✓	✓	✓	✗	✓	✓
✗	✓	✗	✗	✗	✗	✓	✓	✗	✓	✓	✓	✓	✓	✓
✗	✗	✓	✓	✓	✗	✗	✗	✗	✓	✓	✓	✗	✗	✗
✗	✗	✗	✗	✗	✗	✗	✓	✓	✓	✓	✓	✓	✓	✓
✗	✓	✗	nearby	✗	✗	✓	✗	✓	✓	✓	✓	✓	✗	✗
✗	✗	✗	✗	✗	✗	✗	✗	✗	✓	✓	✓	✓	✗	✓
✗	✗	✗	nearby	✗	✗	✓	✓	✓	✓	✓	✓	✗	✗	✗
✗	✗	✗	nearby	✗	✗	✗	✗	✗	✓	✓	✓	✓	✗	✗
✗	✗	✗	✗	✗	✗	✗	✗	✗	✗	✓	✓	✗	✗	✗
✗	✗	✗	nearby	✗	✗	✗	✗	✗	✓	✓	✓	✓	✗	✗
✓	✓	✗	nearby	✗	✗	✗	✗	✗	✗	✓	✓	✓	✗	✗

MID-ATLANTIC SKI RESORTS MILEAGE FROM MAJOR CITIE

Region	Resort	PA Harrisburg	PA Philadelphia	PA Pittsburgh	DE Wilmington	DE Dover	NJ Atlantic City	NJ Lakewood	NY New York City	NY Albany	NY Syracuse	MD Baltimore	MD Cumberland	MD Frederick	MD Salisbury	DC Washington, DC	VA Charlottesville	VA Fredericksburg	VA Norfolk	VA Richmond	VA Roanoke	WV Bluefield	WV Charleston	WV Huntington	WV Martinsburg	WV Morgantown	WV Parkersburg	OH Cincinnati
PENNSYLVANIA RESORTS	Alpine Mtn	134	112	313	175	129	174	118	169	89	159	202	267	209	233	240	348	299	446	352	431	527	480	544	228	339	481	596
	Big Boulder	111	102	288	164	118	164	127	196	97	166	192	244	186	223	231	325	284	243	338	408	504	467	521	205	316	458	571
	Jack Frost	111	102	288	164	118	164	127	196	97	166	192	244	186	223	231	325	284	243	338	408	504	467	521	205	316	458	571
	Blue Knob	116	217	90	233	211	279	275	410	294	364	166	53	118	271	163	200	210	358	264	283	341	276	330	105	125	267	392
	Blue Mtn	107	85	307	148	102	147	118	199	110	187	175	240	182	206	213	321	272	419	325	404	500	463	517	201	312	454	574
	Camelback	119	111	296	173	127	173	122	191	93	164	200	251	194	232	239	333	297	445	351	416	512	474	528	212	324	466	579
	Doe Mtn	76	61	276	124	78	123	133	227	111	207	134	208	151	182	174	286	227	374	281	373	469	431	485	169	281	423	548
	Elk Mtn	144	145	321	208	162	207	168	174	139	111	225	276	219	266	264	358	317	465	371	441	537	499	553	237	349	491	603
	Hidden Valley	143	244	60	261	238	306	302	438	321	392	194	58	145	299	191	227	238	385	291	310	279	214	268	133	60	207	332
	Montage Mtn	126	127	303	190	144	190	41	185	121	129	207	259	201	249	246	340	299	447	353	423	519	482	536	220	331	473	586
	Seven Springs	150	250	60	267	244	313	308	444	327	398	200	53	152	305	197	233	244	392	298	316	278	213	267	139	60	206	332
	Shawnee Mtn	56	162	157	178	156	224	220	328	234	270	142	127	118	255	182	231	210	358	264	314	410	350	404	111	200	341	466
	Ski Denton	163	266	202	295	244	328	315	259	276	155	249	217	244	353	289	364	342	489	368	447	483	418	472	236	265	364	465
	Ski Liberty	49	139	184	152	132	202	197	345	228	299	64	105	35	170	81	167	128	276	182	250	346	328	382	47	177	291	456
	Ski Roundtop	15	109	205	119	87	171	167	310	194	264	70	137	73	182	109	221	162	310	216	302	398	360	414	98	209	351	476
	Whitetail	77	178	157	187	176	240	236	372	255	326	97	75	49	202	94	162	141	288	195	245	341	298	352	41	148	262	428
	Blue Marsh	49	99	241	125	90	161	148	262	145	224	130	181	124	194	169	263	222	370	276	346	445	404	458	142	254	396	521
	Boyce Park	195	295	21	312	289	357	353	489	372	376	245	109	197	350	242	278	289	436	343	361	295	230	224	184	77	190	315
	Mount Tone	137	130	313	193	147	192	141	187	113	138	217	269	212	257	257	350	310	457	364	443	530	492	546	230	341	483	596
	Mystic Mtn	159	360	74	268	267	322	318	454	337	408	188	38	140	293	185	196	232	379	286	279	267	202	256	127	52	166	335
	Mountain View	281	405	114	403	380	467	454	397	414	257	359	223	310	464	356	392	403	550	456	440	400	335	389	298	184	255	336
	Ski Sawmill	113	217	221	245	199	279	266	257	226	154	200	177	194	303	239	328	392	440	346	411	465	400	454	207	249	390	504
	Spring Mtn	104	36	304	99	53	98	89	231	115	222	126	237	180	195	222	126	237	180	276	401	497	460	514	198	309	451	576
	Tanglwood	159	130	336	193	147	193	134	159	97	160	220	291	234	251	259	373	317	465	371	456	513	514	568	252	365	506	619
	Tussey Mtn	83	188	141	205	182	251	246	324	223	266	169	114	150	281	208	261	242	390	296	344	402	337	391	142	196	304	429
MD	Wisp Ski Resort	188	281	85	274	273	343	339	474	358	428	194	45	146	299	191	187	238	386	292	243	259	194	248	133	43	157	352
W. VIRGINIA	Alpine Lake	202	303	117	296	295	365	361	496	379	450	216	67	168	321	213	185	196	343	250	239	236	171	225	127	33	136	345
	Canaan Valley	200	301	123	268	293	363	359	494	378	448	214	65	166	293	170	158	192	323	223	212	236	175	229	123	68	149	384
	New Winterplace	379	463	267	418	432	517	522	673	551	628	359	258	311	443	317	195	260	360	261	104	34	78	132	282	188	161	285
	Snowshoe	284	368	195	323	337	422	427	579	456	533	264	132	217	349	222	115	179	279	180	146	157	147	201	188	116	180	354
	Silvercreek	284	368	195	323	337	422	427	579	456	533	264	132	217	349	222	115	179	279	180	146	157	147	201	188	116	180	354
	Timberline	215	316	138	281	308	378	374	509	393	463	229	80	181	306	180	147	184	312	212	201	222	176	230	138	76	152	392
VIRGINIA	Bryce	193	276	262	232	245	330	335	487	364	441	172	133	125	257	131	97	117	262	162	151	247	278	332	78	188	302	484
	Massanutten	175	258	244	214	228	312	317	469	346	423	155	115	107	239	113	46	88	203	103	112	208	239	293	96	206	238	446
	The Homestead	271	354	243	310	325	409	413	565	443	519	251	146	203	335	209	89	154	259	154	72	141	159	213	174	164	242	366
	Wintergreen	231	286	300	230	255	340	345	525	374	479	182	171	163	255	140	20	85	185	85	101	197	228	282	134	244	310	434
NORTH CAROLINA	Beech Mtn	450	534	405	489	503	588	593	744	622	698	430	391	382	514	388	266	331	362	332	160	120	216	270	353	326	299	361
	Sugar Mtn	463	547	418	502	516	601	606	758	635	712	443	404	396	528	401	280	344	371	345	174	134	229	283	366	339	312	352
	Appalachian Mtn	466	549	408	505	519	603	608	760	637	714	446	406	398	530	404	282	347	353	323	166	123	219	273	369	329	302	352
	Cataloochee	581	664	552	620	634	719	723	875	753	829	561	522	513	588	512	397	476	451	421	291	221	363	315	484	473	446	331
	Sapphire Valley	592	676	563	631	645	730	735	887	764	841	572	533	525	599	530	409	488	462	432	303	232	374	325	496	484	457	406
	Scaly Mtn	631	714	601	670	684	768	773	925	803	879	611	571	563	638	569	447	526	501	470	341	267	413	396	534	522	496	370
	Ski Hawksnest	495	578	437	534	548	632	637	789	666	743	475	435	427	559	433	311	376	385	355	195	152	248	302	398	358	331	358
	Wolf Laurel	563	647	456	602	616	701	706	858	735	812	543	447	496	570	501	380	459	433	403	274	160	267	254	467	377	350	384

OH				KY			TN					NC						SC				FL					GA				
Cleveland	Columbus	Dayton	Toledo	Bowling Green	Lexington	Louisville	Chattanooga	Knoxville	Johnson City	Nashville	Memphis	Asheville	Charlotte	Fayetteville	Raleigh/Durham	Winston-Salem	Wilmington	Columbia	Charleston	Greenville	Florence	Jacksonville	Miami	Orlando	Tallahassee	Tampa	Atlanta	Augusta	Albany	Columbus	Savannah
393	493	564	491	811	668	694	834	723	606	875	1080	676	611	569	524	537	610	702	784	706	657	966	1300	1103	1117	1160	846	768	1024	952	828
368	468	539	466	786	645	669	811	700	583	850	1052	653	588	554	509	514	118	679	769	683	643	951	1286	1089	1094	1145	823	745	1001	929	813
368	468	539	466	786	645	669	811	700	583	850	1052	653	588	554	509	514	118	679	769	683	643	951	1286	1089	1094	1145	823	745	1001	929	813
211	289	366	310	607	454	490	685	574	458	671	873	527	463	480	435	387	521	553	670	558	569	852	1187	989	968	1046	697	620	875	289	714
390	476	553	488	794	641	677	807	696	579	858	1060	649	584	541	496	510	582	675	757	679	630	938	1273	1076	1096	1132	819	741	997	925	800
376	475	546	474	794	653	677	818	767	591	858	1060	660	596	567	522	522	608	687	782	691	656	964	1299	1102	1102	1158	831	753	1009	937	826
397	445	522	495	763	610	646	775	664	548	827	1029	617	553	497	452	478	538	644	712	648	585	894	1229	1031	1059	1088	788	710	966	445	756
400	500	571	499	819	678	702	843	732	616	883	1085	685	621	587	542	547	628	712	802	716	675	984	1319	1121	1127	1178	856	778	7034	500	846
182	230	307	280	547	392	430	580	469	394	611	813	497	433	508	463	387	549	523	640	528	596	822	1157	959	939	1016	668	590	846	774	684
383	483	554	481	801	660	684	826	715	598	865	1067	668	603	569	524	529	610	694	784	698	658	966	1301	1104	1109	1160	838	760	1016	944	828
181	229	306	279	547	392	430	579	468	393	611	813	497	432	514	467	387	555	523	639	527	602	821	1156	959	938	1015	667	589	845	773	683
282	364	441	380	682	529	565	717	606	489	746	948	559	494	480	435	420	521	585	695	589	569	877	1212	1015	1000	1071	729	651	907	835	739
251	362	433	360	680	543	563	823	718	622	744	948	691	627	612	567	552	653	717	827	722	700	1009	1343	1146	1133	1203	862	784	1040	968	871
305	353	430	404	667	506	554	653	642	425	725	929	495	430	398	353	356	439	521	613	525	487	795	1130	933	936	989	665	587	843	771	657
374	376	451	424	692	539	575	704	593	477	756	958	546	482	432	387	407	473	572	647	577	520	829	1164	966	998	1023	716	639	894	823	691
278	326	403	376	638	477	527	647	536	420	702	904	489	425	411	366	350	452	515	626	520	499	808	1143	945	930	1002	659	582	837	766	670
370	418	495	468	736	583	619	748	638	521	800	1002	590	526	492	447	457	533	451	707	621	581	890	1224	1027	1032	1082	761	683	939	867	751
139	212	289	237	530	393	413	596	485	410	594	796	514	449	559	514	404	600	540	656	544	556	838	1173	976	955	1032	684	606	862	790	700
393	493	564	491	811	670	694	836	725	608	875	1077	678	613	580	535	538	620	704	795	709	668	976	1311	1114	1119	1171	848	771	1026	955	839
210	232	309	308	542	381	453	568	457	382	606	818	486	421	502	456	376	543	512	629	516	590	810	1145	948	927	1040	656	578	834	763	672
91	233	304	207	551	414	434	694	589	515	615	817	618	554	673	628	508	714	644	761	649	661	943	1278	1080	1059	1137	788	711	966	897	805
301	401	472	399	719	582	602	813	702	586	783	985	655	591	562	517	516	603	681	777	686	650	959	1294	1096	1096	1153	825	748	1003	932	821
425	473	550	524	791	638	674	804	693	576	855	1057	646	576	493	448	514	534	657	708	671	581	890	1224	1027	1058	1084	810	724	946	917	752
416	515	586	514	834	693	717	858	747	631	898	1100	700	636	587	542	561	727	802	731	675	984	1319	1121	1142	1178	871	793	1049	977	846	
247	346	417	345	646	516	528	747	636	519	709	911	586	524	512	467	449	553	615	727	619	600	909	1124	1046	1030	1103	759	681	937	865	771
222	250	327	320	533	372	445	560	449	374	597	799	477	413	508	463	367	549	503	620	508	520	802	1137	939	918	996	647	570	825	754	664
236	243	320	334	511	350	422	537	426	351	575	777	455	390	466	355	345	507	393	443	427	317	625	960	763	794	819	567	459	682	673	487
260	281	358	358	515	354	426	537	426	651	579	781	457	392	440	328	318	481	483	599	487	439	781	1116	919	898	975	627	549	805	733	643
341	240	272	392	418	257	329	335	224	149	407	611	253	188	262	246	143	373	279	395	283	295	577	912	716	694	771	423	345	601	529	439
314	321	341	412	487	326	399	458	347	272	530	753	376	311	333	296	266	437	402	518	406	418	700	1035	838	817	894	546	468	724	652	562
314	321	341	412	487	326	399	458	347	272	530	753	376	311	333	296	266	437	402	518	406	418	700	1035	838	817	894	546	468	724	652	562
282	289	366	381	516	355	427	523	412	337	580	782	446	381	429	317	307	470	472	588	476	428	770	1105	908	887	964	616	538	794	722	632
366	414	491	464	617	456	529	553	442	326	625	829	395	331	378	267	257	419	422	538	426	378	720	1055	858	837	914	566	488	744	672	582
383	379	432	482	578	417	490	515	404	287	587	791	357	292	319	228	218	360	383	499	387	339	681	1016	819	798	875	527	449	705	633	543
361	321	353	460	499	333	410	442	331	247	514	718	317	252	259	223	178	350	343	460	347	311	642	977	779	758	836	487	410	665	594	504
421	389	421	520	567	406	479	503	393	276	575	779	345	281	301	189	188	342	371	488	376	300	670	1005	807	786	864	516	438	693	622	532
479	378	413	530	339	282	358	260	149	47	332	236	106	129	213	196	95	324	220	337	152	236	519	853	656	565	713	294	287	472	401	381
492	391	403	558	330	273	349	251	140	38	323	527	96	137	221	205	104	332	237	348	142	244	530	865	667	555	737	284	270	462	391	392
482	381	412	533	348	277	349	269	158	26	341	545	97	120	203	187	86	314	211	327	143	227	509	844	647	556	703	285	277	463	392	371
578	434	383	538	270	253	329	153	80	102	263	467	38	168	279	285	184	394	186	297	91	263	479	813	616	446	628	175	219	353	282	341
637	510	458	613	345	328	404	175	155	117	338	542	53	378	321	296	195	367	159	269	60	236	452	786	589	427	609	156	165	334	263	314
616	473	422	577	279	292	368	151	119	152	280	484	88	181	338	335	234	384	176	287	80	253	464	784	563	392	576	121	175	299	228	331
511	410	409	564	336	279	355	257	146	44	329	533	78	119	213	219	118	346	219	330	124	226	512	847	649	537	719	266	252	444	373	374
530	371	454	591	323	306	382	244	133	45	316	520	19	155	262	267	166	395	173	284	78	250	466	800	603	491	673	220	206	398	326	328

13

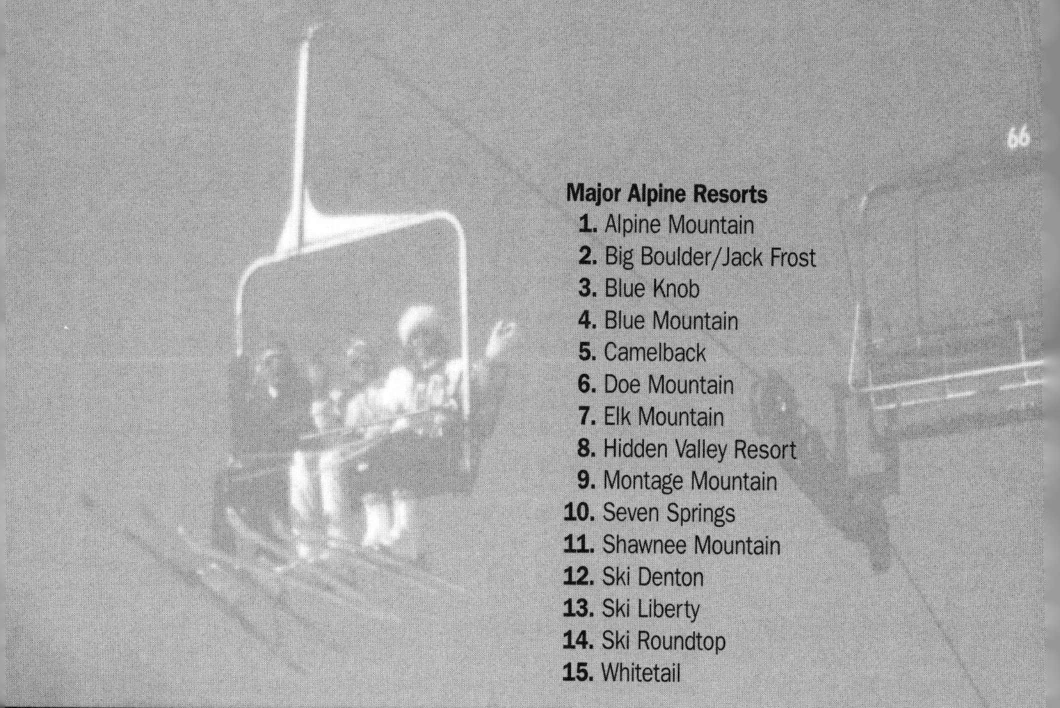

66

Major Alpine Resorts
1. Alpine Mountain
2. Big Boulder/Jack Frost
3. Blue Knob
4. Blue Mountain
5. Camelback
6. Doe Mountain
7. Elk Mountain
8. Hidden Valley Resort
9. Montage Mountain
10. Seven Springs
11. Shawnee Mountain
12. Ski Denton
13. Ski Liberty
14. Ski Roundtop
15. Whitetail

ALPINE RESORTS:
PENNSYLVANIA

Other Alpine Ski Areas
16. Blue Marsh
17. Boyce Park
18. Mount Tone
19. Mystic Mountain
20. Mountain View at Edinboro
21. Ski Sawmill
In Addition: Laurel Mountain
22. Spring Mountain
23. Tanglwood
24. Tussey Mountain

14

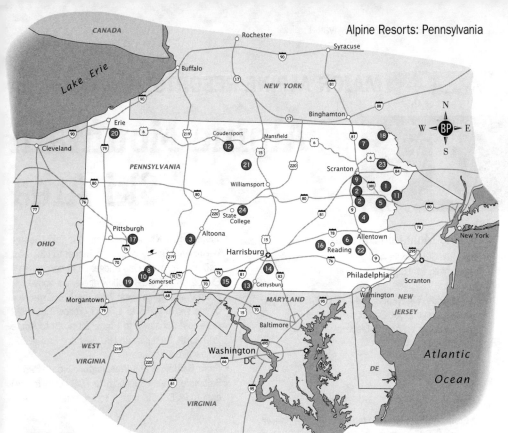

W ith over 30 ski areas, Pennsylvania currently ranks third among all states in total alpine ski facilities, behind New York (59) and Michigan (43). (Downhill giant Colorado has 28 sprawling resorts.) Most of Pennsylvania's ski areas are clustered inside or near the tourist-laden Pocono Mountain range, while a batch of resorts lie in the bountiful snow region of the Laurel Highlands, located one hour southeast of Pittsburgh. A handful of others are scattered throughout the state, including southern Pennsylvania's Liberty, Roundtop, and Whitetail, which attract mammoth skier markets from nearby Washington, DC and Baltimore.

After the state's first private slopes and chair lift opened in what would later become mega-resort Seven Springs, the first commercial ski areas began to surface in the 1950s. Though its mountains and plateaus were but small bumps compared to what was being offered in New England, several eastern Pennsylvania ski areas established themselves, as skeptics scoffed at the notion of skiing in the "Banana Belt"—a region deemed more suitable for agriculture than skiing. Big Boulder brought several metropolitan areas to the forefront of alpine skiing, relying on a pioneering snowmaking system that was first developed on its mountain. Now-closed Laurel Mountain had a more naturally conducive location, serving Pittsburgh-area skiers during its heyday in the 1950s with the benefit of over 100 inches of snowfall per year. As the 1970s rolled around, an onslaught of ski areas opened—primarily in the Poconos—to a demanding number of Mid-Atlantic skiers. *See Pocono Mountain Lodging list on page 194.*

Today the state is highly regarded for its beginner to intermediate mountains, with abundant bunny terrain and smooth, well-groomed novice track. Nearly all of its ski areas offer solid instruction that caters to young and old alike. And nine resorts host the nationally recognized SKIwee program—a *SKI* magazine-sponsored childrens' training program that combines teaching, supervision, and play time.

What many Mid-Atlantic skiers don't realize is that upper intermediate to advanced skiing does exist in Pennsylvania—albeit in somewhat limited quantities. Trail networks filled with diverse, challenging terrain can be found at Blue Knob, Seven Springs, Elk, Montage, and Blue Mountain. And strong intermediate trails surround some surprisingly steep terrain at numerous other areas, including Ski Denton, Jack Frost, and Camelback.

15

MAJOR ALPINE RESORTS: PENNSYLVANIA

Alpine Mountain Ski Area

Alpine Mountain Ski Area

P.O. Box 309, Route 447
Analomink, PA 18320

Information/Ski Report: (717) 595-2150
Reservations: 1-800-233-8240
Credit Cards: VISA, MC, Discover
Operating Hours:
8 a.m.-5 p.m. daily
Season: December to March

Getting There

- **From southern NJ:** Take the Garden State Parkway north to 287 north to I-80 west to PA Exit 52. Take Exit 52 off I-80 west, then left onto Route 447 north. Follow Route 447 10 miles to Alpine Mtn.

- **From metro NY and northern NJ:** Take George Washington Bridge or Lincoln Tunnel to I-80 west to Delaware Water Gap Bridge. From here take PA Exit 52 off I-80 west. Follow directions above.

- **From Philadelphia area:** Take the N.E. Extension of the PA Turnpike to Exit 33. Follow Route 22 east past Allentown to Route 33 north to Route 209 north, then pick up I-80 east and PA Exit 52. Follow directions above.

- **From Baltimore and Washington:** From I-695 in Baltimore, take I-83 north to I-81 north to I-80 east to PA Exit 52, then follow directions above.

Background

A rguably the least-visited of the many Pocono ski areas, Alpine Mountain can promise two things: You won't lose sight of anyone in your group, and you'll ski the trails five times over in a day without losing time waiting in lines. The resort is also one of Pennsylvania's oldest ski areas, having opened up shop here in the southern Poconos during the late 1950s under the name Timber Hill Ski Area. Ownership changed hands in 1983, taking on Alpine Mountain as its new moniker.

Though it markets mostly intermediate terrain, Alpine Mountain falls into the beginner category, with straight, wide trails over just 500 feet of vertical drop. Its strength more realistically lies in its varied winter activities, both on-site and just off the mountain. In conjunction with Wilderness Recreations, the resort maintains a snowmobiling center and rental shop on its own course served by 100 percent snowmaking. Additionally, a new snow tubing facility has been added to the mountain, snowboarders have a park filled with aerial obstacles, and snow skaters are welcome on the trails, with skate rentals available. Nearby at Evergreen Park, a cross-country skiing center operates when a five-inch snow base covers its nine-hole golf course. Penn Hills Resort offers ice-skating with rentals and lessons in its indoor rink as well.

Mountain Stats

Base Elevation: 600 feet
Summit Elevation: 1,150 feet
Vertical Drop: 550 feet
Longest Run: 3,500 feet
Primary Slope Direction: North to northeast
Slopes and Trails: 3 beginner, 10 intermediate,
  5 advanced
Skiable Terrain: 60 acres
Lifts: 2 quad, 1 double

Uphill Capacity: 5,800 skiers per hour
Average Annual Snowfall: 55 inches
  1995-96 season: 110 inches
Skiable Days:
  1995-96 season: 100
  1994-95 season: 95
Snowmaking: 100% of area
Night Skiing: None

As for downhill skiing, Alpine is a small, single-face mountain with 18 short slopes and trails, three of which were cut four years ago. Its gentle terrain caters to a primary skier base of families, as well as scout, school, and church groups. Just seven trails flow from the summit, with numerous built-in connector slopes and cat tracks. Despite its lackluster reputation among Pocono resorts, Alpine is an ideal place for newer skiers. Many guests just learning the sport will find their confidence rising as they ski most of the trails, no matter what the difficulty rating.

Trail Profiles

There aren't many options here for skiers seeking advanced terrain. Alpine's five black diamond trails are nothing short of simple cruising runs. The exception is *The Bumps*—an extension of the intermediate *Roller Coaster* trail that serves up modestly sized moguls on a fairly steep, straight drop, finishing near the base lodge. The mountain's left side holds Alpine's two most challenging runs. *Power Line* and intermediate *Outer Edge* have a few steep dips and partial turns built into the terrain.

Beginners won't be let down with the trail network's wide and nicely groomed track. *Alpine Way* is a 3,500-foot novice cruising run that offers a panoramic view of the Pocono Mountains from its summit and a running creek at its base. It uses all 500 feet of Alpine's vertical drop on gentle, rolling terrain that's nearly 100 feet wide. Carving the intermediates on the mountain's right side won't be too difficult either. They're pitched only slightly steeper than the green runs, and wide enough to negotiate any gradual turns.

You might guess a resort such as this would have extensive bunny hill areas for kids and uninitiated adults. Surprisingly, there isn't much

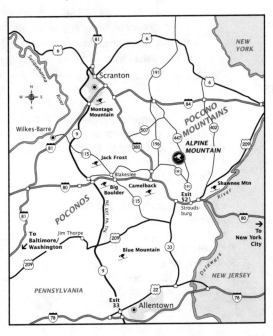

available. The two areas in front of the base lodge reserved for learning skiers are less than spacious and situated inappropriately at the runout of four steeper, faster trails. What the resort lacks in beginner terrain is made up for in childrens' instruction programs, which serve two different age groups. Alpine also offers free winter start specials leading up to the Christmas holidays, including complementary beginner lessons and rentals on selected days.

Snowboarding

Alpine Mountain converted its secluded intermediate *Rockaway* trail into the Original Sin Snowboard Park for the 1996-97 season. Employees and snowboarders combined to create a snowboard only park with 20 changing obstacles that included jumps, gaps, spines, and wales. The park has a decent downhill pitch and a width nearly equal to its length, which means there's ample room for runouts. Regrettably, it operates during day hours only, like the rest of the mountain, and boarders have to negotiate the park without a lift. Unless you have undying energy, be prepared to trek over to the Alpine quad chair, reach the summit, and carve back down the mountain's right side to get back to the park.

The resort is otherwise conducive to boarders, holding numerous races and events from December through February, including the eight-year-running Ski and Snowboard Bump Contest in January. All slopes are open for boarding, though many use the trail network just as a warm-up for the park.

Snowboard Rentals
- 70 sets: Original Sin: $20/day

Snowboard School
- 25 instructors: ski school rates apply

Lift Tickets/Rentals/Services

Alpine has only three lifts—two summit-reaching quad chairs and a bunny slope double chair. Remarkably, the longest lift line last season was a mere three minutes. Considering its limited terrain and the fact that skiing ends abruptly at 5 p.m. daily, lift tickets are much cheaper than what its Pocono rivals offer. Without enough yearly skier visits to necessitate night skiing, Alpine simply doesn't offer any.

Lift Tickets
- 8 a.m.-5 p.m.: weekday $23, weekend $30
- Ages 10 & under: weekday $19, weekend $26
- Afternoon tickets available at 1 p.m.
- Children 6 and under ski free
- 20% discount for ages 62+
- Group rates for 15 or more skiers
- Season passes from $295-$395

Ski Rentals
- 800 sets: Rossignol, Dynastar
- Weekday $16, Weekend/Holiday $18

Special Programs
- Racing Clinics for ages 7-18
- Adaptive Ski Programs for the hearing and visually impaired

Base Lodge Facilities
- Indoor/outdoor cafeteria, pizza shop, lounge, ski/rental/gift shops, lockers, game room
- Day Care offered 9 a.m.-4 p.m. daily at the base lodge

Ski School
- PSIA certified: 100 instructors: Private $35; Group $15
- Learn-to-ski package: $44-$50, includes ticket, lesson, rental
- Five-week childrens' ski/snowboard program (weekends) for ages 4-12: $200-$210/child
- Alpine Adventurers program for ages 10-14: $80/child
- One-day kids program: $60

Other Winter Sports

On-site snowmobiling course with snowmaking, operating daily: ($1/2$-hour ride: single $27, double $40)
Cross-country skiing, weather permitting, at nearby **Evergreen Park** *(see page 196)*
On-site five-lane snow tubing area with surface lift—new for 1997-98 season; call for rates
Sled Dog snow skate rentals: $20/day; snow skating instruction offered
Indoor ice-skating at Penn Hills Resort, daily from 10 a.m.-9 p.m. (rentals and instruction available; (717) 421-7721)
Pony and carriage rides at Colony Village, Analomink; (717) 595-3150

Lodging/Dining/Aprés-Ski

Located six miles north of East and West Stroudsburg, Alpine Mountain is just an hour drive from New York City and less than two hours from Philadelphia. Guests can plan an affordable slopeside stay at the resort's luxurious Alpine Village on the mountain's summit, or at several resorts, villages, and inns nearby. All the trappings of urban life can be found in the Stroudsburgs, while nearby tourist attraction Colony Village offers year-round horseback and carriage rides, museum tours, restaurants, and pubs.

Lodging
On-site
Alpine Village slopeside chalets w/indoor pools, whirlpools, fully furnished/fireplace; 1-800-233-8240

Nearby
Penn Hills Resort, Analomink, 3 miles from resort, w/saunas, whirlpools, fireplace
Penn Estates Resort, Analomink, 6 miles from resort, villas/homes, fully furnished, indoor pools, whirlpools, fireplace
Penn Skiers Motel, 3 miles from resort
Resort packages include midweek lift ticket, weekend discounts. Call 1-800-233-8240, (717) 421-6464 for info

Other
Brookview Manor B&B Inn, Canadensis, 10 minutes from resort; 1-800-585-7974, (717) 595-2451
Hillside Lodge, Canadensis, restaurant, fireplace, Jacuzzi, Murder Mystery Weekends; 1-800-666-4455, (717) 595-7551
Martinville Streamside Cottages, Canadensis; (717) 595-2489
Village Court Motel & Cottages, Canadensis; (717) 595-7888
Laurel Grove Inn & Resort, Canadensis; 1-800-842-0497, (717) 595-7262

Pine Knob Inn, Canadensis, circa 1847 country inn, restaurant/pub; 1-800-426-1460
Budget Motel, East Stroudsburg; 1-800-233-8144, (717) 424-5451
Howard Johnsons Plaza Hotel, Stroudsburg; 1-800-777-5453, (717) 424-1930
Paramount Motel, East Stroudsburg; (717) 421-2141

Dining/Aprés Ski
On-site
Cafeteria, pizza shop, lounge w/entertainment on weekend afternoons

Nearby
Wayside Colony Saloon, Analomink, tavern/restaurant; (717) 595-3368
Reflections Night Club, at Penn Hills Resort; (717) 421-6464
Barley Creek Brewery/Restaurant, Tannersville; (717) 629-9399
Taylor's Pub at Colony Village, Canadensis, sports bar/restaurant; (717) 595-7710
China Buffet, East Stroudsburg; (717) 476-7658
Classy Sassy's, Cresco; (717) 595-2680
Cappuccinos Ristorante, Cresco; (717) 595-2833

Calendar of Events

December
- Free beginner lessons and clinics
- Gregg Neck Boat Yard Annual Race
- Alpine Challenge Cup Races (throughout season)
- Christmas Day $15 special

January
- Winter Ski & Snowboard Festival

- Microbrewery Weekend—sample tasting, giant slalom races
- Snowboard races

February
- Festivals, family events/promotions, races, discount days

Big Boulder/Jack Frost Mountains

Big Boulder/Jack Frost

P.O. Box 702
Blakeslee, PA 18610

Jack Frost/Big Boulder Ski Report:
1-800-475-SNOW
Big Two InfoLine/Lodging:
1-800-468-2442
Jack Frost Information: (717) 443-8425
Big Boulder Information: (717) 722-0100
Credit Cards: AE, MC, VISA, Discover
Internet: http://www.big2resorts.com
Operating Hours:
Jack Frost:
    8:30 a.m.-4 p.m. weekdays
    8 a.m.-4 p.m. weekdays
Big Boulder:
    9 a.m.-10 p.m. weekdays
    8 a.m.-11 p.m. Saturday
    8 a.m.-10 p.m. Sunday
Season: December to late March

Getting There:

Jack Frost:
- **From the N.E. Extension of the PA Turnpike:** Take Exit 35 to Route 940 east. Follow signs 4 miles to Jack Frost on the left.
- **From New York/New Jersey:** Take Exit 43, then right onto Route 115 north, left on Route 940 west, follow signs 4 miles to Jack Frost on right.

Big Boulder:
- **From the N.E. Extension of the PA Turnpike:** Take Exit 35, following signs to I-80. Take I-80 east to PA Exit 43 and turn right onto Route 115 south. Turn right onto Route 903 south and follow signs to Big Boulder.
- **From New York/New Jersey:** Take I-80 west to Exit 43, then left onto Route 115 south. Turn right onto Route 903 south and follow signs to Big Boulder.

Background

With its modest plateaus and inconsistent snowfall, Pennsylvania's Pocono region hardly seemed an appropriate site to try and mirror the success of the emerging western and New England ski resorts of the 1940s. Nonetheless, Big Boulder established itself on a wing and a prayer—a new snowmaking system would combat the region's common winter thaws to bring thousands of ready-minded skiers from three different major metropolitan areas.

Commercial snowmaking was actually first introduced in the U.S. here at Big Boulder. In the early 1940s, pioneering local inventor John Garish was able to produce artificial snow by tinkering with a garden hose, sprinkler, and varying water pressures. And although he received little credit, his work enabled the resort to operate on a limited basis, and paved the way for the snowmaking industry boom.

Big Boulder also holds the distinction of being Pennsylvania's first commercial ski area. The resort celebrated its 50th anniversary during 1996-97 with torchlight parades and fireworks, live entertainment, and other special events each Saturday of the season. The resort's success as a family and couples destination prompted the creation of nearby Jack Frost Ski Area in 1972, which complements Big Boulder's beginner and family reputation with steeper, upper-intermediate terrain. "The Big Two" are separated by a distance of six miles, offer a reciprocal lift ticket, and are renowned for their impeccable snowmaking and grooming and posh vacation lodging.

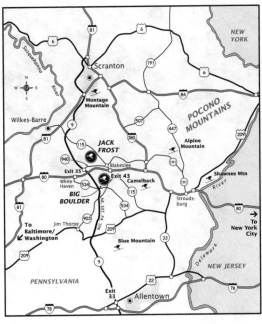

Mountain Stats

Base Elevation: Jack Frost: 1,400 feet; Big Boulder: 1,700 feet

Summit Elevation: Jack Frost: 2,000 feet; Big Boulder: 2,175 feet

Vertical Drop: Jack Frost: 600 feet; Big Boulder: 475 feet

Longest Run: Jack Frost: 3,200 feet; Big Boulder: 2,900 feet

Primary Slope Direction: North (both mountains)

Slopes and Trails: Jack Frost: 4 beginner; 8 intermediate; 8 advanced; Big Boulder: 5 beginner; 4 intermediate; 4 advanced

Skiable Terrain: Jack Frost: 75 acres; Big Boulder 55 acres

Lifts: Jack Frost: 1 quad, 2 triples, 4 doubles; Big Boulder: 2 triples, 5 doubles

Uphill Capacity: Jack Frost: 10,800 skiers per hour; Big Boulder: 9,600 skiers per hour

Average Annual Snowfall: Jack Frost: 55 inches; 1995-96 season: 96 inches; Big Boulder: 60 inches; 1995-96 season: 105 inches

Skiable Days: Jack Frost: 1995-96 season: 105 days; Big Boulder: 1995-96 season: 107 days

Skier Visits: Jack Frost: 1995-96 season: 140,000; Big Boulder: 1995-96 season: 150,000

Snowmaking: 100% of both areas

Night Skiing: Jack Frost: Trails close at 4 p.m. daily; Big Boulder: 100% of slopes, Sunday-Friday until 10 p.m., 11 p.m. Saturday (beginning late December)

Trail Profiles

The trail system at Jack Frost manages to squeeze a lot of pitch out of its small 600-foot vertical drop, with suit-up-and-ski access off the resort's inverted summit lodge. Though not considered an expert mountain by any stretch, eight short but sweet black diamonds on the east face

make up for lack of length with some deceptively challenging steeps. Runs are mostly straight, with few bends. On the other hand, they're quite narrow, offering a variety of pitches and some unforgiving drops. Billed a double black diamond, *Elevator's* swift drop runs straight down the fall line. The trail ends before you know it, but it's Jack Frost's most electrifying run by sheer steepness alone. Bordering *Elevator* on both sides, and nearly as steep, are *Floyd's Folley* and *River Shot* and their 1,000-foot runout. Skiers and snowboarders can also create their own jumps on parts of intermediate *Exhibition* and *Dematte's Demise* trails, where they'll find longer landing strips than in the snowboard and halfpipe area.

Frost's limited beginner terrain lies due left from the summit lodge. Three short slopes on an easy 11-percent grade are served by two chair lifts, while the ski school teaches on the near-flat *School Slope*. Instruction is solid at Jack Frost and may be a better bet on weekends than Big Boulder, where class sizes are bigger and the teaching areas busier.

Six miles away at Big Boulder, wide and well groomed trails are designed for neophyte and developing skiers. The resort's reputable ski school uses two small parcels that are sheltered from other trails to teach beginners the basics. The next step for learning skiers may be the wide, easy tracks of *Little Boulder* and *Edelweiss*, each served by its own lifts.

There aren't too many steeps on the 475-foot-vertical mountain, but advanced skiers and snowboarders can break off for a run down *Draufganger* (German for "daredevil") and its winding, sharp downhill. One of the other two black diamonds—*Upper Sitzmark* or *Big Boulder*—gets bumped out with some sizable moguls. Compensating for a lack of pitch, several trails offer an array of hidden jumps, dips, and natural bends fashioned into quarterpipes, including *Merry Widow* and *Midway* slopes. *Bunny's Elbow* is aptly named—it's an easy, straight run leading to a 160-degree switchback that's just right for skiers looking to work on their turning.

Weekends at Jack Frost and, to a greater degree, Big Boulder feature crowds of voluminous proportions. Guests who leave behind the daily grind are often met with lift lines as packed as rush-hour subways. Most of the weekend traffic at Big Boulder is centered on the triple and two double lifts that run to the central summit, while Jack Frost's Diversion chair lift gets swallowed up by beginner skiers and snowboarders. Big Boulder does a lot of night business, especially for snowboarders (Jack Frost visitors have to clear out by 4 p.m.). However, night skiing doesn't begin at Big Boulder until late December, weather permitting, with trails closing at 4 p.m. until that time.

Snowboarding

For eastern Pennsylvania snowboarders, the Bonk Yard at Big Boulder is the destination of choice. Boarders create their own hits around a sizable 400-foot halfpipe that's maintained to near perfection. Last year's creations included big-air jumps, walls, rail slides, barrels, 12-foot mailboxes, chutes, and truck tires, with the terrain changing weekly to suit competitions. Riders can hit aerial maneuvers with plenty of room for long, smooth landings. The Yard sits off the black diamond *Big Boulder* trail, at the entrance to the half-pipe, and is open under strong lights nightly. Usually not open until mid-season, the park may get going earlier this year if the resort can manage it.

Big Boulder's trails are wide, straight, and somewhat slow, but countered with jumps, berms, and small hits on the winding *Upper Sitzmark*, black diamond *Merry Widow*, and *Big Boulder* trails. Events are also a staple at Big Boulder, where Generation X Sundays feature a snowboard competition series over the course of eight weekends. Included are Big Air, Slalom, and Boardercross events and awards, as well as raffles for free snowboards.

Jack Frost sees fewer visitors than its more snowboard-minded sister mountain, closing at an early 4:30 p.m. But they do have a 500-foot deep halfpipe, in addition to steeper terrain on expertly groomed trails. Halfpipe Alley shoots off the intermediate *Lehigh* trail with some tabletops and a few other hits on the narrow wooded run. Unlike Big Boulder's Bonk Yard, Jack Frost doesn't mix up its obstacles much or let boarders design their own work. Advanced riders usually prefer the Bonk Yard's steeper pitch over Halfpipe Alley's slower roll. Jack Frost does manage to keep its halfpipe open much of the season under varying conditions, though.

Neither resort has an exclusive lift for its park areas, so boarders have to long-ride the chairs back to the summit areas. Halfpipe and park riders at Jack Frost may face an extra-long wait on the Diversion chair lift, shared by beginner and intermediate skiers using several bordering trails. Both resorts run snowboard demo days throughout the season at which time boarders can sample tasty rides from major manufacturers.

Snowboard Rentals

(Jack Frost)
- 200 sets: Morrow, Joyride, Rossignol

(Big Boulder)
- 350 sets: Joyride

Lift Tickets/Rentals

Adult lift tickets are pretty steep at both mountains, which is why the resorts have set up an affordable program for juniors. Skiers and snowboarders ages six to 15 can ride any session for just $20; children under six ski free. Guests can use one lift ticket for both mountains, but with no available shuttle service, they'll have to find their own way between resorts.

Lift Tickets
(Jack Frost & Big Boulder)
- Open-4 p.m.: weekday $32, weekend $40
- Noon-close: weekday $32, weekend $40
- Open-12:30 p.m. or noon-4 p.m.: $27, $35
(Big Boulder)
- Open-close: weekday $35, weekend $45
- 4 p.m.-close: weekday $20, weekend $25
(Big Boulder/Jack Frost)
- Ages 6-15 and 62-69: $20/all times

- Night ticket at Big Boulder includes free midweek snow tubing
- Midweek rates apply all week before Christmas
- Group rates for 15 or more skiers

Ski Rentals
(Jack Frost)
- 2,400 sets
(Big Boulder)
- 2,200 sets
- Rates: $20/adult, $15/ages 15 and under
- Numerous shops nearby offer cheaper rentals

On-Site Services

Day Care
(Big Boulder)
- Available with nominal charge from open to 5 p.m. (including lunch); half-day sessions; and 5 p.m. to close
(Jack Frost)
- Same as Big Boulder, but no night session

Ski/Snowboard School
- Jack Frost/Big Boulder: PSIA certified: Over 100 instructors: Private $40/hour; Group $20/hour

- Kids' C'n Ski (ages 3-8): $50 w/rental, $35 w/o (includes lift ticket, three hours supervision)
- Kids' C'n Ride (ages 6-8) snowboarding, same rates apply
- Discovery Package for first-time skiers and snowboarders
- Womens' Two-day Seminars
- Learn-to-Ski Specials
- Adaptive Ski School: Solid program offered at Jack Frost

Other Winter Sports

The Big Two also offer much more than downhilling for its main clientele of families, couples, and snowboarders. Snow tubing is offered at both resorts, with Big Boulder maintaining one of the country's largest tubing facilities. The resort hosts 12 chutes and four lifts, and tallied a whopping 75,000 tubing visits during the 1995-96 season. Both Frost and Boulder have groomed cross-country ski trails when natural snow permits. Jack Frost offers a wooded snowmobiling course, equipped with snowmaking, grooming, and rentals. And Jack Frost is the only Mid-Atlantic ski area currently offering paintball. "Splatter" is open year-round throughout 2,500 acres of Pocono woodlands.

Big Boulder
- **2-mile cross-country skiing course**, contingent on deep natural snow base, off Edelweiss chair lift summit area, with trail access to Hickory Run State Park. Rentals/lessons available; trail fee $10, rental/trail fee $20.
- **Snow tubing** (on-site): 12 chutes, 4 lifts, exclusive kids' area, and family area with 4- to 6-person group tubes available. Rates—open to 4 p.m.: $17; half day or 4 p.m.–close: $12; open-close: $22.

Jack Frost
- **9-mile cross-country ski course** (weather dependent) near the tennis court area, with rentals and lessons available at the cross-country ski center. Trail fee $10; group lesson, trail guide fee $15; rental and trail fee $20; group lesson, rental, and fee $35.
- **Tundra Run snowmobiling course**, located off the summit with snowmaking, grooming, and rentals. Trail rates: $27/single, $40/double (rates per half-hour).
- **Snow tubing** (on-site): 5 chutes, new Launch Pad expert chute, 2 lifts, group rates available, Big Boulder rates apply.
- **Splatter paintball** (on-site): 2,500 wooded acres, available year-round, with full rental equipment.

Lodging

Midweek packages (minimum 2 nights) include lift tickets & meals; ages 8 and under stay, ski, & eat free.

On-site
(Jack Frost)

Snow Ridge Village townhomes (up to 8 people/unit), w/kitchen, fireplace, dining room, all appliances, some units w/hot tubs. Call for rates.

(Big Boulder)

The Villages lakeside townhomes and condos (up to 8 people/unit), 2-3 bedroom units, same amenities as Snow Ridge Village, without hot tubs. Call for rates.

Nearby
Over 30 bed and breakfasts/country inns, seven couples' resorts, numerous cabins/chalets/rental homes, and 60 hotels/motels are within 20 miles of both Jack Frost and Big Boulder. Call 1-800- 762-6667 for free travel information/reservations or (717) 424-6050 for immediate tourist information.

Guests can base themselves on both mountains in the resorts' fully equipped houses, condominiums, and townhomes. There's just one full-service restaurant on the mountain, but numerous establishments can be found five to 10 minutes away along Route 940. The surrounding area is packed with family and couples' resorts, country inns, and lakeside communities that offer stately lodging and winter recreation such as cross-country skiing, snowmobiling, sledding, tobogganing, and ice-skating. Refer to the chart on *page 194* for a complete listing of lodging and winter sports in the Pocono region.

With the abundance of alpine and four-seasons resorts in the Pocono region, the number of nearby tourist trappings and attractions is no surprise. For a nice getaway, try the Water Gap Trolley that winds through the Delaware Water Gap National Recreation Area. Within this national recreation area are natural and historic points of interest along the Kittatinny Ridge and a 25-mile stretch of the Appalachian Trail. Some of the other activities you'll be sure to find literature on during a trip here include pony, carriage, and sleigh rides; outdoor tours; museums; and shopping at Pocono factory outlets and country craft stores. The two resorts are also well known for their numerous festivals held from spring through early fall. Jack Frost's Irish Festival runs each

Memorial Day Weekend, and the treasured Pocono Blues Festival is held each July at Big Boulder. For information and a free Poconos Travel Guide covering all lodging, restaurants, indoor/outdoor attractions, and events, call 1-800-762-6667.

Jack Frost

E-2000 Bar/Lounge, with live weekend entertainment
* Cantina Bar/Lounge
* Cafeteria, pizzeria, outdoor barbecue

Big Boulder

On-site

Blue Heron Grille overlooking Big Boulder Lake (on Lake Shore Drive), with casual dining, weekend buffet
* Cafeteria
* Pizzeria in Double Decker building

The Cellar Nightclub, w/live weekend entertainment

Glass House Bar/Lounge

Dining/Aprés-Ski

On Lake Shore Drive in Lake Harmony (just outside resort)

Lake Harmony Lodge Sports Bar Cafe, (717) 722-8368

Shenanigan's of Lake Harmony, (717) 722-1100

Close Quarters Restaurant, (717) 722-8127
* Numerous restaurants/lounges nearby along Route 940

Blue Knob

Blue Knob

P.O. Box 247
Claysburg, PA 16625

Ski Report: 1-800-458-3403
Information/Lodging: 1-800-458-3403, (814) 239-5111
Credit Cards: AE, MC, VISA, Discover
Internet: http://www.nb.net/~blueknob
E-mail: blueknob@nb.net
Season:
December to late March
Operating Hours:
9 a.m.-10 p.m. daily

Getting There

* **From Philadelphia and Harrisburg:** Take the Pennsylvania Turnpike to I-99 (Route 220) north to Osterburg, then Route 869 west to Pavia. Follow signs to Blue Knob.
* **From northern Pennsylvania points:** Take I-80 south or Route 22 east to I-99 (Route 220), heading south to East Freedom. From East Freedom, take Route 164 west and follow signs to Blue Knob.
* **From Washington/Baltimore:** Take I-95 north to I-695 west to I-70 north. Then take the Pennsylvania Turnpike west to I-99 (Route 220) north to Osterburg. From Osterburg, take Route 869 west to Pavia and follow signs to Blue Knob.

Background

Blue Knob is, without question, the most challenging mountain in the Mid-Atlantic region south of New York. And it just got tougher. A whopping 12 new trails have been cut for the 1997-98 season that are certain to bring a measure of respect to Pennsylvania skiing. The four-seasons resort has the state's second-highest vertical drop (1,072 feet) and hosts a diverse selection of steep descents, extreme gladed runs, open bowls, and fast, narrow chutes. It's also Pennsylvania's highest skiable mountain at 3,172 feet, just 41 feet shy of the state's tallest point on Mt. Davis in southwestern Huntington County.

Blue Knob's story is an interesting one. Some sixty years ago, the resort's summit lodge area was the site of a World War II Air Force radar station whose gracious workers would traverse pristine, self-cut trails right from their base. It wasn't until the late 1950s, though, that the mountain's potential for commercial skiing was realized. The occupants of a single-engine airplane flying over the mountain on a clear May afternoon happened to gaze down on the mountain, marveling at the thick snow still holding so well into spring. The same group opened the mountain for business in 1963. Today the top quarter of the mountain's land is state-park owned—the remainder of the ski area is privately leased.

Mountain Stats

Base Elevation: 2,100 feet
Summit Elevation: 3,172 feet
Vertical Drop: 1,072 feet
Longest Run: 9,200 feet
Primary Slope Direction: North
Slopes and Trails: 6 beginner, 14 intermediate, 14 advanced
Skiable Terrain: 100 acres
Lifts: 2 triples, 2 doubles, 3 surface tows

Uphill Capacity: 5,200 skiers per hour
Average Annual Snowfall: 120 inches
  1995-96 season: 171 inches
  1994-95 season: 110 inches
Skiable Days
  1995-96 season: 120
  1994-96 season: 110
Snowmaking: 72% of area
Night Skiing: 20% of area, nightly until 10 p.m.

A laid-back but festive resort, the Knob is a throwback to ski areas of the 1960s, with music cranking all day from its three-quarter station. The inverted summit lodge allows instant park-and-ski access, with easier terrain off the top and advanced track on the lower half. Though the slopes are monitored by ski patrol, downhillers are generally allowed more freedom—and sometimes transgressions—than other regional resorts.

But no resort is without its drawbacks. At Blue Knob, though, the problem is beyond its control. Although the mountain receives some of Pennsylvania's lightest and longest-lasting snow—averaging well over 100 inches per year—it's also one of the coldest skiing experiences south of Vermont.

The north-facing mountain is prone to extreme wind and cool conditions. And when the sun goes down at Blue Knob, icy conditions tend to rule the mountain. Temperatures routinely run 10 to 15 degrees colder than the lower-lying town of Altoona, 20 miles away. The resort does guarantee a free return voucher to skiers not satisfied with the conditions (redeemable within one hour of purchase).

Ten of Blue Knob's 34 trails rely solely on natural snow, including the new glade runs. Fortunately, the mountain's altitude and north-facing slopes allow them to stay open long after the last snowfall. The 1995-96 season featured a record 171 inches of snow. Skiing typically blossoms here in spring, running through March and early April. Four-wheel-drive vehicles come highly recommended during storm periods: The climb to the summit lodge is long, slow, and fashioned like some of Blue's undulating trails. Before the ascent, the flat drive along picturesque Route 869 winds past old churches and a covered bridge. Also, bring a camera for chair lift shots of scenic Overland Pass en route to the summit.

Trail Profiles

Natural conditions aside, the mountain is quite sizable for the Mid-Atlantic. The Knob is highly regarded for its steep, narrow trails, contoured with shifting pitches through the hardwoods of Mt. Laurel. But already-satisfied regulars can't wait for the 1997-98 season: Those trails will take a back seat to the resort's 12 newly introduced runs. Advanced glade and bowl trails—true rarities in the region—are the hallmarks of the new terrain. Traversing the steep, tree-lined powder stashes of *East Wall Glades, Ditch Glades, Bone Yard Glades,* and *Mine Shaft Glades* will conjure up images of western skiing like few other resorts on the east coast can. Also being introduced this season, black

diamond *Upper Stembogen Bowl* is an enormously wide, steep bowl that's fed from the narrow *East-Wall Traverse* trail. These trails will run without the benefit of additional chair lifts at first, but the new terrain will open up the entire mountain to more of Pennsylvania's best skiing. Guests who prefer to pound the lower half's steeper terrain have a midstation off the Route 66 double chair.

Be warned, though: Blue Knob's lower-mountain terrain is indeed for advanced skiers only. The gladed trails and *Upper Stembogan Bowl* show no deviation from their natural topographical state. Don't be surprised to encounter cliffs, rocky outcroppings, chutes, changing snow conditions, and numerous natural obstacles in their paths. There's nothing even remotely comparable to this terrain in the Mid-Atlantic, so exercise extreme caution when entering these areas.

The advanced *Stembogen* trail (extending from the new *Upper Stembogan Bowl*) is a serpentine, terraced trail with quick drop-offs through a relentless spate of high-banking turns. One of the state's steepest top-to-bottom slopes can be found on true double diamond *Extrovert*. It's a wicked, bumpy run down the fall line, offering three pitches at 39 degrees, and packed high with beastly moguls. More steep, narrow track is featured on *Lower Shortway*, which offers the option of breaking out among the trees on either *Mine Shaft Glades* or *Bone Yard Glades*.

Many of Blue's intermediate trails are expert by Mid-Atlantic standards, including *Expressway*—

a long cruising run filled with some fairly challenging steeps. Not a mountain for neophyte skiers, the resort does offer two easy bunny hills off the summit. After conquering these, novices can graduate to nearby *Mambo Alley (Upper and Lower)* and its nearly two miles of twisting, beginner track. *Condo trail* is the only other wide, easy cruiser, with a few jumps available for snowboarders.

Snowboarding

Blue Knob presently has a small snowboard area on the beginner *Condo* trail with a few relatively tame jumps. An exclusive park has been tentatively planned for the 1997-98 season, but likely won't be constructed for another year. The same area formerly held a modest halfpipe. Grooming difficulty and constantly drifting snow accounted for its demise. Until the new park is created, boarders won't be let down on the mountain's variety of expert terrain on the lower half. Be sure to check out the *Upper Stembogan Bowl* and the many gladed trails that were newly cut for this season. Boarders will also find the rest of the mountain filled with bumps, dips, curves, and dipsy-doodles.

Snowboard Rentals
- 40 sets: Kemper, Oxygen: $15-$25

Snowboard School
- 3 instructors: Day, twilight sessions: $25; Half day, night sessions: $15

Lift Tickets/Rentals/Services

Surprisingly, lift tickets are moderately priced and long lift lines rare, despite slow and somewhat outdated lifts. Even if guests finish the entire mountain in a day, they may wish to get a second helping, which is why slopeside condominiums were built off the beginner Condo trail. All units come fully equipped and include fireplaces, and the Clubhouse Restaurant and Bar sits right next door. The ski lodge is basic and somewhat tight quartered, but skiers will find everything they need without venturing far.

Lift Tickets
- 9 a.m.-5 p.m.: weekday $22, weekend $32
- 1 p.m.-5 p.m.: weekday $17, weekend $25
- 1 p.m.-10 p.m.: weekday $22, weekend $32
- 6 p.m.-10 p.m.: $17
- 9 a.m.-10 p.m.: weekday $30, weekend $37
- Reduced rates for ages 12 and under and 65+
- Group rates, multi-day packages available

Ski Rentals
- 1,500 sets: Atomic, Fischer, Tyrolia, and Elan: $12-$20

Ski School
- 35 instructors: PSIA certified; Private: $30/hour; Group: $20/hour

- Learn to Ski package: $35
- Kinderski Program (ages 4-10)
- Mountain Mashers (ages 9-16)

Racing
- NASTAR offered on *High Hopes* trail, weekends beginning at 11 a.m.
- USSA Junior Ski Racing/Training Team for ages 8 and up

Summit Lodge Facilities
- Ski and rental shops, ski school, cafeteria, lounge, lockers

Day Care
- Available 9 a.m.-5 p.m. for ages 2 years and older; $3/hour, reservations required on weekdays

Other Winter Sports

- **Cross-country skiing** on Blue Knob's golf course and a large network of surrounding trails *(see page 209)*
- **Sleigh rides** and **ice-skating** at the condominium area
- **Skis of all types** welcome on the trail network

The Knob, in recent years, has also felt the impact of Telemark skiing's reemergence. Tele-skiing is allowed on all slopes (no rentals), though the mostly narrow trails don't generally suit the Scandinavian-bred skiing variation. Blue Knob's neighboring golf course and surrounding backcountry trails are Nordic nirvana for cross-country skiers of all levels. And even after this season's massive alpine terrain expansion, the mountain still holds a seemingly unlimited number of undesignated, unmarked—but loosely restricted—side trails on which daring experts can blaze. Skiers will find some imposing headwalls and nasty drops on these side trails.

Winter activities don't end after you leave the mountain. Cross-country skiing, snowmobiling, and winter hiking abound in the Laurel Highlands, and nearby streams and lakes hold some of Pennsylvania's best ice fishing. When the snow finally clears, the four seasons resort offers miles of mountain biking/hiking trails, a nine-hole golf course, tennis courts, indoor/outdoor pools, and a Jacuzzi, sauna, and steam room.

Calendar of Events

December
- Winter Festival

January
- BK Alpine Dual Slalom Challenge
- Marianne Andrews Memorial Telemark Race

February
- Tavern Race
- Washington, DC Ski International Slalom/Giant Slalom

- Joe Selecky-Ski Vertical for Cancer

March
- Annual Spring Fling: snowboard events, downhill mogul contests, snow mountain bike race, music, and barbecue
- County Appreciation Days

Lodging/Dining/Aprés-Ski

Outside of the resort's condominiums and 10 privately owned slopeside and nearby homes, the next available options are roughly 20 minutes away. Altoona and Bedford have numerous bed and breakfasts and hotels/motels. Tourist attractions include the working colonial village of Old Bedford, Raystown Lake, and several antique shops and stores in Blue Knob's surrounding villages.

Lodging:

On-site:
- Privately owned slopeside and nearby chalets, condos, studios, and lofts, with pool, Jacuzzi; rates $135-$390/2 days (Call 1-800-458-3403)

Blue Knob slopeside condominiums: (1-2 bedrooms, studios, and lofts) with kitchen, fireplace, balcony, pool, Jacuzzi, sauna

Nearby:
Beford's Covered Bridge Inn B&B: Schellsburg, 18 miles from Blue Knob, 6 rooms, cottage, private bath, country decor; rates $65-$95/night, (814) 733-4093

Hickory Hollow Farm B&B: Schellsburg; (814) 733-4639

Station Inn B&B, Cresson: 5 suites with private baths, 1-800-555-4757

Holiday Inn-Altoona: restaurant/lounge; (814) 944-4581

Ramada Inn-Breezewood: restaurant, pool/Jacuzzi/sauna; 1-800-535-4025

Beford, Pennsylvania (25 miles from Blue Knob)

Quality Inn: Arena Restaurant/Lounge; (814) 623-5188

Best Western: with hot tub, exercise room/sauna, restaurant/lounge; 1-800-752-8592

Judy's Motel: 12 rooms, ski lift packages; (814) 623-9118

Dining/Après-Ski
On-site

Ski lodge lounge, with live weekend music, open until 10:30 p.m.

The Clubhouse, restaurant/bar, located at the condo area

Nearby (Claysburg)

Ranch House Family Restaurant, along Rt. 220, (814) 695-8825

Village Inn Restaurant, RD 1; (814) 239-5191

Peggy's Diner, RD 2; (814) 239-2196

Dane Anthony's Restaurant, RD 1; (814) 239-8382

Blue Mountain

Blue Mountain
Box 216
Palmerton, PA 18071

Ski Report: 1-800-235-2226
Information: (610) 826-7700
Credit Cards: AE, MC, VISA, Discover
Internet: http://www.com.aminews/bluemountain
Season:
Early December to mid-March
Operating Hours
8:30 a.m.-10 p.m. weekdays
7:30 a.m.-10 p.m. weekends/holidays

Getting There

- **From Allentown:** Take Route 145 (MacArthur Road) north, approximately 9 miles to the "Y" intersection at the far end of a long bridge. Bear right here, traveling 3 miles to the light in Cherryville. Go straight on Blue Mountain Drive for 3 miles through Danielsville to the entrance sign past the top of the mountain.

- **From I-80 (NY/NJ and central PA):** Follow I-80 to Exit 46A and Route 209 south. Follow 209 south 14 miles (follow 209 closely from 4-lane highway) to the village of Gilbert. At Gilbert, turn left off 209 at the stoplight next to the bank. Follow signs for 13 miles to Blue Mountain.

- **From Harrisburg, Washington and points south:** Take I- 270 west to Route 15 north to Harrisburg. From Harrisburg, take I-81 north to I-78 east all the way Exit 15 (Route 22 east) toward Whitehall. Take Route 145 north (MacArthur Road), approximately 9 miles to "Y" intersection at end of bridge, bearing right. Then travel 3 miles to the light in Cherryville. Go straight on Blue Mountain Drive for 3 miles through Danielsville to the entrance sign past the top of the mountain.

Background

Blue Mountain's success as a southern Pocono Mountain resort was built on two things: location and determination. The resort has two urban markets within its grasp—Allentown and Philadelphia—17 and 75 miles away, respectively. And a generous trail offering fit skiers from novice to advanced abilities. Of Blue's 20 slopes and trails, three are over one mile long. Its headliner trail—*Challenge*—is one of the Mid-Atlantic's steeper and more invigorating runs.

Local developer Ray Tuthill started the ski area in the mid-1970s in an effort to keep his construction employees' time cards punched year-round. Initially dubbed Little Gap Ski Area, Tuthill would later change the resort's name to the more appealing Blue Mountain. While ownership hasn't changed, the resort has unveiled major modifications in terrain—and philosophy—during the last few years. In addition to cutting four new trails three years ago, Blue became the final Mid-Atlantic ski area to release its ban on snowboarding. The resort had previously maintained its trail network for skiers only. But soaring snowboarding profits at surrounding Pocono mountains finally caught up with Blue's top brass, which decided to allow boarding in February of the 1996-97 season to the delight of area riders.

Mountain Stats

Base Elevation: 592 feet
Summit Elevation: 1,645 feet
Vertical Drop: 1,082 feet
Longest Run: 6,400 feet
Primary Slope Direction: North
Slopes and Trails: 9 beginner, 5 intermediate,
  6 advanced
Skiable Terrain: 75 acres
Lifts: 1 high-speed quad, 4 doubles,
  1 T-bar, 1 rope tow

Uphill Capacity: 8,400 skiers per hour
Average Annual Snowfall: 25 inches
  1995-96 season: 80 inches
  1994-95 season: 20 inches
Skier Visits
  1995-96 season: 206,000
  1994-95 season: 225,000
Snowmaking: 100% of area
Night Skiing: 100% of area, nightly until 10 p.m.

Like most Pocono ski areas, Blue can be a tight squeeze on weekends. The resort's investment in a high-speed quad lift has paid its dividends, though. The mountain's uphill capacity has since doubled with the addition of the Comet superquad. A good share of business is also conducted on midweek nights, especially for school and community groups and Philadelphia-area skiers, with the entire trail network open until 10 p.m. nightly.

What Blue can't offer in terms of a strong wintry climate it makes up for with snowmaking technology. With just 20 to 25 inches of average yearly snowfall, the mountain relies on constant man-

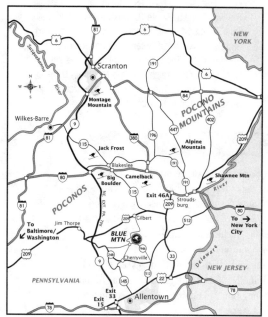

made gunning and grooming, usually done during both day and night hours. Don't dare leave home without hat and goggles, should you encounter rapid-firing snow blowers on some of the trails.

Blue also carries the dubious distinction of owning Pennsylvania's highest vertical drop of 1,082 feet. By extending its beginner terrain a mere 50 feet on a near-flat grade, the resort was able to claim the crown over Claysburg's Blue Knob Resort. Vertical drop, or rise, represents one of the ski resort industry's premiere marketing ploys, and Blue literally went the distance to distinguish itself in that regard. The resort also aggressively bills itself the closest major ski area to Philadelphia—a title that realistically goes to Doe Mountain (55 miles away).

Trail Profiles

Though Blue Mountain doesn't measure up to Blue Knob's diverse trail network, the resort does offer some fairly strong advanced trails. The east summit's double diamond *Challenge* tops off with an electrifying headwall, running straight down the fall line before hitting 350 feet of vicious drop on *The Falls*. A new mogul runoff was built off the top section of *Challenge* for bump skiing. The other notables are *Main Street*—a 3,300-foot straight, steep shot to the mountain's midway point—and *The Chute*, with its narrow descent over a short 700 feet of track.

The recent terrain expansion of four trails includes *Paradise*—one of the region's longest continuous runs (6,400 feet). It's a picturesque beginner cruising run off the east summit that twists and snakes from top to bottom and is conveniently fed by the Challenge super quad lift. Developing skiers will also find the long, winding, slow-moving terrain of *Burma Road* to their liking.

What Blue lacks is a series of long intermediate trails. Better skiers may discover a half day or night session is more than enough to satisfy them. The best blue runs are the recently lengthened *Sidewinder* trail, *Lazy Mile*, and the serpentine *Switch Back*, which has over 3,800 feet of moderately steep terrain.

Snowboarding

At last, the final major Mid-Atlantic resort to lift its restriction on snowboarding is Blue Mountain. Since Blue just recently opened the mountain to the sport, don't expect the resort to establish a complete snowboarding environment just yet. If enough snowboarders roll in this season, they may have their own park before too long. Nonetheless, the mountain is new grounds for boarders, who will discover a variety of terrain that's steep and wide enough to sustain big carving turns. Aggressive boarding—and self-construction of snow-mound jumps—might likely be monitored with great scrutiny, so look out for Blue's ski patrol.

Lift Tickets/Rentals/Services

Lift Tickets
- 8:30 a.m.-12:30 p.m.: weekday $25, weekend (7:30 a.m.) $28
- 8:30 a.m.-5 p.m.: weekday $31, weekend $39
- 12:30 p.m.-5 p.m.: weekday $25, weekend $28
- 12:30 p.m.-10 p.m.: weekday $31, weekend $39
- 4 p.m.-10 p.m.: weekday $23, weekend $25
- Reduced rates for ages 7-12 & senior citizens
- Group Rates for 15 or more skiers

Ski Rentals
- 3,100 sets: Elan, K2, Atomic, Rossignol, Saloman (Step-in System)
- Adult: $16-$20
- Ages 7-12: $12-$13
- High-performance skis available

Ski School
- PSIA certified: 300 instructors, Private $40; Group $17; Beginner $17
- SKIwee Program (ages 4-12): $35-$55
- First-time Package: $30-$40
- Adaptive Ski Program

Main (Summit) Lodge Facilities
- Two cafeterias, ski school, day care, ski and rental shops, lockers

Base Lodge Facilities
- Ticket and rental shops, snow tubing, vending area, lockers

Day Care
- Free midweek service 8:30 a.m.-9 p.m.; weekends: $2/hour

Other Winter Sports/Events

If you're thinking of bringing the kids for an afternoon, Blue has you covered. Childrens' skiing programs abound on several bunny slopes, a large snow tubing park is now available, and there's a free baby-sitting service midweek for infants from six months to five years of age (with nominal hourly charges on weekends). The snow tubing park was introduced last year off the base lodge, with further expansion set for the 1997-98 season. Presently it has five slides, each 800 to 1,000 feet long, and two rope tow lifts.

Events, races, and sponsored festivities are staples each weekend, both day and night. Blue is also one of the stops on the Subaru Master the Mountain tour—a program stressing racing, new trends in equipment, and skier/snowboarder safety.

Other Winter Sports
- **Snow tubing** with five lanes, each 800-1,000 feet long, with two rope tow lifts
- **Telemark skiing** allowed on all trails; no on-site rentals

Calendar of Events
- Events/entertainment held most weekends

January
- Free Learn-to-Ski Day (w/reservations)
- Foster's Blue Mtn Challenge Race Series

February
- Subaru Family Day
- Coca-Cola Day in SKIwee
- Northeast PA Ski Council Race
- McCall Ski Cup
- Mack Bulldog Challenge Race
- Eastern PA Ski Council Race

March
- Winter Carnival
- Slalom Races, Torchlight Parades

Lodging/Dining/Après-Ski

Despite having both summit and base lodges and parking, Blue hasn't followed the Pocono trend of upgrading to a full-fledged resort, committing its resources instead to the trail system. Nevertheless, guests will find everything they need at Blue's summit lodge. The smaller valley lodge holds a second ticket office, rental shop, and snow tubing tickets. There are tentative plans to expand its base facilities.

Because of its location and abundance of nearby accommodations that include bed and breakfasts, cottages, and motels, the resort offers no on-site lodging. The historic town of Jim Thorpe, known as "Little Switzerland," serves as a popular ski-and-stay vacation, 25 minutes from Blue. This quaint, endearing downtown—site of the Jim Thorpe Inn—has an old railroad station that runs trains for tourists, a bevy of specialty and craft shops, and ongoing light displays during the winter holiday months.

Lodging
Nearby
Grassy Hill B&B, overlooking Blue Ridge Country Club; (610) 826-2290

Lakeview Lodge B&B, log cabin-style lodging; private bath, balcony, fireplace; (610) 377-8344

The Inn at Jim Thorpe B&B, downtown, 22 rooms w/private bath; 1-800-329-2599

Sheraton Inn Jetport, Allentown, indoor pool/sauna/Jacuzzi, restaurant; 1-800-383-1100

Days Inn, Allentown, children stay free; (610) 395-3731

Hampton Inn, Fogelsville, fitness room/sauna; (610) 391-1500

Comfort Inn, Fogelsville, Fogey's Cafe & Lounge, fitness room; 1-800-951-7800

Allentown Hilton, restaurant/sports bar, pool/sauna/fitness room; 1-800-445-8667

Barn House Village, Bath, PA, 12 country suites, lounge; (610) 837-1234

Allentown Comfort Suites, restaurant/pub, fitness room; (610) 437-9100

Mahoning Court Motel, Leighton, restaurant; (610) 377-1600

Dining/Après-Ski

On-site

Cafeteria, summit lodge pub w/live music/dee jay Thursdays, karaoke Saturdays

Nearby (Palmerton)

Bert's Steakhouse & Restaurant; (610) 826-9921
Covered Bridge Inn; (610) 826-5400
Fireline Inn; (610) 852-3400
Tony's Pizzeria; (610) 826-6161
Hunan House Chinese Restaurant; (610) 826-4567

Camelback

Camelback Ski Area

P.O. Box 168
Tannersville, PA 18372

Ski Report: 1-800-233-8100
Information: (717) 629-1661
Credit Cards: AE, VISA, MC, Discover

Internet: http://skicamelback.com
E-mail: camelback@silo.com

Operating Hours
8:30 a.m.-10 p.m. weekdays
7:30 a.m.-10 p.m. weekends

Season: Mid-December to late March

Getting There

- **From Philadelphia:** Take the N.E. Extension of the PA Turnpike to Lehigh Valley Exit 33. Follow Route 22 east to Route 33 north to I-80 west and PA Exit 45 at Tannersville. Follow signs to Camelback Resort.
- **From metro NY/NJ:** Take I-80 west to PA Exit 45 at Tannersville. Follow signs to Camelback Resort.
- **From Scranton:** Take Route 380 east to I-80 east to PA Exit 45 at Tannersville. Follow signs to Camelback Resort.
- **From Washington/Baltimore:** Take I-95 north to 695 north toward Towson, then I-83 north, I-81 north, and I-80 east to PA Exit 45 at Tannersville. Follow signs to Camelback Resort.

Background

While Pocono Mountain ski areas seem mired in their reputation as honeymoon and family destinations, one such resort has worked hard to distinguish itself from the others. Camelback has spent a lot of dough in upgrades over the last five years: cutting new trails, increasing its uphill lift capacity and lighting, developing an impressive snowboard park and halfpipe, and building a separate snow tubing park to top off the resort.

The opening of Big Pocono Ski Area in 1950-51, which ran sporadically for four years before hurricanes Connie and Diane struck in 1955, closing the operation, preceded Camelback's rise. The hurricanes dumped millions of gallons of water on the mountain, causing massive runoff and destruction and taking the lives of more than 50 local residents. Skiing was resurrected a few years later when Pennsylvania entrepreneurs Jim Moore, Terry Lloyd, and Daniel Horan teamed with

Austrian Walter Foeger, an expert skier and Austrian Davis Cup tennis player, to design a new trail system here on the north face along the Pocono plateau's southern ridge. The resort's new name was announced after geological maps revealed the mountain as "Camelback," attributed to its double-hump profile from the south. The resort skirted bankruptcy twice in the early going, but an aggressive new snowmaking system helped it survive in an area New England skiers mockingly refer to as the "Banana Belt."

Mountain Stats

Base Elevation: 1,250 feet
Summit Elevation: 2,050 feet
Vertical Drop: 800 feet
Longest Run: 1 mile
Primary Slope Direction: South-southwest
Slopes and Trails: 19 beginner, 8 intermediate, 6 advanced
Skiable Terrain: 139 acres
Lifts: 2 high-speed quads, 1 quad, 2 triples, 7 doubles

Uphill Capacity: 18,600 skiers per hour
Average Annual Snowfall: 40 inches
  1995-96 season: 114 inches
  1994-95 season: 23 inches
Skiable Days
  1995-96 season: 116
  1994-95 season: 102
Snowmaking: 100% of area
Night Skiing: 80% of area, nightly until 10 p.m.

Trail Profiles

Camelback's terrain caters mostly to skiers of beginner and mid-level ability, punctuated by wide, well-groomed green and blue runs. There are also several options for skiers seeking stronger runs, with four short black diamonds on the mountain's upper-third tier and the longer, steeper *Cliffhanger* trail on the mountain's far-eastern end. Though it's not quite as ominous as its name implies, *Cliffhanger* uses all of the mountain's 800 feet of vertical drop, boasting plenty of steep dips and drops and a quick elbow turn over its 4,000-plus feet of track. It's the expert's choice at Camelback—seldomly skied, completely secluded, and accessible from the Sullivan high-speed quad lift. Although subject to extreme ice or slow mush, the four short-lived advanced runs on the upper west section drop steeply off the bat before running out into more gradual, intermediate terrain.

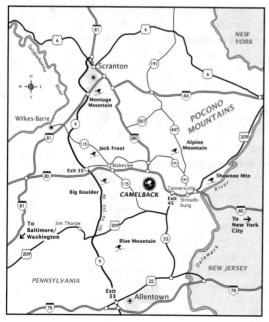

The resort isn't a mogul paradise, but *Margie's Delight* and the narrow *Rocket* take turns as ungroomed bump fields. Racing, on the other hand, is given more attention. The Corona Camelback Challenge Series is an expertly run slalom racing program held on the left side of the wide, intermediate-pitch *Raceway* trail, served by its own convenient triple chair. Skiers can open it up with giant slalom turns on the other side of *Raceway*.

Camelback also has an outstanding learning environment. First-time skiers and snowboarders can use two broad areas of little gradient, each with two double chair lifts for easy access. *Little Caesar*, via the Stevenson Express, takes novice skiers down the west face through the *Sun Bowl* for a long, continuous cruising run. Another gradual cruiser is *Marc Antony*—the resort's longest run at over one mile. *Near East* was erected a few years ago to connect *Julius Caesar and Upper Moore's Ramble* trails, easing the task of negotiating the entire mountain.

And the big news for the 1997-98 season is the addition of a one-mile advanced novice trail on the far end of the trail system, next to the advanced *Cliffhanger*. The scenic *Nile Mile* trail will be the resort's widest run, at nearly 100 feet, and contoured over an 18- to 22-percent pitch, which should prove well for skiers and snowboarders of all abilities. It's Camelback's hope that *The Nile Mile*, serviced by the Stevenson Express high-speed quad, will alleviate some of the congestion of the central blue and green trails.

Snowboarding

Camelback didn't fool around when it set out to create a freestyle snowboard haven a few years ago. Its seven-element, 25,000-square foot snowboard park and halfpipe can be found on the *Laurel Glade* beginner trail. The well-maintained pipe ranks among the Mid-Atlantic's best—400 feet long and 40 feet wide, culminated by a phat gap jump at the finish. And the resort isn't finished yet. The snowboard areas are being redesigned for the 1997-98 season, and a new Pipe Dragon grooming apparatus will preserve the halfpipe for supreme conditions.

An adjacent snowboard park is slightly less ambitious but features a solid set of gaps, fun boxes, a log slide, and a quarterpipe, which may not be constructed in coming years. The 800-foot park has extra-broad track for wide-arcing turns.

Unfortunately, its gentle pitches aren't quite steep enough for long airtime on the jumps. The resort is considering converting the area into a skier-welcome terrain park—to the dismay of territorial snowboarders. Good lighting keeps the park and pipe open nightly until 10 p.m., with the Meadows quad lift serving the snowboard area and a neighboring beginner trail.

For those who prefer to shred the trails, Camelback is a cruising paradise. Most boarders here don't mind the trails' sometimes-soupy conditions. In fact, they usually prefer it that way; their boards will carve through anything. Make sure to check out this season's new trail—*The Nine Mile*. It has a green/blue difficulty rating, but it's definitely steep and wide enough for strong turns.

The resort offers lots of snowboard events and promotions, including the Brave New World Snowboard Challenge and the running Boardercross series on weekends.

Snowboard Rentals
- 230 sets: Rossignol, K2, Kemper, Avalanche—mostly step-in bindings
- Day $26; Half day $18

Snowboard School
- 15 instructors: ski rates apply

Lift Tickets/Rentals/Services

At the base of the mountain lies Camelback's new snow tubing facility, complete with seven runs and three tow lifts. The area is equipped for night tubing and has its own ticket and parking areas. The sprawling resort's home base is by the gigantic clock tower, and skiers will find four lodges with numerous food venues and comfortable après-ski lounges. In case you arrive *sans* skis, two separate rental shops just replaced their fleet with brand-new equipment. Lift ticket prices are on par with other Pocono ski areas—a bit on the expensive side—but the resort offers numerous discounts and incentive packages.

Surrounded by Big Pocono State Park, Camelback offers 14 outdoor activities from spring to fall, including hiking, biking, scenic chair lift rides, a water slide, and the Alpine Bobsled Slide that sits among the resort's ski trails.

Lift Tickets
- 7:30 a.m.-5 p.m.: weekday $39, weekend $33
- 7:30 a.m.-12 p.m.: weekday $25, weekend $33
- 12:30 p.m.-5 p.m.: weekday $25, weekend $33
- 12:30 p.m.-10 p.m.: weekday $33, weekend $39
- Open-close: weekday $40, weekend $46
- 5 p.m.-10 p.m.: weekday $24, weekend $26
- Discount rates for kids 46" tall to 10 years, and ages 65-69
- Civil service, student, and Monday discounts
- 3-day ticket and frequent skier discounts
- Group rates for 15 or more skiers

Ski Rentals
- 3,200 sets: Elan
- 650 new shaped skis (150 sets for children)
- Day $20; Night $15

Ski School
- PSIA certified: 200 instructors; Private $42/hour; Group $18/hour

Childrens' Programs
- Sugar Bears ski discovery program, ages 4-6, includes rental, 3 hours instruction, play time, lunch; full day $65, half day $50
- Skiing/Boarding Bears, ages 7-12; midweek $70, weekend $75

- Grizzly Bears, ages 7-12, with lesson, rental, 3-hour time; midweek $55, weekend $60
- Snow Cats, ages 13-16, workshops for snowboarders; $35/day
- Adult Masters Program, $40/day

Base Lodge Facilities/Summit Lodge area
- Ski school, rental shop, restaurants, lounges, cafeterias, pizza bar, childrens' learning center, day care, lockers

Racing
- Corona Camelback Challenge Series, run like NASTAR, held weekends 1 p.m. on *Racetrack* trail

Recreational Racing Class
- Adult $40/day; junior $35/day

Day Care
- Children 12 months to 4 years, 7:30 a.m.-5 p.m. weekends (8:30 a.m. from December 16 to season's end), $3/hour or $24/day

Other Winter Sports
- Seven-lane **snow tubing** park at the base of the mountain, with 3 tow lifts; operating noon-9 p.m. midweek, 8:30 a.m.-9 p.m. weekends; $10/half day; $17/full day

Calendar of Events

January
- Chevrolet Winter Ski Carnival
- The N'Ice Ice Challenge
- CHEX Winter Party Mix Weekend
- Demo Days

February
- PSIA Clinic

- U.S. Ski Team Passport Ski Festival
- Annual Mountain Division Ski Day

March
- Brave New World Snowboard Challenge
- Event weekends until season's end

Lodging/Dining/Après Ski

Though the resort lacks slopeside lodging, guests can shack up just across the mountain in a limited number of townhomes and condominiums at Northridge. Most overnighters choose from over 25 motels within 10 minutes' drive, all of which offer ski-and-stay packages. The Cameltop Restaurant, open from May to late fall, sits high atop Camelback Mountain with a panoramic view of the scenic Poconos. And the energy doesn't end when the sun goes down—Camelback's après-ski scene thrives in its base lodge lounges.

Lodging
Nearby

Tannersville
Northridge Condominiums across from Camelback mountain; (717) 629-1661
Hojo Inn, Tannersville; 1-800-441-2193, (717) 629-4100
Hill Motor Lodge, Tannersville; (717) 629-1667

Nearby Bed and Breakfasts
Brittania Country Inn, Swiftwater; (717) 839-7243
Holiday Glen, Swiftwater; (717) 839-7015
Farmhouse B&B, Mt. Pocono; (717) 839-0796
Memorytown B&B, Mt. Pocono; (717) 839-1680
Mountain Manor Inn, Marshalls Creek; 1-800-MANOR47, (717) 223-8098

Other Nearby Lodging:
Holiday Inn, Bartonsville; 1-800-231-3321, 1-800-828-6879 (PA)
Comfort Inn, Bartonsville; 1-800-822-3275, (717) 476-1500
Countryside Cottages, Bartonsville; (717) 629-2131
Knights Inn, Bartonsville; 1-800-KNIGHTS, (717) 629-8000
Caesars Paradise Stream, Mt. Pocono; 1-800-233-4141, (717) 839-8881

Dining/Après-Ski
On-site
Base lodge: 2 cafeterias, 2 lounges, pizza bar, deck grill
Glen Lodge: cafeteria, lounge, deck grill
Sunbowl Complex: cafeteria
Cameltop: cafeteria
Main lodge lounge open until 10 p.m. nightly, live music Friday-Sunday 2 p.m.-6 p.m., Saturday 3 p.m.-7 p.m.

Nearby
Barley Creek Brewing Co./Restaurant, Tannersville, 1 mile from mountain, 6 home brews, live music Thursday-Sunday; (717) 629-9399
The Inn at Tannersville, (717) 629-7056
Romano's Pizzeria, at Crossings Factory Stores, Tannersville; (717) 620-2600
Smuggler's Cove, Tannersville; (717) 629-2277
Shannon Inn & Pub, East Stroudsburg, live Irish music; (717) 424-1951
Bailey's Steakhouse, Mt. Pocono; (717) 839-9678
Fanucci's, Swiftwater; (717) 839-7097
Ribs & More, Bartonsville; (717) 421-7444
Lee's Japanese Restaurant, Bartonsville; (717) 421-1212
Marco Polo's Restaurant & Lounge, Reeders; (717) 629-6151

Doe Mountain

Doe Mountain Ski Area

101 Doe Mountain Lane
Macungie, PA 18062

Ski Report: 1-800-682-7107
Information: (610) 682-7100/7108
Credit Cards: AE, VISA, MC, Discover

Operating Hours
9 a.m.-10 p.m. weekdays
8 a.m.-10 p.m. weekends

Season: Mid-December to late March

Getting There

- **From Philadelphia area:** Take the N.E. Extension of the Pennsylvania Turnpike to the Quakertown exit and head right on Route 663 south to Pennsburg. At Pennsburg turn right on Route 29 north to the junction with Route 100 at Hereford. Cross Route 100, following it 4 miles to Doe Mountain.
- **From NY/NJ and points north:** Take I-78 west or Route 22 west to the Trexlertown exit. Follow Route 100 south to Macungie, and turn right on Church Street. Follow Church Street 5 miles to Doe Mountain.
- **From Baltimore, Washington, and points south:** Take I-95 to Route 202 north (Pennsylvania) to 100 north to Hereford. Turn left at the junction with Route 29 (at Turkey Hill Mini Market), and follow Route 29 for 4 miles to Doe Mountain.

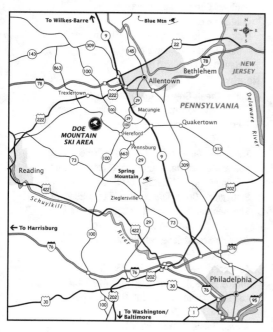

Background

Doe Mountain skiing began in the mid-1960s when seven Philadelphia-based men purchased several parcels of land in a low-lying region between Allentown and Reading. Having opened in 1966 with two slopes and a T-bar and rope tow, the ski area today comprises 15 trails and seven lifts. Seeking to upgrade its image from simply being the closest sizeable ski resort to Philadelphia (55 miles), Doe has completed numerous expansion projects over the last eight years, including the addition of *Timberline*—a 7,400-foot beginner cruising run. A fairly steep black diamond trail on the east face next to *Timberline* is currently under development, and a six-lane snow tubing park is set to open for the 1997-98 season as a complement to the downhill area. The tubing park will sit in a separate area and have its own lodge and parking lot.

Mountain Stats

Base Elevation: 600 feet
Summit Elevation: 1,100 feet
Vertical Drop: 500 feet
Longest Run: 7,400 feet
Primary Slope Direction: North-northeast
Slopes and Trails: 6 beginner, 6 intermediate,
 3 advanced
Skiable Terrain: 90 acres
Lifts: 1 triple, 3 doubles, 2 rope tows, 1 T-bar

Uphill Capacity: 7,000 skiers per hour
Average Annual Snowfall: 40 inches
 1995-96 season: 120 inches
 1994-95 season: 45 inches
Skiable Days
 1995-96 season: 92
 1994-95 season: 78
Snowmaking: 100% of area
Night Skiing: 93% of area, nightly until 10 p.m.

Located near scenic Lehigh Valley, Doe's primary markets are Philadelphia, Allentown, Reading, and Wilmington. Although the area is regarded primarily as a local daytime destination for beginners and intermediates, Doe does a good bit of night business as well. Unfortunately, a temperate climate with little natural snowfall often keeps hopeful local skiers tied up calling Doe's toll-free ski report. An aggressive snowmaking system compensates admirably for its natural shortcomings, but trails are sometimes closed in poor conditions.

Snowboarding

Doe Mountain sports both a halfpipe and snowboard park, located on the north side in front of the base lodge. The 300-foot halfpipe was built five years ago and is effectively maintained by Doe's snow groomers. Jumps are occasionally built at the bottom of the pipe. The neighboring, 700-foot snowboard park last year hosted rail slides, fun boxes, barrels, and other changing obstacles. To reach the park and pipe, snowboarders can either take one of two double lifts to the summit or make the trek from the base with boards in tow.

The halfpipe is well lit for night boarding, and the park should be fully illuminated by the 1997-98 season. The pipe and park prohibit skiers, while snowboarders are restricted from both the *Extreme* advanced trail and *Timberline* beginner trail. Snowboard competitions at Doe are centered mainly on the halfpipe, with two new events held last season. Annual events include the Cool Runnings Sean Spearman Memorial Snowboard Competition and Doe's Snowboard Competition.

Snowboard Rentals
- 200 sets: Nale (Elan), Kemper
- Weekday $25, weekends $30

Snowboard School
- 12 instructors
- Private lessons only; ski school rates apply

Trail Profiles

An initial glimpse of the mountain and its modest 500-foot vertical won't strike a chord of fear in too many skiers. The resort is without much intermediate and expert terrain, featuring mostly short cruising runs. Its 13 slopes and trails are designed to build confidence on a variety of twists and straightaways. To Doe's credit, they don't designate every cat track and extension on the mountain as a trail—a common promotional ploy practiced by many Mid-Atlantic resorts. The beginner-friendly mountain is easy to negotiate, with few intersecting slopes, and skiers can typically enjoy the entire area without waiting in lengthy lift lines.

Doe sports just three short advanced trails, most notably the *Extreme*—a small but challenging mogul run with a decent pitch throughout its 2,000 feet. The *Upper Moose* trail also occasionally holds some bumps, otherwise serving as the designated racing course. Heavily traveled

Timberline isn't nearly as winding as the trail map indicates, but does offer a few sharp drops. The resort also welcomes cross-country and Telemark skiers on its trails.

The resort is realistically for novices, who will have a hard time getting in over their heads almost anywhere on the mountain. First-time skiers have two expansive learning areas served by their own two rope tows and a double chair. Doe's ski school is first-rate; children just getting into skiing and snowboarding should take advantage of the resort's small class sizes and personal instruction.

Lift Tickets/Rentals

Lift Tickets
- 9 a.m.-1 p.m.: weekday $22, weekend (8 a.m.) $30
- 9 a.m.-5 p.m. weekday $27, weekend $35
- 1 p.m.-5 p.m.: weekday $22, weekend $30
- 1 p.m.-10 p.m.: weekday $27, weekend $35
- 5 p.m.-10 p.m.: Monday-Thursday $20, Friday-Sunday $24
- Reduced rates for ages 6-12 and 62-69
- Group rates for 15 or more skiers; daily specials, season passes available

Ski Rentals
- 2,200 sets-Elan
- 100 shaped skis, 20 high-performance skis; Tyrolia bindings, Solomon boots
- Weekdays $16-$20
- Weekends $17-$25
- Rates vary by lift ticket

Services/Other Winter Sports

Ski School
- Over 100 instructors: PSIA certified, Private $39/hour; Group $18/hour
- Three-week childrens', teen, and adult programs
- Learn-to-Ski package

Racing
- NASTAR held on *Doe Run* trail, Saturday and Sunday 11 a.m.

Base Lodge Facilities
- Ski school, cafeteria, bar & grill, ski/rental shop, lockers

Day Care
- Offered 9 a.m.-9 p.m. in base lodge, free on weekdays

Other Winter Sports
- **Snow skating,** with rentals available
- **Telemark** and **cross-country skiing** permitted on slopes, no rentals

Calendar of Events
December
- Christmas Eve discount tickets
- Anniversary/New Year's celebration/events

January
- Cool Runnings Annual Sean Spearman Memorial Snowboard Competition
- Parachute Ski Competition

February
- Ski Slalom Race (prize money)
- Annual Snowboard Contest
- Annual Mogul Competition

Lodging/Dining/Aprés Ski

There's no lodging at Doe, primarily because few guests drive more than 45 minutes to get here. Skiers can base themselves in nearby Allentown and Reading in a pinch, while a handful of restaurants are located within miles of the mountain.

Lodging
Nearby
Landis Store Bed & Breakfast, Landis Store; (610) 367-0598
Cab Frye's Motel, Palm; (610) 679-5955
Sheraton Inn Jetport, Allentown; (610) 266-1000
Cloverleaf Motel, Allentown; (610) 395-3367
Comfort Inn, Allentown; (610) 391-0344
Comfort Suites, Allentown; (610) 391-0344
Hampton Inn, Allentown; (610) 391-1500
Holiday Inn, Allentown; (610) 391-1000
Globe Inn, East Greenville; (610) 679-5948

Dining/Aprés-Ski
On-site
Cafeteria, bar & grill, with live music on some weekends
Nearby
Buckeye Tavern, Macungie; (610) 966-4411
Red Lion Inn, Macungie; (610) 845-2900
Italiano Delite, Macungie; (610) 366-7166
Salvatore's Pizzeria, Macungie; (610) 966-2844
Bally Hotel, Bally; (610) 845-2440
Inn at Maple Grove, Alburtis; (610) 682-4346
Olde Millside Inn, Palm; (610) 679-9558
Topton House Restaurant, Topton; (610) 682-4536

Elk Mountain

Elk Mountain Ski Area
RR3, Box 3328
Union Dale, PA 18470

Ski Report: 1-800-233-4131
Information: (717) 679-2611
Credit Cards: MC, VISA, Discover

Operating Hours
8:30 a.m.-10 p.m. daily
Season: Early December to April

Getting There
- **From Binghamton and northern New York points:** Take I-81 south to Exit 64 and follow signs for Elk Mountain.
- **From Philadelphia, western Pennsylvania, southern New Jersey, or Delaware:** Take the N.E. Extension of the PA Turnpike (Route 9) to Exit 39, then follow I-81 north. Take Exit 63 to Route 374 east toward Elk Mountain.
- **From Washington/Baltimore:** Take I-695 toward Towson, then I-83 north to Harrisburg. From Harrisburg follow I-78 north/east for 20 miles to I-81 north. Take Exit 63 to Route 374 east toward Elk Mountain.
- **From NY City or northern NJ:** Take I-80 west to I-380 west. Follow I-380 west to I-81 north. Take Exit 63 to Route 374 east, following signs for Elk Mountain.

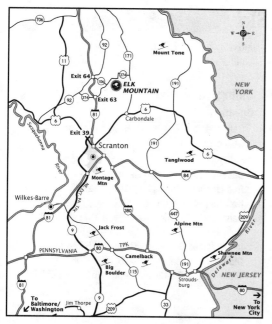

Background

Elk Mountain is situated in the state's northeast corner in the Endless Mountains range, just miles from the Pocono Mountain border and 20 miles from the New York state line. The atmosphere here is quiet and comfortable, with little in the way of lavish amenities. Norway Spruce and red and white pines are planted nearly every year to provide a unique flavor for the region—it's a Pennsylvania resort with a European mindset. Elk's mainstays agree the resort is a rare bird in the state. The resort has its own distinct character and soul.

One of Pennsylvania's first commercial ski areas, Elk surfaced in 1959 when businessmen Ralph Lomma and Gus Steppacher cut three slopes, strung up a 2,200-foot T-bar, and built a small base lodge to accommodate up to 600 skiers per day. Two years later, five expert trails and a host of intermediate runs were erected along with the resort's first double chair. Elk has since grown into one of Pennsylvania's most varied and challenging ski areas, doubling its skiable acreage in the last decade with the addition of nine new trails.

Mountain Stats

Base Elevation: 1,693 feet
Summit Elevation: 2,693 feet
Vertical Drop: 1,000 feet
Longest Run: 1.75 miles
Primary Slope Direction: North
Slopes and Trails: 6 beginner, 9 intermediate, 11 advanced
Skiable Terrain: 235 acres
Lifts: 1 quad, 5 doubles
Uphill Capacity: 5,400 skiers per hour

Average Annual Snowfall: 50 inches
  1995-96 season: 115 inches
  1994-95 season: 65 inches
Skiable Days
  1995-96 season: 125
  1994-95 season: 110
Skier Visits
  1995-96 season: 100,000
Snowmaking: 98% of area
Night Skiing: 30% of area, nightly until 10 p.m.

With a solid vertical drop of 1,000 feet, Elk has an abundance of advanced terrain with 9 blues and 11 black diamonds throughout its 235 acres. The mountain isn't quite as steep as the North Face at nearby Montage Mountain. Still, only Blue Knob has more intermediate and advanced skiing available in the state.

The resort is highly regarded by seasoned skiers who enjoy its long, narrow runs filled with steep drops, tight turns, and bountiful moguls. Elk's somewhat isolated location accounts for modest lift lines and limited congestion, though it's not too far north of other Pocono resorts. The resort hasn't needed to install new lifts in some time, despite an uphill capacity of only 5,400 skiers per hour.

Trail Profiles

Elk's trails are noticeably longer and consistently steeper than most of its Pocono rival areas. When there's a good natural snow base, skiers in the know will often head right here to Elk. The mountain's left face holds the steepest terrain, where eight black diamond trails are conveniently lined up across the mountain face. *Mohawk, Iroquois,* and *Tuscarora* trails are all narrow and steep, resembling classic New England trails. Big bumps and jumps are featured on *Seneca* and *Tunkhannock,* which has a nasty headwall. *Slalom*—regrettably one of just two black diamonds lit for night skiing—has some satisfyingly steep pitches, while *Lackawanna* is often left ungroomed toward the top of the trail for mogul seekers. Regulars will be happy to learn that snowmaking is being added to *Tecumseh,* which formerly ran only with enough natural snow.

Elk is also proud to announce a new addition to the trail system. The intermediate *Mahican* trail was cut above *Tioga* for some more continuous cruising, and will have snowmaking, but no lights. Other intermediate notables include *Delaware* trail and its extension, *Delaware Chute*—a long, undulating run with a sustained pitch typical of the entire mountain. *Kickapoo* features three tight switchbacks before dumping onto the lower section of *Wissahickon.* On the far right end of the mountain is *Lenape*—a long, undulating cruising trail and a favorite for intermediates.

For true beginners, two wide, open areas sit off the lodge, with SKIwee programs for ages 3 to 5 and 4 to 7, and the Elk Mountain Rangers program for ages 7 to 12. The best novice trail is *Lehigh*—a scenic 1.75-mile beginner run with views over the mountain's western face. Unfortunately, it tends to close in the absence of natural snowfall.

Snowboarding

Traditionally a mountain committed to the definitive alpine ski experience, Elk gave in to the snowboard phenomenon last year by cutting a 200-foot snowboard park off the beginner West Slope trail. The new park was a bit on the small and tame side, but there's room for growth. Hits included some moderate gaps and tabletops and a small quarterpipe. The resort may add more obstacles and bigger jumps for the 1997-98 season. Elk is also considering building a halfpipe to complement the park. Restricted to skiers, the park operates under lights until 10 p.m. nightly, with access off the Middle Chair lift.

Without a complete snowboarding arena at Elk, carving-minded boarders will happily stick to the trail network's diverse selection of runs. The mountain's east face trails have the right sustained pitch and plenty of switchbacks for speed and big slalom turns.

Snowboard Rentals
- 100 sets: Burton, $30/day or twilight session; $20/night
- Boots only: $11

Snowboard School
- 15 instructors (ski school rates apply)

Lift Tickets/Rentals/Services

Lift Tickets
- 8:30 a.m.-4:30 p.m.:
  weekday $30, weekend $38
- 8:30 a.m.-12:30 p.m. or 12:30-4:30 p.m.:
  weekday $24, weekend $29
- 12:30 p.m.-10 p.m.:
  weekday $30, weekend $38
- 4:30 p.m.-10 p.m.: $20 all week
- 8:30 a.m.-10 p.m.:
  weekday $35, weekend $43
- Reduced rates for ages 7-12 and 65+

Ski Rentals
- 1,000 sets: Elan (Shaped skis new for 1997-98 season)

- Adult: Weekend/holiday $20, Weekday $18,
  Night $15; Children/seniors: Weekend/holiday
  $14, Weekday $14, Night $12

Ski School
- PSIA certified: 85 instructors, Private $38/hr.,
  Group $18/1.5 hours; First-time skiers' package $30-$35

Base Lodge Facilities
- Ski/rental shops, restaurants/cafeteria, day
  care, downstairs lockers

Day Care
- Offered daily, reservations required

Racing
- Junior slalom racing program

Elk is primarily a day-tripper area, with just four trails and the beginner slopes operating under lights. But consistently is the resort's trademark. It's always one of the last Mid-Atlantic mountains to close each year. Season ticket holders are guaranteed at least 100 skiable days per year, and they have the luxury of instant lift access near the parking area, without the check-in wait. Otherwise, guests have to take a short shuttle ride from the parking lots uphill to the base lodge. In addition to savings from season passes, Elk offers "Big and Friendly Book" rates with coupons toward tickets, equipment, and lessons; generous group discounts for 20 or more skiers; and reduced midweek packages. Seniors and college students have $10 lift tickets on designated weekdays.

Other Winter Sports

- **Cross-country skiing** at nearby Starlight Lodge *(see page 198)*, Ararat Lodge *(see Lodging)*, and two miles away on a new course behind Chet's Restaurant/Lounge
- **Ice-skating** two miles away at Carousel Bed & Breakfast *(see Lodging)*

Calendar of Events

January
- WinterFest
- Learn-to-ski day
- Anna Kilgore Memorial Race
- Randy Turner Memorial Race

February
- Ski/snowboard demo days
- Wilburger Memorial Race

- USCSA Slalom
- USCSA Giant Slalom

March
- Spring Carnival

Lodging/Dining/Après Ski

Though night skiing is limited, guest may not want to leave after an afternoon of riding and sliding. Elk's base lodge area has two restaurants and the Wintergarden Lounge, with live music on Wednesday and weekend afternoons. Child care is offered on an hourly basis, with 24-hour advanced reservations required.

There's no lodging directly on the mountain, but over 25 motels and bed & breakfasts are within 20 miles. Three quaint bed and breakfast houses lie within five miles—the Victorian-style Carousel B&B, Whiffy Bog B&B, and The Ski Habit B&B. Numerous country inn restaurants and taverns are also a short drive away. And antique enthusiasts can visit Carriage Barn Antiques in Clarks Summit (717-587-5405), or call the Top of the Endless Mountains Antique Dealers Association of Susquehanna County to find the dozen or so other antique shops surrounding Elk Mountain (1-800-769-8999).

Lodging

Contact Elk for complete listing of nearby bed and breakfasts and motels

Nearby

Carousel B&B, Union Dale, 9 rooms w/private bath, ski discounts, on-site ice-skating, rates $65-$85/night; (717) 679-2600

Stone Bridge Inn/Restaurant, Union Dale, 12 rooms w/fireplace, indoor pool/hot tub, tavern overlooking Elk Mountain; (717) 679-9200

Oliveri's Crystal Lake Hotel, Carbondale, restaurant/piano bar, rooms w/Jacuzzi; (717) 222-3181

Ramada Inn, Clarks Summit, steak house/bar/cafe; (717) 586-2730

Orazzi's Blue Ridge Inn, Carbondale, restaurant/lounge, rooms w/Jacuzzi; (717) 282-7224

Lodge at Newton Lake, Carbondale, country lodging; (717) 222-3622

Ararat Lodge, Thompson, restaurant/lounge, cross-country ski trails, hot tubs; (717) 727-3174

Holiday Inn, 1-800-HOLIDAY

Motel 81, Dalton; (717) 563-1157

Mountain View Motel, Clifford; (717) 222-5000

Dining/Après-Ski

On-site

Two restaurants (fine dining and casual), cafeteria

Wintergarden Lounge, with live music Wednesdays 3 p.m.-7 p.m., weekends 3 p.m.-6 p.m., open until 11 p.m.

Nearby

Stone Bridge Inn/Restaurant, Union Dale, elegant dining, bands on some weekends, quiet atmosphere; (717) 679-9500

Chet's, two miles from Elk, bar food, bands on Saturdays

Mother Tucker's, Union Dale; (717) 679-2980

Oliveri's (see Lodging listing)

The Windsor Inn, Jermyn, reasonably priced menu and late-night tavern; (717) 876-4600

Mountain View Restaurant/Lounge, Clifford, home-style cooking; (717) 222-5000

Hidden Valley Resort

Hidden Valley Resort

4 Craighead Drive
Hidden Valley, PA 15502

Ski Report: 1-800-443-SKII
Information: (814) 443-2600
Group Information: 1-800-848-3849
Lodging Information: 1-800-458-0175

Internet: http://www.hiddenvalleyresort.com
Credit Cards: VISA, MC, Discover

Operating Hours

9 a.m.-10 p.m. daily

Season: December to late March

Getting There

- **From Pittsburgh:** Take the Pennsylvania Turnpike (I-76). At Donegal take Exit 9 onto Route 31 east for 8 miles, following signs to Hidden Valley.
- **From Cleveland:** Take I-80 to the Pennsylvania Turnpike (I-76). Follow directions from Pittsburgh.
- **From Columbus:** Take I-70 east into Pennsylvania. At I-70/76 east (PA Turnpike), follow directions from Pittsburgh.
- **From points east:** Take the Pennsylvania Turnpike west to Exit 10 (Somerset). Follow Route 31 west for 10 miles to Hidden Valley.
- **From Washington/Baltimore:** Take I-695 to I-70 west (or I-270 to I-70 from Washington) into Pennsylvania. Then take the Pennsylvania Turnpike west, following directions from points east.

Background

Nestled in a pristine setting in southwestern Pennsylvania's Laurel Highlands, Hidden Valley Ski Resort has emerged as one of the state's premiere family and learning ski areas. Hidden Valley doesn't quite measure up to the mega-resort posture of neighboring Seven Springs, offering instead a low-key approach in a quiet, European-resort mold. Its terrain is solidly beginner to intermediate, punctuated by wide, gentle cruising slopes and meticulous grooming. Alpine skiing here is often overshadowed, though, by the activities and amenities of the four-seasons resort, as well as one of the state's best cross-country trail systems.

The site on which Hidden Valley now stands began as a mom and pop restaurant and country inn in 1949. Proprietors George and Helen Parke converted some of their 125 acres into a small ski area in 1955, installing a rope tow and two slopes to accommodate a growing number of skiers from Pittsburgh (65 miles away) and surrounding areas. The Parkes later sold the property in 1983 to

Washington, DC developer Kettler Brothers, Inc., which added additional terrain and helped gradually transform the area into one of the east coast's most well-rounded four-seasons resorts.

Mountain Stats

Base Elevation: 2,390 feet
Summit Elevation: 3,000 feet
Vertical Drop: 610 feet
Longest Run: 1 mile
Primary Slope Direction: North
Slopes and Trails: 6 beginner, 6 intermediate, 5 advanced
Skiable Terrain: 85 acres
Lifts: 1 quad, 2 triples, 3 doubles, 2 handle tows
Uphill Capacity: 12,000 skiers per hour
Average Annual Snowfall: 150 inches
　1995-96 season: 226 inches
　1994-95 season: 180 inches

Skiable Days
　1995-96 season: 114 days
　1994-95 season: 103 days
Skier Visits
　1995-96 season: 200,000
　1994-95 season: 185,000
Snowmaking: 98% of area
Night Skiing: 93% of area, nightly until 10 p.m.

Those tired of skiing the artificial corn snow and mush of many eastern Pennsylvania mountains should look no further. Hidden Valley sits directly in line with the snow belt that carries southward through West Virginia. Snowfall sometimes reaches 175 inches per year here on Laurel Mountain. When the slopes aren't blanketed with powder, the resort ensures perfectly textured snowmaking and grooming on the entire trail network.

Hidden Valley is highly regarded for its patient, conscientious ski school and friendly atmosphere. The resort defines the beginner skier experience, with most of the mountain holding novice cruising terrain and learning slopes. Many ski areas restrict their green runs to the lower half of the mountain, but aspiring skiers here can gain confidence from the summit. By not limiting beginners to one section of the mountain, the resort offers novices green runs on both the north summit and the valley lodge areas. Beginners should be able to negotiate the wide, low-pitched terrain of the resort's novice and intermediate trails without too much difficulty. For the uninitiated, there's a bunny slope with its own lift directly off the base lodge—the site of Hidden Valley's ski school. Lift tickets are modestly priced compared to other Mid-Atlantic resorts. Plan your trip here if you're just starting out or introducing the sport to others, as there may not be a more laid-back resort on the east coast.

Trail Profiles

The intermediate *Continental* and beginner *Mile-long* trails are the resort's most traveled runs. Centrally located *Continental* is expertly groomed on extra-broad terrain, while the north summit's *Mile-long* trail is a long, easy, serpentine run, cutting through the gorgeous hardwoods of Laurel Mountain.

To compliment the mountain's mostly novice terrain, the north summit area was constructed in 1988 to include three black diamond trails. But Hidden Valley's intermediate to advanced terrain lacks both substance and variety, which is why local diehards prefer the bigger and more challenging Seven Springs Resort. Hidden Valley's most challenging runs are *Thunderbird* and *Chabe*. *Thunderbird* has a steep headwall off the summit but gradually peters out on steadier pitches. *Straight Shot* trail is the resort's only showcase mogul run. Its wide track is groomed on one half, leaving the other partially bumped for mogul mashers. Despite just a quad lift serving the entire north summit, lines rarely form here, with most activity centering on the valley lodge area. If you want to traverse untracked powder, make an early run for the north summit.

Snowboarding

Most would agree that Hidden Valley's terrain is generally suited to beginner snowboarders. That's why the resort committed its resources to building an impressive boarding playground. At the bottom of the *Jaguar* trail is a 400-foot halfpipe with 10-foot sidewalls and full snowmaking, grooming, and lights. Next door is the resort's new 600-foot snowboard park, currently available during day hours only. The 1996-97 park offered some pretty good tabletops, rails, and ramps as standards hits, as well as some occasional chutes and tubes. Boarders will have more freedom to create new hits this year.

What snowboarders really need here is for the resort to string up a J-bar lift. Without convenient uphill transportation, freestyle boarders use one of four different chairs. They have to either shred down the mountain from the summit or walk, board in tow, to get back to the park.

Halfpipe and freestyle boarding play a major role in the resort's annual Winter Carnival, which hosts several competitions and events. And Sundays are racing days at Hidden Valley, with giant slalom ski and snowboard competitions. For snowboarders-in-the-making, a patient and well-staffed snowboard school operates several good instructional programs.

Snowboard Rentals
- Over 200 sets: Burton, Hooger, some Oxygen (100 sets with step-in bindings) $30/board, including boots

Snowboard School
- 10 instructors; $20/1.5-hour session
- Snowboard clinics (ages 6-16) offered Sundays

Lift Tickets/Rentals/Services

Lift Tickets
- 9 a.m.-6 p.m.: weekday $20, weekend $34
- 1 p.m.-10 p.m.: Monday–Friday $20-$25, weekend $34
- 4 p.m.-10 p.m.: Monday–Thursday $15, Friday–Saturday $25
- Reduced rates for ages 6-12 and 65-69
- Group rates for 15 or more skiers

Ski Rentals
- 2,000 sets: Integrated Rossignol System (step-in bindings) Adult $18, junior/senior $14, ages 5 and under $10; High-performance skis $25

Ski School
- PSIA certified: 130 instructors, Private $40/hr., Group $15; First-time skiers' package $30-$40
- Mountain Munchkins childrens' program (ages 3-5), with ski instruction, play time, lunch; half day $30, full day $50, rentals $5

- Junior Ski Program (ages 6-12) 10 a.m.-3 p.m. weekends, $50/child, rentals extra
- Ski Camps and Youth Racing Clinics (ages 6-16)

Base Lodge Facilities
- Food court, restaurants, lounges, ski/rental shops, basket check, gift shop

Day Care
- For children 18 months to 8 years of age, available 9 a.m.-6 p.m.; $5/child, additional $5 for lunch

Racing
- Sunday afternoon ski and snowboard competitions

Adaptive Skier Program: By appointment only
- During January, the resort hosts a special adaptive skier program and a Pennsylvania Special Olympics day

Other Winter Sports

- **Cross-country skiing:** Over 25 miles of marked, groomed trails and over 25 miles of mostly ungroomed trails through adjacent state parks; see Laurel Ridge State Park *(page 196)* and Kooser State Park *(page 211)*
- **Snow tubing**, with surface tow, at the North Summit Center; $12 per 4-hour session; night tubing available under lights starting at 6 p.m.
- **Snowshoeing** allowed on all trails; rentals ($10/person) offered at the North Summit Center
- **Horse-drawn sleigh rides** at the North Summit Center; $5/person; offered weekends and, by appointment, weekdays

Hidden Valley bolstered its activity-filled mountain with the addition of the Jeep Eagle Winter Fun Center during the 1996-97 season. Located at the golf club area, the facility introduced horse-drawn sleigh rides and snow tubing to the resort. The center also serves as a warming stop in its acclaimed 50-mile backcountry trail system atop Laurel Mountain. The resort will once again be a host site for SkiFest—a national celebration of cross-country skiing held at selected touring centers throughout the United States. Hidden Valley was also picked to host Pennsylvania's fifth annual Sled Dog Weight Pull—a two-day event covered under the rules of the International Sled Dog Racing Association. Siberians, Samoyeds, Malamutes, Pit Bulls, Boxers, and other top east coast dogs compete in different weight classes to pull 250-pound sleds a total of 16 feet.

Skiing and other winter sports are just some of the components of the 2,000-acre four-seasons resort and conference center. Golfers know Hidden Valley to be one of the Mid-Atlantic's best golf courses, while 30 miles of mountain biking and hiking trails accompany almost every spring to summer activity imaginable.

Lodging/Dining/Aprés-Ski

Since the resort is fairly remote, it offers an abundance of on-site lodging that includes town homes, single-family houses, and an inn. Restaurants and lounges seem to be around every corner of the resort. If you're planning a Hidden Valley vacation and don't want to stay on the mountain, the town of Somerset is 12 miles away. Numerous Victorian bed and breakfasts, chain motels, and restaurants can be found there.

Lodging

On-site (call 1-800-458-0175)

- Studios and suites at The Inn; rates from $52-$105/person per night
- One- to three-bedroom fully equipped condos, town homes, and single-family homes
- The Lake House, with cheaper lodging for couples and groups

Nearby (town of Somerset)
Bed and Breakfasts

Glades Pike Inn B&B, Route 30, 6 miles from resort, 5 rooms w/antique setting, $70-$85/night; 1-800-762-5942, (814) 443-4978

Bayberry Inn B&B, 11 rooms, lounge, $40-$55/night; (814) 445-8471

The Inn at Georgian Place, 11 rooms, posh setting, $95-$180/night; (814) 443-1043

Somerset Country Inn, 6 rooms; (814) 443-1005

Motels

Budget Inn, (814) 443-6441

Hampton Inn, 1-800-HAMPTON

Ramada Inn, 1-800-272-6232

Days Inn-Somerset, 1-800-325-2525

- Call Somerset County Chamber of Commerce for complete listing of lodging/restaurants; (814) 445-6431

Dining/Après-Ski
On-site
Clock Tower Restaurant, with adjoining bar

Slopeside Lounge and the new slopeside **Glaciers Pub**, with live weekend entertainment

Hearthside Restaurant at the conference center, open year-round

Snowshoe Lounge and Escapades Club, with live entertainment

Mountain Deli (conference center)

Nearby
Laurel Mountain Inn, 3 miles from resort, steakhouse/pub; (814) 443-2741

Myron's Restaurant at Ramada Inn, Somerset, Exit 10 Pennsylvania Turnpike; (814) 443-4646

Cafe Fratelli, Somerset; (814) 445-4477

Montage Mountain

Montage Mountain
1000 Montage Mountain Road
Scranton, PA 18505

Ski Report: 1-800-GOT-SNOW
Information: (717) 969-SNOW
Credit Cards: AE, MC, Discover

Operating Hours
9 a.m.-10 p.m. weekdays
8:30 a.m.-10 p.m. weekends

Season: Mid-November to late March

Getting There
- **From NY and points north:** Take I-80 west into PA, get on I-380, and follow it to I-81 south. Take Exit 51 (Montage Mountain Road) and follow signs to Montage.
- **From eastern PA and Philadelphia area:** Take N.E. Extension of PA Turnpike to Exit 37 (I-81 north). Follow I-81 north to Exit 51 and follow signs to Montage.
- **From Washington/Baltimore, and points south:** Take I-95 north toward Baltimore, then I-695 west to I-83 north. Take I-83 north to I-81 north to Exit 51. Follow signs to Montage.

Background

One of the most recent ski resorts to hit the east coast, Montage Mountain began in the 1984-85 season as a private, nonprofit corporation, run by a volunteer board of directors in an effort to bring additional tourism to the region. Because of overwhelming maintenance costs, the resort was turned over in 1991 to Lackawanna County, the securer of the ski area's debt. It made more sense for the county to own and operate the resort since it serves as the broker of the region's tourism trade. The county also owns the Lackawanna County Stadium and its AAA affiliate Red Barons baseball team.

Situated just beyond the Pocono Mountain range, Montage has distinguished itself as a market-niche resort for advanced-intermediate skiers and snowboarders. *SKI* magazine listed Montage number 58 in its ninth annual readers' survey of favorite U.S. ski areas. The resort doesn't have the lavish amenities found at nearby Pocono ski areas—or the time-killing lift lines, for that matter, a sacrifice to which the regulars happily concede. That's not to say there aren't sizable crowds here—skiers will just get more downhill runs than more popular Camelback and Shawnee resorts. Snowboarders coming to Montage will find an outstanding park filled with aerial jumps on a 4,000-foot trail of intermediate pitch.

Mountain Stats

Base Elevation: 960 feet
Summit Elevation: 1,960 feet
Vertical Drop: 1,000 feet
Longest Run: 6,300 feet
Primary Slope Direction: North to northeast
Slopes and Trails: 8 beginner, 6 intermediate, 7 advanced
Skiable Terrain: 130 acres
Lifts: 1 quad, 3 triples, 1 double, 2 tow bars
Uphill Capacity: 8,300 skiers per hour
Average Annual Snowfall: 45 inches
  1995-96 season: 114 inches
  1994-95 season: 23 inches

Skiable Days
  1995-96 season: 120 days
  1994-95 season: 102 days
Skier Visits
  1995-96 season: 180,000
  1994-95 season: 160,000
Snowmaking: 100% of area
Night Skiing: 100% of area, nightly until 10 p.m.

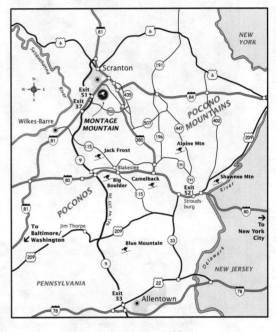

The resort's three-face system offers a solid 1,000-foot vertical on wide but mostly straight trails between towering spruce stands. The trail design restricts the number of intersecting slopes, effectively separating green, blue, and black runs. Despite lacking a lot of winding track on its 21 slopes and trails, the terrain is solidly intermediate, with six black diamond slopes that should satisfy many experts. Montage has more of an advanced-skier reputation than most of its Pocono competition. The terrain on its North Face is quite steep for Pennsylvania standards. There are also several small areas offering baby green turf off the mountain's gentle summit, with a double chair and two surface tows. Two neighboring beginner cruising runs have their own triple lift to the summit as well.

Montage's only true likeness to western resorts is that guests can ski under constant snowfall, albeit the artificial stuff. Snow guns fire on the North Face practically all day, creating manmade blizzards. So be prepared with the right facial and head accessories. The top, right part of the mountain, facing partly east, is more exposed to the sun than the lower section, requiring constant snowmaking. The North Face holds snow longer and requires a consistent, deep base because of its sheer steepness.

Trail Profiles

Two enticing double black diamond trails are featured on the North Face—the newly cut *White Lightning* and *Boomer*. *White Lightning* is self-billed as one of the state's steepest runs with its 70 percent pitch, which measures in at about 37 degrees (terminology used by road departments to measure the grade of roads). The trail is certainly a steep thigh burner, but some argue that Pennsylvania's biggest drop can be found at one of its least-known resorts—Ski Denton in the north-central section of the state (see page 66). Nonetheless, 1,800-foot *White Lightning* is an exhilarating cliff-like run down the trail's double fall line. Its steepest point, unlike black diamonds at many other resorts, lies toward the trail's finish. *Boomer* is another thrilling run. It's 700 feet longer and slightly less mogul-packed than *White Lightning*. Neighboring *Smoke* offers steep pitches around the midway point and a nice switchback on its runout.

Last season, Montage kept *White Lightning* filled with moguls most of the season so skiers wouldn't fly down its steep terrain at breakneck speeds. The trail was groomed with a winch cat groomer only when moguls formed out of control. *Boomer* and *Smoke* have traditionally served as the resort's bump trails, but were groomed more consistently last season with the addition of *White Lightning*.

Skiers and snowboarders can race down long, continuous stretches of 6,500 and 6,300 feet on

Fast Track and *Runaway* trails, respectively. Upper parts are more narrow and serpentine before turning into wider and steeper black diamond track, particularly on the steep pitch toward the end of *Lower Fast Track*. Few advanced skiers get out on these two trails, opting instead for the North Face section, but the steeps are well worth it toward their finishes. The problem with *Runaway* and *Fast Track* is that skiers have to ride the lengthy Long Haul chair lift to get to that side of the mountain, traversing lengthy and leisurely terrain before accessing the trail-ending steeps. Other good intermediates include *Spike* and *Switch*—two terraced runs that level off after strong initial drops.

Snowboarding

Boarders air it out at Montage. The resort proudly hosts one of the Mid-Atlantic's biggest and most diverse snowboard parks. Montage's North Face is the site of this exclusive park and its series of monster jumps on 4,000 feet of the former (converted) intermediate *Whistler* trail. A halfpipe and park were located under the Iron Horse chair lift years ago, but the terrain was too flat for thrill-seeking boarders. So the pipe was removed and the park relocated to the now-converted *Whistler* trail.

Last season the boarder-friendly resort allowed guests to design obstacles at their own discretion. Hits included several gaps, spines, a quarterpipe, and a rail slide. The park is long and wide, with ample space to carve and accelerate between its big-air jumps, and has more than enough run-off after the jumps. The Iron Horse triple lift serves the park, which continues into the night under full lights.

The rest of the mountain is open for shredding. The popular North Face is steep enough to satisfy good boarders, while the mountain's upper half is used mostly by developing riders. The 1997-98 season will feature more competitions, events, and promotions. To complement the successful park, management is considering adding a terrain park so skiers can perform their own aerial maneuvers.

Snowboard Rentals
- 60 sets: Kemper and Hammer: $18/all times

Snowboard School
- 5 instructors: Private $35/hour; Group $15 per 1 1/4 hours

Lift Tickets/Rentals/Services

Lift Tickets
- 9 a.m.-10 p.m.: weekday $28, weekend $35
- 9 a.m.-12:30 p.m.: weekday $24, weekend $28
- 12:30 p.m.-10 p.m.: weekday $28, weekend $35
- 5 p.m.-10 p.m.: weekday $18, weekend $18
- 20-25% discounts for children ages 6-10
- Children under 5 ski free
- Season Pass: $450

Ski Rentals
- 1,500 sets: Dynastar with Solomon boots/bindings $15-$18 (Shaped skis to be introduced for the 1997-98 season)

Ski School
- PSIA certified: 20 instructors: Private $35/hour; Group $30/1 1/4 hours

- SKIwee for ages 5-10, daily 10:30 am-12:30 p.m., 2-4 p.m., and 6-8 p.m.: $45 w/rentals, $37 without

Base Lodge Facilities
- Food court, restaurants, lounges, ski/rental shops, basket check, gift shop

Day Care
- For children 18 months to 8 years of age, available 9 a.m.-6 p.m., $5/child, additional $5 for lunch

Racing
- NASTAR held on *Switch* trail weekends 10 a.m.-3 p.m. and Tuesday nights

Other Winter Sports

Last year Montage hosted the four-day Keystone Winter Games Winter Sports Festival, with racing events including giant and modified-giant slaloms, a dual slalom, a freestyle mogul event, and a first timers' race. Most other downhill events are held on the *Spike* and *Cannonball* advanced slopes, and the freestyle Snowboard Park Jam is a big hit annually. Outdoor ice-skating is available at nearby Lackawanna Stadium. Additionally, cross-country skiing clinics are held on a nearby one-mile course, and annual five- and 10-kilometer cross-country ski races are held in February at nearby Wilkes-Barre Municipal Golf Course.

- **Cross-country skiing**, conditions permitting, 30 miles away at Promise Land State Park
- **Ice-skating** nearby at Lackawanna Stadium

Calendar of Events

December
- PA Interscholastic Racing Series (through February)

January
- Mid-winter Fun Fest
- Annual Mid-Atlantic Montage Bump Challenge
- Subaru Master of the Mountain Series

February
- Keystone Winter Games—amateur ski/snowboard competitions
- Pennsylvania Winter Olympics
- National Ice Carving Championships

March
- March Madness—races, events, and games

Lodging/Dining/Aprés-Ski

Without any slopeside lodging or full-dining establishments, Montage is still an ideal family ski resort. The closest lodging is one mile from the mountain, and there's no shortage of beds nearby. Over 30 hotels, motels, and inns are all within a short drive, as well as shopping malls, movie theaters, and restaurants. The resort's cafeteria and pub run until 10 p.m. nightly, while unlimited dining and aprés-ski can be found close by in populous Scranton and Wilkes-Barre. Although the resort is a bit further than other Pocono areas for guests driving from southern points, access to the mountain is relatively quick and easy off Interstate 81.

Lodging
Nearby

Woodlands Inn & Resort, Wilkes-Barre, 179 rooms, indoor pool, Jacuzzi, health club, restaurant, lounges w/band and dj, call for rates; 1-800-897-8991, (717) 824-9831

Hampton Inn/Marvelous Muggs Restaurant & Pub, on Montage Mtn., 129 rooms, indoor pool, hot tub, excercise room, free breakfast, rates $75-$80/night; 1-800-HAMPTON; (717) 342-7002

Ponda-Rowland Inn (B&B) at Rowland Farm, Dallas, PA, w/ 2 fireplace suites & rooms for families, rates $75-$95/room; 1-800-854-3286

Victoria Inns/Jad's Place dining, JP's Lounge, Pittston (1 mile from Montage); 1-800-937-INN5, (717) 655-1234

Big Bass Lake, Gouldsboro; 1-800-762-6669, (717) 842-7600

Holiday Inn, Scranton; 1-800-HOLIDAY, (717) 654-3300

Econo Lodge, Scranton; 1-800-424-4777

Knights Inn, Scranton; 1-800-662-4084

Kelley's Inn, Gouldsboro; 1-800-432-5253

Dining/Aprés-Ski
On-site

Cafeteria and pub open until 10 p.m.

Nearby

Arcaro & Genell's, Old Forge; (717) 457-5555

The Dough Company, Wilkes-Barre; (717) 824-1003

The Lobster Trap, Wilkes-Barre; (717) 825-6909

Tom & Jerry's, Scranton; (717) 344-1771

Smith's Restaurant, Scranton; (717) 961-9192

Gabello's Pizza

* Variety of bars in nearby Scranton area, notably Tinks and Whistlers, Rascals in Dickson City, and Jim Dandy's in Chinchilla

Seven Springs

10

Seven Springs Mountain Resort

Road 1
Champion, PA 15622

Ski Report: 1-800-523-7777
Information: 1-800-452-2223, (814) 352-7777
TTY Reservations: #18143527313
Credit Cards: MC, VISA, Discover
Internet: http://www.7Springs.com

Operating Hours
9 a.m.-10 p.m. Sunday-Thursday
9 a.m.-11 p.m. Friday-Saturday

Season: December to April

Getting There

- **From Pittsburgh:** Take the Pennsylvania Turnpike (70/76) east to Exit 9 and Route 31 east. Follow Route 31 east to Route 711 and turn right. Turn left onto County Line Road, traveling 7 miles to Seven Springs entrance.
- **From Philadelphia and eastern points:** Take the Pennsylvania Turnpike (70/76) west to Exit 10 and Route 31 west. Turn left at Pioneer Park campground. Go 4 miles to the stop sign, turning right onto County Line Road. 5 miles to the resort.
- **From Washington/Baltimore:** Take I-695 (from Baltimore) to I-70, into Pennsylvania. Get on the Pennsylvania Turnpike (70/76) traveling west. Follow the directions above.

Background

S ome things get better with time. At least that's the case with Seven Springs, one of the Mid-Atlantic's oldest ski areas and also one of its best. The resort consistently ranks as a top east coast family ski destination, welcoming an astonishing 400,000-plus visitors per year. The resort provides a sprawling, amenity-laden base facility, welcoming guests with a barrel of apple grogs and a large grill firing kielbasa and sauerkraut.

Located one hour southeast of Pittsburgh, the resort began in 1932 as a series of private vacation cabins owned by Pittsburgh merchant Adolph Dupre. Hunting and fishing were the summertime staples, but it was the winter possibilities that intrigued Dupre. An avid skier, he would capitalize on the region's snow-filled bounty in 1935 by introducing the area's first skiing rope tow and alpine slope. Today the resort is still Dupre owned and operated—and probably much more than he ever imagined.

While the 1970s featured record-setting skier visits at Seven Springs, as well as frequent 40-minute lift waits, the next two decades would bring about a

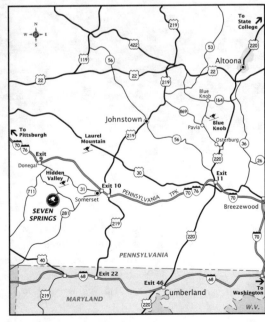

change for the better at the resort. The North Face section was cut in the early 1980s and has been expanded considerably over the last 15 years to provide extra terrain for all abilities. The resort also runs a yearly assessment of the mountain, constantly adding, widening, and regrading terrain; increasing snowmaking and lights; and upgrading lifts and amenities. The front-side lifts were recently rearranged, completely separating the beginner slopes from other trails. This learning area formerly sat at the bottom of an intermediate trail, causing all sorts of mayhem between faster and slower skiers.

Mountain Stats

Base Elevation: 2,240 feet
Summit Elevation: 2,990 feet
Vertical Drop: 750 feet
Longest Run: 1.25 miles
Primary Slope Direction: North to northeast
(North-facing side and east-facing side)
Slopes and Trails: 15 beginner, 10 intermediate,
5 advanced
Skiable Terrain: 500 acres
Lifts: 3 quads, 7 triples, 3 handle bar tows,
5 rope tows

Uphill Capacity: 24,600 skiers per hour
Average Annual Snowfall: 100 inches
1996-97 season: 53 inches
1995-96 season: 234 inches
1994-95 season: 96 inches
Skier Visits
1995-96 season: 450,000
1994-95 season: 386,000
Snowmaking: 95% of area
Night Skiing: 75% of area, Friday-Saturday until 11
p.m., 10 p.m. midweek

Seven Springs used to rely on mostly natural snow mixed with some sparse snowmaking. At its 3,000-foot elevation, the area gets an average of 100 inches of snow per year, and a record 234 inches was collected during the 1995-96 season. Snowmaking coverage and grooming have been superb in recent years, especially with some of this decade's lean winters. *Turtleneck* trail and a few of the connecting bypasses don't have snowmaking, but all the main trails are equipped with the manmade crystals. Ski seasons have been extended to last well into March, and the resort is

typically among the last Mid-Atlantic ski areas to close each year. Seven Springs regulars love warm, spring skiing on the resort's slushy, mashed potato terrain.

The resort has yet to invest in a detachable high-speed quad, and it could use one, despite having 18 strategically located—but somewhat archaic—chair lifts. Amazingly, the uphill lift capacity is over 24,000 persons per hour—an indication of the kinds of crowds the resort draws. Weekend and holiday peak hours can mean long lift lines, but it's the trails that are sometimes saturated beyond normal comfort zones. Unfortunately, there's no limit on ticket sales. Congestion is fueled by the hordes of skiers arriving from Mid-Atlantic and southern regions for weekend and week-long vacations. An efficient operating system does its best to ease parking and monitor skier traffic patterns. The best bet for maximizing your number of runs and escaping arduous lift lines is to ski the North Face early, as heavy weekend traffic builds on the front base like an urban beltway's rush hour. This side also tends to get pretty windy, so dress appropriately in colder conditions.

Snowboarding

Snowboarders have it all at Seven Springs: solid terrain, a big-air snowboard park, and a large connecting halfpipe. The park's size has quadrupled since its inception years ago, and last season's playground hosted an array of aerial hits that included six jumps and a tabletop, rail slide, and quarterpipe. The 400-foot-long, 50-foot-wide halfpipe also got high marks last year. It's groomed regularly by a Pipe Dragon grooming machine designed specifically for pipes.

Seven Springs has a staff dedicated to maintaining the park and pipe—freestylers are for the most part restricted from constructing their own jumps. Skiers can also roam free in the park, though boarders don't much appreciate the invasion of turf. There's a rope tow for the halfpipe, as well as a chair lift above it so guests can watch boarders in action. And a sound system cranks music in the park all day.

As far as the terrain goes, there's enough variety to keep carving boarders content for a full day. The width and pitches on *North Face Slope* and *Giant Steps Slope* are just right for boarders to cut sweeping giant-slalom turns. Some of the growing number of annual snowboard events held here include the Mid-Atlantic Snowboard Series and the FatAir Snowboard Contest.

Snowboard Rentals
- 400 sets: Burton, including boots and bindings
- New step-in bindings for 1997-98 season
- Day $29; Night $19

Snowboard School
- 15 instructors: Private $40/hour; Group $18/1.5 hours

Trail Profiles

Despite a modest vertical drop of 750 feet, the mountain's enormous 500 acres of skiable terrain features 30 slopes and trails to provide a solid skiing and snowboarding experience for all levels. The North Face is the choice for the resort's advanced clientele. The steep headwalls on aptly named *Giant Steps Slope* and *Gunnar Slope* run quickly to a cross-trail mid-shelf, with more steep drops and runouts toward the bottom. And the width and pitch on *North Face Slope* and *Giant Steps Slope* allow skiers to make fast, giant-slalom turns and let their skis run over the terraced terrain. Double diamond *Goosebumps* on the Front Face is the resort's steepest, and possibly shortest, trail. The top headwall of *Gunnar* on the other side is nearly its equal in pitch. Three trails on the Front Face are left ungroomed for stumpin' and bumpin'. *Goosebumps* is moguled out the whole way down the short, narrow trail, but often gets rutted with icy bumps by day's end. Blue run *Stowe*, the site of the resort's mogul races, has a nice vertical and is pocketed with bumps down the trail's right side. Black diamond *Avalanche* also features mogul mounds on one side.

The resort's average vertical drop aside, the steeps don't stop after finishing the five advanced trails. Several blue runs have somewhat daunting drops, including wide-open but short-lived *Tyrol* and *Stowe*. The network of blue and green trails between the two faces offers more narrow, serpentine track, while there are some glade sections on *Alpine Meadows Slope* and a narrow chute on *Little North Face Trail*.

Terrain for beginners is also quite substantial. First-time skiers have a secluded ski school learning area with its own rope tow lift between the two mountain sides and another small section at the bottom of *Fawn Lane* that uses a handlebar tow. A good bet for novices is *Lost Boy Trail*— a narrow, 1.25-mile cruiser with gradually changing pitches stretching across the bottom of the North Face. And the north summit's *Turtleneck Trail* winds leisurely through the mountain's hardwoods, with many turning opportunities and two connecting slopes to provide a longer run. The resort offers top-notch childrens' instruction in its Tiny Tot Ski School and Junior Program. Run like the national standard SKIwee program, Tiny Tot offers a mix of indoor/outdoor ski instruction and supervised play time for ages four to seven.

Lift Tickets/Rentals/Services

Lift Tickets
- 9 a.m.-7 p.m.: weekday $32, weekend $39
- 1 p.m.-10 p.m.: Monday-Thursday $32, Sunday $39
- 1 p.m.-11 p.m.: Friday $32, Saturday $39
- 4:30 p.m.-10 p.m.: Sunday-Thursday $24
- 4:30 p.m.-11 p.m.: Friday-Saturday $24
- 20-25% discounts for children 11 and under
- Friday night to Sunday special: $72
- Children under 5 and adults 70+ ski free

Ski Rentals
- 3,000 sets: Rossignol, K2, Dynastar; Nordica and Rossignol boots
- 450 sets of shaped skis; Day/twilight session: adult $19.50, child $14.50
- Night: adult $15.50, child $11.50; Weekend: $37.50, $27.50

Ski School
- 250 instructors: PSIA certified: Private $40; Group $18

- Junior Program (ages 7-12) offered daily, 10 a.m.-3 p.m., $50-$70; rentals extra
- Tiny Tot Ski School (ages 4-7), offered daily; rates: $40-$55
- Learn-To-Ski program, offered daily; rates: $30-$39, includes rental, group lesson, and lift ticket

Base Lodge Facilities
- Indoor swimming and new (main lodge) hot tubs open to lodge guests and the public, two game rooms, miniature golf, bowling, exercise room, roller skating/roller blading, Swedish massage, specialty shops, rental and equipment shops

Day Care
- Walking age and older; offered 8:30 a.m.-4:30 p.m. and 6 p.m.-10 p.m. on weekends; rates: full day $30, half day $22

Racing
- NASTAR offered daily on *Giant Steps Slope*, with races at 1 p.m.

Other Winter Sports

On-site
- **Snow tubing** with five 400-foot chutes and one handle tow lift
- **Horse-drawn backcountry sleigh rides** offered daily from 10 a.m.-8 p.m.; rates: $10/person
- **Sledding** hill
- Snowmobiling not offered for 1997-98 season

Nearby
- **Cross-country skiing**, weather permitting, at Hidden Valley Ski Area *(see page 197)*, Laurel Ridge State Park *(see page 196)*, and Kooser State Park *(see page 211)*
- **Ice-skating** and **ice fishing** 12 miles away in Somerset

Calendar of Events

December
- Giant Slalom Series/annual races

January
- Mid-Atlantic Snowboard Series
- Womens Skiing Program
- Kids' Days
- Pennsylvania Special Olympics

February
- WinterFest Celebration
- USCSA Allegheny Conference Championships
- Miller Mogul Challenge

March
- Subaru Master the Mountain Series
- FatAir Snowboard Contest
- American Cancer Society's Snowshine Festival
- Snow Volleyball Tournament

Lodging/Dining/Après-Ski

To say that skiing here is trivialized by the resort's array of indoor activities and amenities is an understatement. The base lodge's entertainment center is akin to a suburban mall and recreation park. The health club, bowling alley, indoor mini-golf, racquetball courts, and roller-rink are all seamlessly connected to a hotel, numerous restaurants and lounges, specialty shops, and game rooms. With all the resort has to offer, extended-day guests are advised to bring thick wallets of cash, several credit cards, and more cash.

Snow Country and *Ski* magazines rated Seven Springs one of their top 50 U.S. ski resorts two consecutive years. The resort is also consistently voted among the top five eastern destinations for skiable acres, snowmaking, slopeside lodging, overall weekend trips, and dining and entertainment. On-site accommodations are extensive—and a bit expensive—with 385 hotel rooms, 12 suites, 16 chalets, and 10 dormitories. Five cabins and 238 family condominiums are also available on resort property, with shuttle bus access to the main lodge. Several midweek ski-and-stay packages are more affordable, and include all resort amenities.

There's not much just beyond the resort for après-ski activity, but then again there's no need to leave. The Foggy Goggle slopeside lounge is a favorite resort watering hole, recently ranked twenty-eighth in America among ski area bars by *Ski* magazine. The Tahoe Lodge also serves as a nice ski break with its summit views.

For out-of-town guests who don't want to spend and spend, bargain lodging can be found off the turnpike in the town of Somerset—a 12-mile drive from Seven Springs. Between the resort and Somerset are 16 bed and breakfasts, 12 hotels/motels, and a few restaurants and pubs.

Lodging

On-site

Slopeside lodging: 384 rooms and 12 suites
Main Lodge: over 800 one- to four-bedroom condos, and cabins for 6-20 persons
- Call 1-800-452-2223 for rates/information.

Nearby (Somerset)

See Hidden Valley—*Lodging, (page 51)*

Dining/Après-Ski

On-site

Twelve eateries (from take-out to gourmet) and 6 bars, including: Helen's Restaurant (gourmet), the Oak Room (traditional/seafood menu), Slopeside Grill (family dining), and slopeside Foggy Goggle lounge. Also, weekend buffets, bands/DJs, Monday night comedy acts.

Nearby

See Hidden Valley—*Dining/Après-Ski, (page 51)*

Shawnee Mountain

Shawnee Mountain

P.O. Box 339, Hollow Rd
Shawnee-on-Delaware, PA 18356

Ski Report: 1-800-233-4218
Information: (717) 421-7231
Credit Cards: AE, MC, VISA, Discover
Internet: http://www.shawneemt.com
E-mail: ski@shawneemt.com

Operating Hours
9 a.m.-10 p.m. Monday-Friday
8 a.m.-10 p.m. Saturday-Sunday

Season: Late November to late March

Getting There

- **From New York City and northern New Jersey:** Take I-80 west to PA Exit 52/Route 209 north. Follow signs to Shawnee.
- **From Philadelphia/Delaware:** Take the N.E. Extension of the PA Turnpike to Route 22 east. Exit in Allentown to Route 33 north onto I-80 east, then take PA Exit 52/Route 209 north. Follow signs to Shawnee.
- **From Washington/Baltimore:** Take I-95 north to I-695 west to I-83 to Harrisburg. Then take I-81 north to I-78 east to Route 22 east past Allentown. Exit in Allentown to Route 33 north onto I-80 east. Follow I-80 east to PA Exit 52/Route 209 north. Follow signs to Shawnee.

Background

Since 1975 Shawnee has been a major player in the busy Pocono Mountain alpine ski scene. Situated just off the Delaware River and the New Jersey border, the ski area was originally developed as an amenity for the historic, recently renovated Shawnee Inn. With several large urban markets under two hours' drive, Shawnee Development Co. began constructing time shares, cutting new trails, and adding more chair lifts during the 1980s. The resort's original inverted summit lodge was also replaced with a larger base-area lodge to accommodate growing numbers of day skiers. Recently acquired by Watershed Realty Company, Shawnee's operation was rescued through debt restructuring in 1992 by a group of local investors and long-standing Shawnee employees.

Regarded as a leading east coast family ski area, Shawnee received the highest overall ranking of the Pocono ski resorts from *SKI* magazine's 1996 eastern U.S. ski area survey. The resort offers exceptional SKIwee and adaptive skier programs and is one of only three Pennsylvania ski areas to host the *SKI* magazine-sponsored MINIriders program, which teaches snowboarding to children ages 7-15. Shawnee is also adding snow tubing to its base area for the 1997-98 season, with six

lanes and two lifts. The resort hosts events for the family nearly each weekend, while parents have the option of dropping off their children at the base lodge's child care, offered from 9 a.m. to 5 p.m. daily. Visitors will find one of the country's largest rental shops at Shawnee, with over 4,000 sets of skis including the new shaped ski variety.

Shawnee consistently attracts a sizable yearly skier base because of its proximity to populous areas in several surrounding states—it's one of the closest major resorts to metropolitan New York and northern New Jersey (1 1/2 hours).

Mountain Stats

Base Elevation: 650 feet
Summit Elevation: 1,350 feet
Vertical Drop: 700 feet
Longest Run: 5,100 feet
Primary Slope Direction: North to northwest
Slopes and Trails: 7 beginner, 10 intermediate, 6 advanced
Skiable Terrain: 125 acres
Lifts: 1 quad, 1 triple, 7 doubles

Uphill Capacity: 12,600 skiers per hour
Average Annual Snowfall: 50 inches
  1995-96 season 96 inches
  1994-95 season 60 inches
Skier Visits
  1995-96 season 115
  1994-95 season 110
Snowmaking: 100% of area
Night Skiing: 95% of area, nightly until 10 p.m.

With an altitude of only 1,350 feet, winter climates aren't customarily conducive to skiing at Shawnee. Two things are guaranteed, though: relentless snowmaking/grooming and, unfortunately, excessive crowds. It's among the first Pocono ski areas to open each season, typically around the Thanksgiving holiday, with snow guns firing over the entire mountain early and often. But the trail system simply isn't big enough to sustain the skier masses. Shawnee's 23 slopes and trails, most of which carry names of noted Native Americans who once populated the Delaware River area, are a bit overstated and misleading. Though the slopes are cut extra wide for the most part, many of them intersect other trails. Others are little more than cat tracks not-so-subtly designed to max out the resort's number of advertised runs.

To combat most weekends' long, movie-theater lift lines and saturated slopes, Shawnee added a new quad lift to the overburdened *Tomahawk* trail. The quad chair raises the resort's lift capacity to a whopping 12,600 skiers per hour. A new computerized ticket system has also been installed to help ease the flow of incoming guests.

Trail Profiles

Shawnee's strength is its cluster of bunny terrain adjacent to the base lodge. Three secluded hills are devoted to the uninitiated skier—*Little Chief, Little Brave*, and the wide-open *Snowdance* slopes, with three double lifts among them. Though beginners will be hard pressed to find long, crowd-free trails on which to build confidence, the wide, gentle track of *Upper* and *Lower Pennsylvania* should serve them well. Remaining green runs—*Pocahontas, Indian Queen, Meadows*, and *Minisink*—are usually less crowded. Unfortunately, they run through the middle of the mountain, intersecting with heavier traveled trails.

Not known as a particularly steep mountain, one short but sweet beauty that sticks out among the others is *Renegade* trail. Its steep headwall off the summit and fast-turning terrain is short lived but compelling. The rest of Shawnee's limited advanced track can be found on the mountain's lower half, covering roughly 500 of the mountain's 700 feet of vertical. Five short black diamonds are lined up across the row, with mogul skiing underneath the double chair on *Tecumseh* trail. These advanced runs, with the exception of *Tecumseh*, should be more appropriately considered strong intermediates. *Tomahawk* hosts a nice mix of drops and runouts on its wide, smooth cruising track.

Delaware is the longest and most varied of the intermediates, with its winding course and steep, dog-leg finish. On the other side of the mountain is *Upper* and *Lower Bushkill*—a long, wide cruiser on a straight path. *Kittatinny* is a baby blue run off the summit that becomes gradually more challenging for novices before running out past beginner *Minisink* and *Lower Pennsylvania*.

Snowboarding

One of the pioneers of east coast snowboarding, Shawnee was the first Pocono resort to build a halfpipe, constructed over a decade ago. Located on the intermediate *Country Club* trail off the west summit, the 400-foot pipe is deep, fairly wide, and somehow maintained without top-of-the-line grooming equipment. Snowmakers run snow guns and a flex tiller on the sides. Once the pipe opens, it's usually golden the entire season. The halfpipe is complemented by a surrounding 900-foot snowboard terrain park and its array of changing jumps and obstacles such as spines, quarter pipes, fun boxes, and table tops.

The park and pipe are both lit for night boarding and are accessible directly off the Country Club double chair (which may operate weekends only) and the Arrowhead and new quad lift. Certain trails may occasionally shut down to boarders, but the otherwise rider-friendly resort hosts the Mid-Atlantic Snowboard Series, featuring both halfpipe and freestyle competitions, with plans for a big-air competition during the 1997-98 season. Affordable season passes are available to boarders and skiers, with additional discounts through Shawnee's Loyal Skier's Club. The resort invested in a new fleet of Burton boards with step-in bindings last year, doubling their rental inventory.

Snowboard Rentals

- 200 sets: Burton, Oxygen; $26/board and boots

Snowboard School

- 20 instructors (Ski rates apply); First-time snowboard package $50-$55, with 1.5-hour lesson, rental, and restricted lift ticket

Lift Tickets/Rentals/Services

Extremely active in racing and events, Shawnee is the only Pocono ski area, and one of just nine in the state, to offer NASTAR (National Standardized Racing), held weekends on the intermediate *Bushkill* trail. Both juniors and adults can sign up for weekend training programs. And the resort's reputable adaptive ski school, partially funded by grants and donations, has taught skiers with disabilities since 1987, with over 500 lessons registered during the 1995-96 season.

Lift ticket rates are consistent with somewhat high-priced Pocono standards, though a number of budget options are available to skiers: affordable group rates, multiday and book discount tickets, Sunday night family discounts, and midweek daily specials for college, professional, and civil service guests. And Shawnee will take a page from nearby Jack Frost/Big Boulder by upgrading its junior lift ticket for the 1997-98 season. For $25, youths up to age 15 can ski or snowboard anytime, any day. Additional coupons can be found inside the *Shawnee Mountain News* and in ski shop brochures.

Lift Tickets

- 9 a.m.-12:30 p.m.: weekday $25, weekend (8 a.m.) $29
- 12:30 p.m.-5 p.m.: weekday $25, weekend $29
- Open-5 p.m.: weekday $31, weekend $39
- 12:30 p.m.-10 p.m.: weekday $31, weekend $39
- 5 pm-10 p.m.: weekday $25, weekend $25
- Open-10 p.m.: weekday $36, weekend $43
- Group rates (20-35% off) for 15 or more skiers

Ski Rentals
- 4,000 sets: Elan, Atomic
- Salomon bindings and boots; Daily $21; Night $16

Ski School
- 300 instructors; Private $40/hour, Group $18/1.5 hours; First-time ski package, w/group lesson, rental, restricted lift ticket: $47-$52
- SKIwee (ages 5-12), Pre-SKIwee (ages 3-4), and Mountain Cruiser programs (ages 10-15): $55/daily, $40/half day ($10 additional fee for rental)
- MINIrider 4-hour snowboarding program for ages 7-15: daily $40, rental $15

Base and Summit Lodge Facilities
- Separate ski and snowboard shops, day care, cafeteria, food courts, pizza bar, cocktail lounges and bars

Day Care
- 8 a.m.-5 p.m. daily

Adaptive Ski School
- By appointment; over 500 lessons taught during 1996 season

Other Winter Sports

On-site
Snow tubing off base lodge, with six 800-foot-long chutes and two lifts (call for rates)
Telemark skiing permitted on all trails

Nearby
Cross-country skiing, sledding, and **ice-skating** at nearby Mountain Manor Inn, (717) 223-8098, 1-800-228-4897. Weather permitting, cross-country skiing is offered on the golf course, with three trails from beginner to intermediate; $6 trail fee, $10 with rental

Calendar of Events

December
- NASTAR race series begins

January
- Dannon Winterfest—events/entertainment

February
- Mid-Atlantic Snowboard Series—

halfpipe/freestyle competition
- Race Against Cancer (giant slalom)
- Subaru Family Weekend w/giant slalom race

March
- Annual Mogul Competition (on *Tecumseh* trail)

Lodging/Dining/Aprés-Ski

With so many lodging options available both just off the mountain and within 10 minutes' drive, the resort keeps all but a few trails open under lights nightly until 10 p.m. The Easy Bumps Saloon serves as the resort's central watering hole and aprés-ski site. When the nearby private chateaus, town homes, and Shawnee Inn fill to capacity, skiers can base themselves in the Stroudsburgs, Marshalls Creek, or Delaware Water Gap, which also offer numerous restaurants, pubs, and activities. Local attractions include the scenic Delaware Water Gap National Recreation Area, 10 miles to the north, and the roaring waters of Bushkill Falls nearby.

(continues)

Lodging

On-site

65-bed ski dormitory in summit lodge,
for groups only (call for rates)

Nearby

Shawnee Inn, restaurant/pub, indoor pool; call
for package rates; 1-800-SHAWNEE, extension
1413

Shawnee Valley, 2- to 3-bedroom
homes/chateaus just off Shawnee Mountain,
with fireplace, kitchen, whirlpool (call for rates);
1-800-SHAWNEE, extension 8970

Shawnee Village & Valley View, villas, townhomes up to 6 and 8 persons, shuttle bus service; 1-800-SHAWNEE, extension 8970

Budget Motel/JR's Greenscene Restaurant; 1-
800-233-8144

Mountain Manor Inn, 5 minutes from Shawnee,
country inn with two restaurants;
1-800-228-4897

Ramada Inn, Delaware Water Gap,
restaurant/sports bar with live weekend entertainment, indoor pool, game room, ski packages; 1-800-228-4897

Shannon Inn, East Stroudsburg, restaurant/live
Irish music on weekends, indoor pool; 1-800-
424-8052

Hillside Lodge, family lodging, dining, with fire-
place/Jacuzzi rooms available; 1-800-666-
4455

Dining/Après-Ski

On-site

Hickory Lick's Restaurant and Bar, with lunch
and light-dinner menu

Easy Bumps Saloon, three cocktail bars

Nearby

Mimi's Streamside Café; (717) 424-6455

* See *Nearby Lodging* above for other dining
establishments

Ski Denton

Ski Denton

P.O. Box 367
Coudersport, Pennsylvania 16915

Ski Report/Information/Reservations:
(814) 435-2115

Credit Cards: MC, VISA, Discover

E-mail: skidenton@penn.com

Operating Hours
10 a.m.-9 p.m. Monday, Friday
1 p.m.-9 p.m. Tuesday to Thursday
9 a.m.-9 p.m. weekends

Season: Early December to late March

Getting There

- **From points north (New York State):** Take Route
16 south to Olean, New York, then Route 417
south to Route 44 south to Route 6 east. Follow
signs to Ski Denton.

- **From Cleveland and Erie:** Take US 90 east to US
17 east to Olean, New York. Then take Route 417
south to Route 44 south to Route 6 east. Follow
signs to Ski Denton.

- **From Pittsburgh:** Take I-79 north to I-80 east to
Route 66 north to Route 6 east to Coudersport.
Follow signs to Ski Denton.

- **From Harrisburg:** Take US 15 north to Route 6
west at Mansfield. Follow signs to Ski Denton.

- **From Washington/Baltimore:** Take I-95 north to I-
695 west, then I-83 north to Harrisburg. Follow US
15 north to Route 6 west at Mansfield. Follow
signs to Ski Denton.

Background

Northcentral Pennsylvania's Potter County is home to more deer than people, which is why Mid-Atlantic skiers are usually surprised to hear there's a pretty good ski area here in this remote section of Allegheny wilderness. Ski Denton is tucked away amidst towering stands of maple trees in one of the state's biggest snow belts. And despite its seemingly small appearance—a 650-foot vertical over 75 acres of terrain—and remote location, Denton attracts just enough of a yearly skier base to earn its keep. Visitors comprise a mix of beginners and families and a growing number of skilled skiers who come to slide down Denton's frequent natural powder base—snowfall averages well over 100 inches per year. Along with 20 slopes and trails, the resort offers a snowboard park, five-track snow tubing run, and virtually endless cross-country skiing terrain on surrounding trails. It's also one of the Mid-Atlantic's friendliest ski areas. A courteous and helpful staff make for a nice change of pace from busier east coast resorts.

The ski area, part of Denton Hill State Park, is concessioned to Denton Hill and Ski Resort, Inc. Commercial skiing began here after a state study in the 1950s determined the property was a natural fit for alpine and Nordic skiing with its heavy snowfall and north-facing mountain. Beginning with just a few trails, a poma tow lift, and no snowmaking, Pennsylvania's park service ran the operation for 20 years. The state then decided the venture wasn't worth running in the red, selling off the property to a few small interest groups. After twice closing shop with no one to take the lease, locals Mike and Joyce Kneffley turned the fledgling business around and have run the mountain each of the last 15 years.

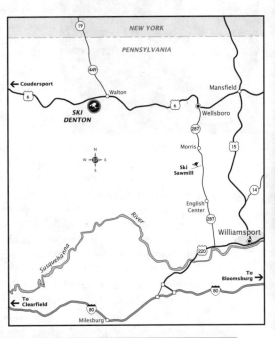

Mountain Stats

Base Elevation: 1,750 feet
Summit Elevation: 2,400 feet
Vertical Drop: 650 feet
Longest Run: 1 mile
Primary Slope Direction: North
Slopes and Trails: 7 beginner, 6 intermediate, 7 advanced
Skiable Terrain: 75 acres
Lifts: 1 triple, 1 double, 2 poma lifts, 1 handle tow

for tubing
Uphill Capacity: 4,200 skiers per hour
Average Annual Snowfall: 100 inches
1995-96 season 132 inches
Skiable Days
1995-96 season: 110
1994-95 season: 112
Snowmaking: 95% of area
Night Skiing: 85% of area, nightly until 9 p.m.

Trail Profiles

The resort is so far removed from metropolitan areas that lift lines are almost nonexistent, even during holidays and peak weekend hours. Most trails are of the green- and blue-level variety, but seven single to triple black diamonds offer several steep, straight drops, albeit painfully short.

Since the mountain never draws big crowds, Denton's advanced terrain is a good bet for skiers seeking untracked powder runs. While the 1,500-foot *Avalanche* trail is distinguished as one of the steepest slopes in the east, skiers will find an even sharper, more challenging drop on a connector chute known as *The Wall*, despite its mere 100 feet in length. Denton regulars swear there's nothing steeper on the east coast than these two recently added runs. The hair-raising *Avalanche*

 features a 68-degree incline on a straight and fairly wide trail (over 70 degrees is considered a cliff). Keep in mind, though, that its double fall line breaks not only straight down, but left, toward the trees, which is where skiers head when they lose it. The top section of *Avalanche* is most difficult, and often quite slick, so dig in your edges and hang tight. The trail is often bumped out late in the season—the lower two-thirds is always well groomed for fast cruising.

The Extreme is classified a triple black diamond—a narrow, steep, and unforgiving gladed chute parallel to *Avalanche*. With the trail's 66-degree descent and narrow 25-foot width, most skiers have to hop their turns, rather than carve, with both determination and accuracy. Two transition areas afford skiers much-needed respites. Denton's abundance of natural snow helps keep the advanced slopes open, and opens up the 100 miles of surrounding cross-country skiing terrain. The resort keeps a low-key approach to racing and events, with few sanctioned races.

The Link is an advanced intermediate trail that the resort sometimes leaves ungroomed for mogul busters. When it is maintained, the trail is a comfortable, easy cruising run. Denton more consistently bumps up *Buck Run* underneath the triple chair. If plans go unimpeded, two additional intermediate slopes off the summit should be finished within the next few years.

Outside of four or five steep areas, gentle slopes serving beginners and novices make up the rest of the mountain. Most intermediate runs can be handled by beginner skiers, who also have the option of shooting down the summit without touching the more advanced terrain, or connecting with less challenging sections of *Avalanche* from two locations. Two secluded green trails over one mile long wind lazily on both sides of the mountain, including the popular *Sidwinder* trail, which is wide enough for developing skiers to practice turning. Denton's patient ski school works out of the *Snowflake* bunny slope—a large, open space off the base lodge that has its own poma lift.

Snowboarding

Because of its inaccessibility from urban areas, snowboarding doesn't fit as strongly into the equation at Denton as other Mid-Atlantic ski areas. The resort is, however, considering two locations, possibly off the centrally located *Liberty Bell* and its triple chair, for a large snowboard park and halfpipe. Denton doesn't presently have the right kind of tiller to create a stable halfpipe, but will purchase the necessary grooming apparatus if snowboard ticket sales continue to rise.

In the meantime, there's an area cleared in the woods where freestylers can build mounds of snow for aerial jumps. Last year, some sizable hits and a horseshoe were cut. The trails themselves are pretty narrow for the most part, and not necessarily conducive to sweeping giant slalom turns that boarders like. But the *Spirit of '76* and *Elm Hollow* trails feature natural banks on both sides that serve as quasi pipes.

Snowboard Rentals
- 15 sets: K2, Morrow; $25/day; $9/two hours

Snowboard School
- 3 instructors: ski school rates apply

Lift Tickets/Rentals/Services

Skiers will find lift tickets cheap, and downright generous, for Mid-Atlantic standards. Denton even went as far as giving lift tickets away one Christmas Eve, drawing a record crowd of 1,400 skiers. And despite its isolated location, night skiing is offered on 17 trails seven nights a week, come hell or high water, until 9 p.m.

Lift Tickets
- 9 a.m.-5 p.m.: weekday (10 a.m.) $18, weekend $25
- 1 p.m.-5 p.m.: weekday $14, weekend $21
- 1 p.m.-9 p.m.: weekday $18, weekend $25
- 5 p.m.-9 p.m.: weekday $14, weekend $21
- 9 p.m.-9 p.m.: $30 weekend
- 10 a.m.-9 p.m.: $21 weekday
- Reduced rates for ages 11 and under; $10 weekday/$15 weekend for ages 65+

Ski Rentals
- 350 sets: mostly Atomic, some shaped skis, demos available; Solomon bindings/boots; $16-$18.50/day; $10/night

Ski School
- PSIA certified: 35 instructors; Private $25/hour; Group $10/hour
- SKIwee $25/three hours
- Learn-to-ski program $33/weekend, $25/weekday

Base Lodge Facilities
- Cafeteria, ski school, rental/ski shops, bunkhouse lodging

Day Care
- None

Adaptive Ski School
- By appointment only

Other Winter Sports

Though cross-country skiing is not permitted on most trails, skinny skiers can access over 100 miles of pristine state park backcountry off the summit or two miles away from the state forestry department. A $4 chair lift ride to the summit connects with a series of ridges that extends over 20 miles before circling back to the resort, where Nordic skiers can run down the beginner trail. Cross-country trails are marked with colored signs, and maps are available from the forestry department.

Cross-country skiing throughout 100 miles of marked, ungroomed track, with trails accessible from the summit lift or two miles away at the forestry department (814-274-8474); no trail fee; rentals available from Denton for $13.50/day.

Sled Dog snow skate rentals available, by the hour or two hours: $3.50-$6.00; resortwide access, except on *Avalanche* trail

Snow tubing area with handle tow, offering five runs separated by small banks on an easy slope (call for rates)

Calendar of Events

December
- Free lift ticket day on Dec. 24 for pre-qualified customers

March
- Family Fun Weekend
- Free lift tickets on last Sunday of season

Lodging/Dining/Après-Ski

Though Denton attracts a lot of families, no day care is offered. Most visitors come from Lancaster County and Harrisburg areas, roughly three hours away. A limited number of chalets are available on-site, as well as group bunk lodging on the third floor of Denton's small base lodge. "Après-Ski" is a term rarely associated with the remote Coudersport/Galeton area. Expect little more than the serenity of a small town. But guests can plan an economical and comfortable overnight stay in a number of bed and breakfasts or motels within 20 miles, with modest rates ranging from $25 to $45 per night.

Lodging

On-site:
- Six fully equipped two-bedroom cabin chalets (up to 6 persons) at the foot of the mountain, with ski-in, ski-out access, living/dining rooms, kitchen
- Bunkhouse quarters in third floor of base lodge for large groups (up to 70 persons)

Nearby:
Bed & Breakfasts:
The Lush Victorian B&B, country lodging, Coudersport; (814) 274-7557
The Poet's Walk B&B, Port Allegheny, with/4 doubles, 1 single; 1-800-646-5731/1068
Kaltenbach's B&B, Wellsboro, with hot tub and Jacuzzis; 1-800-722-4954
Blackberry Inn B&B, Smethport, 45 minutes from Denton; (814) 887-7777

Motels/inns/Rental homes:
Pine Log Motel & Cabin Run, Galeton, 1 mile from Denton; (814) 435-6400
Potato City Motor Inn, near Denton, fine dining restaurant/pub; 1-800-867-7133
Antlers' Inn, restaurant, ski packages; (814) 435-6300
Evergreen Lodge (cabin rentals), Coudersport, 2 miles from Denton; (814) 435-6395

Westgate Inn, Coudersport, restaurant; (814) 274-0400
Coach Stop Inn, Wellsboro, fine dining restaurant/lounge; 1-800-829-4130
Penn Wells Hotel, Wellsboro, restaurant, indoor pool; 1-800-545-2446
Comfort Inn, Mansfield, restaurant/lounge, Jacuzzi rooms, ski packages; 1-800-822-5470
Susque Homestead & Chalet, Ulysses, PA, fireplaces; (814) 435-2966

Dining/Après-Ski

On-site:
Cafeteria

Nearby (Coudersport)
Mosch's Tavern & Country Inn; (814) 274-9932
Laurelwood Inn; (814) 274-9220
Sweden Valley Inn; (814) 274-7057
The Original Italian Pizza; (814) 274-0455

* See *Lodging* above for more dining establishments

Ski Liberty

13

Ski Liberty

P.O. Box SKI
Carroll Valley, PA 17320-0703

Ski Report: 717-642-9000
Information: 717-642-8282
Credit Cards: VISA, MC, Discover

Internet: http://www.skiliberty.com

E-mail: skiliberty@skiliberty.com

Operating Hours
9 a.m.-10 p.m. weekdays
8 a.m.-10 p.m. weekends

Season: Late November to mid-March

Background

Just north of the Maryland border in Caroll Valley lies Pennsylvania's Ski Liberty—one of Baltimore and Washington, DC's closest and most visited alpine destinations. The resort was acquired in 1972 when it was known as Charnita Ski Area, re-opening in 1974 as Ski Liberty. The same conglomerate that claims nearby Ski Roundtop and New York's Ski Windham in the Catskills also owns Liberty.

Mountain Stats

Base Elevation: 580 feet
Summit Elevation: 1,186 feet
Vertical Drop: 606 feet
Longest Run: 5,200 feet
Primary Slope Direction: Northeast-northwest
Slopes and Trails: 6 beginner, 6 intermediate, 4 advanced
Skiable Terrain: 100 acres
Lifts: 3 quads, 3 doubles, 1 J-bar, 1 handle tow
Uphill Capacity: 10,920 skiers per hour

Getting There

- **From Baltimore:** Take I-695 to I-795 north to Route 140 west (Route 140 west becomes Route 16 west at the Pennsylvania line). Follow 16 west and turn right on Route 116 east for 3 miles. Liberty is on the right.
- **From Washington and Northern Virginia:** Take I-495 north to I-270 north to Frederick, MD. Then follow Route 15 north to Emmitsburg, PA. Exit onto South Seton Avenue, following South Seton to the traffic light. Turn left onto Route 140 west (becoming Route 16 west at the Pennsylvania line). Take Route 16 west to Route 116 east and turn right. Follow this for 3 miles to Liberty on the right.
- **From York, Pennsylvania:** Follow Route 30 west to the square in Gettysburg. Take the three-quarter turn on Baltimore Street. Travel one block and turn right at the stop light onto Route 116 west (Middle Street). Follow this for 10 miles to Liberty on the left side.

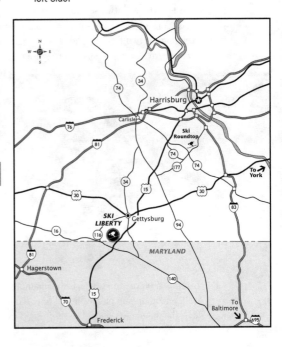

Average Annual Snowfall: 28 inches
1995-96 season: 62 inches
1994-95 season: 46 inches

Skier Visits:
120,000-200,000 per year
Snowmaking: 100% of area
Night Skiing: 100% of area, nightly until 10 p.m.

The mountain—a near-replica of nearby Ski Roundtop—appears modestly sized from the parking lot. It is, in fact, a mountain of limited terrain. With just 16 slopes and trails, Liberty's strength is its two mountain faces, which effectively separate skier traffic by ability. The back side holds some deceptively steep pitches directly off the summit, despite only 606 feet of vertical drop, while novice terrain makes up the majority of the busier front face. New for the 1997-98 season are major upgrades for the popular snowboard park and halfpipe. The resort is also building a terrain park on the front side's mid-station area so skiers can enjoy their own snowboard-type obstacles, including bumps, spines, and tabletops.

Lean winters, low altitude, and sun exposure force Liberty into running a top-notch snowmaking and grooming operation. Skiers essentially take whatever conditions they can get around here. Trails are smoothly packed and groomed, but often succumb to icy conditions come nightfall. Like so many other Mid-Atlantic resorts, Liberty's snowmakers have to dig and groom the snow into a hard, granular, blended pack because of the otherwise late-night freeze and resulting ice. Since guests may also be subject to virtual manmade blizzards, wearing goggles comes highly recommended. Snow blowers often have to work around the clock to keep the trails open. Another reputation the resort has formed is its aggressive and sometimes over-zealous ski patrol, which will quickly stamp the ticket of anyone caught skiing or snowboarding recklessly.

Trail Profiles

With the Mid-Atlantic's relatively small mountains and plateaus, beginner turf is usually the rule and not the exception. But for first-time skiers and snowboarders, it doesn't get much better than Liberty, with two separate learning areas on opposite sides of the front face. The *First Class Area* is one of the region's most substantial true beginner sections. Liberty facilitated the area by stringing up two lifts: a quad chair lift and mid-station handle tow. On the other end is *Alpine Run*, where learning skiers can practice on a slightly stronger-pitched hill. Both areas have been

designated "Family Ski Zones" and "Slow Skiing Areas." The heavily traveled, one-mile-long *Dipsy Doodle* trail is the only continuous beginner run on the mountain—something the mountain could use more of. It does offer the option of forking off to the broader, easier *Don't Worry* slope on the back face.

Skiers offer many different opinions of Liberty's trail system, but there's no question the back side is quite steep—and painfully short lived. Black diamonds *Ultra*, *Eastwind*, and *Strata* each drop sharply off the summit before flowing into more intermediate track at the trails' midway points. *Eastwind* can be Liberty's most challenging trail when it's left ungroomed and bumped. *White Lightning*, on the front face, is the mountain's best-kept secret with its 90-degree left turn, headwall, and changing pitches in fall line. *White Lightning* and neighboring *Blue Streak* are coined after the mountain's once-densely wooded summit that served as the site of a lucrative moonshine distillery years ago.

Liberty's best intermediates are the wide, masterfully groomed *Heavenly* and *Blue Streak* trails. *Heavenly* is typically the more congested of the two as the resort's main artery from the front to back side. It has a steep initial drop that breaks into a fast-carving turn before barreling out into extra-wide cruising track. *Blue Streak* is mistakenly billed a black diamond trail, and should test well, unless moguls are left to form, for mid-level skiers. Liberty's most recent addition—*Sidewinder*—is a baby blue run that allows an easier route down the back side than the black diamonds. The resort recently introduced lighting to and widened *Lower Strata*, opening up some more good terrain for skilled skiers descending the steeper stretches of *Upper Strata*.

Snowboarding

A major destination for Washington, DC- and Baltimore-area snowboarders, Liberty sports both a park and halfpipe on the far-right end of the mountain's main lodge side. The park has been expanded each of the last three seasons, tripling its size and number of big-air obstacles. During the 1996-97 season, the secluded park was built up pretty well with changing hits such as tabletops, spines, some smaller jumps, and quarter-pipes. Its best feature may not be of substance, but of comfort: A convenient J-bar lift was added a few years ago for easy access.

The halfpipe has always been somewhat of a dis-appointment, being a bit on the small side and often unavailable during warm fronts. But that's old news. *Big* changes are in store for the 1997-98 season. The resort is enlarging and moving the pipe to a bet-ter-suited location adjacent to the park, and adding a sound system to blast the area with music. A new Scorpion grooming machine, developed out of California, will be shared with sister resort Ski Roundtop to more effectively groom the walls and

transitions of the pipe—a problem that has consistently plagued Liberty's halfpipe. Despite the overhaul, area boarders may still consider Roundtop's pipe the better of the two, with a longer and deeper base relative to Liberty's.

The park and pipe both operate under lights nightly until 10 p.m. Boarders can carve the entire mountain, but like nearby Whitetail, Liberty's ski patrol will flag, stamp, and dismiss snowboarders they consider "haz-ardous." The resort welcomes speed and air on its designated boarding areas, though, and will be running a halfpipe and Boardercross competitive series throughout the coming season. For those who want to try board-ing for the first time, Liberty's Boarderline Snowboard Shop has one of the east coast's largest rental fleets, and instructional programs are available from the ski school.

Snowboard Rentals
- 320 sets: K2, Mistral; mostly step-ins
- $22-$26 weekday; $23-$29 weekend

Snowboard School: 28 instructors (ski school rates apply)

Lift Tickets/Rentals/Services

Come prepared—lift tickets don't come cheap here. Luckily, the resort's time-increment ticket system allows visitors a lot of flexibility. If you think you'll wind up packing your gear for Liberty more than six or seven times a season, consider purchasing the Ski Advantage Card. The $69 sea-son-long pass allows 40 percent off all lift tickets and 25 percent off NASTAR racing at Liberty, Roundtop, and New York's Ski Windham. Skiers and snowboarders can also return their lift tick-ets within one hour of purchase if not completely satisfied, with a guaranteed return-trip voucher.

Liberty's flex ticket system, offers four- and eight-hour blocks from time of purchase, which helps reduce lift lines and bottlenecks at peak hours. The flex system is a necessary function of Liberty's, with droves of skiers making the 60-mile trip from the Washington/Baltimore area for both weeknight and weekend skiing. Lift ticket sales are limited, though, to curb lengthy lift lines and overburdened slopes.

The resort is constantly upgrading both its terrain and services, and it must do so to accommodate the constant flow of its guests. The remodeled base lodge area is now a sprawling series of connected buildings, with several food venues to choose from, a restaurant/tavern, separate children's learning center and rental shop, and the adjoining 40-room hotel. There's also a new restaurant at the base of the back side.

Lift Tickets
- Weekend: $33/4 hours, $37/8 hours, $24/5 pm-10 p.m.; Weekday: $25, $29, $24
- $4 discount for ages 6-10
- 50% off for ages 65+ midweek only
- 40% ticket discounts with Ski Advantage Card ($69/person)

Ski Rentals
- 2,300 sets: Elan, Rossignol, Dynastar, Atomic
- 200-300 sets of Parabolic skis
- $20-$23 weekday; $20-$26 weekend

Ski School
- PSIA certified: 240 instructors
- Private $41/hour; $30/half-hour; Group $19/hour (Lessons held daily at 10 a.m., noon, 2 p.m., 7 p.m.)
- Childrens' Learning Center

- Ski Camp offered daily for ages 4-10, reservations required, half-day $50-$60, full day $60-$74
- Limited and all-mountain ski or snowboard learning packages

Base Lodge Facilities
- Ski/Childrens' Learning Centers, lockers/basket check, Lost and Found, snowboard shop, rental/repair shops, cafeteria/restaurant/tavern/food courts, hotel, day care

Day Care: Ages 1-10; $5/hour; Offered Monday-Thursday 9 a.m.-5 p.m., Friday 9 a.m.-9:30 p.m., weekends/holidays 8 a.m.-9:30 p.m.

Racing: NASTAR held on *Be Happy* intermediate trail on Tuesdays, Thursdays, weekends, and holidays

Adaptive Ski School: By appointment only

Calendar of Events

January
- Pennsylvania Learn-to-Ski-Free Day
- Washington Ski International Race
- Sunday Triple Crown Races (through February)

February
- Liberty Winter Carnival: slalom races, bump contests, entertainment

- WHFS Ski Festival: several bands, snowboard competitions, fun events

March
- Annual Beach Party: races, contests, entertainment

Lodging/Dining/Aprés-Ski

With its central location to urban markets (and limited terrain), most Liberty guests are in and out the same day. Otherwise, the resort's 40-room base-side hotel and the nearby private Carroll Valley Resort Hotel usually have rooms available. If you're going to ski and stay overnight, a good choice is historic Gettysburg. It's an easy 10-mile drive from Liberty, and has a broad selection of quaint bed and breakfasts in the heart of its downtown area, several chain motels, and turn-of-the-century restaurants and taverns. History buffs and shoppers will appreciate the numerous Civil War-era museums, guided tours, and specialty shops in town.

Lodging

On-site

- 40-room slopeside hotel, $79-$89/night, $139/luxury suite; (717) 642-8282

Carroll Valley Resort Hotel; 1-800-548-8504

Nearby

Bed & Breakfasts

Maplewood Inn B&B, Fairfield, 3 miles from Liberty; (717) 642-6290

The Windborne Farm B&B, Fairfield; (717) 642-5436

Old Appleford Inn, downtown Gettysburg, 10 miles from Liberty; 1-800-275-3373

The Tannery B&B, downtown Gettysburg; (717) 334-2454

The Herr Tavern B&B/Restaurant, Gettysburg; 1-800-362-9849

The Brickhouse Inn B&B, downtown Gettysburg; 1-800-864-3464

Farnsworth House B&B/Restaurant, Gettysburg; (717) 334-8838

Gettysburg motels

Holiday Inn; 1-800-HOLIDAY
Days Inn; 1-800-325-2525
Hampton Inn; 1-800-426-7866
Larson's Quality Inn; 1-800-228-5151

Dining/Aprés-Ski

On-site

- Food court, pizza/pasta shop, deck with barbecue/entertainment

Ski Liberty Tavern/Restaurant, 11 a.m.-1 a.m. weekends, occasional live entertainment

Nearby (Gettysburg)

Gettysburg Hotel/Restaurant, historic mansion, circa 1797, fine dining; (717) 337-2000

Dobbin House, historic restaurant/bar, downtown; (717) 334-2100

The Pub, popular Gettysburg tavern; (717) 334-7100

Cashtown Inn, Cashtown; (717) 334-9722

Ski Roundtop

Ski Roundtop

925 Roundtop Road
Lewisberry, PA 17339

Ski Report: (717) 432-7000
Information: (717) 432-9631

Internet: http://www.skiroundtop.com
E-mail: skiroundtop@skiroundtop.com
Credit Cards: VISA, MC, Discover

Season
Late November to late March

Operating Hours
Weekdays 9 a.m.-10 p.m.
Weekends 8 a.m.-10 p.m.

Getting There

- **From Harrisburg:** Take I-83 south to Exit 15. Turn left on Route 177 then right on Pinetown Road. Turn left on Moore's Mountain Road, then right on Roundtop Road.
- **From Baltimore:** Take I-83 North to Exit 13. Turn left on Route 177 then right on Pinetown Road. Turn left on Moore's Mountain Road, then right on Roundtop Road.
- **From Washington, DC and points south:** Take I-95 to 495 north, then I-270 to Route 15 North. Turn right at the first traffic light in Pennsylvania, then right on Old York Road. Turn left at the next light onto Route 177, left on Pinetown Road, then left on Roundtop Road.

Background

Just 20 miles from Ski Liberty sits Lewisberry's Ski Roundtop—both owned by the conglomerate Snow Time, Inc. Roundtop was originally the brainchild of a group of ski-minded businessmen from the nearby town of York. For years they would make the long northward trek to carve Vermont's formidable mountains. Hoping to establish a resort on one of the small plateaus in their own neck of the woods, the group knew they would have to overcome poor natural conditions that included an average annual snowfall of just 30 inches. The resort could only operate with an advanced snowmaking system and a north-facing mountain in this region the snow gods seemed to overlook. What they had going for them was demographics, with Baltimore just 75 miles away and Harrisburg, Lancaster, and York all within a short drive. Since opening in 1964 with just two slopes and a single chair lift, Roundtop has expanded to 15 runs, and now has a family snow tubing area and a respected snowboard park and halfpipe.

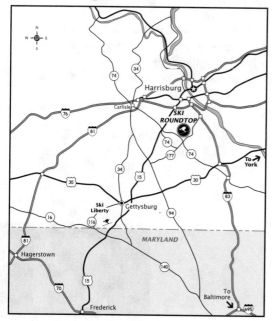

Mountain Stats

The mountain itself is the spitting image of Liberty, both with small vertical drops of just 600 feet. You might wonder how Roundtop could even be that big, judging from base-lodge views. And considering the trail network's lack of variety, many guests end up skiing the same four or five trails over and over again. That's why Roundtop adopted its flex ticket system, offering four- to eight-hour blocks from time of purchase. More experienced skiers will use the four-hour ticket to get their runs in, without getting locked into a more expensive day-long investment.

Roundtop, like many of the Mid-Atlantic's resorts, offers perfectly groomed cruising and learning terrain. Essentially a family area, the resort offers a supervised day care facility for children 18 months and older, and runs a limited adaptive ski school program with three-track skiing and instruction available.

Base Elevation: 755 feet
Summit Elevation: 1,355 feet
Vertical Drop: 600 feet
Longest Run: 4,100 feet
Primary Slope Direction: North
Slopes and Trails: 6 beginner, 5 intermediate, 4 advanced
Skiable Terrain: 100 acres
Lifts: 2 quads, 1 triple, 2 doubles, 2 j-bars, 2 tow lifts, 1 carpet lift

Uphill Capacity: 11,000 skiers per hour
Average Annual Snowfall: 30-40 inches
  1995-96 season: 80 inches
  1994-95 season: 20 inches
Skier Visits
  100,000-200,000 annually
Snowmaking: 100% of area
Skiable Days
  1995-96 season: 110
  1994-95 season: 95
Night Skiing: 93% of area, nightly until 10 p.m.

Trail Profiles

Advanced skiers won't likely find enough challenging terrain to keep them occupied for a full day, but there are three or four trails worth checking out. Roundtop's left summit holds two black diamond runs—*Ramrod* and *Gunbarrel*—with steep drops off the summit followed by more sustained pitches, each with roughly 4,000 feet of terrain. One of the two trails is left partially ungroomed for mogul busters, as is the midway section of *Lafayette's Leap*. *Barrett's Trail* is the one exception to the mountain's otherwise straight runs. It has more of an intermediate pitch than its black diamond rating suggests, but it's a fun, narrow run with a width of roughly 20 feet. It also has the mountain's best switchback toward its runout finish. *Minuteman* is by far the most heavily traveled of the intermediates. It is extra wide and well textured—ideal for lower- to mid-level skiers looking to perfect their turns.

As expected from a family ski area, beginner slopes are substantial at Roundtop, and four of its ten lifts serve the cluster of green runs. The *Discovery* area and *Izzy Bear Children's Learning Area* are flat parcels off the main lodge exclusively for first-timers and instruction. The mountain's beginner design is not without its flaws, though. One such blemish is the absence of a long, slow cruising trail from the summit. Novice skiers may be able to negotiate the steady pitches of the resort's intermediate runs, but there's no available trail on which to build confidence after finishing the three short beginner slopes. To make matters worse, the three main beginner runs aren't completely separated from faster terrain, as skiers on *Barrett's Trail* funnel into these slow zones.

Snowboarding

Snowboarders can shred in one of the area's best halfpipes, located in its own area in front of the main lodge. The pipe—nearly 300 feet long and 40-feet wide—also has its own J-bar lift. Both Roundtop and Liberty are major destinations for area boarders, but many prefer Roundtop's better-maintained halfpipe. The resort used a big excavator to groom its halfpipe last year, keeping the pipe open more frequently than Liberty. The two areas will now share a newly purchased Scorpion groomer, which should prove more efficient and powerful than the noted Pipe Dragon groomer. A sound system will also be added to the halfpipe area for 1997-98.

A 200-foot snowboard park is located on a chute between intermediate *Minuteman* and advanced *Lafayette's Leap* trails. Its ramps, tabletops, and gaps are sizable enough, but the park's small pitches keep boarders from getting enough speed to catch big air time. The park could also stand to have its own J-bar lift like the halfpipe offers. Boarders currently have to use the quad chair off the *Minuteman* trail or walk themselves.

All trails are open to boarding, and both the park and pipe are well lit until 10 p.m. nightly. Halfpipe competitions are held during Roundtop's annual Spring Ski Fest in early March, and the Edge Snowboard Series offers ongoing competitions and events, beginning around Christmas. The resort will also host a series of 18 events during the 1997-98 season that includes halfpipe competitions and a new Boardercross series (a slalom-like race for four to six riders, with numerous jumps and obstacles). The events will be heavily promoted and may feature major national sponsors.

Snowboard Rentals
- 300 sets: K2, Kemper, Mistral
- Weekday $22-$26; Weekend $23-$29

Snowboard School: 25 instructors

Lift Tickets/Rentals/Services

Roughly 90 percent of the resort's skier base comes from nearby Harrisburg and York, as well as Lancaster, Baltimore, and Washington, DC. Considered slightly less crowded than nearby sister resort Ski Liberty, guests may get more runs per day at Roundtop. Along with its staggered lift ticket operation, Roundtop's Skier Guarantee allows a free return voucher for any skier or snowboarder who leaves within one hour of ticket purchase.

Lift Tickets
- 8 hours: weekday $29, weekend $36
- 4 hours: $25, $32
- 5 p.m.-10 p.m.: $24 all week
- Reduced rates for ages 6-10
- Frequent skier card—40% discounts

Ski Rentals
- 2,300 sets: mostly Atomic; 150 Elan parabolic and other high-performance skis
- Weekday $19-$22; Weekend $21-$25

Ski School
- 200 instructors: mostly PSIA certified
- Private $41/hour; $30/half-hour; Group $19/hour
- Learn-to-ski/snowboard packages

Base Lodge Facilities
- Main lodge/food court, outdoor barbecue, ski shop, ski school, tickets/rentals, lockers

Day Care: Ages 1-10; $5/hour; Offered Monday-Thursday 9 a.m.-5 p.m., Friday 9 a.m.-9:30 p.m., weekends/holidays 8 a.m.-9:30 p.m.

Racing: NASTAR held on the intermediate *Exhibition* trail Fridays 6:30 p.m.-9 p.m., weekends 11 a.m.-3 p.m.

Adaptive Ski School: By appointment only

Other Winter Sports
Five-lane **snow tubing** area offered weekdays 4 p.m.-9 p.m., weekends 10 a.m.-9 p.m.; $7/hour

Calendar of Events

December
- Apple Subaru Race

January
- Subaru Master the Mountain: mini clinics
- Continental and Lawrence Subaru Races
- WTPA-FM late-night ski events: two each in January, February

February
- Cumberland/Lancaster Valley races

March
- Spring Ski Fest: races, competitions, music, events

Lodging/Dining/Aprés-Ski

As for aprés-ski, it isn't a term much used here. Adults are sometimes disappointed to learn there's no chance of sipping on a cold one after a session on the slopes. As is the case with nearby Whitetail Ski Resort, Roundtop makes its home in one of Pennsylvania's dry townships.

Few Roundtop guests drive very far to get here, so there's no need for lodging on the mountain. For a change of pace, a few bed and breakfasts are short drives away in the towns of Wellsville and Mechanicsburg—a large suburb of Harrisburg, which also has several chain motels.

(continues)

Lodging

(continued)

Nearby
Bed & Breakfasts

Warrington Farm B&B, Wellsville, 5 miles from Roundtop; (717) 432-9053

Moore's Mountain Inn B&B, Mechanicsburg (6 miles), restored brownstone tavern, circa 1798, 3 rooms, private bath, $75/night; (717) 766-3412

Motels

Hampton Inn, Mechanicsburg (10 miles); 1-800-HAMPTON

Super 8 Motel, Etters (7 miles); (717) 938-6200

Fairfield Inn, New Cumberland (14 miles); 1-800-228-2800

Sheraton Inn, Harrisburg (20 miles); 1-800-644-3144

Dining/Aprés-Ski

On-site
Food court, outdoor barbecue

Nearby
Lewisberry

Silver Lake Inn; (717) 938-4894

BC's Family Restaurant; (717) 938-9208

Allen's Eatery; (717) 938-4702

Mechanicsburg

Ale House (Ye Old); (717) 763-8929

Bert Brothers Family Restaurant; (717) 697-6591

Whitetail

15

Whitetail Ski Resort

13805 Blairs Valley Road
Mercersburg, PA 17236

Ski Report: (717) 328-5300
Information: (717) 328-9400
Credit Cards: AE, MC, VISA

Internet: http://www.skiwhitetail.com

Season: December to late March

Operating Hours
8:30 a.m.-10 p.m. daily

Getting There

- **From Pennsylvania and points north:** Take I-81 south to Exit 3 (Route 16) in Greencastle, PA. Then follow Route 16 west towards Mercersburg. Follow signs to Whitetail Ski Resort.
- **From Washington, DC, and points south:** Take I-495 north around DC toward Bethesda, Maryland. Get on I-270 north to I-70 to Exit 18 (Route 68). Go through a traffic light in Clear Spring, Maryland, and follow snowflake signs 6 miles to Whitetail.
- **From Baltimore:** Take I-695 to I-70, then follow the directions above.
- **From Pennsylvania points west:** Take I-76 (PA Turnpike) east to Breezewood, PA, then I-70 into Maryland to Exit 18 (Route 68). Go through the light in Clear Spring and follow signs to Whitetail.

Background

"Ten years in planning, ten months to build" is the phrase most often used by Whitetail management when referring to the resort's creation. Just seven years old, the resort is the most recent major ski area to open in the U.S.—and one of the region's sleekest operations. Situated 1,800 feet high on Two Top Mountain in south-central Pennsylvania's Tuscarora Mountain range, Whitetail has served as a necessary alternative to the busy Washington, DC, and Baltimore ski scenes. Despite the mountain's southern-exposed slopes and infrequent snowfall, the privately owned land was developed into a ski resort with two factors in its favor: 900-plus feet of vertical drop and proximity to two very profitable urban markets.

The ski area is now owned by the conglomeration Whitetail Ski Company, whose long-term plans are to develop the site into a four-seasons resort. Ownership also projects nearly doubling the trail network to 30 runs, occupying ample space on the mountain's outer edges. Located just miles past the north-central Maryland state line, Whitetail is primarily a day retreat, though it recently opened 30 slopeside town homes for rent or purchase.

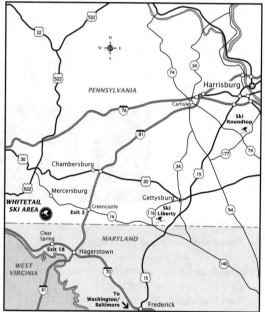

Mountain Stats

The resort is one of only two ski operations in the country to offer reservations for skiing, and skier limits are routinely set at 4,500 when all trails are open. The base lodge is both spacious and ultra-modern, with exceptional services and amenities and a true western-resort atmosphere. Another unique development strategy in creating Whitetail was designing a trail system that would completely separate its terrain by skier ability. The resort's three-face network features a secluded beginner area with access off four chair lifts; a five-trail intermediate section of long, wide, and smooth cruising runs; and a short but steep black diamond area. *Snow Country* magazine gave Whitetail its 1992 Best Overall Resort Design Award, and the publishers of *Ski* and *Skiing* magazines awarded it their Silver Eagle Award for environmental excellence in area design.

Even with Whitetail's skier-limit policy in effect, expect strong crowds on weekends. That's why the resort invested in what it calls the Whitetail Express Quad. It's one of the Mid-Atlantic's fastest high-speed detachable quad chair lifts, transporting 3,000 skiers per hour with a three-minute lift time. The quad is the only chair on the heavily skied intermediate face, though, and skiers who want to reach the neighboring advanced section must take the lift and ski down before they can access the Expert's Choice quad lift. The mountain's two summit areas provide panoramic views and photo opportunities of the hillsides and valley. From the summit, you'll likely spot the indigenous Whitetail deer that roam unencumbered throughout the resort's 1,600 acres of hunting-free property.

Whitetail's biggest drawback, though, is its notorious south-facing mountain. Both natural and manmade snow tends to dissipate quickly, leaving snowmakers and groomers with the arduous task of keeping the mountain clean and skiable. The conditions don't suffer too dramatically, but skiers may find some of the more advanced terrain closed during warm, winter days.

Base Elevation: 865 feet
Summit Elevation: 1,800 feet
Vertical Drop: 935 feet
Longest Run: 1 mile
Primary Slope Direction: South
Slopes and Trails: 6 beginner, 8 intermediate, 3 advanced
Skiable Terrain: 108 acres
Lifts: 1 high-speed quad, 2 quad, 1 double, 2 surface tows
Uphill Capacity: 11,200 skiers per hour

Average Annual Snowfall: 38 inches
  1995-96 season: 88 inches
  1994-95 season: 40 inches
Skier Visits
  1996-97 season: 190,000
  1995-96 season: 240,000
Snowmaking: 100% of area
Skiable Days
  1996-97 season: 70
  1995-96 season: 100
Night Skiing: 70% of slopes, including snowboard park and pipe, until 10 p.m. daily (back side closed at dusk)

Trail Profiles

The resort's wide, open terrain is suited more for the intermediate skier than its main competition—nearby Ski Liberty. Whitetail's Two Top Mountain is bigger and slightly more challenging, comparable to Maryland's Wisp Mountain. *Angel Drop* and *Home Run* trails are long, broad seamless cruisers with some nice dips, turns, and changing pitches. With just three advanced trails, the mountain lacks enough terrain to satisfy experts for very long. Nonetheless, the back side is plenty steep, most notably the mogul-packed *Exhibition* and *Bold Decision* trails.

First-time and developing skiers congregate on the beginner side's three slopes and three bunny hills. The resort offers a SKIwee children's program that's first-rate, and over 200 ski instructors cater to all ages and levels of skiers and snowboarders. Something to remember: Once learning skiers acclimate themselves to the short, beginner slopes, they'll find a big difference in difficulty between the novice runs and the heavier-pitched intermediates.

Snowboarding

When Whitetail opened in 1991, the timing was just right to market the resort with a focus on the country's fastest-rising sport. With both a halfpipe and a snowboard park, hundreds of boarders from the Baltimore and Washington, DC, area make Whitetail their home away from home. One of the best aerial arenas around, the park was recently relocated and expanded on the beginner side's *Stalker* trail, where guests will find tabletops, spines, mailbox slides, and some smaller walls and quarterpipes. Creative juices may have peaked a few years ago when a Volkswagen bus was hauled into the park and filled and topped with snow, forming a sizable jump.

The resort groomed the park out to be an expert area toward the start and finish of the 1996-97 season, doubling and tripling the size of their spines and tables. Management toned down the park after one particularly nasty mid-season injury, but beefed it up again in late February with a 20-foot spine, along with a posted sign declaring the park an advanced freestyle area only. The nearby halfpipe didn't fare as well last season, operating sporadically with mediocre grooming and disagreeable weather. The pipe was built high inside the outer left ridge of the beginner *Snow Park* trail, and boarders have just two feet of tree-lined platform with a small follow-through area at the finish.

The park's obstacles will be redesigned again this year, and a full list of competitions and events, including a new Boardercross series, is being scheduled. Several good instructional programs are available for young and learning riders, and the Underground Snowboard Shop will tune up your board and fix your bindings or straps in little time. To accommodate those who want to shred beyond sunset, the pipe and park operate under strong lights nightly.

Snowboard Rentals
- 250 sets: Rossignol, Burton (Ski rates apply to lessons and rentals)

Snowboard School: 25 instructors

Lift Tickets/Rentals/Services

Whitetail and nearby Liberty are Baltimore and Washington, DC's most accessible ski areas, both within 95 miles. Don't expect to belly up to the bar after pounding the slopes, though. This tiny Pennsylvania township is dryer than the Sahara, and security vans roam the parking grounds to enforce the no-alcohol decree. Calling ahead and reserving lift tickets a few days before your trip also comes highly recommended on weekends, especially for those skiers arriving after morning. Without reservations, skiers may find themselves denied without warning after suiting up on peak weekends. Don't be surprised either to find fewer trails operating than the resort advertises. The snowboard park is usually counted as a trail, and other slopes sometimes close mid-day during sloppy weather periods. The resort's recently expanded World Wide Web site is a viable alternative to calling the resort for current ski conditions. The site features daily video clips and still photos depicting the day's conditions.

Whitetail does offer some perks uncommon for the Mid-Atlantic region, including a free ski check and a nominal $2 charge to continue skiing into evening sessions. Sadly, the advanced back side isn't lit for night skiing, leaving just three intermediate slopes and the beginner area during later hours. Pegged for the 1997-98 year is the new Peak Performance Camp—a day-long adult teaching program with video analysis, lift ticket, and meals provided.

Be warned that Whitetail's ski patrol will toss any skier/snowboarder it finds skiing recklessly and dangerously. To counter that reputation, the resort makes itself unusually responsive to customer suggestions.

Lift Tickets

- 8:30 a.m.-5:30 p.m.: weekday $30, weekend $39; Noon-10 p.m.: $30, $39
- 8:30 a.m.-12:30 p.m.: $25, $34
- 12:30 p.m.-5:30 p.m.: $22, $30
- 5 pm-10 p.m.: $25
- 8:30 am-10 p.m.: $48
- Reduced rates for ages 7-12 and 65-69; others ski free
- Season passes; frequent skier club card; group discounts for 25 or more skiers

Ski Rentals

- 300 sets: Dynastar, Rossignol with Solomon boots/bindings
- $20/weekday; $25/weekend

Ski School

- PSIA certified: 280 instructors; Private $43/hour; Group $18/1.5 hours
- Whitetail Academy (intermediate-advanced skiers)

- Childrens' Programs: SKIwee, Mountain Adventures program (ages 8-12); Beginner packages
- Quick Carve program designed for intermediate/advanced skiers to learn snowboarding

Base Lodge Facilities
- Day/night care for children ages 1-12, restaurant/food court, ticket/rental shops, free ski and basket checks, sports shop, snowboard shop

Racing: NASTAR, Whitetail Race Team for ages 8-18, and an adult race team offered Wednesday nights on *Home Run* trail

Adaptive Ski School
- Lessons available by appointment; 100 sets of parabolic rental skis, including Rossignol and Elan
- Whitetail hosts the "Disabled Sports USA Ski Spectacular" each year in February or March

Calendar of Events

January

- PA Learn-to-Ski Day, early January
- Winterfest—charity races/ice sculpture competitions
- Demo Days
- Womens' Special Program Days (through March)

February

- Snowboard Boardercross Series
- Peak Performance Camps (through March)

March

- Disabled Sports USA Ski Spectacular
- Jimmie Heuga's Toyota Ski Express—fund raiser for MS
- Spring Games—bump contests, snowboard events, pond skimming, paintball

Other Winter Sports

Telemark skiing permitted on all slopes (telemark rentals available, lessons by appointment)

Summer Activities

When the ski season ends, mountain biking takes over the slopes. Whitetail's popular mountain biking center offers guests the chance to fly down the mountain and be transported back up the trails on a chair lift. The biking center runs numerous races and demo days. Also during the summer months, Whitetail hosts scenic chairlift rides, hiking, and camping.

Lodging/Dining/Aprés-Ski

Lodging

On-site

30 fully equipped slopeside townhomes. Call (717) 328-9400 for information

Nearby

Bed & Breakfasts

Breezee Hill Farm, Clear Spring, MD; (301) 842-2608

Fox Run Inn, Mercersburg, PA; (717) 328-3570

Metcalfe's B&B, Mercersburg, PA; (717) 328-5317

The Mercersburg Inn (& Restaurant); (717) 328-5231

The Steiger House, Mercersburg, PA; (717) 328-5757

(continues)

(continued)

Motels
  Holiday Inn, Hagerstown, MD; 1-800-422-2SKI
  Econo Lodge, Hagerstown, MD; 1-800-258-0127
  Comfort Inn, Greencastle, PA; (717) 597-8164
  Howard Johnson Plaza-Hotel, Hagerstown, MD;
     1-800-732-0906

Dining/Aprés-Ski
On-site
Windows Restaurant, the Marketplace (fast food)
 * No alcohol served at Whitetail, by township law
Nearby (Mercersburg)
  James Buchanan Pub & Restaurant;
     (717) 328-3008
  Foot of the Mountain Restaurant;
     (717) 328-2960
  Mansion House; (717) 328-5090
  Fox's Pizza Den; (717) 328-3699
 * Several other restaurants and bars located 20
   miles south of Whitetail in Hagerstown,
   Maryland, off I-70

PENNSYLVANIA'S **OTHER ALPINE SKI AREAS**

Blue Marsh

Blue Marsh

P.O. Box 609
Bernville, Pennsylvania 19506

Ski Report/Information: (215) 488-6399/6396
Credit Cards: MC

Operating Hours
9 a.m.-10 p.m. Monday-Saturday
9 a.m.-6 p.m. Sunday

Season: Mid-December to mid-March

Getting There

- **From Philadelphia:** Take the PA Turnpike (70/76) west to I-176 north toward Reading, then take 422 west. Pick up Route 183 and follow signs for Blue Marsh.
- **From Baltimore:** Take I-695 toward Towson, then I-83 north to Harrisburg, PA. Take I-78 east from I-83 toward Allentown, then take Route 61 south toward Reading. Pick up Route 183 and follow signs to Blue Marsh
- **From upper Delaware:** Take Route 41 into Pennsylvania, then Route 10 north past PA Turnpike. Pick up I-176 to Reading, then follow directions above from Philadelphia

Background

Just outside the town of Bernville—10 miles north of the outlet-store mecca of Reading—there's a learn-to-ski center called Blue Marsh. It sits at an elevation of just 590 feet on gently rolling Pennsylvania countryside. The region is lucky to get hit with one or two sizable snow blasts each year. And with only 300 feet of vertical drop, the slopes are a natural fit for beginners and children. In fact, on any given day here, you'll probably see nothing but parents and their kids. That's mainly a result of the ski center having turned its focus over to tubing—the fastest-growing winter resort activity outside of snowboarding.

General Manager Joseph Aichholz, who served as the official snowmaker for the 1980 Winter Olympics in Lake Placid, New York, cut Blue Marsh's first snow tubing runs next to the T-bar lift near the base lodge. *The Little Tube* area has four lanes on a 75-foot vertical drop and a tow lift to transport guests back up the hill. Then, with tubing visits sometimes reaching 1,000 on peak weekends, a second section was constructed last season on the area's opposite side. *The Big Tube* features five lanes, tube tow, and a 105-foot vertical, offering guests faster downhill times and bigger bumps. Aichholz also has plans to build a half-mile-long tubing run with several turns, bends, and banks of 50 to 65 degrees.

Mountain Stats

Base Elevation: 290 feet
Summit Elevation: 590 feet
Vertical Drop: 300 feet
Longest Run: 3,500 feet
Primary Slope Direction: North to northeast
Slopes and Trails: 1 advanced, 6 intermediate, 5 beginner

Skiable Terrain: 30 acres
Lifts: 1 triple, 1 double, 1 tow lift, 2 poma lifts
Uphill Capacity: 5,400 skiers per hour
Average Annual Snowfall: 35 inches
Snowmaking: 100% of area
Night Skiing: Monday-Saturday until 10 p.m.

Trail Profiles

Skiing at Blue Marsh has certainly been overshadowed by the advent of snow tubing, but the center still caters to its long-standing beginner clientele. One advanced trail is advertised, but only relative to the other downhill runs. Realistically, *Main Street* is a straight intermediate slope that's just steep enough to move downhill at a nice speed. The 11 remaining slopes are short and easy. There's ample room on the wide-open *Jug Handle* slope to master turning techniques, while neighboring runs offer some gradual bends on more narrow track. *Outback Run* was added a few years ago to provide a leisurely, serpentine trek around the hill's perimeter.

Snowboarding

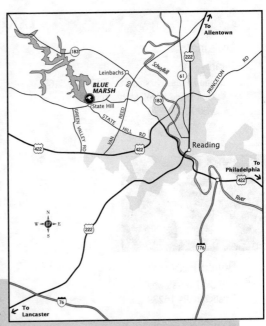

The Snowboarder's Whale Park, under the triple chair lift, mixes in some small jumps with wide terrain for developing boarders. The park isn't equipped for air-time maneuvers, considering the trail's gradual pitch. It's a good area for learning snowboarders to practice their carve turns and stops.

Snowboard Rentals: $15-$18; Boots $5

Lift Tickets/Rentals/Services

Large crowds are rare at Blue Marsh—more so on the slopes than its tubing areas. You'll find most of the activity centered on the two teaching areas in front of the small base lodge. Blue Marsh runs the popular SKIwee program for children ages five and under, and offers junior instructional programs and first-time-skier packages for adults and children. Regrettably, day care is not an available option here, but the modest yet comfortable base lodge was built with kids in mind: A cafeteria, sun deck, and game room are offered.

Lift Tickets
- 9 a.m.-5 p.m.: weekday (10 a.m.) $16, weekend $24
- 10 a.m.-1 p.m.: weekday $10, weekend $18
- 1 p.m.-5 p.m.: weekday $13, weekend $21
- 1 p.m.-10 p.m.: $17, $24 (Saturday)
- 4 p.m.-10 p.m.: $16, $17 (Saturday)
- Open to close: $20, $26 (Saturday)
- Ages 10 & under: $3 off any ticket
- Ages 5 & under ski free (1 child per adult)
- Ages 65+: $10 ticket/all times
- Monday day tickets $5; Wednesday Ladies Nights; Saturday family specials

Ski Rentals: Adult $16; Ages 10 & under $12
Ski School
- Private $35/person; Group $10/1.5 hours

- SKIwee (ages 5 & under) $38/child, includes rental, lesson, lift ticket
- First-time-skier package $25/weekday, $30/weekend; $5-$10 upgrades to all lifts

Base Lodge Facilities: Cafeteria, sun deck, rental shop, lockers, game room

Other Winter Sports
- **Ice-skating, ice fishing** at Blue Marsh Lake
- 2 separate **snow tubing** areas, each with five lanes
  5 p.m.-10 p.m.: weekday $10
  9 a.m.-1 p.m.: weekend $12.50
  1 p.m.-5 p.m.: weekend $12.50
  5 p.m.-10 p.m.: Saturday $12.50
- * Discount group tubing rates available

Lodging/Dining/Aprés-Ski

Lodging

Nearby

Econo Lodge, Wyomissing; (610) 378-5105
Wilson World Hotel, Morgantown;
1-800-342-2276

Dining/Aprés-Ski

Nearby (Bernville)

Old 22 Inn; (610) 488-1458
Burkey's Restaurant; (610) 488-6394
Jocko's Restaurant/Pizzeria; (610) 488-0831
Jefferson Drive-in; (610) 488-6166

Boyce Park

Boyce Park
675 Old Frankstown Road
Pittsburgh, PA 15239

Ski Report: (412) 733-4665
Information: (412) 733-4656
Credit Cards: VISA, MC

Operating Hours
2:30 p.m.-10 p.m. Monday-Thursday

9 a.m.-4:30 p.m. and 5 p.m.-10:30 p.m. Friday-Sunday

Season
Late December to late March

Getting There

• **From the Pennsylvania Turnpike (70/76), near Pittsburgh:** Take Exit 6, Monroeville, then follow orange belt signs to Boyce Park main entrance.

Background

With an average annual snowfall of 70-plus inches, Pittsburgh might seem like an opportune site for a ski area. Unfortunately, there aren't any sizable plateaus to hold one. Undeterred, Boyce Park went forward anyway in 1968, playing host to a strict clientele of families and learning skiers. Just 20 miles northeast of downtown Pittsburgh, Boyce began as a privately owned facility and has since turned over the reigns to Allegheny County.

Mountain Stats

Base Elevation: 1,072 feet
Summit Elevation: 1,232 feet
Vertical Drop: 160 feet
Longest Run: 1,300 feet
Primary Slope Direction: Northeast
Slopes and Trails: 3 beginner, 6 intermediate
Skiable Terrain: 25 acres
Lifts: 2 doubles, 2 handle tows, 1 poma lift
Uphill Capacity: 2,000 skiers per hour
Average Annual Snowfall: 70 inches
  1995-96 season: 120 inches

1994-95 season: 70 inches
Skiable Days
  1995-96 season: 76 days
  1994-95 season: 70 days
Skier Visits
  1995-96 season: 30,000
  1994-95 season: 25,000
Snowmaking: 100% of area
Night Skiing: 78% of area (7 of 9 trails), Friday-Sunday until 10:30 p.m.

Trail Profiles

The ski area is flat—flat as a pancake, with just 160 feet of vertical drop. But the terrain here serves beginners well on nine wide, gradual slopes. *Sun Bowl* and *Casper* are short, broad runs designed for children and first-time skiers. Although no child care is offered, the Tiny Tot Ski Program for ages four to six is held on Saturdays from 10 a.m. to 3 p.m., and includes a lift ticket, lesson, rental, and lunch.

Snowboarding

Beginning and learning snowboarders make up almost half of Boyce Park's skier base, even when their half-pipe isn't running. The pipe has operated each of the last four seasons on the bottom of the *Alpine* slope whenever conditions allowed, often not until February. Depending on the amount of snow, the modest, night-equipped pipe is roughly 150 feet long and 30 feet wide, with a fairly deep base and a handle tow for access. Unfortunately, the mountain's paltry vertical drop doesn't allow much speed to get through the halfpipe. Plans to build a small, adjacent snowboard park are also underway. Presently Boyce offers no snowboard school.

Snowboard Rentals: 50 sets: Burton; $15/day

Other Winter Sports

For guests interested in racing and practicing their slalom turns, Boyce offers free NASTAR timing runs with gates and jumps. NASTAR runs are held Friday through Monday on *Powder Run* slope—a two-tiered, 714-foot hill of boulevard width. When at least five inches of snow cover the area, cross-country skiers can traverse 2.7 miles of marked Nordic trails throughout Boyce Park, with rentals available from the ski lodge.

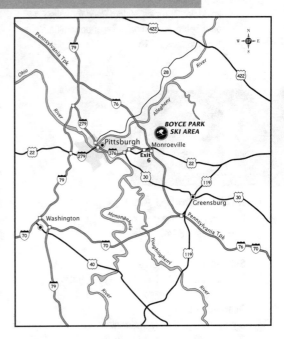

Cross-country skiing offered on 2.7 miles of marked, ungroomed track through woodlands and hiking/bike trails, with a few narrow and steep sections, or easier options around them; no trail fee; rentals at ski lodge: $7 weekend, $6 weekday

Ski Runner rentals $8 (slightly smaller than the Sled Dogs)

Sledding slope open with natural snow on Indian Hill near ski lodge, not affiliated with Boyce Park, no rentals

Lift Tickets/Rentals/Services

With a total of five lifts, weekend lines are usually under five minutes. The longest waits typically occur on Martin Luther King day, averaging 20 minutes. The area recently overhauled its two double chairs with new motors, switches, and slow-down capability. When it's not snowing here, a pretty good SMI Snowmaking System blankets the entire area, laying down six inches to a foot of manmade powder overnight. And with the limited terrain available, it's not surprising that Boyce extends the cheapest lift tickets in the Mid-Atlantic.

Lift Tickets
- 2:30 p.m.-10 p.m. Monday-Thursday: adult $8, ages 6-17 $6, age 60+ $6
- 9 a.m.-4:30 p.m./5 p.m.-10:30 p.m. Friday-Sunday: $12, ages 6-17 $10, age 60+ $10

Ski Rentals: 1,000 sets: Look Interval System; $8 rental/all sessions

Ski School:
- 12 instructors: PSIA certified; Private $20/1.5 hours; Group $10; Semi-private $13

- Tiny Tot Ski Camp for ages 4-6: Saturdays 10 a.m $40

Racing
- NASTAR timing runs offered free, normally Friday night through Monday night

Base Lodge Facilities: Cafeteria, rentals, ski school, upper-level lodge observatory, video games, pool table

Dining/Après-Ski
- Cafeteria at ski lodge

Calendar of Events/Lodging

Calendar of Events

February
- Mini-Junior Olympics Slalom Race for ages 5-12
- Adam Zebroski Memorial Race: downhill slalom races for ages 13-18

Lodging

Nearby (Monroeville):
Days Inn, 1-800-325-2525
Holiday Inn, 1-800-465-4329
Harley Hotel, Pittsburgh, 1-800-321-2323
Radisson Hotel, 1-800-333-3333
Red Roof Inn, 1-800-843-7663

18

Mount Tone

Mount Tone Ski Area
P.O. Box 766
Moscow, PA 18444

Ski Report: (717) 798-2300
Information: 1-800-747-2SKI, (717) 842-2544

Operating Hours
6 p.m.-10 p.m. Friday-Saturday
9 a.m.-4:30 p.m. Saturday-Sunday

Season: Late December to mid-March

Getting There
- **From Pennsylvania and New York State:** Follow I-81 toward Pennsylvania's northeast section, and take Route 171 (a few miles from the New York State border) past Susquehanna. From there take Route 370, following signs for Mount Tone.
- **From I-84 in New York State:** Follow I-84 west to I-380 north to I-81 north, and follow directions above.
- **From I-80 in New York/New Jersey:** Follow I-80 west to I-380 north to I-81 north, and follow directions above.

Background

Mount Tone is a family ski area and ski camp nestled in the village of Lake Como, five miles from the New York state border in northeastern Pennsylvania's Wayne County. The area has operated as a quaint alpine getaway since the mid-1950s, utilizing two separate small plateau faces. It was first known as Snow-Hill Ski Area, and holds the distinction of being home to the first triple chair lift east of the Mississippi River, installed in 1972. The two-face system features beginner-ability terrain throughout nine short slopes. An extremely affordable lift ticket is valid on both sides, with a hayride shuttle (or five-minute walk) servicing the two sections.

Mountain Stats

Vertical Drop: 450 feet
Longest Run: 1,300 feet
Primary Slope Direction: North-northeast
Slopes and Trails: 2 beginner, 4 intermediate, 3 advanced
Skiable Terrain: 25 acres
Lifts: 1 triple chair, 1 rope tow, 1 handle tow, 1 T-bar
Average Annual Snowfall: 65 inches
   1995-96 season: 115 inches
   1994-95 season: 65 inches
Snowmaking: 90% of area
Night Skiing: Lights on the north face (right side) Friday-Saturday until 10 p.m.

Trail Profiles

Mount Tone's smaller east plateau features three easily negotiable trails, three lifts, and all base lodge facilities, including a full-service cafeteria and ski and rental shops. It's also the site of the well-received *Beach Club* snow tubing park, which holds four lanes, full snowmaking, and a T-bar lift. Next door is a small expanse of bunny terrain and its own rope tow lift. Slightly more challenging track can be found on the north face, though just a single T-bar lift serves the entire side. *Solitude* is a short-lived run that culminates in a sweet elbow turn before funneling into the straight, easy course of *El Capitan*. There's also some gradual turning terrain on the novice *Winding Way* trail. Snowboarders have a wide terrain park toward the end of *Heaven's Gate* trail, with a few modest jumps and obstacles over the plateau's 450 feet of vertical. A warming hut greets tired guests at the summit.

Other Winter Sports

For cross-country skiing enthusiasts, 15 kilometers of terrain is available off the smaller (east) summit area. Mount Tone maintains a marked, ungroomed trail network with varying levels of difficulty, suitable for novice to intermediate Nordic skiers. Additionally, ice-skating is offered free on Mount Tone's base-area pond.

Other Winter Sports
Four-lane snow tubing park; rates—$5/three-hour session, available at 10 a.m., 1 p.m., and 7 p.m.
Cross-country skiing on 15 kilometers of Mount Tone's marked, ungroomed loop system; trail fee $7, rentals $7
Ice-skating on Mount Tone's base-side pond (no charge, no rentals)

Information/Events

Mount Tone's ski camp features inclusive weekend rates that offer lift tickets, on-site lodging, and meals. Families and youth groups make up the primary skier base. Management restricts its operating hours from Friday evenings to Sunday afternoons, and a limited ticket sales policy ensures crowd-free skiing.

Weekends at Mount Tone are filled with events and activities. Outdoor barbecues, ski races, snow sculpting, and winter volleyball are some of the day events, while movies and dee jays play in the base lodge's meeting room at nights.

Lift Tickets/Rentals/Instruction
Call 1-800-747-2SKI or (717) 842-2544 for information
Base Lodge Facilities
Cafeteria; ski, rental, and gift shops; repair/tuning shop
Calendar of Events
January
- Sloppy Slalom Ski Races
- Winter Carnival

February
- Snowshoe Expeditions
- Snowboard Races
- Snow Tube Races

Lodging
On-site
- Near-slopeside, fully furnished ski dormitories
- Nearby country inn

Dining/Après-Ski
- Full-service cafeteria (liquor not sold on-site)

Mystic Mountain

Mystic Mountain/Nemacolin Woodlands Resort
P.O. Box 188, Route 40 east
Farmington, PA 15437

Ski Report: 1-800-422-2736
Information: (412) 329-8555
Credit Cards: MC, VISA, AE

Operating Hours
10 a.m.-10 p.m. weekdays
9 a.m.-10 p.m. Saturday
9 a.m.-6 p.m. Sunday

Season: December to mid-March

Getting There

- **From Wash/Balt:** Take I-70 west or 270 north past Hagerstown, then I-68 west past Cumberland. From Cumberland, follow Rte 40 north at the Rte 219 intersection. Follow this to Farmington, PA, and signs for Nemacolin/Mystic Mtn.

- **From eastern Pennsylvania:** Take the Pennsylvania Turnpike (76/70) west, then Route 220 south to I-68 west. Follow directions from previous page.
- **From Pittsburgh:** Take the Pennsylvania Turnpike (70/76) east, then Route 119 south to Route 40 south/east toward Farmington and signs for Nemacolin/Mystic Mountain.

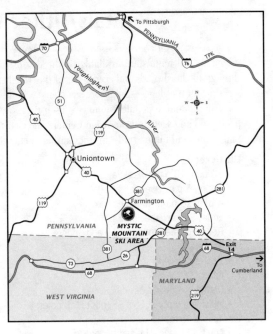

Background

With the considerable amount of snowfall that blankets the Laurel Highlands region of southwest Pennsylvania, a fourth ski area was just waiting to emerge. Three years ago, Nemacolin Woodlands Resort opened its doors to downhillers at Mystic Mountain. Skiing, though, is just one component—and a small one— of the posh, 1,000-acre four-seasons resort. Overshadowing the sport is the resort's myriad of other winter activities, luxurious base amenities, and year-round lodging in the French Renaissance-molded hotel and surrounding condominiums. *Town & Country* magazine recently recognized Nemacolin's spa as one of its 10 Best in America, and the four-star Golden Trout restaurant has also won acclaim from *Bon Appetit* magazine.

Nemacolin resides in the small town of Farmington, which is 16 miles southeast of Uniontown and just a few miles from historic Fort Necessity, where George Washington's first military engagement, in the French and Indian War, took place.

Mountain Stats

Base Elevation: 1,730 feet
Summit Elevation: 2,030 feet
Vertical Drop: 300 feet
Longest Run: 2,600 feet
Skiable Terrain: 25 acres
Average Annual Snowfall: 100 inches

Snowmaking: 100% of area
Slopes and Trails: 2 beginner, 3 intermediate
Uphill Capacity: 2,000 skiers per hour
Lifts: 1 quad lift, 1 surface lift
Night Skiing: 100% of area, Monday-Saturday until 10 p.m.

Mystic Mountain offers only five downhill slopes. Skiing was designed merely to complement the peak seasons at Nemacolin Woodlands and to serve as a day area for locals. There's always the option of shacking up in style at Nemacolin and making the 30-minute trip north to Seven Springs or Hidden Valley. But for guests who want to be pampered and just take a few turns out on the slopes, Mystic may be enough. The five slopes are gradual cruising runs over just 300 feet of vertical drop, with the longest slope extending to 2,600 feet. The resort does have a good ski school, geared toward young children. And the benefit of learning the sport at a brand-new ski area means having new rental equipment at your disposal as well. Childcare is offered at the Nemacolin Woodlands activities center, just below the ski area.

Rentals/Other Winter Sports/Lodging

The resort's golf course is used by cross-country skiers during winter months. Course trails are fully groomed, and rentals are available by the day or half-day. Horse-drawn sleigh rides are also offered through the hardwoods and evergreens of the Allegheny Mountains' Laurel Highlands. Snowboarding is welcome on the slopes—the resort has plans to build a halfpipe within the next few years.

During the more popular summer season there are two PGA golf courses, seven indoor and outdoor pools, and an excellent Equestrian Center. The resort's new Adventure Center offers 30 miles of mountain biking and hiking trails, in-line skating, a climbing tower, beach volleyball, and a rope course.

Lift Tickets:
- 10 a.m.-10 p.m.: weekday $12
- 9 a.m.-6 p.m.: weekend $19
- 4 p.m.-10 p.m.: weekend $14
- Friday-Sunday special: $40
- Reduced rates for ages 11 and under

Ski Rentals
- 100 sets: Salomon: weekday $12; weekend $12
- Night session: $10
- Individual rentals: Skis $8, boots $6, poles $3

Snowboard Rentals
- Adult $24, ages 11 and under $18
- Night session $10, $6
- Individual rentals: Snowboard $20, boots $8

Ski School
- Private $35/hour; Group $15/1.5 hours

- Kids' Club Program (ages 4-7); Youth Ski Program (ages 7-12)

Other Winter Sports
- **Cross-country skiing** on the fully groomed golf course; rentals: full day $15, half day $10; trails open daily until dusk
- **Horse-drawn sleigh rides**

Base Lodge and Resort Facilities
- Ski/rental shop, activities center, Golden Trout restaurant, numerous restaurants/lounges, pizza shop, two indoor pools, full spa, fitness center

Lodging: On-site
- 40 condominiums and 68 inn rooms, with 124 additional rooms under development

Mountain View at Edinboro

Mountain View at Edinboro

P.O. Box 447
Edinboro, PA 16412

Ski Report/Information: (814) 734-1641
Credit Cards: VISA, MC

Operating Hours
Monday-Thursday 3 p.m.-9 p.m.
Friday 3 p.m.-10 p.m.
Saturday-Sunday 9:30 a.m.-10 p.m.

Season: December to late March

Getting There

- **From Erie:** Take I-79 south to the Edinboro exit and follow Route 6N, heading east. At the traffic light in Edinboro, continue straight for 4 miles, then turn right on Sharp Road. Follow signs 2 miles to Mountain View.
- **From I-90 in Ohio and New York state:** Take I-90 into Pennsylvania to I-79 south. Follow the directions above.
- **From Pennsylvania points south:** Take I-79 north (or I-80 west to I-79), then follow the directions above.

Background

Mountain View is the only alpine ski area in remote northwestern Pennsylvania, located in the tri-state strip between Ohio and New York. It sits just 20 miles from Lake Erie, in line with the Great Lakes snow belt that dumps some of Pennsylvania's heaviest powder.

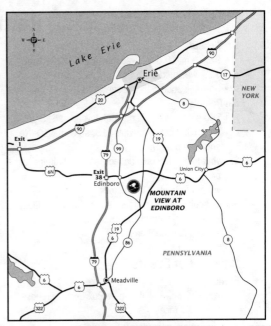

Formerly known as Mount Pleasant, the family ski area shut down in 1992 after 20 years of operation, only to resurface again in 1992 under a group of dedicated skiers and employees. They formed the Edinboro Ski Association, Inc., a nonprofit membership-owned and operated ski club, to continue business. The slopes are open to the public, but the association may attempt to privatize the facility, thereby limiting the area to a total of 300 families and their guests.

Mountain Stats/Trail Profiles

Base Elevation: 1,200 feet
Summit Elevation: 1,550 feet
Vertical Drop: 350 feet
Longest Run: 2,800 feet
Skiable Terrain: 25 acres
Average Annual Snowfall: 120 inches
Snowmaking: 60% of area

Slopes and Trails: 4 beginner, 4 intermediate, 1 advanced
Skier Visits: Averages 8,000 annually
Lifts: 3 (all T-bars)
Uphill Capacity: 2,400 skiers per hour
Night Skiing: 100% of area: Monday-Thursday until 9 p.m.; Friday-Sunday until 10 p.m.

The modest mountain, which rises to 1,550 feet, offers nine slopes on a small 350-foot vertical drop. Trails are of strictly beginner difficulty—eight are on the narrow side and one is a wide-open bowl. Five runs are covered by adequate snowmaking. There are just three T-bars for uphill transport, but lift lines have never factored into the equation. It's not surprising that a few of Pennsylvania's big resorts draw more skier visits on one peak day than Mountain View amasses in a year. Knowing that, the facility specializes in instruction, teaching lots of children in the area. The *Lower Meadow* section off the base lodge holds most instructional programs, including Snow Kids—a five-week series of lessons for small children. Mountain View also hosts several local schools during the week, and is presently contracting with nearby Edinboro University to set up an introductory skiing course.

Other Winter Sports

Downhill skiing is the only winter sport offered here, but good cross-country terrain is within a short drive at Elk Valley Touring Center in the town of Girard.

Nearby
Cross-country skiing at Elk Valley Touring Center, *(see page 207)*
Snowmobiling trails in surrounding area

Rentals/Other Information

Lift Tickets
- 9:30 a.m.-10 p.m.: weekday adult $20, student $15; weekend $24, $17
- Half-day: adult $15, student $10

Ski Rentals
- 350 sets: mostly Elan; Weekday: adult $13, student $8; Weekend: adult $18, student $10 (No snowboard rentals)

Snowboarding: Resortwide access, no halfpipe or park

Snowboard School: 2 instructors

Ski School: 30 instructors, some PSIA certified; Private $25/hour; Group $15/hour
- Intramural school programs

Calendar of Events

February
- Winter Carnival, with Snow Box Derby, firehose races, ski races
- Snow Box Derby days
- Ski and Snowboard Race Day

Base Lodge Facilities

Mountain View's two-tiered base lodge is small but comfortable, with a roaring fireplace, snack bar, and rental shop.

Nearby Lodging
Ramada Inn; (814) 734-5650
Raspberry House B&B; (814) 734-8997

Dining/Après-Ski

Nearby (Cambridge Springs)
Riverside Inn; (814) 398-4645
Cambridge Family Restaurant; (814) 398-2613
Betty's Restaurant; (814) 398-8673

21

Ski Sawmill

Ski Sawmill
P.O. Box 5-B
Morris, PA 16938

Ski Report/Information: 1-800-532-7669
Credit Cards: VISA, MC

Operating Hours
10 a.m.-9:45 p.m. Monday-Friday
9 a.m.-11:45 p.m. Saturday
9 a.m.-8 p.m. Sunday
Season: Mid-November to late March

Getting There

- **From Williamsport:** Take Route 220 west to Route 287 north past English Center, and follow signs to Sawmill.
- **From points east:** Take I-80 west to I-180, passing Williamsport, then follow to Route 220. Pick up Route 287 north past English Center, and follow signs to Sawmill.
- **From points west:** Take I-80 east to Route 220 north toward Williamsport, then take Route 287 north, and follow signs to Sawmill.

Background

Pennsylvania has a lot of family ski areas, but few are as affordable as north-central Pennsylvania's Ski Sawmill. Its value packages offer one of the Mid-Atlantic's cheapest lift tickets and rentals. Midweek skiers and snowboarders need just $11 for a slope pass and $7 for equipment rentals. The 28-year-old resort draws most of its visitors from Williamsport—home of the Little League World Series—and surrounding towns.

Trail Profiles

The area's eight slopes are short, gradual, and easily negotiable over 515 feet of vertical drop. An attentive, PSIA-certified ski school teaches predominantly young children on *Lower Area*—its base-lodge bunny slope, with several instruction packages offered. For faster skiers, three trails are just steep enough to ensure relatively quicker runs: *Chainsaw, Double Bucker,* and *Saw Dust Trail.* Timed racing trials are also available on weekends, and snowboarders have a park filled with a few modest jumps and obstacles.

Mountain Stats

Base Elevation: 1,700 feet
Summit Elevation: 2,215 feet
Vertical Drop: 515 feet
Longest Run: 3,250 feet
Skiable Terrain: 15 acres
Average Annual Snowfall: 45 inches
Slopes and Trails: 2 beginner, 3 intermediate, 3 advanced
Lifts: 1 double, 2 t-bars

Uphill Capacity: 3,200 skiers per hour
Snowmaking: 100% of area
Night Skiing: 100% of area, weekdays until 9:45 p.m., Saturdays 11:45 p.m., and Sundays 8 p.m.

Other Information

Sawmill is essentially a day area, but late-night skiers have use of the slopes until 11:45 p.m. on Saturdays with a half-price lift ticket. Overnight guests can shack up in Sawmill's slopeside 32-room base lodge or fully equipped houses and cottages.

Lift Tickets
• $11 midweek/all times
• $23.95 weekends; Ages 7-12: $11.98
• Ages 6 and under ski free

Ski Rentals
• $18 weekends
• $7 weekday
• Ages 7-12 $12.50

Ski School
• PSIA certified; Private $30/hour; Group $12/hour; Children $26.50/hour
• Learn-to-Ski Package: weekend $39.95, $29.95 ages 12 and under, midweek value specials

Lodging
On-site
• 32-room lodge at base, weekday $32/night, $130/weekend
• Fully furnished house and cottage rentals

* Ski & Stay Packages: $116/person includes Friday-Sunday lift tickets, Friday-Saturday slope-side lodging (children free with parents); Call 1-800-532-7669 for information/rates

Nearby
* 14 hotels/motels near area (call 717-353-7731/7521 for listing)
Canyon Motel, Williamsport; (717) 724-1681
Sherwood Motel, Wellsboro; (717) 724-3424
Penn-Wells Hotel, Wellsboro; (717) 724-2111

Dining/Après-Ski
On-site
• Restaurant (weekends only), lounge/cafeteria
• **Inn 287**—restaurant and bar

Nearby
• **Gary's Place Restaurant & Tavern**, Morris; (717) 353-6641

In Addition: Laurel Mountain

Laurel Mountain

Located 12 miles east of Ligonier along Route 30
Elevation: 2,750 feet

Average Annual Snowfall: 100 inches
Information: Contact Linn Run State Park;
(412) 238-6623

Western Pennsylvania's Laurel Highlands regions is home to Laurel Mountain—a popular ski area that closed commercially in the mid-1980s. But when the mountain gets hit with some of the region's frequent heavy snowfall, a loyal contingency of local advanced skiers drive out to the northernmost tip of Laurel's Appalachian Mountain ridge to take a turn down its considerably steep trails. Without operating chair lifts, however, they have to hoof it back up the mountain in order to get another run. Park-and-ski access is available, thankfully, since the area formerly housed an inverted summit lodge. The ski area's parking lots are gated shut, but there's plenty of space along Laurel Summit Road.

Located near Seven Springs and Hidden Valley resorts, the resort was originally the property of the Mellon family (of Rolling Rock brewery fame). Its heyday was during the 1950s and 1960s, when skiers from Pittsburgh and local areas took advantage of the Highland's bountiful powder-filled winters to traverse Laurel's slopes. The Mellons cut some trails and strung up a rope tow before leasing the resort to the state, but the ski area succumbed to financial problems and eventually closed. Soon after, the lodge went down in flames, raising questions about possible insurance fraud. The resort re-opened with a new lodge, but went out of business yet again, and hasn't operated since.

Despite the absence of chair lifts, all trails are open to downhillers. The terrain here is also excellent for Telemark and nordic skiers, with plenty of wide track for giant-slalom turns. Since the area is no longer groomed, beware of any natural obstacles including rocks, outcroppings, and other growths. *Upper* and *Lower Wildcat* are the signature expert runs, both quite long and steep. On the far left of the mountain is *Dream Highway*—an undulating intermediate trail that culminates in a difficult, tight turn onto the *Rocky Corner* trail. *Innsbrook* is a wide, serpentine trail through the hardwoods—a favorite run for mid-level skiers. It winds down to Midway Cabin, which until last year was open to guests for breaks. The cabin was built in the 1930s by the Mellons, but is now completely boarded up and shut down. A warming hut with an open-door policy is still available at the bottom base for brown-bag lunching and respites from Laurel's thigh-burning descents and miserable uphill climbs.

Laurel is still state-owned, under the jurisdiction of Linn Run State Park. Efforts have been underway for years to resurrect commercial skiing here on the mountain. A portion of an estimated $18 million investment has been raised to re-open the resort, but there's been some difficulty getting the remainder. Plans, though presently in limbo, are to develop Laurel into a classic, western-prototype skier's mountain, without the amenities—and costs—of bigger resorts.

Getting There
- **From Pittsburgh:** Take Route 30 east and follow to the top of Laurel Mountain, turning right on Laurel Summit Road, then travel 2 miles to Laurel Mountain Ski Area.
- **From the Pennsylvania Turnpike:** Take Exit 9 (Donegal) and follow to Route 711 north to Route 30, turn right on Laurel Summit Road, then travel 2 miles to Laurel Mountain Ski Area.

Spring Mountain

Spring Mountain

Box 42
Spring Mount, PA 19478

Ski Report: (610) 287-7900
Information: (610) 287-7300
Credit Cards: VISA, MC

Season: Mid-December to mid-March

Operating Hours
10 a.m.-10 p.m. weekdays
9 a.m.-10 p.m. Saturday
9 a.m.-9:30 p.m. Sunday

Getting There

- **From Philadelphia:** Take the Schuylkill Expressway and exit at King of Prussia, Route 202 south. Then take the 422 Expressway West to the Collegeville Exit and follow Route 29 north to Schwenksville. Follow signs to Spring Mountain.
- **From Wilmington, Delaware:** Take I-95 to Route 202 north, then take the 422 Expressway West. Follow directions above.
- **From western points:** Take the Pennsylvania Turnpike (70/76) east, then 422, and follow directions above.

Background

Spring Mountain has operated since 1963 as a family ski area for the nearby Philadelphia area. The ski center sits just 528 feet above sea level on a small plateau in Western Montgomery County. It's a good place for skiers to pick up the sport, with private and group instruction for all ages. Wiith little snowfall during most winters, Spring relies heavily on snow guns that fire around the clock. All trails are open under lights nightly, but most skiers come for the afternoon, particularly school and church groups. The ski area's only true selling points are its instruction, learning environment, and one-hour proximity to Philadelphia. The lodge has a cafeteria and fireplace, but no overnight accommodations aside from year-round, on-site camping.

Mountain Stats

Base Elevation: 108 feet
Summit Elevation: 528 feet
Vertical Drop: 420 feet
Longest Run: 2,220 feet
Skiable Terrain: 15 acres
Average Annual Snowfall: 35 inches
Slopes and Trails: 4 beginner, 3 intermediate, 1 advanced
Lifts: 1 triple, 3 doubles

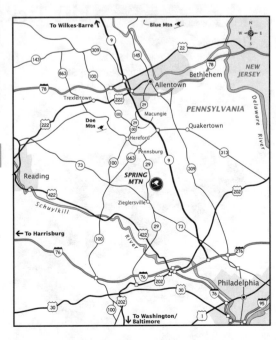

Uphill Capacity: 8,000 skiers per hour
Snowmaking: 100% of area

Night Skiing: 100% of slopes, Monday-Saturday until 10 p.m., 9:30 p.m. Sunday

Trail Profiles

Spring's limited terrain features two small faces: four short, contoured slopes on one side and a low-pitched hill, nearly as wide as it is long, on the other. A triple and double chair and two rope tows serve the area. Seeking to improve its ant-hill image, Spring recently cut a steeper, more advanced trail called *Edelweiss*, though it hasn't yet opened for skiing. It's been a proposed trail for years and was due to open for the 1996-97 season, but poor natural conditions and lack of snowmaking have kept it shut down.

Snowboarding

Spring has tried to upgrade its dime-store skiing reputation by creating a snowboard-friendly environment. A terrain garden and small halfpipe were built a few years ago on the wide track of *Drifter Trail*. Lacking the right equipment, the pipe was closed during last year's lean winter. There's not much challenging turf to offer on Spring's slopes, so boarders can make their own obstacles in the garden and pipe. Last year they considered hauling in a stripped car to use as a jump. The snowboard area operates under lights after sunset, but Spring needs to set up a J-bar for its boarders. The Rocktop Ridge double chair is the current means of uphill transport.

Snowboard Rentals
- 40 sets: Kemper and Hammer
- Weekday: $16/4 hours, $20/6 hours
- Weekend: $20/4 hours, $25/6 hours

Snowboard School: 4 instructors

Lift Tickets/Other Information

Lift Tickets
- Weekday $16; Weekend $20
- 5 p.m.-10 p.m. (9:30 p.m. Sunday) $16
- Seniors $8, ages 6 and under ski free
- Group rates for 15 or more skiers

Ski Rentals
- 1,500 sets: Elan, some SCX high-performance skis
- Weekend $17; Weekday/evening $15

Ski School
- 60 instructors: PSIA certified: Call (610) 287-8344 to reserve instruction
- Private $35/hour (up to 3 persons $65/hour)
- Group $15/hour (5-person minimum)
- Learn-to-Ski and childrens' packages

Base Lodge Facilities: Cafeteria, ski school, rentals, lockers

Lodging
Nearby
Holiday Inn; (215) 368-3800
Kaufman House; (215) 234-4181
Bed & Breakfast of Valley Forge; (215) 783-7838
Guest Quarters; (215) 843-8300
Days Inn; 1-800-329-7466

Tanglwood

Tanglwood Ski Area

P.O. Box 165
Tafton, Pennsylvania 18464

Ski Report/Information/Reservations: 1-888-226-SNOW, (717) 226-9500
Internet: http://www.tanglwood.com
E-mail: tnglwood@ptd.net
Credit Cards: VISA, MC, AE, Discover

Operating Hours
9 a.m.-10 p.m. Monday-Saturday
9 a.m.-5 p.m. Sunday

Season: Early December to mid-March

Background

Overlooking Lake Wallenpaupack in the Pocono Mountains, Tanglwood Ski Area has hosted family and novice skiers each of the last 30 years. Locals may remember the resort as Paper Birch Mountain. The family-operated business turned over in 1972 to Tanglwood—a development company that essentially used the ski resort to sell properties in the area. The resort was sold again last year to a new company, retaining its name.

Mountain Stats

Base Elevation: 1,335 feet
Summit Elevation: 1,750 feet
Vertical Drop: 415 feet
Longest Run: 1 mile
Primary Slope Direction: North
Skiable Terrain: 35 acres
Average Annual Snowfall: 65 inches
  1995-96 season: 90 inches
  1994-95 season: 60 inches
Snowmaking: 100% of area
Skier Visits
  1995-96 season: 45,000
  1994-95 season: 45,000

Getting There

- **From New York/New Jersey:** Take I-80 west into Pennsylvania, then Route 447 north to Route 390 north. Pass I-84 on 390 and follow signs for Tanglwood. From I-84, take Exit 7, Route 390 north, and follow signs.
- **From I-81:** Follow I-81 toward Scranton, then I-380/80 to I-84 east to Route 390 north. Follow signs to Tanglwood.
- **From Philadelphia:** Take the N.E. Extension of the Pennsylvania Turnpike past Wilkes-Barre, then connect with I-81 north to I-380/80, then I-84 east, then Route 390 north. Follow signs for Tanglwood.

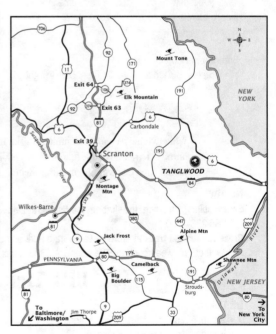

Slopes and Trails: 2 beginner, 3 intermediate, 4 advanced
Night Skiing: 100% of area, Monday-Saturday until 10 p.m.
Lifts: 2 doubles, 2 t-bars, 1 rope tow
Uphill Capacity
  4,300 skiers per hour

Tanglwood's trail system features 100 percent snowmaking and full grooming, and all nine runs are well lit for night skiing, six days per week until 10 p.m. The terrain is much easier and less congested than bigger Pocono areas, and the rates more affordable. The resort issues credit for a future visit to any skier not satisfied, within one hour of ticket purchase.

Trail Profiles

Tanglwood is a good choice for learning skiers in the populous Scranton and Wilkes-Barre areas. It contrasts well with the intermediate to advanced terrain of Montage Resort. The resort's summit base offers a wide beginner area that covers just 70 feet of vertical drop and uses a rope tow lift. Surrounding the beginner turf are the remaining eight runs comprising novice to intermediate track, despite trail ratings advertised as more difficult. The narrow, serpentine *Weasel* trail runs on a steady grade over 2,600 feet of track. More advanced skiers have one worthy trail: *Wildcat's* wide, straight course is filled with moguls and bumps. The trail overlooks scenic Lake Wallenpaupack—one of Pennsylvania's largest manmade lakes. Tanglwood's best novice trail is *Big Bear*. It winds slowly from the summit over one mile of terrain.

Snowboarding

Tanglwood built a snowboard park last season to accommodate an influx of young boarders. The 350-foot-long, 100-foot-wide park experienced some growing pains, but a series of rail slides, tickers, trick boxes, and plastic barrels proved to be a good start. The park will open late for the 1997-98 season, likely in January. Boarders also have resort-wide access on Tanglwood's tame terrain.

Snowboard Rentals
- 25 sets: Burton and Smelly Tuna: Day/twilight $20, night session $17

Other Winter Sports

While winter recreation is limited to skiing and snowboarding at Tanglwood, leisurely cross-country ski trails can be found nearby at both Promised Land State Park and Bruce Lake National Area (snowfall permitting). Rentals are available at both areas.

Nearby
Snowmobiling, sledding, ice-skating, ice fishing at Lakeside Resort, 10 minutes from Tanglwood, 1-888-233-4130
Cross-country ski trails at Promise Land State Park and Bruce lake Natural Area, within 10 minutes.
Paintball offered year-round at Pike County AMBUSH, Inc., 1-888-2AMBUSH

Lift Tickets/Other Information

Lift Tickets
- 9 a.m.-5 p.m.: weekday $29, weekend $18
- Half day: weekday $15, weekend $22
- 1 p.m.-10 p.m.: weekday $18, weekend $29
- 5 p.m.-10 p.m.: weekday $15, weekend $20
- 9 a.m.-10 p.m.: weekday $29, weekend $39
- Reduced lift tickets for ages 6-12
- $15 lift ticket/all sessions before Christmas and after February

Ski Rentals
- 800 sets: Elan and Atomic: Day/twilight $18, night $15

Ski School
- 20 instructors: PSIA-certified: Private $35/hour; Group $18/hour
- Free ski or snowboard group lesson with Learn-to-Ski package
- Childrens' programs: SKIwee (ages 5-12), weekends only: full day $55, half day $45

- Junior Racing Program
- Learn-to-Ski and childrens' packages

Snowboard School: 4 instructors

Summit Lodge Facilities: Slopeside restaurant and lounge, ski/rental shop, lockers, game room

Calendar of Events

March
- Tanglwood Winter Carnival (first weekend in March)

January
- Annual Coors Light Jim Nicol Memorial Adult Racing. Series (each Wednesday through season's end)

Lodging

On-site
- 14 slopeside condominiums, call for rates

Nearby

Comfort Inn, Lake Ariel, 20 minutes away, 1-800-523-4426

Keley's Inn The Poconos, Gouldsboro, w/indoor pool, hot tub, English pub, 1-800-432-5253

Lakeside Resort, Greentown, 1-888-233-4130

Dining/Aprés-Ski

On-site

Restaurant, Last Lift slopeside lounge, with live entertainment on Saturdays

Nearby

Ehrhardt's Lakeside Restaurant, 1 mile from resort, seafood, steaks, etc.; (717) 226-2124

AJ's Fireplace family restaurant, Tafton; (717) 226-2701

Critters Restaurant, Route 390, Tafton; (717) 226-9002

Tussey Mountain

Tussey Mountain Ski Area

Route 322
Boalsburg, PA 16827

Ski Report: 1-800-733-2754
Information: (814) 466-6810/6266
Credit Cards: MC, VISA, AE, Discover

Operating Hours
Noon to 10 p.m. weekdays
8 a.m. to 10 p.m. weekends
Season: December to late March

Getting There

- **From State College:** Take 322 east through Boalsburg, then follow signs to Tussey Mountain.
- **From I-80:** Take Route 322 east, then follow signs to Tussey Mountain.

Background

There's a little-known ski area in tiny Boalsburg that's been serving local families and students for the last 15 years. Tussey Mountain, located five miles east of Penn State's University Park campus, offers eight short slopes and trails over its 500-foot vertical drop. Little has changed since Tussey's inception—at least as far as skiable terrain is concerned. A bold snowboard terrain park was added just last season, though, to fill the void. More lift tickets are sold to skiers than to boarders, but the ratio is quickly shifting with the success of the new terrain park. And Tussey jumped on the snow tubing bandwagon by building a large park, nearly as long and steep as some of its ski trails.

When the ski season ends at Tussey, spring activities take over: there's a golf course and driving range, an amphitheater for concerts, and new family fun center.

Mountain Stats

Base Elevation: 1,310 feet
Summit Elevation: 1,810 feet
Vertical Drop: 500 feet
Longest Run: 4,100 feet
Primary Slope Direction: North to northeast
Skiable Terrain: 72 acres
Average Annual Snowfall: 48 inches
    1995-96 season: 75 inches

Snowmaking: 85% of area
Slopes and Trails: 3 beginner, 3 intermediate, 2 advanced
Night Skiing: 85% of area, Monday-Saturday until 10 p.m., Sunday until 9 p.m.
Lifts: 1 quad, 1 poma lift, 2 handle tows
Uphill Capacity: 4,800 skiers per hour

Trail Profiles

Not surprisingly, beginners rule the majority of the mountain. Tussey's solid ski school teaches neophytes on a large bunny slope area. And once that's mastered, two beginner slopes offer an easy trek down a short distance. The favorite post-novice trail at Tussey is *Grizzly*—an entry-level black diamond run with wide track and just enough drops for a fast ride. It's also their designated bump trail, groomed only when the moguls form beyond control. Possibly the most challenging trail here, using most of Tussey's 500-foot vertical drop, is *Tuscarora*. The upper half of the run is steepest and also gets the occasional bump treatment. Weekend racing time trials are held on this top section.

Snowboarding

Tussey formed a pretty good terrain park on the bottom 250 vertical feet of an intermediate trail, covering nearly two-thirds of its width. During the 1996-97 season, the park consisted of two spines shaped into quarterpipe-type terrain on both sides, four tabletops with multiple airs, and a few rail slides scattered throughout the course. There's just enough of a pitch to get some good speed for the jumps, and boarders can construct new obstacles at their own discretion. A new halfpipe was built last season, but it operated sporadically and with little fanfare. The ski area may not run a pipe this year until they've invested in new machinery to properly groom it.

The park, also open to skiers, is well lit nightly until 10 p.m. Tussey's snowboard school offers freestyle, freeriding, and carving lessons.

Snowboard Rentals: 35 sets: Airwalk, some K2s; Airwalk boots and bindings

Snowboard School: 11 instructors

Lift Tickets/Rentals/Services

Tussey's trails all form around a quad chair lift that was strung up a few years back to ease often-heavy weekend lift lines. Saturdays tend to stay pretty busy around noon, but crowds filter out by late afternoon after guests get in their runs. Tussey offers an affordable lift ticket, but unfortunately for parents, no day care.

Lift Tickets
- Weekday $20, half day $16, two hours $10
- Weekend $24, half day $20, two hours $14
- Night $18
- Reduced rates for ages 7-10 and 65+
- under 6 ski free

Ski School
- 62 instructors: 75% PSIA certified
- Private $28/hour; Group $14/1 1/2 hours

- Childrens' half-day ski program; Cub House Learning Center for ages 3-6

Base Lodge Facilities
- Restaurant, cafeteria, lounge, ski shop/rentals, lockers

Other Winter Sports

Other Winter Sports

On-site
700-foot **snow tubing** park with a 200-foot vertical drop: $14/full day, $10/half day, 5 runs/$4

Nearby
Cross-country skiing, weather permitting, nearby at Stone Valley Recreation Area *(see page 202)*
Racing: Recreational standard racing held on weekends

Calendar of Events

February
- USSA Race
- Winter Carnival

Lodging/Dining/Aprés-Ski

Lodging

Nearby (call 814-466-6810 for information)
- Bed & Breakfasts in historic town of Boalsburg
- Nittany Lion Inn
- Holiday Inn State College
- Ramada Inn
- Days Inn

Aprés-Ski/Dining

On-site
Cafeteria/lounge with grill menu

Nearby (Historic Boalsburg)
Duffy's Boalsburg Tavern, 18th century dining; (814) 466-6241
The Village Eating House; (814) 466-6865

ALPINE RESORTS:
MARYLAND/WEST VIRGINIA

MARYLAND:
25. Wisp Ski Resort

WEST VIRGINIA:
26. Alpine Lake
27. Canaan Valley
28. New Winterplace
29. Snowshoe/Silver Creek
30. Timberline

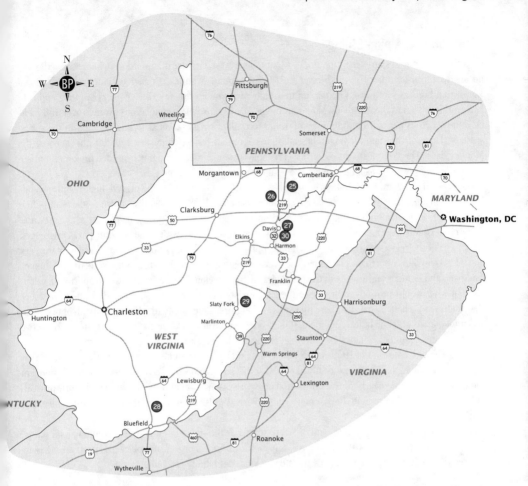

Maryland Alpine Skiing

Deep in the corner of Maryland's western Panhandle region lies Wisp—the state's only downhill ski area. This remote strip of the state sits due north of West Virginia's spacious Monongahela National Forest, with a wintry climate that's unique in Maryland. Wisp is right in-line with an Allegheny Mountain snow belt that runs southward through the Mountaineer State, picking up considerable amounts of powder at its 3,000-foot altitude.

With a limited mountainous region from which to survey, Wisp may continue as Maryland's only alpine ski destination for some time. But there has been talk, and serious planning, in recent years to introduce a second resort to the region. Near the town of Emmitsburg, which is just miles from the Pennsylvania border and Whitetail Resort, a modestly sized plateau has been considered for several years now. Since ski areas are often five to 10 years in the making, regional skiers will have to take a wait-and-see attitude.

In the meantime, cross-country skiing has never taken a back seat in Maryland. Not far from Wisp are two state parks that serve as premiere Nordic skiing spots: Herrington Manor and New Germany State Parks offer excellent trail systems that operate typically from January into late March when snowfall permits.

West Virginia Alpine Skiing

As the "East Coast's answer to the Rocky Mountains," West Virginia is an outdoor winter wonderland—an aberration in an otherwise mild lower East Coast climate. Within the massive Monongahela National Forest that borders southwest Virginia, an unusually arctic microclimate exists. Winters are long and cold here in this section of the Allegheny Mountain range. Yearly snowfall accumulations average over 150 inches, and numerous peaks exceed altitudes of 4,000 feet, allowing its ski areas to linger long into the spring seasons. Three of the state's five commercial alpine ski areas reside within the 200,000-plus acres of the Monongahela. The ski industry has served as a reliable economic source and much-needed broker of tourism in West Virginia, which has long ranked as one of the poorest states in the U.S.

Commercial skiing in the Mountaineer State began nearly 40 years ago in the rugged, high-country woodlands of Canaan Valley. Weiss Knob Ski Area, which opened in 1959, is generally known as the South's first ski area. The area surrounding the defunct resort now belongs to White Grass—one of the East Coast's premiere cross-country touring centers. It would be another decade before West Virginia's state park service took advantage of the region's substantial snowfall, stepping up in 1971 to establish Canaan Valley State Park and Ski Area. The resort complemented the warmer seasons, which began to lure Mid-Atlantic hikers, canoeists, and outdoor enthusiasts to the pristine wilderness region. Canaan's success also spurred development of what would turn out to be one of the East Coast's biggest ski resorts. Privately owned Snowshoe Resort attracts a phenomenal skier base that spans the entire eastern seaboard, offering a wealth of overnight accommodations and amenities. Adjoining, family-oriented Silver Creek was incorporated later, and the two facilities combine to make Snowshoe Mountain Resort the largest ski area in the Mid-Atlantic.

Skiing's growth spurt in the 1970s led developer David Downs to scout a new resort in the Canaan Valley region. Snowmaking had been practically mastered at this point, and would combine with the area's frequent snowstorms to provide nearly four months of skiing per season. Timberline Four Seasons Resort, just two miles from Canaan Valley State Park, opened in the early 1980s and serves up the state's most challenging and varied terrain.

New Winterplace, on the southern end of West Virginia, is the state's latest addition to commercial skiing. Though its winters don't pack the same force as its northeastern cohorts, Winterplace also posts strong yearly skier visits, operating more on aggressive snowmaking and refined grooming.

Wisp
Ski Resort

Wisp Ski Resort
Deep Creek Lake
McHenry, MD 21541

Information/Reservations: 800-462-9477/301-387-4911
Credit Cards: MC, VISA, AE, Discover
Internet: http://www.gcnet.net/wisp

Season: Mid-November to late-March

Operating Hours
8:30 a.m.-10 p.m. Tuesday-Saturday
8:30 a.m.-4:30 p.m. Sunday-Monday
* Noon-9 p.m. weekdays before December 16 and
from March 10 to close

Getting There

- **From Washington:** Take I-495 north to I-270 north to Frederick, Maryland. Take I-70 west to Hancock, then I-68 west past Cumberland. Take Exit 14A to US 219 south toward McHenry, then follow signs to Wisp.
- **From Baltimore:** Take I-70 west to Hancock, then follow signs from Hancock above.
- **From Pittsburgh (via Morgantown, West Virginia):** Take I-79 south to I-68 east at Morgantown and follow to Exit 4 at Friendsville, Maryland. Then take Route 42 south to US 219 south to McHenry, and follow signs to Wisp.

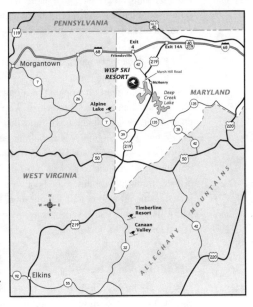

Background

There's an unusual microclimate in Maryland's western panhandle that contrasts with the state's otherwise temperate conditions. Downhill skiing does exist in Maryland, and only here at Wisp—the sole alpine beneficiary of Garrett County's strong winters. The ski area is perched 3,100 feet high atop the Allegheny's Marsh Mountain, just miles from both West Virginia and Pennsylvania. Wisp's base lodge and east ridge sit directly off beautiful Deep Creek Lake—the state's largest inland lake with more than 65 miles of shoreline.

Wisp is no secret to Mid-Atlantic skiers—it's one of the longest running operations in the region. Skiing was crafted here in 1955 by the Helmuth Heise family to complement the development of nearby Will O'the Wisp—a woodsy retreat that has since evolved into a solid four-seasons resort. The success of Wisp is a testament to the vision of Heise, who is still at the helm today.

Mountain Stats

Base Elevation: 2,470 feet
Summit Elevation: 3,080 feet
Vertical Drop: 610 feet
Skiable Terrain: 80 acres
Primary Slope Direction: North to northeast
Average Annual Snowfall: 91 inches
  1996-97 season: 57 inches
  1995-96 season: 260 inches
  1994-95 season: 191 inches
Slopes and Trails: 4 beginner, 12 intermediate, 7 advanced
Longest Run: 1.5 miles

Lifts: 2 triples, 3 doubles, 2 surface tows
Uphill Capacity: 9,120 skiers per hour
Snowmaking: 90% of area
Skier Visits
  1995-96 season: 188,000
  1994-95 season: 176,000
Skiable Days
  1996-97 season: 137
  1995-96 season: 149
  1994-95 season: 102
Night Skiing: 90% of area, Tuesday to Saturday until 10 p.m.

Notwithstanding the resort's smallish 610-foot vertical drop, Wisp's network of 23 slopes and trails is largely intermediate, with surprisingly steep terrain on seven black diamonds. There's an assortment of bumps, dips, and jumps scattered throughout the advanced terrain, and the blue runs are well groomed and contoured for cruising. What brings loyal skiers back to Wisp time and again, though, is its supreme conditions, both natural and artificial. The area gets three times more snowfall, on average, than its main competition—Pennsylvania's Ski Liberty and Whitetail Resort—and had a record 211 inches dumped during the 1995-96 season. Powder tends to stick around a bit longer here as well, thanks to its 3,100-foot summit and north-facing mountain. And during dryer times, Wisp's airless snowmaking system provides a solid corduroy texture on all but three trails. Balanced conditions also translate into more skiable days at Wisp, where 125-day seasons are the norm.

A high-speed quad lift wouldn't be a bad idea for the trail network, but weekend and holiday lift lines are kept in check because of Wisp's somewhat remote location. The skier base here is divided between Washington, DC and Baltimore, and to a lesser degree Columbus, Ohio, and Charleston, West Virginia. Many Baltimore and Washington skiers opt for the shorter route to Pennsylvania's more crowded Ski Liberty and Whitetail Resort. Still, others know the terrain here is more varied and the conditions superior, and will make the longer drive to Wisp. Guests may discover trailhead visibility to be poor, so be sure to check out the trail map billboards that are posted at the lift station and summit areas. There shouldn't be any problem finding Wisp's ski patrol. The highly visible staff was awarded the prestigious Eastern Division Outstanding Patrol award for the 1995-96 season.

Trail Profiles

Steeps are an easy find on three black diamonds directly off Wisp's base lodge. The resort's biggest and most continuous drops are on *The Face*, with its unforgiving fall-line descent. Neighboring *Squirrel Cage* and *Devil's Drop* appear short and direct on the trail map, but they're steep enough to guarantee lots of difficult turning. Though it's only available with enough natural snow, *Devil's Drop* offers a fairly tight chute between trees at the trail's midsection. The resort also has an eye for racing, with strong programs for both adults and juniors, including the national standard NASTAR and numerous annual race events on the steep, wide slalom-turning *Squirrel Cage* trail. An efficient midstation deposits skiers onto the three black diamond runs.

Also without the benefit of snowmaking, *Bobcat Bowl* offers a taste of glade skiing on a long runout through the trees. *Odin's Chute* is a fast drop that flows into the smoothly contoured track of *Down Under* and *Boulder*. And the east ridge section, formed in 1980, features the black diamond *Main Street* trail. It's a near replica of the three advanced runs on the front face, but with breathtaking views of Deep Creek Lake.

Wisp's 11 blue trails are of moderate steepness and length but offer a slew of twists and bends, in addition to shifting widths on the mountain's expertly groomed track. Notable mid-level runs include *Down Under*, which winds steadily down to the east ridge triple lift, and the natural powder-only *Deer Run*.

Wisp's beginner terrain is less selective. Two long practice trails (covering nearly three miles between them) and a small bunny hill are available. *Possum* skirts the plateau's scenic woodlands and the resort's golf course. The trail runs out into the wide-open terrain of the *Chipmunk* slope extension, combining for an easy 1.5-mile run. *Wisp Trail* runs parallel to *Possum* for a second leisurely, mile-long trek. The *Belly Flop* bunny slope, with rope tow, is set in the midst of the base lodge's traffic flow. Though the resort lacks extensive novice terrain, parents shouldn't dismiss Wisp as a learning option: The SKIwee and MINIrider (snowboard) programs are first-rate.

Snowboarding

Most of Wisp's trail system is steep and wide enough for fast, big-turning snowboarders, but it's the halfpipe and terrain park that bring out some of the region's best riders. Located underneath Chair One and next to the snowboard park, the four-year running halfpipe is 400 feet long and 35 feet wide, with 10-foot sidewalls. It can be accessed by taking either the bunny slope rope tow or shredding down *Boulder Run* via Chair One. The pipe requires a lot of work from the snowboard crew and their tillers, but managed to operate on a fairly steady basis during the tame winter of 1996-97.

The neighboring, 500-foot Devil's Arena snowboard park begins with a slight downhill drop to initiate some speed before the first gap jump. Freestyling boarders can also perform tricks on spines, tabletops, log slides, snow mounds, and a quarterpipe. The park was set up for the 1996-97 season and will undergo several upgrades to better accommodate snowboarders. Territorial boarders, however, must relent to skiers: The terrain park is open to anyone who dares enter. Two major snowboard competitions are held at Wisp: January's Phat Air halfpipe events and March's Winterfest Weekend, featuring freestyle events in the park. Additional races and events are pegged for the coming season. Both the park and pipe are well lit during normal night skiing hours.

Snowboard Rentals
- 125 sets: Rossignol, some K2
- Board $22, with boots $26, boots only $18

Snowboard School
- 14 instructors; Private $38/hour; Group $15/hour

Lift Tickets/Rentals/Services

Lift Tickets

- 8:30 a.m.-4:30 p.m. or 1 p.m.-10 p.m.: weekend $40, weekday $32; Saturday through Sunday afternoon $74; three-day holiday $105
- 1 p.m.-4:30 p.m. or 4:30 p.m.-10 p.m.: weekend $25, weekday $21
- * 25%-35% discounts for ages 6-11
- * Half price tickets for ages 65-69; 70+ ski free all times; children under 6 ski free
- * Two-for-one lift ticket specials on Mondays
- * Early and late season (season's open to December 15 and March 10 to close): weekend full day/twilight $32, half day/night $21; midweek $14/all times

Ski Rentals

- 1,200 sets: Rossignol, Elan (Solomon step-in bindings); 30 shaped skis: $16-$19
- * $12 rentals during early and late seasons
- * New Rossignol Winter Adventure Center: rentals and instruction in parabolic skis, snowboards, and snow runners

Ski School

- 80 instructors: PSIA certified: Private $38/hour; Group $15/hour
- Beginner ski package: Weekend Junior Ski and Guide Program
- SKIwee program for ages 4-12; rates $59/day, $45/half day; MINIrider snowboard instructional program for ages 7-12
- Little NASTAR Racer Day Camp

Base Lodge Facilities: Rental/ski shops, lockers/basket check, information office, ski school, two restaurants, two lounges, pastry and pizzeria shops

Adaptive Ski School: Handicapped skiers accommodated, but no specific program; free midweek lift passes for handicapped, blind, and deaf skiers, half price on weekends/holidays

Racing: NASTAR offered weekends and some weekdays on advanced *Squirrel Cage* trail

Day Care: Willy Wisp Children's Center, run daily at the base lodge

Calendar of Events

December
- Rossignol Demo Days

January
- Molson Ski Challenge
- Wendy's Ski Family Challenge
- Snowboard Halfpipe Competition
- Wisp Memorial Super NASTAR Giant Slalom

February
- Wisp Cup Super NASTAR
- Blue Ridge Race Series
- Maryland Special Olympics Winter Games

March
- Maryland Governor's Cup Races
- Winterfest Weekend (ski races, bump contests, halfpipe competitions)

Other Winter Sports

For snow sport enthusiasts, Garrett County is a virtual winter playground. Aside from Wisp's reputable snowboard park and halfpipe, opportunities abound for cross-country skiers and snowmobilers in surrounding state parks and forests. Ice fishing and sleigh riding ars also popular winter activities at nearby Deep Creek Lake.

When the snow melts the four-seasons resort is transformed into a recreational haven. Wisp schedules mountain biking and hiking on marked trails, scenic chairlift rides, and whitewater rafting trips on the Youghiogheny River. It also offers an 18-hole golf course that ranks among Maryland's best. Water sports are another big draw on the expansive Deep Creek Lake: Rentals are available for nearly every type of boat at several local marinas, and fly fishing and water skiing programs are run on-site at the lake. Brown, rainbow, and brook trout fishing can also be found in nearby Garrett County streams. One of the region's popular fall festivals is the annual McHenry Highland Festival, featuring bagpipe bands, Scottish country and highland dancers, and Scottish foods, shops, and athletic events. For information on any of the following, call the Deep Creek Lake/Garrett County Promotion Council at 301-334-1948.

On-site
- **Sled Dog** snow runner rentals, permitted on all trails
- * **Snow tubing** park expected to open for 1998-99 season

Nearby
Cross-country skiing at New Germany State Park *(see page 224)*, Herrington Manor State Park *(see page 225)*

Snowmobiling permitted on 35 miles of marked state forest trails (call Garrett County's Promotion Office, 301-334-1948 for information/maps) and in state parks with valid snowmobile permits; additional snowmobile trails at Deep Creek Lake: 301-387-5563;

Ice fishing, sleigh riding at Deep Creek Lake

Lodging/Dining/Aprés-Ski

As for the base lodge, it's not full of flash but is comfortable and well equipped in a European resort likeness. Both families and aprés-skiers have plentiful dining and lounging opportunities, with two restaurants, two pubs, and several eateries. The resort's slopeside hotel offers several different ski packages with lift tickets and meals; also in great supply in the area are house and condominium rentals, motels and inns, and bed and breakfasts. Guests who want to break away from the slopes can hit some of the area's many shops and stores, including the Christmas Chalet in McHenry, Inglenook Gift & Craft Shop, and eight specialty shops at Oakland's Grand Central Station.

Lodging

On-site
- 168-unit slopeside hotel at base area, with restaurants/pub, indoor pool/Jacuzzi, new fitness center and racquetball courts (call 1-800-462-9477/(301) 387-4911 for rates)
- Camping facility two miles away

Nearby
Will O'The Wisp condominium suites and rooms (call (301) 387-4911 for information)

Alpine Village, Oakland, lakeside chalets and efficiency rooms with fireplaces, dining and shopping within walking distance; 1-800-343-5253/(301) 387-5534

A&A Realty, Vacation rentals, McHenry, 1-800-336-7303

Timberlake Rentals, Oakland; (301) 387-0336

Comfort Inn—Deep Creek Lake; 1-800-228-5150

Lake Breeze Motel; (301) 387-5503

Lakeside Motor Court; (301) 387-5566

Bed and Breakfasts:
The Country Inn Bed and Breakfast, McHenry, (301) 387-6694

Carmel Cove Inn B&B, Deep Creek Lake, (301) 387-0067

Lake Point Inn B&B, Deep Creek Lake, walking distance to Wisp; 1-800-523-LAKE

Red Run Lodge B&B, Deep Creek Lake, 1-800-898-7786

Harley Farm B&B, Deep Creek Lake, (301) 387-9050

Dining/Aprés-Ski

On-site
The Bavarian Room restaurant, **Pizzazz Pizzeria**, **The Gathering** sandwich shop, cafeteria, **Shenanigans Lounge**, 23 Below Lounge, with live weekend entertainment

Nearby (McHenry)
The Four Seasons Dining Room, five miles away at Will O'the Wisp

The Silver Tree Inn, Route 219/Glendale Bridge Road; (301) 387-5524

Pizzeria Uno restaurant/pub; (301) 387-4866

JG's Pub, Route 219; (301) 387-6369

Cornish Manor Victorian restaurant, circa 1868, fine dining, live piano music

Country Kitchen Restaurant, Route 42; (301) 746-5583

Dominick's New York Style Italian Pizzeria, Deep Creek Drive; (301) 387-6800

Le French Cafe, Route 219; (301) 387-5900

McClive's Lakeside Restaurant & Lounge, Deep Creek Drive; (301) 387-6172

Alpine Lake

Alpine Lake Resort

Route 2, Box 99-D2
Terra Alta, West Virginia 26764

Ski Report/Information: 800-752-7179
Local: 304-789-2481
Internet: http://www.wvweb.com/www/
ALPINE_LAKE.html
Credit Cards: AE, MC, VISA

Operating Hours
9 a.m.-4 p.m. Thursday-Monday
6 p.m.-10 p.m. Friday and Saturday

Season: Late November to late March

Getting There
- **From Pittsburgh:** Take I-79 south to I-68 East in Morgantown, then take Route 7, turn left onto Lime Plant Road, and follow 4 miles to Alpine Lake Resort.
- **From Washington/Baltimore:** Take I-70 (I-495 to I-270 to I-70 from Washington, DC) to I-68 through Western Maryland's Panhandle, then take Route 7, and follow directions above.
- **From Charleston:** Take I-79 north to Morgantown, then take I-68, and follow directions above.

Background

Alpine Lake is the smallest and least visible of West Virginia's alpine ski resorts, with just six slopes to offer downhill enthusiasts. The resort is better known for its cross-country ski touring center, but learning skiers often come here to test their skills unencumbered by crowds. The ski area lies 3,050 feet high in the Preston County section of the Allegheny Mountain range, just east of Morgantown and West Virginia University. The facility was a hunting

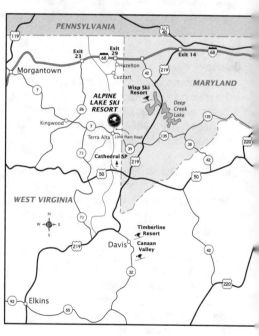

and fishing club until 1969, when it was purchased under the name Mountaintop Vacationland Resort. Financial difficulties would allow Morgantown industrialist J.W. Ruby to eventually take over the property. He then expanded the area and gave it the moniker Alpine Lake. The four-seasons resort now encompasses 2,300 acres of Allegheny woodlands and features a stocked 148-acre lake, an 18-hole golf course, and an indoor Olympic-size pool.

Mountain Stats

Base Elevation: 2,600 feet
Summit Elevation: 3,000 feet
Vertical Drop: 400 feet
Longest Run: 3,300 feet
Primary Slope Direction: North
Average Annual Snowfall: 120 inches

Slopes and Trails: 4 beginner, 2 intermediate
Lifts: 2 poma lifts, 1 tow lift
Uphill Capacity: 900 skiers per hour
Snowmaking: 90% of area
Night Skiing: 100% of area, Friday-Saturday until 10 p.m.

Trail Profiles

The pint-size downhill terrain at Alpine Lake is a natural fit for novice skiers and small children. Trails are both gentle and wide, and crowds are few and far between, with spacious room for beginners to practice turning and stopping. Alpine has constructed a new black diamond trail that occupies all of 400 feet of the small plateau's vertical drop, but it's a run usually handled by mid-level skiers with relative ease.

Other Winter Sports

The popular cross-country skiing center offers rentals, lessons, and trailhead warming huts. Telemark skiing has also taken off here at Alpine, with Tele and cross-country races held annually on a designated Telemark site. Other options for families and children include a sledding hill with rope tow and an ice-skating rink with rentals. Snowboarding is welcomed on the slopes, but the resort is presently without a park or halfpipe.

On-site
- **Cross-country skiing** at the Terra Alta Touring Center
- **200-yard sledding hill** with rope tow: Friday 4 p.m.-8 p.m., weekend noon-6 p.m.; rates $3.50/hour; $9/day
- **Ice-skating rink** with rentals available at the base lodge
- **Telemark skiers** permitted on downhill slopes

Lift Tickets/Rentals/Services

Lift Tickets
- 9 a.m.-6 p.m./1 p.m.-10 p.m.: weekend-adult $23, junior $17
- 9 a.m.-10 p.m.: weekend-adult $28, junior $21
- 9 a.m.-1 p.m./1 p.m.-5 p.m.: weekend-adult $17, junior $13
- 5 p.m.-10 p.m.: weekend-adult $14, junior $11
- 4 p.m.-10 p.m.: Friday-adult $19, junior $15
- * Call resort for midweek availability and rates
- * Group rates for 20 or more skiers

Ski Rentals
- Adult: $19/day, junior $15
- Adult half day/night $16, junior $13

Ski School
- * Call 1-800-752-7179/(304) 789-2481 for instruction and rate information

Base Lodge Facilities: Restaurant and snack bar, lounge, rental shop, ski shop/boutique

Lodging/Dining/Après-Ski

Although downhill skiing is not at a premium at Alpine Lake, the resort offers affordable weekend getaway packages that include lodging, alpine or Nordic lift tickets, an Olympic-size indoor swimming pool, and hot tubs/saunas. It's also a popular lodging destination for nearby Wisp Ski Resort in McHenry, Maryland. Aside from locals, visitors come mostly from nearby Pittsburgh and Washington, DC, which is a three-hour drive. Call ahead to confirm trail openings on weekdays.

Lodging
On-site
42 units and suites with indoor heated pool, hot tubs, saunas, fitness center (call for rates)

Nearby
See Maryland's Wisp Ski Resort, *Nearby Lodging*, page 113

Après-Ski/Dining
On-site
Restaurants and lounges on-site

Nearby
See Wisp Ski Resort, *Nearby Après-Ski/Dining, page 113*

Canaan Valley

Canaan Valley Resort
Route 1, Canaan Valley State Park
Davis, WV 26260

Information: 800-622-4121/304-866-4121
Credit Cards: VISA, MC, AE, Discover

Internet:
http://www.wvweb.com/www/cvresort.html

Operating Hours
9 a.m.-4:30 p.m. Monday-Thursday
9 a.m.-9 p.m. Friday-Sunday

Season: December to late March

Getting There
- **From Washington, DC:** Take I-66 west to I-81 south. Near Strasburg, VA, exit onto Route 55 west through Petersburg, West Virginia, heading to Harman. At Harman take Route 32 north to Canaan Valley. Follow signs to Canaan Valley Ski Area.

- **From Baltimore and points north:** Take I-70 west to Hancock, Maryland, then I-68 west to Cumberland. Follow Route 220 south through Keyser, West Virginia, to Route 50 west at New Creek, then take Route 93 west to Davis. From Davis, follow Route 32 south to Canaan Valley Ski Area.

- **From Richmond, VA:** Take I-64 west to I-81 north to Harrisonburg. At Harrisonburg take Route 33 west to Harman, West Virginia, then follow 32 north to Canaan Valley Ski Area.

- **From Pittsburgh and points north:** Take I-79 south to Morgantown, West Virginia, then pick up I-68 east to Route 42 south at Friendsville, Maryland. From there follow Route 219 south at McHenry to Thomas, West Virginia, then take Route 32 south to Canaan Valley Ski Area.

- **From Columbus, Ohio:** Take I-70 east into Pennsylvania, then take I-79 south to Morgantown, West Virginia, and follow directions above.

- **From Charleston:** Take I-79 north to Weston. Exit onto Route 33 east to Harman. At Harman pick up Route 32 north to Canaan Valley Ski Area.

Background

Nestled in a high alpine valley on the Allegheny's Cabin Mountain is Canaan Valley Ski Resort—West Virginia's second commercial ski area. Off-piste, or backcountry, skiing first began in this remote wilderness area in the late 1940s after pilots reported abundant amounts of snow that frequently held strong here long into April. The ski resort is part of a 6,000-acre state park that features the country's second largest inland wetland—home to white-tail deer, black bear, fox, wild turkey, beaver, and waterfowl.

Some 30 years ago, 3,000 acres of the wilderness area was donated privately to West Virginia, with the stipulation that the state would pick up the tab and match the acreage, turning the area into a state park. A nine-hole golf course was erected first, and the resorts's first ski trails and chair lifts followed shortly after in 1971. And just a few years ago, the nation's five-hundredth wildlife preserve was established a few minutes from the resort.

Mountain Stats

Base Elevation: 3,430 feet
Summit Elevation: 4,280 feet
Vertical Drop: 850 feet
Longest Run: 1.25 miles
Primary Slope Direction: Northwest
Skiable Terrain: 80 acres
Average Annual Snowfall: 155 inches
  1996-97 season: 87 inches
  1995-96 season: 260 inches

Skiable Days
  1996-97 season: 120
  1995-96 season: 120
Slopes and Trails: 10 beginner, 14 intermediate, 10 advanced
Snowmaking: 85% of area
Lifts: 1 quad, 2 triples
Uphill Capacity: 6,100 skiers per hour
Night Skiing: 30% of area, Friday-Sunday until 9 p.m.
*May operate day skiing only for 1997-98 season

At 4,280 feet above sea level, Canaan sits on one of the highest skiable mountains east of the Mississippi, with neighboring Timberline Ski Area only two miles away. Over 150 inches of snow typically cover the northwest-facing peak of Canaan, which is one of the few Mid-Atlantic ski areas to depend more on natural powder than snowmaking. Most of the area's snow comes off the Great Lakes, providing a light powder that doesn't pack very hard, while smaller batches of snow drop from southern storms, impacting the mountain and valley with bigger but wetter snowfalls. Canaan's natural base takes some time to build during the season's start, but generally packs tighter and longer for a late finish. When it's not snowing here, skiers and snowboarders will find some of Canaan's best trails, specifically its wide-open glade sections, closed due to lack of snowmaking.

Although Canaan Valley is a fairly long hike for most metropolitan-based visitors, it's very much worth the trip when its fresh powder opens up the entire mountain. Even with the Mid-Atlantic's dreadful 1996-97 ski season, Canaan managed 87 inches of snow. The resort may not be quite as busy as Timberline, but lift lines can swell on weekend peak times with just a quad and triple chair reaching the summit, and a midstation off the quad. Weekend guests visiting the region have the option, and often take advantage, of skiing both mountains—traversing more difficult Timberline one day and winding down on Canaan the next.

Trail Profiles

In a natural bowl recessed between two mountains, Canaan's trails run against a backdrop of inspiring vistas and scenery. It's an ideal novice and intermediate skier's mountain, with wide, boulevard slopes running down 850 feet of vertical. The trail system is smaller than its 34 advertised slopes and trails—skiers may be hard pressed to find that many. But that's all forgotten when they discover the mountain's real gem—the Weiss Meadows section and its sampling of glade skiing on wide-open, tree-lined terrain. *Weiss Meadows 3* trail is a huge expanse of slalom-turning

terrain, as wide as it is long, with a narrow, contoured chute through the trees on *Weiss Road*. Faster skiers will find some nice steeps on the short-lived *Weiss Drop*. *Meadows 3* ends up being open only half the season on average, as natural conditions permit. *Meadows 2*, unlike the other runs, is equipped with snowmaking, but it's always the last trail on the mountain to receive it.

Advanced skiers usually prefer neighboring Timberline's bigger mountain and tighter, steeper black diamonds, but Canaan has a few strong trails of its own to complement the modest expanse of gladed terrain. *Gravity* is the resort's steepest and most challenging trail, with a headwall off the summit and solid, sustained pitches over 3,300 feet of track. Snowmakers blow extra snow on the trail, then groom it out and carve it to make the pitch even steeper, allowing moguls to form toward the top for bump skiers.

On blue trail *Valley Vista*, skiers can carve under a chair-lift audience before dropping onto steeper track on *The Face*. The beginner area is set in its own area, with two broad hills served by a triple lift, and the adjacent *Bunny Buster* trail caters to small children at its base lodge location. *Dark Side of the Moon*, Canaan's tribute to Pink Floyd, is a gentle, mile-long panoramic cruiser looking out over the mountain. Regrettably, it operates only when there's enough of a natural snow base. *Dark Side* and *Prosperity* were cut just a few years ago with intended snowmaking, but management hasn't agreed to start covering the trails just yet. Occasional warm snaps shut the trails down, and it may be a few years before they decide to provide artificial cover. Some classic novice runs that do feature snowmaking include *Timber Trail*—a 6,000-foot meander off the northwest summit that eases developing skiers into slow-moving turns and gradual, confidence-building gliding.

Snowboarding

Canaan Valley had no snowboard park or halfpipe last year, but the resort is leaning toward adding a terrain park at some point during the 1997-98 season. However, since Canaan is a state park, there's a lot of bureaucratic red tape and approval stages to deal with, which means it may be a while before snowboarders have their own haven. The resort is considering one of three different mountain locations for a park and/or halfpipe in the meantime. Until then, boarders can carve it out on Canaan's boulevard-width intermediate runs; long, undulating beginner runs; and wide-open true glade trails in the Weiss sections.

Riding Canaan's frequent natural powder is somewhat of a rare treasure in the Mid-Atlantic, so snowboarders are starting to make Canaan Valley and Timberline a change-of-pace stop. The terrain at Canaan offers fewer steeps and bumps than its neighboring mountain, but its wide trails provide a solid environment for both big-turning shredders and developing boarders.

Snowboard Rentals: 100 sets; Day/twilight $25; Half-day/night $18
- Alter Ego Sports (off-mountain), specializing in snowboards/rentals, 304-259-2219/866-4698

Snowboard School: 6 instructors, ski rates apply: Ride Ranger instruction program for boarders ages 10 and over

Lift Tickets/Rentals/Services

Skiers get a lot of vertical for their buck here in isolated Canaan Valley. Lift tickets are much cheaper here than at comparable Mid-Atlantic resorts. Night skiing isn't much factored into the equation, though. Just 11 slopes and trails currently have lights, and the resort is considering making the transition to a daytime-only operation because of dwindling night ticket sales and competition with nearby Timberline.

Lift Tickets:
- 9 a.m.-9 p.m.: weekday $27, weekend $36
- 9 a.m.-4:30 p.m.: weekday $22
- 12:30 p.m.-9 p.m.: weekend $27
- 4:30 p.m.-9 p.m.: Friday $17, weekend $23
- * Discount rates for ages 12 and under
- * Multiday discounts available, reduced rates offered during value ski seasons (before Christmas and after February)

Ski Rentals: $16/all adult rentals; $13/ages 12 and under

Off-mountain Rental Shops:
- The Ski Barn/demo ski center, full fleet of shaped and regular skis, snowboards, tuning service, 304-866-4444

Ski School:
- 30 instructors: PSIA certified;
- Private: $39/hour; Group: $15/1.5 hours
- SKIwee programs for ages 4-6 and 7-12

Base Lodge Facilities
- Lodge 1: ticket office, information, ski and rental shops, lockers, ski school
- Lodge 2: day care, lockers, cafeteria, pub

Day Care: Available at base lodge, reservations suggested

Racing: NASTAR held weekends and some mid-week days on intermediate *Ramble* trail

Calendar of Events

Races, events, and demo days held periodically throughout ski season

January
- Special Olympics Winter Games

March
- Annual Governor's Cup ski race (slalom and giant slalom) on *Ramble* trail
- Annual Spring Thing weekend—events, races, festivities

Other Winter Sports

Cross-country and Telemark skiers are welcome at Canaan, where consistent snowfall ensures plentiful opportunities during most seasons. The resort's Nordic ski center sits one mile from the ski lodge, with a connector trail that accesses an ungroomed, 18-mile trail system of wide-open meadows and backcountry wilderness. Skinny skiers can also traverse the eight-mile Blackwater/Canaan trail and the Dolly Sods Wilderness Area from the resort's summit, while both Blackwater Falls State Park and the acclaimed White Grass Touring Center are just a few miles away.

On-site
- **Cross-country skiing** at Canaan's touring center*(see page 231)*
- Lighted, outdoor **ice-skating** rink, with rentals, overlooking the Allegheny Mountains

Nearby
- **Cross-country skiing** at White Grass Touring Center, 1 mile from Canaan *(see page 229)* and

Blackwater Falls State Park, also with **tobogganing/sled run** *(see page 234)*
- Additional **Nordic skiing** trails in the rugged, ungroomed Dolly Sods Wilderness Area
- **Ice fishing** on the Blackwater River

Lodging/Dining/Après-Ski

Canaan, like Timberline, is a destination ski resort with a multitude of lodging and dining options. Guests can base themselves at Canaan's 250-room lodge two miles from the slopes, or at a selection of mountain cabins and year-round campsites. The amenity-filled resort is a favorite site for corporate trips, with several conference rooms available in the spacious lodge. Weekend and vacation skiers also have over 500 private home and condominium properties rented and sold by local realtors and development companies, as well as numerous bed and breakfasts, inns, and motels in Canaan Valley and the nearby towns of Davis and Thomas.

Sparsely populated Davis is the highest elevated incorporated town east of the Mississippi, and combines with the nearby borough of Thomas to offer a host of restaurants, pubs, art and photography stores, and antique and specialty shops. Thomas, two miles north of Davis, is home of the landmark Christmas Shop and Eagles Nest stores, open year-round. Also within driving distance is the picturesque Seneca Rocks-Spruce Knob National Recreation Area, the natural formations of Smoke Hole and Seneca Caverns (open year-round with constant 56-degree temperatures), and Harper's Old Country Store. Built in 1902, Harper's is one of the state's oldest continuously operated businesses, situated in front of scenic Seneca Rocks and Spruce Knob—West Virginia's highest point (4,861 feet).

Summer seasons at the resort bring out thousands of vacationing urban dwellers seeking refuge from the east coast's muggy heat. Canaan's cool mountain air combines with an average summer temperature of 75 degrees to make the resort's numerous outdoor activities even more appealing. Some of Canaan's offerings include a 72-par golf course, tennis courts, Olympic-size swimming pool, chair lift rides overlooking scenic mountain vistas, and 18 miles of hiking trails that wind through Canaan's network and rise to the towering peak of Bald Knob.

Lodging

On-site/State Park Area
- **Canaan Valley Resort State Park**, 2 miles from ski area: 250-room lodge (1-4 bedroom units, efficiencies, suites from $49-$119/night); indoor pool, hot tub, saunas, fitness center, table tennis/game rooms
- 23 mountain cabins (1-4 bedrooms) with fireplaces, full kitchens; rates $125-$194/night
- 34 year-round campsites with electrical hookups (no running water during winter)

On-site and Nearby

Canaan Realty, 104 chalets and 5 condo properties slopeside or nearby, with fireplaces, hot tubs, large decks; personal checks only for rentals; 1-800-448-0074

Northpoint, Canaan Valley, popular cross-country ski lodging, bordering Monongahela National Forest with 30-mile Nordic/hiking/biking trail system; 46 large, modern fireplace units include chalets and cabins with hot tubs, and townhomes and log cabins; views of Timberline and Canaan slopes; all units (sleeping 4-14 persons) fully furnished with full kitchens; rates $285-$700 per 4 nights; 1-800-542-8355

Black Bear Resort/Condos, Davis, 44 cottages and 6 condos with full kitchen, living/dining room, fireplace, Jacuzzi; 12 inn rooms with Jacuzzi; indoor pool; restaurant/lounge; rates $110-$200 nightly per unit; 1-800-553-2327

Deerfield Village Resort and Restaurant, Canaan Valley, 125 villas with full kitchen, fireplace (most with Jacuzzis); restaurant; shops/groceries/ski rentals; rates (2-night minimum) $125-$180/night, up to 10 persons $250/night; 1-800-342-3217

Alpine Lake Resort; 1-800-752-7179 *(see pages 114, 227)*

Mountain Top Rentals, Canaan Valley, 90 units: condos, cabins, chalets, and large homes at Timberline and close to Canaan ski areas; most with fireplaces, some with hot tubs/Jacuzzis; all units with full kitchens; also 20 efficiency condos in Davis, with kitchenettes, at Pendletonheim; rates at Mountain Top $240-$900/3 nights for 2-16 people; 1-800-624-4341

Yokum's Vacationland, Seneca Rocks, 30 miles from Canaan, 45-50 units, including fireplace/Jacuzzi cabins, motel units with kitchenettes, efficiency apartments, and home trailers, all with private baths; winter campground with showers and electrical hook-ups; restaurant and deli on-site; rates from $30-$95/night; 1-800-772-8342

Nearby Bed and Breakfasts

Meyer House B&B (the Green Gables of Davis), large 5-room country house, circa 1885, popular lodging for cross-country skiers, 1 mile from Blackwater Falls State Park trails, also skiing out the back door along Blackwater River leading to the canyon; 4 restaurants close by; rates $65-$85/2 persons nightly; (304) 259-5451

Bright Morning B&B, Davis, 10 miles from Canaan, 8 rooms with private bath; dining room with breakfast/lunch (also open to non-guests); rates $60 nightly/2 persons; (304) 259-5119

Pour Victoria B&B, circa 1883 Queen Anne Victorian inn, with antique furnishings, 20 minutes from Canaan in Parsons; (304) 478-1103

Hill House B&B, Davis, circa 1890 Victorian house, 3 rooms with shared bath, kitchen and living room privileges; full country breakfast; rates $75 nightly/2 persons; (304) 259-5883

White Oak B&B, Parsons, 25 miles from Canaan Valley, 4 single rooms and 1 suite with 3 rooms, kitchenette, fireplace; breakfast extra; restaurants nearby; rates $45/double, $35/single; (304) 478-4705

Other Nearby Lodging

Mountain Aire Lodge, Davis, at entrance to Blackwater Falls State Park, 11 standard, affordable rooms, restaurant next door; 1-800-553-0724

Best Western Alpine Lodge, Davis; (304) 259-5245

Montwood Motor Inn; (304) 463-4114

Tucker Country Inn; (304) 478-2100

Windwood-Fly Inn; 1-888-359-4667

Village Inn; (304) 866-4166

Dining/Aprés-Ski

On-site

- Cafeteria, pub, pizza cellar
- Nearby Canaan Lodge offers fine dining at the Aspen Dining Room and Laurel Lounge

Nearby

White Grass Natural Foods Cafe, Canaan Valley; (304) 866-4114

Body and Soul Cafe, Thomas, coffee bar/light menu, art/gift/book shop, live jazz/blues/folk music, poetry, and storytelling; (304) 463-4458

Golden Anchor & Portside Pub, Canaan Valley, acclaimed seafood menu; (304) 866-2722

Tucker Country Inn, Parsons, homestyle meals and baked breads, desserts; (304) 478-2100

Amelia's Restaurant/Yeager's Bar at the Windwood-Fly Inn, Canaan Valley; 1-888-359-4667

(continues)

(continued)

Oriskany Inn Restaurant/Lounge, fine dining at the entrance to Timberline Resort; (304) 866-4514

Sirianni's Cafe, Davis, well-known family restaurant with Italian menu; (304) 259-5454

The Sawmill Restaurant at Best Western, Davis, country cooking with affordable menu; (304) 259-5245

Blackwater Lodge Restaurant/Lounge, Davis; (304) 259-5216

Joe's Italian Supper Club & Lounge, Davis, breakfast-dinner; (304) 463-4291

The Front Porch, Seneca Rocks, gourmet casual dining and clear views of Seneca Rocks and surrounding Allegheny Mountains; (304) 567-2555

New Winterplace

New Winterplace Ski Resort

P.O. Box 1
Flat Top, West Virginia 25841

Ski Report: 800-258-3127
Information/Reservations: 800-607-SNOW
Local: 304-787-3221

Credit Cards: MC, VISA, AE, Discover

Internet: http://wwweb.com/www/Winterplace.html
E-mail: M4264@aol.com

Operating Hours
9 a.m.-10 p.m. weekdays
8 a.m.-10 p.m. weekends

Season: Early December to late March

Getting There

• **From Charleston:** Take I-77 south to Exit 28, Flat Top, and follow signs 2 miles to New Winterplace.

• **From Huntington:** Take I-64 east to I-77/I-64 south. Follow directions above.

• **From Washington, DC:** Take I-66 west to I-81 south to I-64 south/west into West Virginia. Then follow I-64 west to Beckley, picking up I-77 south. Take Exit 28, Flat Top, and follow signs 2 miles to New Winterplace.

• **From Charlotte, North Carolina and Columbia, South Carolina:** Take I-77 north through Virginia, then take Exit 28, Flat Top, West Virginia, and follow signs 2 miles to New Winterplace.

• **From Raleigh/Durham and Greensboro, North Carolina:** Take I-40 north/west to I-77 north, then follow directions above.

Background

Flat Top Mountain is home to New Winterplace—West Virginia's only major alpine ski area outside the expansive Monongahela National Forest. The 15-year-old resort is located between the towns of Beckley and Princeton, in the state's southern region bordering Virginia.

Though far removed from any metropolitan areas, Winterplace still has demographics in its favor. It's one of the South's favorite ski destinations, luring guests from Charlotte, Raleigh/Durham, and Columbia, South Carolina, as well as more locally based skiers from Charleston and Huntington. The resort's 27-trail network far surpasses North Carolina's biggest ski areas, and offers slopeside condominiums and a long list of nearby facilities. The resort is also easily accessible from Interstate 77, just two miles off the major four-lane highway. It's a distinction that's heavily marketed by the resort since the region averages 100 inches of snow per year. Southern skiers especially cherish the opportunity to carve through natural powder, but are generally less inclined than northerners to drive on it, which is why the resort's convenient highway access helps draw a strong yearly skier base.

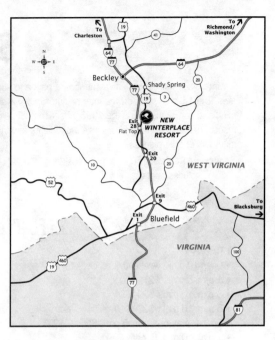

Mountain Stats

Base Elevation: 2,997 feet
Summit Elevation: 3,600 feet
Vertical Drop: 603 feet
Longest Run: 1.25 miles
Primary Slope Direction: North
Skiable Terrain: 90 acres
Annual Snowfall: 100 inches
   1996-97 season: 65 inches
   1995-96 season: 140 inches
Snowmaking: 100% of area
Slopes and Trails: 11 beginner, 12 intermediate, 4 advanced
Night Skiing: 90% of area, nightly until 10 p.m.

Lifts: 2 quads, 3 triples, 2 doubles, 2 surface lifts
Uphill Capacity: 13,000 skiers per hour

Jammed slopes and interminable lift lines have long been the scourge of skiing at Winterplace, but ownership responded during 1996-97 by increasing the uphill capacity and adding new terrain. A much-needed quad lift was strung up next to the triple chair on the advanced section, and another new quad reaches the often-congested mid-summit area. Four new trails introduced last season have also helped distribute the flow of traffic. Nonetheless, skiers can still bank on large crowds on just about any weekend or holiday. Snow tubing will be introduced this year as an alternative to skiing and snowboarding: eight lanes and two surface lifts make up the new tubing park.

Trail Profiles

The mountain's two-face system separates the limited advanced terrain from the more prevalent beginner track. One major drawback at Winterplace, however, is the resort's awkward trail design: Two chair lifts are required to reach the summit. Most of the resort's trails are on the short side, but beginners have over one mile of continuous cruising on the summit's *Ridgerunner* trail—an easy jaunt leading down to the base. There's also considerable bunny turf and slow-skiing terrain off the base lodge. Of the four new trails Winterplace cut last season, *Wood's Run* is the most notable. It's a long, narrow beginner run off the summit that zig zags along the outskirts of the trail network down to the new quad lift.

Seasoned skiers won't find too many challenges on the mountain: There's only 600 feet of vertical drop, and not all of it is on the advanced face. The resort's four black diamond trails are somewhat steep, but short-lived and rarely bumped out with moguls. The steepest drops can be found on the wide-open summit bowl, which flows into more narrow, tree-lined terrain on the advanced *Plunge* and *Nosedive*. *Turkey Chute* and *Drop Off* are blue runs disguised as black diamonds on satisfyingly pitched cruising terrain. Winterplace hosts the popular NASTAR time-trial racing program on the intermediate *Look At Me* trail.

Snowboarding

Winterplace has an exclusive snowboard park and surface lift in a centrally located, tree-lined cul-de-sac area. The 1.5-acre park, off the intermediate *Snow Field* trail, featured snowboarder-created tabletops, hips, rails, and gap jumps during the 1996-97 season. Winterplace didn't hold any competitions last year, but the resort is otherwise ripe with riders. Strong lights keep the park open nightly, and boarders have the entire mountain at their disposal.

Snowboard Rentals: 150 sets: K2, Rossignol; $23-$30 (includes boots)

Snowboard School: 45 instructors, ski rates apply; Beginner snowboard package: $30-$50

Lift Tickets/Rentals/Services

Lift Tickets
- Open-10 p.m.: weekend $39, weekday $27
- 1 p.m.-5 p.m.: $27, $20
- 3 p.m.-10 p.m.: $29, $24
- 5 p.m.-10 p.m.: $27, $19
- Open-1 p.m. or 1 p.m.-5 p.m. Sunday $27
- 1 p.m.-10 p.m. Sunday $29
- * Reduced rates for ages 6-12; 5 & under ski free
- * Multiday discounts on lift tickets and rentals

Ski Rentals:
- Over 2,000 sets: Rossignol, Elan, Dynastar;
- Adult $14-$18, junior $11-$14;
- Parabolic (shaped) skis $23-$28

Ski School:
- 200 instructors: PSIA certified;
- Private $30; Group $14
- SKIwee program for ages 4-11, with half-day and full-day sessions; call for rates (800-607-SNOW)
- Learn-to-ski or snowboard package, weekday $20-$30, weekend $40-$50, includes beginner lift ticket, rental, lesson; full-mountain beginner package also available
- Shaped ski instruction and rental package $30

Adaptive ski program: No formal program, but skiers are accommodated, with adaptive ski rentals available

Base Lodge Facilities
Ski/rental shop, Ski School/SKIwee program, group rental area, ski accessory shops, ski and boot lockers, day care, restaurants/lounges

Day care: Offered daily at base lodge, half or full day, 24-hour reservations required (call 800-607-SNOW)

Racing: NASTAR held daily on *Look at Me* trail

Calendar of Events
- * Mountain Bike Slalom Snow Races held each weekend
- * Family Fun Day Saturdays, with events and giveaways

January
- Annual Winter Carnival
- Annual West Virginia Shovel Race Championship

Other Winter Sports
On-site
- 8-lane snow tubing park with 2 surface lifts; call for rates
- Telemark skiing allowed on all slopes

Nearby
- Cross-country skiing 35 miles away at Pipestem Resort State Park *(see page 236)*

Lodging/Dining/Aprés-Ski

Nighttime is the right time at Winterplace, with most of the day-ticket crowds long gone but the revelry continuing under lights. Over 90 percent of the trails and a snowboarding terrain park are equipped with lights. The Snowdrift Lounge runs until midnight with live music and entertainment on weekends, and the Mountain House is a mid-mountain restaurant/lounge that also hosts live bands. In all, the resort has five eateries and three lounges.

Beyond the limited slopeside lodging at the Winterhaven Condos, numerous bedding options are available just off the mountain and in both Princeton and Beckley (10 miles). Overnight guests have the choice of basing themselves at luxury inns, affordable motels, or century-old bed & breakfasts. Winterplace's sister resort, Glade Springs, is a 10-minute drive from the mountain, offering free shuttle service between the two.

Lodging

On-site

- **Winterhaven Condos**—36 slopeside rooms with kitchenettes, hot tubs/spas, and fireplaces; rates $160-$300/night (up to six persons); (304) 787-3202

Nearby (10 minutes)

Appalachian Resort Inn, with restaurant, one-half mile from resort; rates $45-$80/night; 1-800-231-0054

Glade Springs Resort (New Winterplace's sister resort), 8 miles away—shuttle service available, with kitchenettes, hot tubs, fireplaces, indoor tennis, exercise room; rates $60-$325/night (up to 8 persons); 1-800-634-5233

Econolodge, 1 mile from resort; rates $45-$78/night; (304) 787-3250

Country Cabins, 14 miles from resort, with kitchenettes, fireplaces; rates $80-$250/night (up to 10 persons); (304) 466-3930

Sleep Inn, Beckley; rates $41-$59/night; (304) 255-4222

Best Western Motor Lodge, Beckley; rates $41-$62; 1-800-528-1234

Comfort Inn, Beckley, with exercise room; rates $41-$61/night; (304) 255-2161

Days Inn, Princeton, with kitchenettes, hot tubs, indoor pool; rates $45-$67; 1-800-222-0511

Hampton Inn, Beckley; rates $64-$76; 1-800-465-4329

Super 8 Motel, Beckley; rates $40-$57; 1-800-848-8888

Bed and Breakfasts:

Historic Hinton Manor B&B, 22 miles from resort; rates $60-$150/night; (304) 466-3930

Dogwood Ridge B&B, 47 miles from resort, with hot tub; rates $65-$120/night; 1-800-816-1255

Dining/Après-Ski

On-site

The Mountain House—mid-mountain restaurant with large deck, stone fireplace, and live weekend entertainment

Snowdrift Lounge, open from 11 a.m. to midnight, with live music/videos

Penguins Mexican/Italian eatery and lounge

Almost Heaven-The Deck at Winterplace

Mountain Mama's Food Court

Nearby

Holiday Inn, Beckley, restaurant/lounge, 17 miles from resort; 1-800-465-4329

Ramada Inn, Beckley, restaurant/lounge, 15 miles from resort; 1-800-341-6455

Snowshoe/ Silver Creek

Snowshoe Mountain Resort (Snowshoe/Silver Creek)

P.O. Box 10
Snowshoe, WV 26209

Ski Report: (304) 572-INFO
Information: (304) 572-1000
Lodging Reservations: (304) 572-5252
Credit Cards: VISA, MC, AE
Internet: http://www.snowshoemtn.com

Operating Hours

Snowshoe: 8:30 a.m.-4:30 p.m. daily
Silver Creek: 8:30 a.m.-10 p.m. daily (Call (304) 572-1000 to confirm new night hours)

Season: Mid-November to late March

Getting There

- **From Washington, DC:** Take I-495 to I-66 west to I-81 south to Staunton, Virginia. Then take Route 250 west to 42 south to Goshen. From Goshen, follow 39 west to Marlinton, West Virginia, and travel 26 miles north on Route 219 to Snowshoe.
- **From Richmond:** Take I-64 west to I-81 north to Staunton. Then take Route 250 west to 42 south to Goshen. From Goshen, follow 39 west to Marlinton, West Virginia, and travel 26 miles north on Route 219 to Snowshoe.
- **From Pittsburgh:** Take I-79 south to Weston, West Virginia, then travel east on Route 33 to Elkins. From Elkins, follow 219 south for 48 miles to Snowshoe.
- **From Cleveland:** Take I-77 south to Parkersburg, West Virginia, then Route 50 east to Clarksburg and I-79 south to Weston. Follow Route 33 east to Elkins, and travel 48 miles south on Route 219 to Snowshoe.

- **From Raleigh/Durham and Greensboro, North Carolina:** Take Route 220 north to Clifton Forge, Virginia, then take I-64 west to White Sulphur Springs. From White Sulphur Springs, follow Route 92 north to West Virginia Route 39 , heading west to Marlinton. Follow Route 219 north 26 miles to Snowshoe.
- **From Atlanta; Columbia, South Carolina; and Charlotte, North Carolina:** Take I-77 north to Beckley, West Virginia, then take I-64 east to White Sulphur Springs. From White Sulphur Springs, follow Route 92 north to West Virginia Route 39 , heading west to Marlinton. Follow Route 219 north 26 miles to Snowshoe.

Background

With an annual visitor count that ranks in the top five percent of North American ski areas, Snowshoe Mountain Resort is the Mid-Atlantic's premiere ski destination. The virtual ski town comprises two ski areas: Snowshoe and Silver Creek, with a combined 53 slopes and trails, same-day reciprocal lift ticket, and shuttle buses servicing both facilities. Snowshoe is the more advanced area of the two and owns Mid-Atlantic's biggest vertical drop of 1,500 feet, all of it on the acclaimed 1.5-mile *Cupp Run*. Silver Creek is the smaller resort, catering primarily to families and developing skiers.

The area was originally developed when Alabama's Dr. Thomas Brigham, who opened North Carolina's Beech and Sugar Mountains, sought to establish a big-time ski resort here in the Monongahela National Forest's Pocahontas County. Dr. Brigham and his crew examined the snow-filled mountain tops of maple, cherry, and red spruce hardwoods, breaking ground in 1973 with nine trails and three chair lifts on the 4,800-foot-high summit of Cheat Mountain. The resort is named after the locally revered Snowshoe Hare, whose survival is a testament to the area's long winter seasons. The white-coated hare is rarely found south of Canada's mountain ranges but manages to make a home here, relying on heavy snowfall coverage and lasting conditions in order to elude predators during the winters. The pristine natural basin is also home to black bear, deer, beaver, bobcat, weasel, wild turkey, and mink.

The entire resort was acquired in 1995 by Intrawest Corporation of Vancouver, British Columbia—the leading real estate developer and mountain resort operator in North America. Intrawest also owns such alpine giants as Vermont's Stratton; California's Mammoth; British Columbia's Blackcomb, Whistler, and Panorama; Colorado's Copper; and Quebec's Mont Tremblant and Mount Ste. Marie. Snowshoe will kick off the 1997-98 with a $12 million capital improvement project that includes the installation of a new high-speed detachable quad lift at Snowshoe; a 40-percent increase in snowmaking at both areas (which should open Silver Creek and *Cupp Run* by late November); and a new snow tubing park, snowboard halfpipe, and night skiing hours at Silver Creek.

Mountain Stats

Base Elevation: Snowshoe: 3,250 feet; Silver Creek: 4,155 feet

Summit Elevation: Snowshoe: 4,848 feet; Silver Creek: 4,818 feet

Vertical Drop: Snowshoe: 1,500 feet; Silver Creek: 670 feet

Skiable Terrain: Snowshoe: 120 acres; Silver Creek: 92 acres

Primary Slope Direction: North to northeast

Average Annual Snowfall: 180 inches
1996-97 season: 95 inches
1995-96 season: 292 inches
1994-95 season: 104 inches

Skier Visits: Snowshoe
1995-96 season: 340,000
1994-95 season: 300,000
Silver Creek
1995-96 season: 70,000
1994-95 season: 80,000

Skiable Days
1995-96: 162
1994-95: 150

Slopes and Trails: Snowshoe: 19 beginner, 9 intermediate, 7 advanced; Silver Creek: 6 beginner, 10 intermediate, 2 advanced

Longest Run

Snowshoe: 1.5 miles

Silver Creek: 1 mile

Lifts: Snowshoe: 1 high-speed quad, 6 triples; Silver Creek: 2 quads, 2 triples, 1 handle tow

Uphill Capacity: Snowshoe/Silver Creek: 19,200 skiers per hour

Snowmaking: 100% of both areas

Night Skiing: Snowshoe: none; Silver Creek: 40% of area nightly until 10 p.m.

Snowshoe is arguably the Mid-Atlantic's busiest resort, with the weekend congestion of a New York City rush-hour subway. The new high-speed quad lift will help filter out much of the resort's mid-section traffic, replacing the heavily used Ball Hooter lift. But what attracts hundreds of thousands of destination skiers from all over the eastern seaboard is the resort's abundance of lodging, restaraunts/pubs, and amenities, as well as the region's most consistent natural conditions. Light, delicate snow—some of the lightest east of the Mississippi River—graces the high-elevation mountain tops. The 1995-96 season featured a virtually insurmountable 292 inches of snow. Both resorts, which now feature 100 percent snowmaking, traditionally begin operations in November and stay open well into March or April.

Trail Profiles

Snowshoe

Snowshoe's north-facing mountain is somewhat of an elliptical bowl, two miles wide by five miles long. Despite the impressive 1,500-foot vertical on *Cupp Run*, the trail system's remaining 34 runs are essentially of beginner and intermediate difficulty and cover substantially less vertical.

Just a few runs can truly be called black diamonds. *Widowmaker* is one of them—a fairly steep headwall and sharp drops precede more gradual terrain over 860 feet of vertical. Mass-marketed black diamond *Cupp Run* boasts constantly changing pitches and terrain throughout its 1.5-mile course, but nothing steep enough to strike fear in skiers. Situated on the mountain's western face, it unfolds from the summit with a solid descent and some bumps, moves on to long cruising track, then enters a mogul field and hits a switchback before winding down on varying trail widths. *Cupp Run* is a long, thigh-burning run for both intermediates and experts, but it's not without its flaws. Guests have to lug their equipment over a few hundred feet of paved road to access the trail, and its western-facing slope requires extensive snowmaking and grooming, especially near the narrow finish. The trail is best served by early-morning risers who can get a few runs in before the course gets packed too hard—and too crowded. Be prepared for a nearly 20-minute ride on its triple chair lift.

Popular mid-level runs include *Upper Ball Hooter*—one of the resort's longer trails. *Lower Ball Hooter* is a terrain park providing a series of jumps and obstacles for skiers and snowboarders. There's also a nicely pitched, serpentine run unencumbered by intersecting trails on intermediate *J Hook*, next to black diamond *Widowmaker*.

Over half of Snowshoe's trails are beginner greens, and most of them are short and easy. Directly facing the summit lodge area are the *Skidder* and *Crosscut* first-time-skier areas and site of the resort's ski school. Narrow, continuous cruising trails are a tough find here: Beginning skiers will discover longer runs that may be less crowded on the intersecting trails *Upper* and *Lower Hootenanny* and *Upper* and *Mid Flume*.

For racers, the NASTAR national recreation racing program is held on a modified giant slalom course on the intermediate *Skipjack* trail.

Silver Creek

Thirty feet lower in altitude lies Silver Creek—a natural fit for beginner and novice skiers with its wide-open and less challenging runs. Its beginner terrain has been expanded this year by 12 acres, and a new quad lift was also added. The *Tenderfoot* bunny hill is ideal for small children and has its own chair lift. Surrounding beginner slopes are plenty wide and easily negotiable, including *Cub Run*, which provides long, narrow, and stable cruising terrain for learning skiers. *Flying Eagle* and *Bear Claw* are rated advanced, but don't expect many steeps here. The mountain was designed for families and beginners and to lighten skier traffic at the larger Snowshoe. Silver Creek's new snow tubing park on the former *Tenderfoot* trail is part of the resort's Family Snow Adventure Area. The park will host four tubing lanes and use a handle tow lift. Both resorts offer numerous ski and snowboard instruction and training programs for children and adults, in addition to child care centers that are open daily.

Snowboarding

Snowboarders share terrain parks with skiers at both Snowshoe and Silver Creek, and have resort-wide trail access. The *Lower Ball Hooter* trail at Snowshoe last year featured modestly sized tabletops, wales, spines, and a quarterpipe. There's no chair lift specific to the park, so boarders have to take the Ball Hooter lift to the summit and wind back down. At Silver Creek, boarders have more options. Though there's less vertical drop on the beginner *Andiamo* trail's park than at Snowshoe, the area will be redesigned this year with more room and new obstacles that include numerous spines and wales. And boarders can shred in Silver Creek's new halfpipe, which will be maintained effectively by a Scorpion pipe groomer. The terrain park and halfpipe are serviced by a triple lift and will feature lights, a sound system, and continuous events throughout the season.

Snowboard Rentals: 63 sets: Rossignol, Morrow; $29 (including boots)

Snowboard School: 6 instructors; Private $40/hour; Group $18/1.5 hours

Lift Tickets/Rentals/Services

Since Snowshoe is primarily a destination resort packed with aprés-ski activities, ownership has seen little need for night skiing—at least until this year. Silver Creek will feature lights on roughly 40 percent of its trails, as well as its snowboard terrain park and tubing area, until 10 p.m. Snowshoe will be without lights for the time being. Guests can use the Snowshoe Hareline Shuttle Service that runs every 30 minutes and transports skiers between areas and to all facilities.

Lift Tickets: (available from Snowshoe's Shaver's Centre and Top of the World; and from Silver Creek Ski Area)
- 8:30 a.m.-4:30 p.m.: weekday $22, weekend $30
- Weekend half-day $22
* Ages 7-12: weekend $22, weekday $14
* Ages 5 and under ski free, discounts for seniors
* Reciprocal lift ticket valid at both Snowshoe and Silver Creek
* Call Silver Creek for new night hours/rates ((304) 572-1000)

Ski School:
- Over 100 instructors: PSIA certified;
- Private $40/hour; Group $40/hour
- Mogul Busters, Brr Rabbit Ski Schools for young children
- Beginner skier/snowboarder package

Ski Rentals:
- 2,300 sets: Rossignol, Edge, Aspen shaped skis, Rossignol CUT skis;
- Adult $19, ages 7-12 $16; CUT skis $21

Adaptive Ski School: Adaptive program offered at Silver Creek

(continues)

(continued)

Summit Lodge Facilities

Snowshoe: Shaver's Centre—ticket sales, customer services/information, lockers, lost & found, ski training center, Souper eatery/Pizzazz Pizzeria, pub, The Connection Night Club/day bar, specialty shops, medical clinic/ski patrol

* Equipment rentals in neighboring Spruce Lodge; day care, rentals/repair, childrens' ski school, and ski shop in Edelweiss Building

Silver Creek: ticket sales, ski and rental shops, lockers, day care, The Cave Entertainment Center, The Deli, Micro-Grocery Mart, Red Oak Lounge, Ski Barn Gift Shop, spa/pool, the Terrace Restaurant

Child Care: Snowshoe: Available daily for ages 2 and older from 8 a.m.-5 p.m.; Silver Creek: Daily for ages 12 weeks and older, 8 a.m.-5 p.m.

Shops
- Why Not Shop
- Fudge Shop
- Shirt Works
- Just Because
- Edelweiss Ski Haus
- Mountain Treasures
- A Cut Above Hair Salon
- The Ski Barn at Silver Creek
- The Grocery Store at Silver Creek
- The General Store

Family/Kids Activities
- The Cave Entertainment Center at Silver Creek
- Shavers Centre Arcade
- Splash Arcade

- Top of the World Game Room
- Miniature Golf at Top of the World
- Arcade at The Inn at Snowshoe

Pools, Spas, and Hot Tubs
- The Splash Pool
- Spa/Pool at Whistlepunk Village
- Masseuse at The Whistlepunk Spa
- Inn at Snowshoe Pool & Jacuzzis*
- Snowcrest Condos Jacuzzis*
- Top of the World Jacuzzis*
- Silver Creek Lodge Pool & Jacuzzis*

(*Resident guests only)

Other Winter Sports

On-site
- New four-lane snow tubing park at Silver Creek on the former *Tenderfoot* trail, serviced by handle tow lift
- Telemark skiing allowed on all slopes at both Snowshoe and Silver Creek (no rentals available)

Nearby
- Abundant cross-country skiing available at nearby Elk River Touring Center *(see page 228)*, Watoga State Park *(see page 237)*, and Monongahela National Forest; Local outfitters/guides include Appalachian Sport in Marlinton ((304) 799-4050) and Cheat Mountain Outfitting & Guide in Durbin ((304) 456-4023)

Summer Activities

The resort also makes a smooth transition into spring and summer, lending its mountain to an excellent mountain biking and hiking trail system and 18-hole golf at the scenic, expertly manicured Hawthorne Valley course. Whitewater sports are a two-hour drive from Snowshoe on the New and Gauley Rivers, and Seneca Rocks (1.5 hours away) offers rock climbing and sight seeing. Closer by is the historical Cass Scenic Railroad State Park, where guests can turn back the clocks to the early 1900s logging era in Pocahontas County, traveling to the near-mile-high summit of Bald Knob on authentic Shay steam locomotives—some of the few left in the world.

Calendar of Events

Calendar of Events

January
- Budweiser Winter Break SkiFest
- Family Channel Tour de Ski
- Absolut Ski Challenge

February
- Miller Lite Cupp Run Challenge Weekend
- Jose Cuervo Games of Winter

- Subaru Master the Mountain Weekend

March
- Subaru Ski Club Bash
- Corona Mars Loco
- Rolling Rock St. Patrick's Weekend

Racing: NASTAR held daily at 11 a.m. and 2 p.m. on Snowshoe's *Skipjack* trail and weekends at 11 a.m. and 2 p.m. on Silver Creek's *Ram's Horn* trail

Lodging/Dining/Aprés-Ski

Few West Virginia towns can match Snowshoe's population during the winter months. The resort offers over 1,200 condominiums, 350 lodge and inn rooms, and numerous private homes. Accommodations range from the luxurious and fully equipped to cheaper, no-frills lodging. And Snowshoe doesn't miss a beat with its aprés-ski scene. The bustling resort offers 12 restaurants and eateries and 10 pubs/lounges, including a full-time Comedy Club and two nightclubs hosting live bands. Guests can also relax in one of the resort's heated pools, saunas, and Jacuzzis, or take a turn in a spa, exercise room, or a massage therapy session. With the night-time revelry in full force, families might feel a bit overwhelmed if it weren't for a slate of childrens' activities that includes miniature golf, three arcades, and an entertainment center, as well as special club nights for the under-21 crowd.

But don't feel that your lodging options are confined to Snowshoe. In the absence of hotels and motels, a long list of bed and breakfasts, inns, cabins, and chalets are available within 30 miles of Snowshoe. Most guests agree, though, that the ski-and-stay experience at Snowshoe is well worth the money. The resort is pretty remote—roughly 20 miles either way to any town—and aside from Snowshoe's general store and The Grocery Store at Silver Creek, the only nearby convenience shop and gas station are near the base of the mountain at Big Spring Station.

Lodging

*Call (304) 572-5252 for rates/further information

On-site

Inn Rooms and Lodges:

The Inn at Snowshoe, at the mountain's base: 150 rooms, with restaurant/lounge, indoor pool, Jacuzzis, sauna/spa, exercise room

Timberline Lodge, located off *Skidder* slope and near commercial areas: 50 rooms with restaurant and lounge in building, access to pool

Spruce Lodge, centrally located/slopeside lodging: 100 less-expensive rooms

Whistlepunk Inn, located off *Whistlepunk* trail and adjacent to Red Fox Restaurant and Whistlepunk Spa: 13 rooms/suites, some with lofts and sun decks

Condominiums:

Camp 4 condominiums, new for 1997-98 season: 17 units

Powderidge, slopeside lodging: 1- and 2-bedroom condos/townhouses

Shamrock, near-slopeside lodging: 1- to 4-bedroom townhouses

Powder Monkey, adjacent to basin slopes and near *Cupp Run*: 2- to 3-bedroom condos, also near Shavers Centre, restaurants, and shops

Stemwinder, near slopes, restaurants, Shavers Centre: 2- to 4-bedroom deluxe townhouse units, some with whirlpools

Snowcrest Village, near-slopeside lodging, close to *Widowmaker* trail: 1- to 2-bedroom units with indoor spas/Jacuzzis/hot tubs

Sundown Hutches, across from Whistlepunk Village, ski-in, ski-out access to *Cupp Run*: 1-, 3-, or 5-bedroom condos

Treetop, centrally located, near-slopeside lodging: 2- to 3-bedroom townhouses

(lodging continues)

(lodging continued)

Wabasso, near-slopeside lodging: 2-bedroom units with loft, fireplace, and deck

Whistlepunk Condominiums, slopeside: 1- to 4-bedroom units with private Jacuzzi tubs; restaurant and pub, spa/massage area, outdoor hot tub and Jacuzzi, free use of pool, nautilus center, sauna

Silver Creek Lodge Condominiums: 240 fully furnished units with heated pool, shops, ski school/rentals, restaurant, pub, Jacuzzi

Summit Condominiums, short walk to slopes, restaurants, Shavers Centre: 3-bedroom units with fireplaces

Top of the World, near *Widowmaker* trail and above Top of the World Commercial Centre: 1-bedroom units, with hot tubs, miniature golf, family game room, restaurant/lounge, shops

Nearby
Bed and Breakfasts:

Slatyfork Farm B&B and cabin rentals, Slatyfork, 2 miles from Snowshoe, 4 rooms (1 with private bath, hot tub), surrounded by cross-country ski trails; (304) 572-3900

Elk River Inn B&B, 4 miles from Snowshoe; (304) 572-3771

Buffalo Run B&B, shared bath, 20 miles from Snowshoe; (304) 456-3036

Jerico B&B, 22 miles; (304) 799-6241

Carriage House B&B, 28 miles; (304) 799-6706

Richard's Country Inn, Huttonsville (pre-Civil War mansion, circa 1835); 1-800-636-7434

Condominiums/Inns/Cabins:

Old Spruce Realty, fully equipped slopeside and nearby condos, with fireplaces, 888-5-SPRUCE/304-572-2946

Overlook Village, Cass, 36 condo/efficiency units, hot tub; rates $45-$99/night; (304) 572-2290

Comfy Camping Cabins, Cass, 2 fully equipped 3- to 4-person cabins; (304) 456-3017/456-4410

Erehwon Cabins, 6 miles from Snowshoe, fully equipped cabin rentals; (304) 572-5140

Seneca State Forest, Route 28, 7 rustic cabins; 1-800-CALL-WVA/304-799-6231

Nakiska Chalets, 6 miles from Snowshoe; (304) 339-6309

Seneca Trail Inn, 4 miles from Snowshoe; (304) 572-2800

Cass Inn, 10 miles from Snowshoe; (304) 456-3464

Dining/Après-Ski
On-site
- 6 restaurants, 5; fast food eateries, 10 pubs/lounges

The Red Fox—award-winning menu
Auntie Pasta's Ristorante
Brandi's at the Inn at Snowshoe
Goodtime Bobby's
Skidder
Terrace Cafe at Silver Creek

Fast Food Outlets:
Pizzazz Pizza
The Souper
The Deli at Silver Creek
Burger Slope
Hoot's Grill

Pubs and Clubs
The Comedy Cellar, at Skidder Restaurant, Tuesday-Saturday
The Connection Nightclub, with live bands, happy hours
Hoot's Pub (at the Top of the World facility), with live music Wednesday-Saturday
Goodtime Bobby's Sports Bar, with billiards, foosball, TV sports
Yodeler's Pub, with large selection of brews and fine cigars
The Red Oak Lounge, with billiards and darts
Skidder Pub
Hole in the Wall Pub
Brandi's at the Inn at Snowshoe
Auntie's Bistro

Nearby
Elk River Restaurant, Slatyfork; (304) 572-3771
Paradise Cafe (Route 219 and Route 66); (304) 572-2210
Papa Joe's Raw Bar & Grill, Big Spring Station, just off Snowshoe Mountain
Suzie's Chic Inn Restaurant, Route 219, Marlinton; (304) 799-0892
French's Diner, Marlinton; (304) 799-9910
Godfather's Pizza, Marlinton; (304) 799-4700

Timberline

Timberline Four Seasons Resort

HC 70 Box 488
Davis, WV 26260

Ski Report: 1-800-SNOWING
Information: (304) 866-4801
Lodging Information: 1-800-633-6682
Credit Cards: VISA, MC
Internet:
http://www.wvweb.com/www/timberline.html

Operating Hours

9 a.m.-4:30 p.m. Monday-Wednesday
9 a.m.-9 p.m. Thursday
8 a.m.-9 p.m. Saturday-Sunday

Season: December to mid-April

Getting There

Timberline is located two miles from Canaan Valley Ski Area on Route 32 in Davis; see directions for Canaan Valley Ski Resort on page 116.

Background

West Virginia's most challenging alpine skiing can be found high atop the Allegheny Mountains in the Canaan Valley region—the birthplace of commercial skiing in the state. Surrounded by thousands of acres of state and federally owned wilderness areas, Timberline Four Seasons Resort can resemble classic northeastern ski areas given the right conditions. It hosts a strong selection of narrow, winding, and tree-lined trails over a variety of pitches, and a reasonable expanse of novice and intermediate terrain.

Based just two miles from Canaan Valley Ski Resort, Timberline was founded 15 years ago by developer David Downs, opening on old logging industry grounds with just a T-bar surface lift and limited snowmaking. Initially, skiers could only reach half of the mountain's available terrain. The less-used and more difficult upper mountain, relying solely on natural snowfall, was only accessible by a slow trip on the resort's Piston Bully snow grooming machine. Timberline took a turn for the better in the mid-1980s when a group of Philadelphia investors purchased the resort and equipped it with a modern lift service and an airless snowmaking system from base to summit.

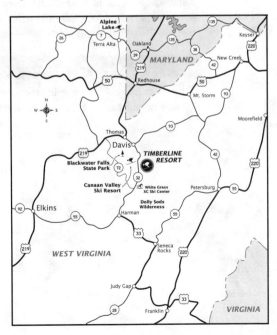

Mountain Stats

Base Elevation: 3,268 feet
Summit Elevation: 4,268 feet
Vertical Drop: 1,000 feet
Skiable Terrain: 91 acres
Longest Run: 2 miles
Primary Slope Direction: North
Average Annual Snowfall: 150 inches
  1996-97 season: 88 inches
  1995-96 season: 235 inches
Skier Visits
  1995-96 season: 118,000

Skiable Days
  1995-96 season: 122 days
  1994-95 season: 116 days
Slopes and Trails: 16 beginner, 10 intermediate, 9 advanced
Uphill Capacity: 4,000 skiers per hour
Snowmaking: 94% of area
Lifts: 1 triple, 2 doubles
Night Skiing: 30% of terrain, Friday-Sunday until 9 p.m.

Timberline's 4,286 foot elevation and average annual snowfall of 150 inches account for ski seasons that normally extend well into March or mid-April. Snowfall here is consistent and strong, somewhat of an aberration for an otherwise-undependable Mid-Atlantic region. A near-record 235 inches dropped during the unusually cold and moist 1995-96 season. But during occasional warm winter periods, Timberline's snowmaking and grooming operation can be suspect. Some of the advanced trails close in the absence of snowmaking, while the two-mile *Salamander* trail has been known to stay open when it's barely skiable. Nonetheless, the resort typically offers over 120 days of skiing per year, and is often the number-one choice for Southern and regional skiers seeking advanced, natural-powder runs in place of notorious "eastern ice" resorts in surrounding states. Timberline's skier visits have increased considerably over the last decade, having surpassed 100,000 each of the last three seasons.

The resort is flawed only by a lackluster lift system that features just three chairs—two of which reach the summit—and an uphill capacity of only 4,000 skiers per hour. Claustrophobic guests should beware of Timberline's "Darth Vader" double chair, which encloses skiers inside a helmeted top that resembles a Volkswagen Bug. It's a long, slow ride to the summit, but the unique chair was designed to shelter skiers from strong winds that tend to plague the north-facing ridge.

Trail Profiles

The resort undertook a sweeping terrain expansion four years ago, adding eight new trails, including two unique black-diamond glade runs that wind through Timberline's hardwoods. The

resort now holds 35 slopes and trails over 91 acres of terrain, but is smaller than its trail count would indicate. Only 10 trails stem from the summit, with numerous slope extensions and cat tracks advertised as runs. Advanced skiers won't be disappointed, though, especially when conditions are ripe: Lots of steep dips and rolls are built into the mountain and its 1,000-foot vertical. Three double-black-diamond trails are short-lived but steep traverses, most notably the headwall off the top of *The Drop* and the near-equal pitches of neighboring *Off the Wall*. And *Thunderdraft's* mogul fields are a true challenge for bump enthusiasts.

A rare find in the Mid-Atlantic region are gladed trails, and Timberline offers two of them for fast-turning, giant-slalom skiers and snowboarders. Double-diamond *Cherry Bowl Glades* is a satisfyingly steep, wide run and thrilling change of pace through Allegheny high-country hardwoods. On the other end of the mountain is *Pearly Glades*. The trail has more of an intermediate pitch but is just as exhilarating. The resort doesn't produce snow on *Cherry Bowl Glades*, *Pearly Glades*, *The Wall*, or *The Drop*.

Possibly the best intermediate trail on the mountain, *Upper* and *Lower Almost Heaven* is a long, continuous run with serpentine terrain that's surprisingly steep on its upper half. The top section of *Upper Dew Drop* is nearly identical in design before dropping into wide and smooth cruising track at its mid-section.

Though most learning skiers head to neighboring Canaan Valley Ski Area, Timberline also lends itself to beginners quite capably. Three small bunny hills facing the base lodge accommodate kids and first-time skiers. A growing childrens' instructional program includes both SKIwee (offered Friday to Monday) and the new Mountain Safari ski and snowboard program for children ages eight to 12. The resort also has one of the Mid-Atlantic's longest trails in *Sidewinder*— a two-mile-long, trench-width run with a slow and gradual pitch. It has several slow-turning areas to help novices craft the technique. *Winterset* is another new addition to Timberline: It follows a long course around the perimeter of the trail system on pleasant, rolling terrain. The remaining green runs are nothing more than a series of cat tracks that intersect more advanced trails.

Snowboarding

Boarders have an exclusive 200-foot halfpipe near the base of *Lower Thunderstruck* and *Plywood Parkway* trails. It's open only with enough natural snowfall, though, since the resort doesn't have the necessary grooming equipment to maintain the pipe in poor natural conditions. Timberline hasn't designated a specific snowboard park just yet, but a few jumps are built off the halfpipe, as well as some spines and jumps on neighboring *Lower Thunderstruck*. Major obstacles are constructed for the resort's U.S. Amateur Snowboard Association-sanctioned Appalachian Boardercross Series, which runs several weekends from January to season's end. The series features freestyle snowboard competitions, big-air competitions, and five separate Boardercross events.

The trail system is otherwise well manicured for snowboarders: There's an assortment of bumps, steeps, turns, and rolls on its intermediate and advanced terrain, and two long cruising runs for beginners. Advanced riders should enjoy carving the steep, tree-lined track of *Cherry Bowl Glades* and *Pearly Glades*, as well as jump-filled *Lower Thunderstruck*.

Snowboard Rentals
- 130 sets: Morrow, Generic
- $17-$24; boots $8-$12

Snowboard School
- 10 snowboard instructors: Ski school rates apply

Lift Tickets/Rentals/Services

Timberline's lift tickets are reasonable considering the solid terrain. The resort hasn't jacked up its prices in five years, and recently instituted early- and late-season discount rates that apply from December 1 to 15 and March 25 to closing date. Its remote location aside, sizable crowds form on weekends, though lift lines are kept in check by nearby Canaan Valley and the ever-popular Snowshoe Resort to the south. On weekdays, the slopes are clean and free of crowds; skied mostly by smaller packs of vacation skiers. A limited number of trails are equipped for night skiing, Fridays through Sundays. The resort also offers child care daily during operating hours.

Lift Tickets

- 8 a.m.-4:30 p.m.: weekday $25, weekend $33
- 8 a.m.-12:30 p.m./12:30 p.m.-4:30 p.m.: $16, $25
- 4:30 p.m.-9 p.m.: Thursday-Friday $16, weekend $20
- 12:30 p.m.-9 p.m.: Thursday-Friday $25, weekend $33
- 8 a.m.-9 p.m.: Thursday-Friday $30, weekend $40
* Ages 6-12: $13-$30; ages 5 and under ski free
* Early and late season reduced rates

Ski School

- Over 100 instructors: PSIA certified
- Private $45/hour; Group $15/1.5 hours

- Introductory ski, snowboard, or Telemark package $25
- SKIwee program (ages 4-11) $55/day
- Mountain Safari (ages 8-12) $65/day

Ski Rentals
- 400 sets: Elan; $12-$21

Adaptive Ski School: By appointment only

Base Lodge Facilities
Cafeteria, pub, rental shop, ski apparel shop, lockers

Child Care: Offered daily at base lodge, $6/hour or $35/day

Racing: NASTAR held on the *Lower Thunderstruck* trail, Thursday-Monday from 1 p.m. until 3 p.m.

Other Winter Sports

Cross-country and Telemark skiing are also hot tickets at Timberline. In addition to allowing Nordic skiing on all slopes and trails, a 10 mile, marked, ungroomed backcountry trail system was recently cut off the downhill area. It meanders through resort property and links with an expansive network in the Monongahela National Forest(Dolly Sods Wilderness Area), at the White Grass Touring Center, and the Canaan Valley State Park system.

Backcountry skiers can use a one-way lift pass to the Herz Mountain summit and head off the mountain to Blackwater Falls State Park at the north end of the valley, Canaan Valley to the south, and Dolly Sods Wilderness Area to the east. Backcountry, Telemark, and cross-country ski equipment is now available for rent from the base lodge. The resort also hosts Nordic events, races, and workshops nearly every weekend of the season. Its wide-ranging calendar of events includes several slalom and giant-slalom Telemark races, the Timberline Nordic Festival, and part of the West Virginia Telemark Race Series. Racing and carving clinics are offered periodically for all abilities; and a new introductory Telemark program teaches the art of the Norwegian-based turning technique. And rounding out the complete Nordic experience, Timberline runs guided backcountry tours, provided there's sufficient snowfall and demand.

On-site

Cross-country skiing on Timberline's 10 mile (17-k) nordic trail system off the summit area, connecting with **Canaan Valley's cross-country trail network** *(see page 231)*, **White Grass Touring Center** *(see page 229)*, **Blackwater Falls State Park** *(see page 234)*, and **Dolly Sods National Forest Area**; full instruction and rentals available at Timberline

Telemark skiing permitted on all trails, with instruction and rentals available

Nearby

Sled run with rope tow at Blackwater Falls State Park

Ice-skating facility at Canaan Valley Resort

Summer Activities

Mountain biking takes charge at the four-seasons resort when the weather turns warm. Twenty miles of mapped and marked trails are available down Timberline's ski trails, on connecting track throughout Monongahela National Forest trails, and in valley locations. Chair-lift rides accommodate bikers, hikers, and sight-seeing spectators for single or all-day passes, from Memorial Day Weekend to October, 9 a.m. to 6 p.m. A long list of other spring to fall activities includes nearby white water rafting and canoeing, swimming, golf, tennis, hunting, fishing, horseback riding, and camping.

Calendar of Events

December
- Holiday Festival Weekend
- Telemark workshops/downhill clinics

January
- Appalachian Boardercross Series (through March)
- Womens' Pro Ski Tour Race Weekend
- Telemark and snowboard workshops
- USSA PARA Giant Slalom

February
- Nordic slalom races and clinics

- West Virginia Telemark Series Race and workshops
- Wendy's WDTV Challenge Series for Cancer

March
- Budweiser White Lightning Slalom pro-am race
- Timberline Norpine (Nordic) Festival
- Allegheny Telemark Series

April
- Local's Cup Weekend/Race

Lodging/Dining/Après-Ski

Vacation skiers can base themselves either slopeside or nearby on the mountain in over 50 fully equipped private rental homes, condominiums, chalets, and cottages brokered by Timberline Realty. The slopeside Herzwoods condominiums have ski-and-stay packages and complementary equipment rentals with a minimum three-night stay. The most affordable times to vacation are during early December and late March when lodging rates drop by up to 27 percent, though you'll be taking your chances with natural conditions and full-slope availability. The towns of Davis and Elkins also offer several bed and breakfasts and lodging opportunities. For a break from the slopes, Timberline guests can go antiquing in numerous shops in Davis and Elkins, or take scenic drives throughout the region's lunar landscape.

Lodging
On-site
- * Call 1-800-633-6682 for on-site lodging information and rates.
- **Herzwoods and Northwoods** slopeside condominiums
- Slopeside homes along *Salamander*, *Winterset*, and *Lower Dew Drop* trails
- Resort homes, cabins, villas, and chalets on the mountain and close-by
- * For complete lodging information in the area, see Canaan Valley Ski Resort, *Nearby Lodging*, page 120.

Dining/Après-ski
On-site
- **Timberhaus Cafeteria**, with outdoor deck barbecue
- **Timbers Pub** (upstairs): slopeside fireplace lounge with trail views and live weekend entertainment

Nearby
- See Canaan Valley, *Nearby Dining/Après-ski*, page 121.

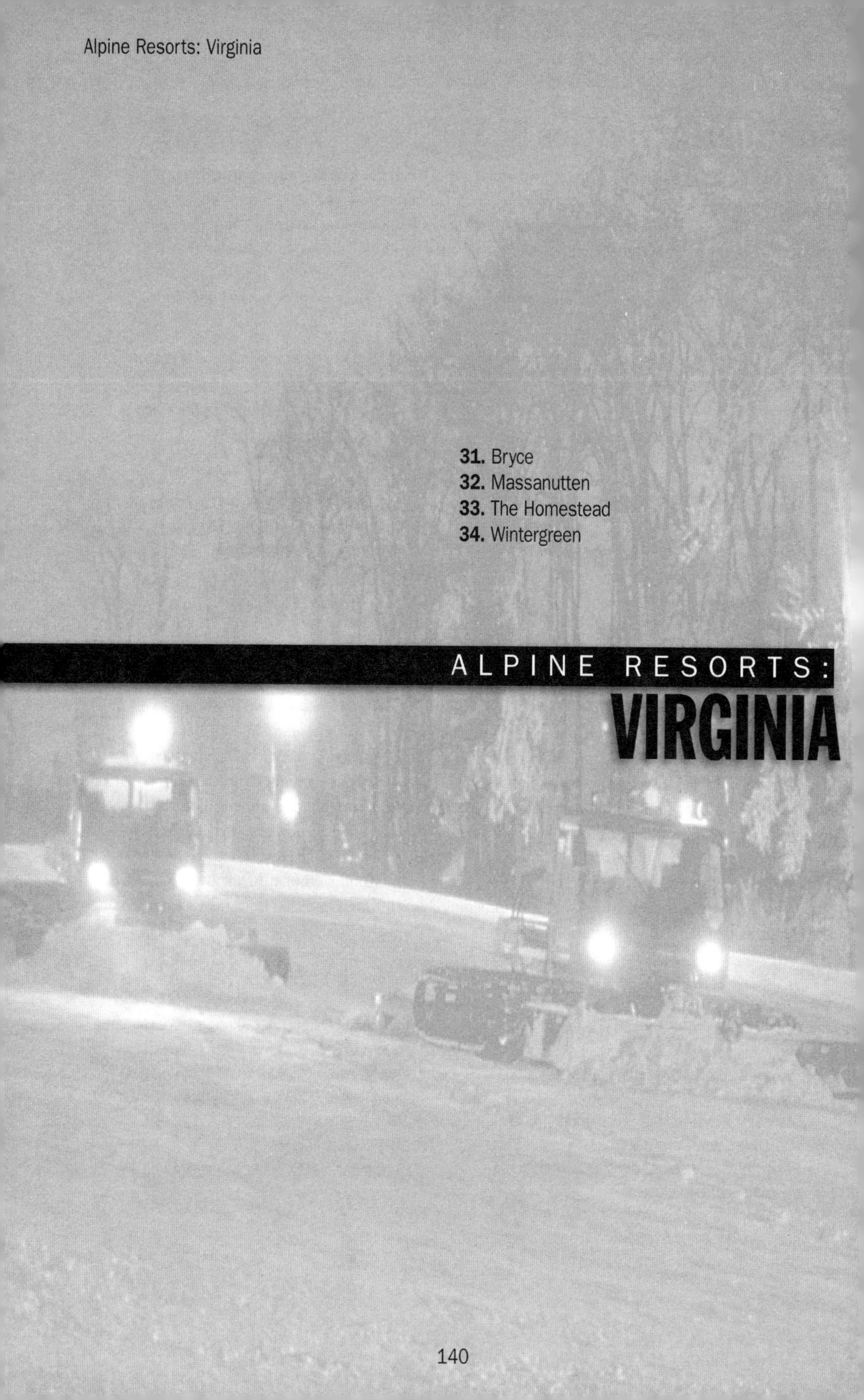

31. Bryce
32. Massanutten
33. The Homestead
34. Wintergreen

ALPINE RESORTS:
VIRGINIA

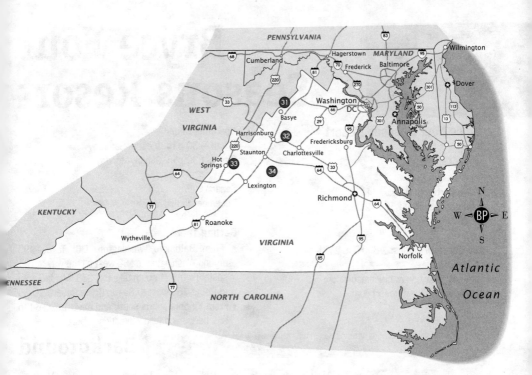

F ew people outside the Mid-Atlantic region would guess that the state of Virginia would be home to several ski resorts. The Old Dominion, for the most part, lacks the wintry climate that neighboring West Virginia's resorts are afforded. Despite Mother Nature's usual neglect, four alpine resorts have prospered with the advent of superlative snowmaking systems: Wintergreen, Massanutten, Bryce, and The Homestead. Each operates as a four-seasons resort, hosting unlimited outdoor activities and comfortable lodging year-round.

Although Massanutten and Wintergreen offer respectable 1,000-foot vertical drops, none of Virginia's ski areas have particularly large or challenging trail networks. Rather, they bill themselves as family resorts. Wintergreen holds the state's most varied terrain off its 3,800-foot-high Blue Ridge Mountain summit. In addition to providing plentiful beginner turf, its more advanced runs are the longest and steepest around. The Shenandoah Valley's Massanutten Resort, near Harrisonburg, is a bit smaller than Wintergreen, and more suited to beginners and intermediates. Massanutten's two best features are its outstanding, jump-filled snowboard park and its proximity to several urban centers, including Washington, DC (a quick two hours away).

Just north of Massanutten is Bryce—a resort truly committed to families, children, and developing skiers. Its modest trail system aside, the nine slopes at Bryce are expertly designed for learning skiers. The Homestead, located a few miles from the West Virginia border, is another area known for solid instruction and programs. Skiing tends to get trivialized by The Homestead's grandiose resort character: posh accommodations, fine dining, European-style spas and pools, and historic southern charm.

Bryce Four Seasons Resort

Bryce Four Seasons Resort
P.O. Box 3
Basye, VA 22810

Ski Report: 1-800-821-1444
Information: (540) 856-2121
Credit Cards: VISA, MC, AE

Lodging reservations: 1-800-296-2121

Internet: http://www.bryceresort.com
E-mail: bryce@bryceresort.com

Operating Hours
9 a.m.-9:30 p.m. Tuesday-Saturday
9 a.m.-4:30 p.m. Sunday-Monday

Season
December to mid-March

Getting There
- **From Baltimore/Washington, DC:** Take I-495 around Washington to I-66 west all the way to I-81 south. From I-81 south take Exit 273 (Mt. Jackson) to Route 263 west to Basye/Bryce Resort.
- **From Virginia points south and east:** Take I-64 to I-81 north, and follow directions above.

Background

National Masters slalom finalist (1987), Horst Locher, and brother Manfred opened Bryce Resort Ski Area in 1965, bringing an Austrian flavor to Virginia's Shenandoah Valley. Bryce is one of the closest ski areas to Washington, DC and Northern Virginia, roughly 90 miles away. Skiers who prefer the skyward route have a 2,500-foot paved landing airstrip adjacent to the resort. The mountain is small and the terrain limited, but the resort's friendly environment is a welcome contrast to the bustling atmosphere of many Mid-Atlantic ski areas.

Mountain Stats

Base Elevation: 1,250 feet
Summit Elevation: 1,750 feet
Vertical Drop: 500 feet
Longest Run: 3,550 feet
Primary Slope Direction: North
Skiable Terrain: 25 acres
Average Annual Snowfall: 30 inches
   1995-96 season: 50 inches
   1994-95 season: 15 inches
Snowmaking: 100% of area
Skier Visits
   1995-96 season: 40,000
   1994-95 season: 36,000
Skiable Days

1995-96 season: 86
1994-95 season: 82
Slopes and Trails
3 beginner, 4 intermediate, 1 advanced

Lifts: 2 doubles, 3 rope tows
Uphill Capacity: 2,500 skiers per hour
Night Skiing: 90% of area, Tuesday-Saturday until 9:30 p.m.

Situated on a low-lying ridge of the Allegheny Mountains that rises to the nearby West Virginia border, Bryce caters almost exclusively to families and beginner skiers. Its controlled-growth philosophy limits crowds, practically guaranteeing a full day of skiing without waiting in arduous lift lines. Bryce's skier base rarely extends north of the Washington, DC area, but the resort worked to widen its appeal last year by investing $500,000 in the construction of its new ski lodge, as well as building 25 slopeside townhouses at "The Ridge."

Trail Profiles

Unlike many Mid-Atlantic resorts, Bryce doesn't unnecessarily advertise black diamonds that don't exist or facilitate its trail count by naming every turn and cat track as a separate run. It focuses instead on providing a solid learning experience and recreational skiing. Four main trails and four smaller slopes are wide, smooth, and well manicured. *White Lightning* and *Bootlegger* trails, coined after the area's once-flourishing moonshine business, are the most popular cruising slopes, offering sustained intermediate pitches. The resort's lone black diamond trail—*Hangover*—is a short, narrow chute connecting to *Revenuer's Run*, which has a fun switchback and a few small gladed sections. The Locher brothers plan to widen *Hangover* and leave it primarily ungroomed and bumped for the 1997-98 season. The wide-open *Locher Bowl* was added off the summit area a few years ago for skiers and snowboarders to cut sweeping, slalom turns. It has a surface lift for those who wish to stick to the upper-third tier of the mountain.

Redeye was expertly designed for beginner skiers to master the art of turning. From the scenic summit, its narrow, steady track becomes increasingly wider and more undulating as it winds down toward the base, providing the perfect arena for novices to negotiate its two switchbacks. Two bunny hills on opposite sides of the base lodge serve as ideal introductory slopes, each with its own rope tow lift and separated from the flow of skier traffic. The patient and highly rated Horst Locher Ski School comes highly recommended for parents who want to introduce the sport to their children in a quiet, peaceful setting. Bryce also has a firm commitment to racing, hosting one of the strongest recreational programs in the South that features clinics and competitions each weekend.

Snowboarding

Bryce permits snowboarding on all eight slopes and trails and is planning to build a snowboard park for the 1997-98 season. The resort won't be able to compete with the gigantic and challenging snowboard park at nearby Massanutten, so it will likely keep its obstacles and jumps geared toward beginning and developing boarders. Call the resort's information line to confirm availability of the planned park.

Snowboard School
• 3 instructors
• Private $39; Group $20

Snowboard Rentals
• 50 sets: Mistral, Burton
• Day/twilight/extended day: $25
• Half-day/night: $20

Lift Tickets/Rentals/Services

Lift Tickets
- 9 a.m.-4:30 p.m.: weekday $23, weekend $37
- 9 a.m.-9:30 p.m.: $33, $47
- Noon-4:30 p.m.: $15, $27
- Noon-9:30 p.m.: Tuesday-Friday $23, Saturday $37
- 5:30 p.m.-9:30 p.m. (Tuesday-Saturday): $15
* Weekend rates reduced for ages 12 and under and ages 65-69 (over 70 ski free)
* Reduced-rate rope tow lift tickets available for beginner area only
* Group discount rates for 20 or more skiers

Ski School
- 50 instructors: PSIA certified
- Private $39/hour; Group $16/hour
- First-time Skier Package (includes ticket, rental, lesson) $39/weekdays, $30/half day and nights, $49/weekends
- SKIwee childrens' program for ages 4-8
  Weekdays: half day $28, with rentals $36
  Weekends: full day $48, with rentals $58; half day $28, with rentals $36

Ski Rentals
- Over 700 sets: Head, Kaestle, Rossignol, and Elan skis; Salomon and Tyrolia bindings; and Salomon boots
- Weekday $13, weekend $15
- Extended weekend (9 a.m.-9:30 p.m.): $20

Racing
- NASTAR racing held on *Bootlegger* trail on weekends and holidays at 3:30 p.m., $5/session
- Competitive Ski Racing Program: weekend training sessions aimed toward USSA-sanctioned races

Base Lodge Facilities
Rental/repair shop, ski boutique, ski school, SKIwee center, first aid center, cafeteria, restaurant, second-floor lounge

Summer Activities

Though not too far removed from eastern West Virginia's prime snow belt, Bryce's 1,750-foot elevation and warmer climate allow disappointingly sparse amounts of powder. The resort compensates adequately with a snowmaking system that covers the entire north-facing trail system. And the skiing doesn't end when the winters do: Grass skiing is now being offered down its trails from mid-June to late October, with lift passes and rentals ranging from $19 to $25. A first-time package includes lift ticket, rental, elbow and knee pads, and instruction. Non-skiers can take a sightseeing lift ride to the summit for a nominal charge. Bryce transformed itself into a four-seasons resort in the early 1970s and currently offers an 18-hole golf course, tennis courts, an outdoor pool, mountain biking trails, horseback riding, and boating/windsurfing on its man-made 45-acre lake.

Calendar of Events

December
- Southern NASTAR Pacesetting
- Shenandoah USSA Slalom/Giant Slalom

January
- Collegiate USSA Slalom and Giant Slalom Race

- Bryce Resort USSA Slalom Race
- Southeastern Race Association Pro-Am Giant Slalom

February
- Washington Ski International Race

Lodging/Dining/Aprés-Ski

Lodging

On-site

200 privately owned studio condominiums, townhouses, and chalets; Call 1-800-296-2121 for information and rates

Nearby

Stony Court at Bryce Resort (townhouses); 1-800-296-0947

The Hill at Bryce (condominiums); 1-800-307-3938

• CMG Properties/Rentals (condos, townhouses, chalets); 1-800-296-2149

• Creekside Realty; 1-800-376-3325
• Motels/hotels 11 miles from Bryce off I-81, Exit 273, at Mt. Jackson

Dining/Aprés-ski

On-site

• **Slopeside Lucio's Restaurant** and **Copper Kettle Lounge**, with entertainment/live music on weekends

Nearby (Basye)

Coleman's Basye Bistro; (540) 856-8187

Mountain Momma Pizzeria; (540) 856-3255

Massanutten Resort

Massanutten Resort

P.O. Box 1227
Harrisonburg, VA 22801

Ski Report/Information: 1-800-207-MASS
Local: (540) 289-9441/4954
Credit Cards: AE, MC, VISA

Internet: http://www.massresort.com
E-mail: skimass@shentel.net

Operating Hours

9 a.m.-10 p.m. daily

Season

Mid-December to mid-March

Getting There

• **From Washington, DC and northeastern points:** Take I-495 around Washington, DC to I-66 west, then take I-81 south at the end of I-66, pick up Exit 247A in Harrisonburg and follow Route 33 east 10 miles to 644; entrance to Massanutten is on the left. *Alternate route: Take I-66 west to Route 29 south past Madison, then turn right onto Route 230 until it ends at Route 33, turning right (west), and follow signs for 30 minutes to the resort.

• **From Richmond:** Take I-64 west (taking the 295 bypass around Richmond), then take Exit 136 (Route 15 north), follow 15 to Gordonsville, and pick up Route 33 toward Massanutten.

• **From Raleigh/Greensboro/Winston-Salem, North Carolina:** Take Route 29 north from Danville, Virginia to Route 250 west, then pick up Route 340 north in Waynesboro, turn left onto Route 649 (Island Fort Road); Turn right at the stoplight onto Route 33 east, following signs for Massanutten.

Background

Between the expansive Shenandoah National Park and Interstate 81 sits Virginia's Massanutten Four Seasons Resort. The area was initially developed by Del Webb, who happened to be co-owner of the New York Yankees during the early 1970s. Webb was also the driving force behind the creation of Arizona's Sun City and several Las Vegas casinos. The entire four-seasons resort has since changed hands to Great Eastern.

Massanutten is unique in that it's the only Mid-Atlantic ski area to exist inside and in conjunction with a residential community. With over 1,000 single-family lots, Massanutten Village sits along the valley below the mountain's ski area, and even has its own police department and road maintenance crew. The resort is considered a "metropolitan" ski area because of its proximity to nearby Harrisonburg—home to James Madison University.

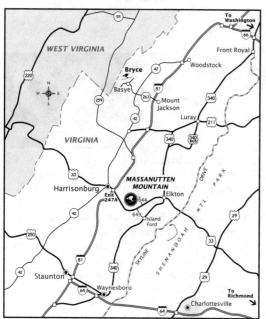

Mountain Stats

Base Elevation: 1,170 feet
Summit Elevation: 2,880 feet
Vertical Drop: 1,110 feet
Longest Run: 4,100 feet
Primary Slope Direction: North
Skiable Terrain: 68 acres
Average Annual Snowfall: 30 inches
Snowmaking: 100% of area
Slopes and Trails
 4 beginner, 6 intermediate, 3 advanced
Lifts
 1 quad, 3 doubles, 1 J-bar
Uphill Capacity
 6,350 skiers per hour
Night Skiing
 100% of slopes, nightly until 10 p.m.

Situated 2,880 feet high on the windy tip of Massanutten Mountain, the resort offers a relatively small alpine trail system, with 13 slopes and trails. The resort is sure to market every inch of Virginia's highest vertical drop (1,110 feet), but you might wonder where the vertical really is after skiing the entire mountain. It lacks truly challenging terrain, suitable more for beginners and intermediates. The trail network is broken up by a mid-section, and requires two lifts to reach the summit. Just two trails flow from the summit—black diamonds *ParaDice* and *Diamond Jim*. There is, however, plenty of room on the mountain for trail expansion, but only time will tell. In the meantime, Massanutten has committed its resources to developing both a model family-ski setting and a wild snowboard haven at the same time. The secluded snowboard park is one the Mid-Atlantic's outstanding aerial arenas: An array of jumps and obstacles offer big-time air to a growing number of boarders from Virginia and Washington, DC. And the resort's newest addition is a snow tubing park that will host six to seven lanes over a vertical drop of 140 feet. The park, located near the snowboarding area, will also have a surface tow lift and operate under lights.

Skiers won't often get the chance to carve down fresh powder here—the area only averages 30 inches per year. But the trail system is well equipped with snowmaking on all slopes and trails. During freezing temperatures, the upper mountain tends to get icy by afternoon. The later parts of the ski season are typically marked by slushy, mashed-potato conditions, which many skiers and snowboarders cherish. A convenient 1-800 number provides current slope conditions and lodging information, and the resort's new World Wide Web site also features the same.

Trail Profiles

The mountain's lower 500 feet of vertical constitutes primarily beginner track. The wide beginner bowl on *Geronimo* is a learning paradise, and has its own double chair, while *Southern Comfort* is a designated slow-skiing area. PSIA-certified instructors expertly teach Massanutten's SKIwee and MINIrider programs. MINIrider is a derivative of the national SKIwee childrens' program, focusing on the fundamentals of snowboarding for ages 7 to 14.

Massanutten cut black diamond trails *ParaDice* and *Diamond Jim* a few years back, adding another 300 feet of vertical for skiers. Both trails have decent pitches on fairly long cruising terrain, with nothing really steep enough to test the experts. The quad lift reaching these trails is slow and arduous, but not without its perks. Keep your eyes open for striking ridge lines and valley views. Skiers will likely find Massanutten's most challenging turf on *Dixie Dare*—a short, narrow trail that throws in a tight elbow turn before flowing into wide-open terrain on *Pacesetter*. The resort often leaves *Dixie Dare* ungroomed for mogul-busting guests.

The resort's mid-level runs are all short but somewhat satisfying. *Rebel Yell* is by far the mountain's most popular blue trail, featuring wide and nicely pitched track that's ideal for turning and carving. *Pacesetter* is the designated racing trail, where NASTAR time-trial runs are held on weekends.

Snowboarding

Massanutten doesn't heavily advertise its snowboard park, but area boarders know it's the place to go for serious freestyling. It is, without question, one of the Mid-Atlantic's premiere parks. The isolated, snowboard-only area is set on a former beginner trail in front of the ski lodge, hosting a relentless series of big-air obstacles to challenge the area's best riders. The 1996 season featured five to seven changing hits, including a quarterpipe, some wales and spines, and a monstrous culminating gap jump, on which boarders have been known to catch over 25 feet of air. The resort formerly held rail slides and tabletops, but now constructs its hits entirely of snow.

A convenient J-bar services the area, and strong lights keep the park open nightly until 10 p.m. There are no plans yet to construct a halfpipe, which would be difficult to maintain considering the region's sporadic snowfall and the resort's lack of a necessary grooming apparatus.

The rest of the trails are open to carving, used mostly by developing snowboarders. Several instructional snowboard programs are offered, including a Skills Improvement Package for novice to intermediate boarders.

The snowboard-friendly resort hosts the Massanutten Intergalactic Race of Champions (MIROC)—a competitive Boardercross series with different age groups held seven weekends from December to March. Freestyle events are also held during the Mid-Atlantic Snowboard Series and the Edge of the World Snowboard Series.

Snowboard School
- 20 instructors
- Private $35/hour; Group $18/1.5 hours
- First-time and Skills Improvement Package $45/weekday, $65 weekend, $35/half day, night

- MINIriders (ages 7-14): weekday $50, weekend $55; includes lift ticket, rental, instruction, lunch (reservations suggested)

Snowboard Rentals
- 300 sets: Mistral, Burton (step-in bindings)
- Ski rental rates apply

Lift Tickets/Rentals/Services

The resort can get crowded on Saturdays—the day of choice for Washington, DC and locally based skiers. Sundays are a better bet to get more downhill time since most area residents are at home watching football. And Massanutten's early- and late-season package features major ticket discounts. Last year, $10 lift tickets were offered during the first three weeks of March for skiers and snowboarders to carve the resort's slushy, man-made snow.

Lift Tickets
- 9 a.m.-4:30 p.m./12:30 p.m.-10 p.m.: weekday $28, weekend $40
- 9 a.m.-10 p.m.: $36, $48
- 9 a.m.-12:30 p.m./12:30 p.m.-4:30 p.m.: $18 (Monday-Friday only)
- 5 p.m.-10 p.m.: $18 (all week)
* Reduced rates for children under 12 and adults ages 62-69
* Early and late season lift ticket discounts
* Group rates available for 15 or more skiers

Ski School
- Over 80 instructors: PSIA certified
- Private $35/hour; Group $18/1.5 hours
- First-time Skier Package or Skills Improvement Package (ski/snowboard): $45/weekday, $65/weekend, $35/half day or night
- Race lessons: weekends at noon, $18/1.5 hours
- Childrens' Programs:
  SKIwee (ages 4-6), Mountain Explorers (ages 7-12): registration 8:30 a.m.-9:30 a.m., class 9:30 a.m.-2 p.m.
  Weekdays $50/child, weekends/holidays $55 (includes lift ticket, rental, instruction, activities, lunch)
* Call 1-800-207-MASS for reservations (24 hours in advance)
** Multiday session discounts available Monday through Friday

Ski Rentals
- Half-day (weekdays) $13
- Night $13
- Day and twilight $18-$22
- Extended day $25-$30

Racing
- NASTAR held Saturdays and Sundays on *Pacesetter* trail, 1 p.m.-3 p.m.; $5/two runs, $1 each additional run; registration at summit of *Pacesetter*
- Junior race team (up to 18 years of age): Wednesdays, Saturdays, and Sundays; $350 fee includes all-season pass and coaching

Adaptive Ski School
Massanutten Adaptive Ski School: a nonprofit educational organization promoting ski instruction for physically handicapped individuals; Program follows the PSIA Adaptive Teaching Model as defined by National Handicapped Sports; Call 1-800-207-MASS or 540-289-4954 for more information

Base Lodge Facilities
- Cafeteria, restaurant/lounges, ski and snowboard shops, ski school, lockers, basket room

Other Winter Sports
New **snow tubing** park set for the 1997-98 season, with 6-7 lanes, tow lift, and lights; call 1-800-207-MASS for rates

Calendar of Events

* **Snowboard demo days** held several weekends throughout the season

December
- Massanutten Intergalactic Race of Champions (MIROC): Boardercross Series held on six weekends from December-March

January
- Mid-Atlantic Snowboard Series (freestyle events)

February
- Edge of the World Snowboard Series (freestyle events)
- Massanutten Challenge
- Giant Slalom race on *Diamond Jim* trail

Summer Activities

Massanutten's mountainous fresh air and multitude of outdoor activities lure thousands of Washington, DC vacationers every summer. Golf, tennis, hiking, swimming, and a reputable mountain bike trail system are available during summer months. And in July, 1997, Massanutten hosted one of the events within the UCI/Grundig Mountain Bike Downhill World Cup Circuit—the world's most prestigious professional mountain bike downhill race series.

Lodging/Dining/Aprés-Ski

Guests will notice hundreds of condominiums toward the top of the mountain. Unfortunately, just about all of them are privately owned timeshares, and only a limited number is available for rent. The Massanutten Tour Company (1-800-207-MASS) will take care of all your lodging needs, either on the mountain or nearby. All area motels and hotels offer ski-and-stay packages.

When visiting Massanutten, be sure to take a drive to the mountain's summit, where miles of hiking trails are available and clear days afford spectacular views of the surrounding hilltops and valleys. Nearby Harrisonburg has a growing downtown, and skiers may want to take some time to check out some of its many antique and specialty shops. Antique stores are also plentiful in nearby New Market, and tourist trap Luray Caverns, open year-round, is only a half-hour drive from the ski area. There are plenty of dining options in Harrisonburg, but not much between there and the resort. One exception is Log Cabin Barbecue, which sits just off the mountain at the Route 33 turnoff. The take-out barbecue joint is a favorite pit stop for hungry, departing skiers.

Lodging

On-site
- Privately owned condominiums, townhouses, and chalets (limited number available for rent); call 1-800-207-MASS for lodging information

Nearby (Harrisonburg)
The Village Inn, with optional deck/whirlpool baths; rates from $37-$53/night; 1-800-736-7355/(540) 434-7355

Shoney's Inn; (540) 433-6089

Days Inn; (540) 433-9353

Dining/Aprés-ski

On-site
- Base lodge cafeteria and **Encounter's Lounge**, with live music most weekends
- **Fareways Restaurant & Lounge**, open year-round at the golf course area

Nearby
Log Cabin Barbecue, just outside the resort on Route 33; (540) 289-9400

Harrisonburg:
Blue Stone Inn & Restaurant; (540) 434-0535

Boston Beanery Restaurant & Tavern; (540) 433-1870

Giuseppe's Italian Restaurant; (540) 432-0200

The Homestead Ski Area

The Homestead Ski Area
State Route 220
Hot Springs, VA 24445

Ski Report/Information: 1-800-838-1766
Lodging: (540) 839-7721
Credit Cards: VISA, MC, AE, Discover

Operating Hours
9 a.m.-5 p.m. Monday-Friday
8 a.m.-10 p.m. Wednesday-Saturday
8 a.m.-5 p.m. Sunday

Season
Mid-December to mid-March

Getting There
- **From Baltimore/Washington:** Take I-495 around Washington to I-66 west, then take I-81 south to I-64 west. Pick up Route 220 north, and follow signs to The Homestead.
- **From Richmond:** Take I-64 west to I-81 south, then pick up I-64 west again to Route 220 north, and follow signs to The Homestead.
- **From Beckley, West Virginia:** Take I-64 east into Virginia to Route 220 north, and follow signs.

Background

Former Austrian national team skier Sepp Kober opened one of the South's first ski areas here at The Homestead in 1959. Located off Interstate 81 and Route 64, just miles from the West Virginia border, the resort entertains a main clientele of family skiers on its small trail network. Skiing is but a small facet of this historic resort better known for its posh accommodations and soothing European-style spas.

The Homestead's story is bound by chapters of early-American history, the earliest written accounts of which date back to 1750. Dr. Thomas Walker, a medical missionary, told stories of numerous Native Americans and European settlers who would flock to the area's natural hot spring waters for their reputed therapeutic benefits. The original Homestead Inn was erected in 1766 near Fort Dinwiddie—a frontier fort that George Washington built as a defense against Native Americans. The inn survived the Revolutionary and Civil Wars, during which time it was acquired by Dr. Thomas Goode, who advertised the professed medicinal healing and rejuvenating powers of the mountain's spring waters. The year 1890 marked the transformation of The Homestead into a full-fledged vacation retreat. It was established by M.E. Ingalls, president of C&O and chairman of the Big Four Railroad, whose family ran the resort through four generations until 1993. The Homestead succumbed to fire in 1901, which destroyed all but the spa, casino, and Cottage Row. A new hotel was erected soon after, though, joined later by several elegantly crafted wings.

Mountain Stats

Base Elevation: 2,500 feet
Summit Elevation: 3,200 feet
Vertical Drop: 700 feet
Longest Run: 4,200 feet
Primary Slope Direction: Northwest
Skiable Terrain: 45 acres

Average Annual Snowfall: 50 inches
1996-97 season: 18 inches
1995-96 season: 60 inches
Snowmaking: 100% of area
Slopes and Trails
3 beginner, 3 intermediate, 4 advanced

Lifts
1 double, 2 tow lifts, 1 J-bar, 1 T-bar
Uphill Capacity
3,000 skiers per hour
Night Skiing: 70% of area, Wednesday-Saturday until 10 p.m.

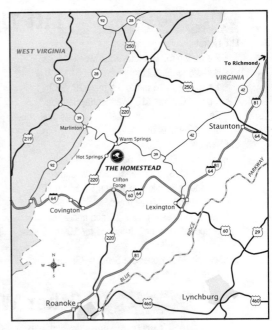

The resort offers over 15,000 acres of year-round recreation from valley to summit, where its alpine ski resort sits 3,200 feet atop a small mountain nestled in the Allegheny Mountain range. Natural conditions aren't much different here than at Virginia's three other ski areas, all plagued by sporadic snowfall, eastern ice, and southern thaws. The Homestead manages 50 inches of snow per year on average, though, and benefits from some occasional residual powder falling wayward off West Virginia's eastern snow belt region.

The terrain is limited, but skiers who want to get their money's worth of runs have the trails free of large crowds commonly seen at other Mid-Atlantic resorts. Lift tickets are generously affordable and controlled by the resort to ease traffic flow. The resort holds 10 slopes and trails throughout its 45 acres, with some additional cat tracks off the summit leading into the mountain's two main runs.

Trail Profiles

Steep drops are few and far between on the mountain and its 700 feet of vertical drop. More advanced track can be found off the summit and the resort's double lift, notably the steep pitch of *The Glades*, which hosts the resort's NASTAR racing program. A tight switchback onto *Goat Trail* extends to wrap-around terrain on *Goat Farm* and *Down Draft*—three black diamonds forming one continuous run. Summit trails close occasionally because of poor conditions and grooming difficulty, so skiers looking to knock out the upper half should call ahead first for updated conditions.

Main Slope is a confidence-building trail for novice skiers, who have a mid-station drop-off option from the double lift that accesses wider track on the trail's lower half. Beginner terrain is found on the mountain's lower tier, which has four lifts. Two extremely wide novice areas punctuate the recreational atmosphere of the resort, and a tiny bunny slope with its own 170-foot tow lift accommodates absolute first-timers. The highly regarded Sepp Kober Ski School offers patient, professional instruction for skiers and snowboarders of all ages.

Snowboarding

The Homestead's family-ski reputation didn't stop it from building a small snowboard park and adjacent halfpipe, built in 1995 to cater to the resort's growing number of boarders. Homestead's above-ground halfpipe is 260 feet long and 20 feet wide, with 6-foot-high walls, but doesn't operate in poor natural conditions. Snowboarders will discover moderately sized jumps and bumps in the resort's snowboard park. Both the park and pipe are conveniently served by a T-bar lift.

Snowboard School
Same rates as ski school, with additional racing and freestyle instruction available

Snowboard Rentals
• Boards: $20/day, boots $7/day
• Night session rental: $12

Lift Tickets/Rentals/Services

Lift Tickets
- 9 a.m.-5 p.m.: weekday $22, weekend $25
- Half-day: $13, $21
- 1 p.m.-5 p.m./6 p.m.-10 p.m.: $22, $32
- 6 p.m.-10 p.m.: $15 (Wednesday-Saturday)
- * Reduced rates for Homestead guests and children 12 and under

Ski Rentals
- 200 sets: Elan skis, Solomon bindings
- Full rental: $16/weekend, $11/weekday
- Individual: $6/skis, $4/poles,$7/boots
- Night rental: $10/all times
- * Reduced rates for ages 12 and under
- * Shaped skis to be introduced for 1997-98 season

Ski School: Sepp Kober Ski School: PSIA certified
- Private $40/1 1/4 hours
- Group $15/1 1/4 hours
- Kids Club Bunny School (ages 5-11), includes ticket, rental, lesson, activities
- Full day, with lunch: $60; Half day: $40

Racing
NASTAR held on *The Glades* trail on Wednesday and weekend afternoons

Base Lodge Facilities
Ski/rental shops, cafeteria/restaurant/lounge, elevated sun deck, ski school, lockers

Other Winter Sports/Activities

As for the resort's amenities and activities, they're nothing short of extensive: The list includes an Olympic-size skating rink, cross-country skiing (weather permitting), horseback and carriage rides, naturally heated indoor pool fed by 104-degree natural hot springs, fitness center, board and table games, aroma and massage therapy in the Homestead Spa, and deluxe accommodations at The Homestead's four-star hotel. And the resort's spring to fall agenda features a championship golf course, fly fishing, shooting facilities, tennis, and bowling.

Cross-country skiing, with rentals and repair services, available with enough natural snow on the golf course below ski area; rental rates: weekend $11, weekday $9; boots $5/all times

Slopeside ice-skating rink, with rentals and instruction; rates: private $20/half-hour, group $10/half-hour

Calendar of Events

January
- **Winterfest Weekends** held during second half of January: ski, snowboard, and skating exhibitions; live music; fireworks; and family events

Lodging/Dining/Aprés-Ski

Lodging

The Homestead Hotel, with over 1,000 beds; rates include weekend and weekday specials from $218/night per couple, with lift tickets and meals provided; Call (540) 839-7721 for rates and information

Dining/Aprés-ski

On-site
The Homestead Dining Room

Sneads Tavern
The Ski Lodge (restaurant/cafeteria)
* Dining service and sports bar in The Homestead's hotel

Nearby (Hot Springs)
Squires Table Restaurant; (540) 965-5577
Country Café; (540) 839-2111
Albert Café; (540) 839-7777

Wintergreen Resort

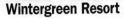

34

Wintergreen Resort

P.O. Box 706
Wintergreen, VA 22958

Ski Report: 1-800-325-7669/(804) 325-2100
Lodging Reservations: 1-800-325-2200
Credit Cards: VISA, MC, AE

Internet: http://www.WintergreenResort.com

Operating Hours
9 a.m.-10 p.m. Sunday-Thursday
9 a.m.-11 p.m. Friday-Saturday

Season
Mid-December to late March

Getting There

- **From Richmond:** Take I-64 west to Exit 107
  (Crozet/Route 250). Head west on Route 250,
  then turn left on Route 151 south. Follow Route
  151 for 14 miles and turn right on Route 664.
  Travel 4 miles to Wintergreen.
- **From Baltimore/Washington:** Take I-495 around
  Washington to I-66 west, then pick up Route 29
  south to Charlottesville. From Charlottesville, take
  I-64 west to Exit 107 (Crozet/Route 250), and
  follow the directions above to Wintergreen.
- *** Alternate Route from Baltimore/Washington:**
  Take I-66 all the way to I-81 south, then pick up I-
  64 east to Exit 99 (Afton/Route 250). Follow 250
  east to Route 151 south. Follow 151 south for
  14 miles, then turn right on Route 664. Travel 4
  miles to Wintergreen.
- **From West Virginia:** Take I-64 east into Virginia,
  then pick up I-81/I-64 north to I-64 east, and follow the **Alternate Route** from Washington, DC
  above.
- **From North Carolina:** Follow Route 29 north from
  Danville, Virginia, to Route 151 north. Travel 21
  miles on Route 151, then turn left on Route 664,
  and follow 4 miles to Wintergreen.

Background

Considering Virginia's limited scope of alpine skiing, Wintergreen is indisputably the
state's most varied ski resort. Situated within 11,000 acres of pristine woodlands
and the expansive George Washington National Forest, the luxurious four-seasons
resort offers a mix of terrain for first-time to advanced skiers. Wintergreen's high-
country land, formerly known as the "Big Survey," was purchased in 1952 by
North Carolina's William Mattox. Twenty years later, Wintergreen Resort would be
developed by Cabot, Cabot & Forbes—the same
company involved in the creation of Hilton Head's
Sea Pines Resort—and celebrated its first ski season
in 1975.

Wintergreen's 3,800-foot plateau reveals picturesque settings of the surrounding Blue Ridge
Mountains, and the resort is bordered by the scenic
Blue Ridge Parkway, just one-half mile from the
entrance to the ski area at Reed's Gap milepost.
Nearly 4,000 acres of surrounding property is privately maintained in its natural splendor, and

Wintergreen's own commitment to preservation was honored in 1987 by the American Hotel/Motel Association's National Environmental Achievement Award. The Appalachian Trail runs through the resort's property along the crest of the Blue Ridge Mountains, and a 30-mile hiking trail system connects at certain points with it. Hiking enthusiasts can check out waterfalls on the *Shamokin* trail and scenic overlooks on the *Highlands Leisure* trail.

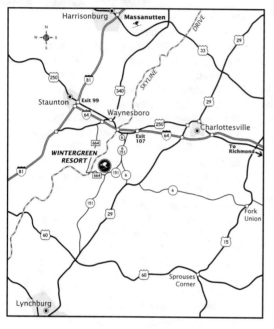

Mountain Stats

Base Elevation: 2,512 feet
Summit Elevation: 3,515 feet
Vertical Drop: 1,003 feet
Longest Run: 1.4 miles
Skiable Terrain: 86 acres
Average Annual Snowfall: 40 inches
    1996-97 season: 28 inches
    1995-96 season: 75 inches
Snowmaking: 100% of area
Skier Visits
    1996-97 season: 156,000
    1995-96 season: 141,000
Skiable Days
    1995-96 season: 99 days
    1994-95 season: 96 days
Slopes and Trails
    7 beginner, 7 intermediate, 4 advanced
Lifts
    4 triple, 1 double
Uphill Capacity: 8,200 skiers per hour
Night skiing: 70% of area, 10 p.m. Sunday-Friday, 11 p.m. Sunday

With an average annual snowfall of just 40 inches, the resort usually depends on an aggressive snowmaking operation. Like Virginia's three other resorts, Wintergreen guests typically ski notorious eastern ice or slush, but the mountain conditions do offer one benefit: The 3,000-foot ele-

vation difference between the summit and valley accounts for 10- to 15-degree temperature variations. This allows the resort to offer same-day ski and golf packages, weather permitting, on its nationally ranked Stoney Creek golf course.

On weekends the resort is packed with families and children from Virginia and Washington, DC. Though a long, beginner cruising run would be a welcome addition to the network of 17 slopes and trails, three wide, easy slopes and a near-flat learning area off the summit lodge accommodate the masses of novice skiers. Multitudes of childrens' instructional programs are offered for different age groups, and the resort's day care welcomes small children, with 48-hour advanced reservations.

Trail Profiles

The Highlands section holds some surprisingly fun terrain on its black diamond trails. The resort blew away long-time bashers of Virginia skiing when its *Upper Wild Turkey* trail was recognized by *Skiing* magazine in a February 1997 feature on east coast resorts. The trail boasts several steep drops and a beastly mogul area. *Lower Cliffhanger* serves up some nice steeps as well. Both *Wild Turkey* and *Cliffhanger* are nearly one mile long with over 1,000 feet of vertical drop; Regrettably, neither is equipped for night skiing. On the western face, 3,000-foot *Big Acorn* is a black diamond trail more deserving of intermediate status but does offer a strong pitch off the summit and boulevard terrain for wide-arcing turns. *Tyro* is one of just two intermediate runs on the mountain, but is fairly aggressive: Its narrow course drops into a switchback that precedes wide-open terrain before a long, ensuing runout.

Snowboarding

A few years ago Wintergreen constructed a modest 450-foot snowboard park on the far-right side of the beginner *Diamond Hill* trail. To keep *Diamond Hill* available for novice skiers, the park was cut a bit smaller and more narrow than it should be: There's not much room for lateral runouts after hitting the three or four changing jumps.

Wintergreen's snowboard park doesn't measure up to rival Massanutten Resort's carnival of aerial obstacles, but if you can catch enough speed on the smallish 200-foot vertical drop, its jumps afford some decent air time. Last year's hits included gaps, rail slides, berms, wales, and tabletops. The resort is without a half-pipe, but snowboarders and employees will occasionally build staggered razorbacks fashioned into quarter-pipes when natural conditions permit. A triple chair lift serves the snowboard park exclusively, and lights keep it well lit until 10 p.m. or 11 p.m. nightly.

Snowboard School
- 6 instructors
- Ski rates apply

Snowboard Rentals
- Over 125 sets: Kemper boards, boots, and bindings
- Ski rental rates apply

Lift Tickets/Rentals/Services

Wintergreen's inverted summit lodge offers a long list of amenities, as well as instant downhill access to the slopes. Though lift tickets and instruction are a bit on the expensive end, the resort does offer a free group lesson with any ski or snowboard rental, occupying a well-staffed ski school on most weekends.

Lift Tickets
- 9 a.m.-4:30 p.m.: Saturday $40, Sunday $38, weekday $32
- 9 a.m.-1 p.m./12:30 p.m.-4:30 p.m.: weekday $22
- 12:30 p.m.-11 p.m.: Saturday $40, Sunday $32, midweek $32
- 5 p.m.-10 p.m.: Sunday-Thursday $17, Friday-Saturday (11 p.m.) $20
- * Reduced rates for ages 6-12 and 60-69; Children under 5 ski free

* Value-season discount rates before Christmas and after March 2
* Group rate discounts for 20 or more skiers

Ski School
- 100 instructors: PSIA certified
- Private $45/hour, $25/half hour
- Group—call 804-325-2100 for new rates

Childrens' Programs:
- Ski Cats (ages 4-12): indoor/outdoor instruction, activities, lunch, rental, beginner lift ticket; rates from $39-$89

(continues)

(continued)

- Mountain Explorers (ages 7-14): offered weekends/holidays 10 a.m.-3 p.m., with 5 hours instruction, practice, lunch; rates $69-$80/day
- Ski Buddy (ages 4 & up): 2 hours skiing supervision; rates $36-$41

Ski Rentals
- 2,400 sets: K2, Head, and Elan SCX (all step-in bindings)
- Midweek day/twilight: adult $21, youth/senior $15
- Weekend day: $26, $20
- Weekday night or half-day: $15, $12
- * Free beginner lesson with rental

Adaptive Ski School
Wintergreen Adaptive Skiing program, run by volunteers, by appointment only; Call 804-823-7026

Racing
NASTAR program on *Upper Diamond Hill* beginner trail; Call 804-325-2100 for scheduled times

Summit Lodge Facilities
Four restaurants, Mountain Inn Conference Center/shopping gallery, Blackrock Village Center, ski center (ticket office, ski school, rentals, lockers and basket storage, child care, Cooper's Vantage restaurant/pub)

Child Care
Available for overnight guests and—by reservation—day skiers; rates $6/hour

Other Seasonal Activities

Wintergreen is one of the Mid-Atlantic's most reputable all-season destination resorts, offering two championship golf courses and a full tennis center, complete with clay and hard courts. Guests also have an extensive hiking trail system, horseback riding, indoor and outdoor pools, boating in 20-acre Lake Monohan, mountain biking throughout the valley, and fishing in creeks and lakes. The Wintergarden Spa features indoor/outdoor pools, hot tubs, an exercise room, saunas, and massage therapy. Wintergreen's summer to fall agenda has special events each weekend, including backpacking excursions, kids' camps, numerous festivals, wine and beer tastings, and fall foliage sight-seeing packages.

Other Winter Sports
On-site
- **Hiking** throughout the resort's 30-mile trail network (Cross-country skiing permitted but not recommended on the trails' narrow, rocky terrain)

Nearby
- **Cross-country skiing** on the Blue Ridge Parkway, (which shuts down to auto traffic at the hint of snowfall), and on numerous adjoining side trails *(see page 250 for more information)*

Calendar of Events
* Ski Appreciation Days offered regularly throughout season

December
- Annual Winter Solstice (snowboard events and demos)

January
- Wintergreen and Blue Ridge Snowboard Event

February
- USSA Ski Race

Lodging/Dining/Aprés-Ski

The resort's slopeside and on-mountain lodging can accommodate up to 1,300 guests in condominiums and houses. There are thousands of privately owned properties around Wintergreen, but only 400 are on the rental market. Dining and aprés-ski options are also incredibly varied here, with five restaurants, several pubs hosting live entertainment, and a cafeteria. Waynesboro is the nearest town with lodging, roughly 20 minutes away, offering bed and breakfasts, cabins, and motels.

Lodging
On-site
Studio to 7-bedroom condominium units and 2- to 7-bedroom houses (mostly slopeside units and fully equipped); Call 1-800-325-2200 for rates and information

Nearby
Bed and Breakfasts:
Trillium House B&B, Wintergreen; 1-800-325-9126
Belle Hearth B&B, Waynesboro; (540) 943-1910
The Iris Inn B&B, Waynesboro; (540) 943-1991
Redwood Lodge B&B, Waynesboro; (540) 943-8765

Cabins
Cabin Creekwood, Lyndhurst; (540) 943-8552
Hibernia, Waynesboro; (540) 943-0070
Royal Oaks, Lyndhurst; (540) 943-6151

Hotels/Motels
The Inn at Afton, Waynesboro; (540) 942-5201
Holiday Inn Express, Waynesboro; (540) 932-7170
Best Western Inn, Waynesboro; (540) 932-3060
Days Inn, Waynesboro; (540) 943-1101

Dining/Aprés-ski
On-site
• 5 restaurants, 1 cafeteria:
The Copper Mine: continental restaurant/lounge, with breakfast & dinner
Garden Terrace Restaurant/Lounge: dinner and aprés-ski
Cooper's Vantage Restaurant & Pub: casual dining and live music six days per week, including blue grass and classic rock

Blue Ridge Terrace: outside bar & grill, weekend lunch hours only
The Gristmill: lounge and cappuccino bar
Pryor's Cafeteria: lunch and dinner
Checkerberry Cabin: mid-mountain lunch/snack facility

Nearby
Broad Street Inn, Waynesboro; (540) 942-1280
Dulaney's Steak & Seafood, Waynesboro; (540) 943-7167
Mulligan's Pub, Staunton; (540) 248-6020
Scotto's Italian Restaurant, Waynesboro; (540) 942-8715
Ciro's Pizza, Waynesboro; (540) 942-5169
Suzanne & Company, Waynesboro; (540) 943-5933

Major Alpine Resorts
35. Beech Mountain
36. Sugar Mountain

ALPINE RESORTS:
NORTH CAROLINA

Other Alpine Ski Areas
37. Appalachian Ski Mountain
38. Cataloochee
39. Sapphire Valley
40. Scaly Mountain
41. Ski Hawksnest
42. Wolf Laurel

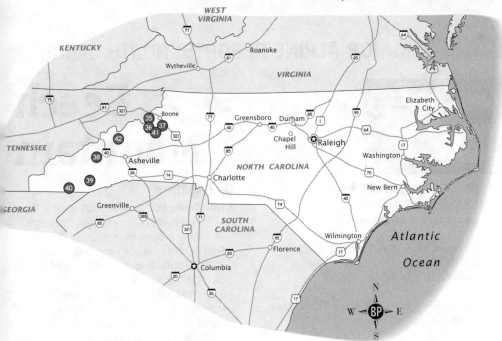

S kiing in North Carolina? Absolutely. The state holds more ski areas than Virginia and Maryland combined. How? The Tar Heel state is able to maintain skiable conditions with a combination of natural and artificial snow. Its eight ski areas are clustered along the far-western strip of the state—several of them perched at mile-high elevations within the Great Smoky Mountains of the Appalachian range. Granted, the considerable snowfall dumps off the Great Lakes don't travel as far south as skiers and resort owners would like, but many Carolina resorts average 60 to 80 inches of powder per year. And the higher elevations help retain both the natural powder and the manmade snow that is gunned virtually non-stop throughout the season. Unfortunately, warmer southern conditions from the Gulf Coast serve to whisk away the effects of winter at the same time.

The state isn't blessed with terribly steep mountains and plateaus, but its ski areas do well with the terrain available. Beech and Sugar are unquestionably the most popular, and most crowded, of Carolina's resorts. As neighbors separated by just a handful of miles, their relationship is symbiotic, and no one can argue their success. Southern skiers don't have the variety of mountains available up north, so they come primarily to Beech and Sugar—two resorts that take the law of supply and demand to excess. There's a huge *demand* for skiing in the South, and the two mega-resorts *supply* visitors with *excessively* priced lift tickets, as well as an abundance of favorable on-site lodging and après-ski options. Still, neither mountain is very large or difficult, which suits the beginner to intermediate majority just fine.

Wolf Laurel, another nearby ski area, makes up for its generally lower-pitched terrain, relative to other Mid-Atlantic mountains, with trail-grooming practices that allow more challenging turf for area skiers and snowboarders. Wolf Laurel continuously spreads its snow out to form contoured obstacles—known as wales—in place of the smooth, level track found at most resorts. The steepest (and shortest) mountain in North Carolina might belong to Hawksnest, which has added new trails in recent years to attract a more advanced clientele. Both resorts have extended their terrain to make snowboarding a big part of the equation, with halfpipes and/or snowboard parks.

The remaining areas in North Carolina are small, comfortable, and geared toward families. Cataloochee, Appalachian, Sapphire Valley, and Scaly Mountain are choice destinations for kids and developing skiers. The latter three are little more than relative molehills, which is why they've focused their resources on teaching and instruction, particularly with regards to children.

159

MAJOR ALPINE RESORTS: NORTH CAROLINA

Beech Mountain

Beech Mountain Ski Resort

1007 Beech Mountain Parkway
Beech Mountain, NC 28604

Ski Report/Information: 1-800-438-2093/
(704) 387-2011
Credit Cards: VISA, AE, MC, Discover

Internet: http://www.skibeech.com
E-mail: skibeech@infoave.com

Operating Hours
8:30 a.m.-4:30 p.m. daily
6 p.m.-10 p.m. nightly

Season
Mid-November to mid-March

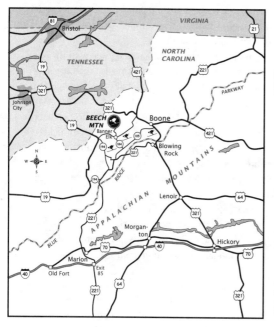

Getting There

- **From Boone, NC:** Take Route 105 south to Route 184 north through Banner Elk, and follow signs for 4 miles to Beech Mountain.
- **From Asheville:** Take I-40 east to Route 221 north to Linville, then pick up 184 toward Banner Elk and follow signs to Beech Mountain.
- **From Charlotte:** Take I-85 or I-77 north to Highway 321 at Gastonia. Follow 321 north toward Boone, then take Route 105 south to Route 184 north through Banner Elk, and follow signs for 4 miles to Beech Mountain.
- **From Virginia:** Take I-81 south into Tennessee, then take Route 23 south to Route 19 and follow signs for Beech Mountain.
- **From Atlanta, GA:** Take I-85 north to Greenville/Spartanburg, then take Route 221 north to 184 and follow signs to Beech Mountain.
- **From Knoxville, Tennessee:** Take I-81 to Johnson City, then take Route 19 into North Carolina, and follow signs to Beech Mountain.

Background

North Carolina's biggest alpine resort is also the highest skiable area among all downhill resorts in eastern North America. At 5,505 feet above sea level, Beech Mountain sits on a windy knob of the Blue Ridge Mountains in western North Carolina. Its towering altitude affords striking views into both Tennessee and Virginia, and reveals the surrounding peaks and valleys, including the 6,300-foot summit of nearby Grandfather Mountain. Beech was also the state's first ski area to incorporate an alpine village resort setting when it opened for the 1968-69 season.

Mountain Stats

Base Elevation: 4,675 feet
Summit Elevation: 5,505 feet
Vertical Drop: 830 feet
Longest Run: 5,000 feet
Primary Slope Direction: North
Skiable Terrain: 100 acres
Average Annual Snowfall: 62 inches
  1995-96 season: 126 inches
  1994-95 season: 84 inches
Snowmaking: 100% of area

Skier Visits
  1996-97 season: 140,000
  1995-96 season: 140,000
Slopes and Trails
  3 beginner, 7 intermediate, 4 advanced
Night Skiing: 100% of trails, nightly until 10 p.m.
Lifts: 1 high-speed detachable quad, 6 doubles, 1 J-bar, 1 rope tow
Uphill Capacity: 8,400 skiers per hour

Roughly two hours from Asheville and 10 minutes from Banner Elk, Beech is generally sardine-packed on weekends but remains exceptionally accommodating to families and developing skiers and snowboarders. Ski resorts are rare commodities in these southern regions, and Beech is a huge attraction for surrounding states, including South Carolina, Tennessee, Georgia, and Florida.

The mountain's mile-high elevation affords one of the coldest climates in the South, and a surprisingly high 60-plus inches of snow is recorded per year on average. The resort is slightly more exposed to the elements than nearby Sugar Mountain—the state's other major downhill ski resort. Despite high elevation and respectable snowfall numbers, wintry conditions tend to be short lived:

The mountain gets bursts of warm air from the Gulf Coast, while northern cold snaps often don't extend this far south. In general, North Carolina skiing is fueled by snow guns and persistent grooming, and Beech's expert snowmaking staff reliably maintains its trail network.

A word to the wise—Bring goggles, face masks, and hats to combat the round-the-clock snow blowers and typically swirling winds. And during storm periods, the road leading to Beech can prove somewhat perilous as it winds steeply upward to the summit, then drops back down to the lodge. Under such conditions, many skiers, particularly families, head off to Sugar Mountain, which is slightly smaller, more accessible, and generally less crowded.

Beech has built a reputation as North Carolina's premiere ski area by marketing the complete family package. The 100-acre resort serves mostly beginners to intermediates on a fairly small system of 14 slopes and trails. Just a few sections are considered challenging for advanced skiers, and Beech would only stand to benefit from cutting some new terrain or improving existing trails. Instead, the resort has added a few twists recently to appeal to a broader base. It continued the rage of Mid-Atlantic snow tubing by debuting the South's first tubing area last year. The 475-foot tubing park off the *Lower Sunny Hall* slope includes three 12-foot-wide flumes and its own chair lift. Night skiing has also been instituted, with strong lights covering the entire mountain. The transition from day to night is plagued, though, by a 90-minute interruption: Trails close at 4:30 p.m. daily so snowmakers can pump the mountain full of manmade snow (when it needs it) before the night session begins at 6 p.m.

Trail Profiles

Novice and intermediate skiers have the run of the mountain on primarily loose, granular-packed, cruising track. A tiny, secluded, introductory-level area with its own rope tow can be found on *College Park*, while neighboring *Play Yard* has similarly easy turf and utilizes a J-bar lift. But these areas often can't accommodate the hordes of beginner skiers who eventually graduate to—and often fill to capacity—the *Freestyle* slope and *Powder Bowl*, revealing one of the resort's blemishes. The trails all funnel into a narrow bottleneck at the mid-station before accessing the beginner areas. Since ugly amounts of traffic form on just about any weekend, many Beech guests opt for the more efficient quad chair, but doing so requires poking through the *Powder Bowl* and navigating around slower skiers. Nonetheless, the resort offers a wide selection of good instructional programs for children, including PEEwee, SKIwee, and Mountain Mashers.

As a rule, there's not a lot of mogul action in North Carolina: Bumpy terrain just doesn't suit the novice to mid-level skier majority. However, sections of the black diamond trail *Southern Star* often hold some challenging bumps over its extra-wide track. *White Lightning* is the only other advanced trail offered, but it's one of the steepest runs in a state otherwise not regarded for its heavily pitched terrain. Bear in mind, though, that both black diamonds tend to pack hard and ice over very quickly.

Top sections of intermediates *Shawneehaw* and *Robbin's Run* provide some more decent vertical, with a more narrow course and an elbow turn on *Lower Shawneehaw*. *Oz Run* is a baby-blue intermediate off the summit's back side that serves to whisk away some of the traffic off the center face. The trail is easily 40 yards wide over the entire run and has a smooth, reliably packed surface over an easy downhill grade. It's also the resort's best means of separating beginners from its monster crowds.

Beech's high-speed quad lift was an obligatory addition to the trail system a few years ago, when lift lines commonly exceeded 30 minutes. The efficient chair provides a fast three- to four-minute ride to the heavily traveled summit. Although this has cut lift lines immeasurably, the quad's lift stations are both awkward and unnatural. Skiers have to hold their balance on a slightly uphill slope while standing in line, which grows quickly tiresome during long weekend waits. And on the dismount, there's a small climb out of the lift shed in place of the usually gradual downhill glide. In all, the resort holds nine lifts, including a notoriously slow double chair on the mountain's back side.

Snowboarding

Beech has a small halfpipe, neither deep, long, nor wide, on a relatively flat beginner slope. Snowboarders tend to drop in for a few jumps, but the pipe is more of a novice arena. While snowmaking is provided on the pipe, the resort doesn't have the necessary equipment to maintain it adequately. Its availability is contingent on colder temperatures.

Snowboarders can carve the resort's 14 trails with few restrictions, but advanced freestylers will find only a few scattered jumps and banks on otherwise smooth cruising terrain. Area boarders tend to choose more snowboard-friendly ski areas such as Hawksnest and Wolf Laurel.

Snowboard School
- 12 instructors
- Private $40/hour
- Group $15/hour

Snowboard Rentals
- 250 sets

Lift Tickets/Rentals/Services

Lift Tickets
- 8:30 a.m.-4:30 p.m.: weekday $27, weekend $41
- 8:30 a.m.-12:30 p.m./12:30 p.m.-4:30 p.m.: $20, $34
- 6 p.m.-10 p.m. Sunday-Thursday: $17, Friday-Saturday $21
* Reduced rates for ages 5-12 and 65+ (15%-25% discounts on tickets, rentals, & lessons)
* Children under 5 ski free
* Group rates for 15 or more skiers
* Coupon books available with discounts on tickets, rentals, & lessons

Ski School
- 125 instructors: PSIA certified
- Private $40/hour, $15/each additional person
- Group $15/hour, $15/each additional person
- Weekday Learn-to-Ski Special: limited lift access, rental, group lesson: $40
- Childrens' Learning Center:
  - PEEwee snow/play program: instruction and day care for 3-year olds
  - SKIwee program: five hours snow/indoor instruction for ages 4-8

- Mountain Mashers ski program: ages 9-14 (Following rates apply to all Learning Center programs: $45/half day, $58/full day)
- Beech Boarders snowboard program, ages 8-14: $75

Ski Rentals
- 3,000 sets
- Weekday, all ages $10-$12
- Weekend/holiday $12-$16
- Bib & coat rental $10 each, $15/both

Adaptive Skier Program
National Handicapped Ski Association event held one weekend each January

Racing
NASTAR scheduled during event weekends

Day Care
Available for children ages 6 months to 3 years from 8:30 a.m.-4:30 p.m., reservations suggested; rates: $7/hour, $50/day

Base Lodge Facilities
Beech Tree Village: outdoor ice skating rink, three eateries and two lounges, Red Baron Snowboard Shop, Ski Beech Sports Shop: rentals and demos, specialty shops, nursery, lockers/ski lock-ups (in 3 locations: ski center building, sports shop, and group sales center)

Other Winter Sports

On-site
- New 475-foot **snow tubing** run with three lanes on *Lower Sunny Hall* slope, accessed by #1 lift; rates: $15/four-hour session, rental included
- 7,800-square-foot **ice-skating rink** at base lodge; rates: $5/session, $5/rental

Nearby
- **Cross-country skiing** (natural conditions permitting) at Mount Mitchell State Park *(see page 252)*, Blue Ridge Parkway *(see page 250)*, Great Smoky Mountains National Park *(see page 251)*, and Pisgah National Forest *(see page 252);* cross-country ski rentals in Banner Elk

Calendar of Events

January
- Winterfest Weekend, first weekend in January, with snowboard programs and events
- Bathing Beauty contest, New Castle dart tournament, and tubing race
- Michelob Light Cup Pro-Am ($3,000 purse) and snowboard series
- USSA Slalom/Giant Slalom Ski Races

February
- Edge of the World Snowboard Series Competition
- Jimmy Heauga Toyota Ski Express: marathon fund raiser for MS, with ski/snowboard races
- Annual White Lightning Slalom Race

Lodging/Dining/Aprés-Ski

Beech Mountain has assumed the name of the small mountaintop area on which it sits. The resort was designed to keep skiers on the mountain, with extensive facilities and recreation opportunities that include several retail shops, restaurants and lounges, nursery, video game facility, outdoor ice-skating, and tourist supplements. Guests can base themselves on the mountain or nearby in one of hundreds of houses, chalets, or other rental units. Reserve your lodging far in advance of your trip: Beech is a big-time destination resort, and accommodations fill quickly. Ten miles away in the college town of Banner Elk, plenty of aprés-ski establishments can be found, as well as one of the region's best snowboard shops at Edge of the World. Beech-bound skiers and snowboarders renting equipment should strongly consider using one of the shops in Banner Elk, if only to spare themselves the often-torturous weekend rental lines at the resort. Most off-mountain shops stay open one hour past Beech's 10 p.m. closing time.

Lodging

* For lodging information, call 1-800-GO-BEECH or Beech Mountain Chamber of Commerce; 1-800-468-5506.

Slopeside and Nearby

• 8,000 total beds include privately owned slopeside lodging and secluded nearby accommodations, including 650 chalets and townhomes, 4 inns, and several bed and breakfasts

• **Accommodations Center & Action Realty**; 1-800-258-6198

Archers Mountain Inn; (704) 898-9004

Beech Alpen Inn; (704) 387-2252

Buchanan's Beech Mountain Rentals, 1- 800-438-2095

4 Seasons at Beech; (704) 387-4421

Pinnacle Inn Resort; 1-800-438-2097

Beechwood Realty, Inc.; (704) 387-4251

Banner Elk/Beech Mountain Rentals; 1-800-845-6164

Beech Mountain Chalet Rentals; 1-800-368-7404

Beech Mountain Realty and Rentals; 1-800-845-6164

Beech Mountain Slopeside Chalet Rentals, Inc.; 1-800-692-2061

Ridgeview Chalet Rentals; (704) 387-2484

Dining/Aprés-ski

On-site

Beech Tree Restaurant & Pub and **View Haus** cafeteria/lounge, open until 10 p.m., with live weekend entertainment some weekends

Nearby (Banner Elk)

Rascals Bar-B-Que & Pub; (704) 387-2266

Beech Alpen Restaurant; (704) 387-2161

Vasarelys Fine Dining Restaurant; (704) 387-4900

Manning House Inn; (704) 898-9669

Smoketree Lodge & Restaurant; (704) 963-6505

Beech Haus Restaurant; (704) 989-4246

Big Chill Bar & Grill; (704) 898-4877

Nick's Restaurant & Pub; (704) 898-9613

Banner Elk Café; (704) 898-4090

Sugar Mountain

Sugar Mountain Resort

P.O. Box 369
Banner Elk, NC 28604

Ski Report/Information: 1-800-SUGARMT
Local: (704) 898-4521
Credit Cards: VISA, MC

Internet: http://www.skisugar.com

Operating Hours
9 a.m.-4:30 p.m. and 6 p.m.-10 p.m. daily

Season
Mid-November to mid-March

Getting There

- **From Virginia and points north:** Take I-81 south to Tennessee Route 91 south, then pick up Route 421 south; take Route 105 south to Route 184 west, and follow 2 miles to Sugar Mountain.

Background

Sugar Mountain couples with nearby Beech Mountain to form the two major players in the limited scheme of downhill skiing below West Virginia. A few years after its inception in 1969 as a four-seasons resort in Blue Ridge Mountain high country, Sugar was rescued from bankruptcy as new owners looked to capitalize on the decade's national ski boom. The ski area has since operated as a separate entity from the four-seasons resort, and benefited from a skier base that stretches across numerous southern states.

Selling lift tickets isn't the only operation happening at Sugar. The resort is also the home of KD Sports, Inc.—the U.S. distributor of Europe's Kneissl skis and Dachstein boots. Gunther Jochl,

- **From Raleigh/Durham and points east:** Take I-40 west to Route 421 north, then pick up Route 105 south to Route 184 west and follow 2 miles to Sugar Mountain. * **Alternate route:** Take I-40 west to North Carolina Route 181 north, then pick up Route 105 north to Route 184 west and follow 2 miles to Sugar Mountain.
- **From Columbia, South Carolina:** Take I-77 north to Route 421 north and follow directions above from Raleigh/Durham.
- **From Asheville:** Take I-40 east past Marion and follow Route 181 north to Sugar Mountain.
- **From Atlanta and points south:** Take I-85 north past Greenville, South Carolina, then take Route 221 north to Route 105 north, and follow Route 184 west for 2 miles to Sugar Mountain.
- **From Tennessee and points west:** Take I-81 north to I-181 south, then pick up Tennessee Route 67 north to Route 321 south. From Route 321, take Route 19E south to Route 194 north, then follow Route 184 east to Sugar Mountain.

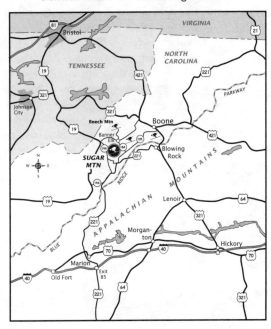

Sugar's general manager, double dips as the owner of Volkl USA Ski Company, which markets equipment for KD. This explains why you might spot some unique variations of skis at Sugar, including the Big Foot— a cross between a snow skate and a ski: 63-centimeters long, metal-edged, and extra wide.

Mountain Stats

Base Elevation: 4,100 feet
Summit Elevation: 5,300 feet
Vertical Drop: 1,200 feet
Skiable Terrain: 110 acres
Longest Run: 1.5 miles
Primary Slope Direction: North to northeast
Average Annual Snowfall: 78 inches
  1996-97 season: 40 inches
  1995-96 season: 100 inches
Skiable Days
  1995-96 season: 137
  1994-95 season: 110

Slopes and Trails
  7 beginner, 9 intermediate, 2 advanced
Uphill Capacity
  8,800 skiers per hour
Snowmaking: 100% of area
Lifts: 1 triple, 4 doubles, 1 T-bar, 1 platter pull, 1 rope tow
Night Skiing: 90% of area, Sunday-Friday until 9 p.m., Saturday 10 p.m.

Defying generally warm southern climates, Sugar's mile-high altitude and sweeping snowmaking system help extend its ski seasons long into March nearly every year. A surprisingly-high average annual snowfall of 78 inches doesn't hurt either, though the snow guns never seem to quit firing on the mountain. The resort sits on a somewhat sheltered bowl, much less exposed to windy conditions that affect nearby Beech Mountain. And Sugar tends to attract more skiers than its counterpart resort after a healthy snowfall hits the region. The trip here is a fairly easy one, with the base lodge on the same level as the road leading to the mountain.

Though the resort offers the state's largest trail count and the Mid-Atlantic's second-longest vertical drop, skiers will discover the mountain to be smaller and the terrain much easier than the numbers suggest. The resort milks every cat track, turn, and connector run—more realistically owning about one-half the 19 slopes and trails it advertises. What Sugar does offer without exception is longer, more continuous skiing than any place around. There's just not that much terrain to choose from. But southern skiers have to take what they can get without traveling long dis-

tances to resorts with more varied terrain. The impressive vertical aside, Sugar is a beginner to intermediate mountain at best, with just two advanced runs available.

Skiers can count on crowds of monstrous proportions on weekends and holidays, though the resort is typically less bustling than Beech Mountain. Four hours would be more than enough time to ski the entire trail network if it weren't for lift lines that make it impossible. The resort is in urgent need of a high-speed detachable quad lift to keep up with its visitor count. There's night skiing available on all but the two black diamonds, but the lighting isn't as strong as Beech's more visible mountain, except during the Christmas holiday when the resort illuminates the mountain with a flashy lights show. First-time guests at Sugar might be shocked at its exorbitant ticket prices, so look for midweek specials, such as college rates and family packages that are often available Sunday through Thursday nights.

Trail Profiles

The satisfying steeps and contours on black diamonds *Tom Terrific* and *Boulder Dash* save Sugar Mountain from complete beginner-level obscurity. The trails are strongly pitched but extremely short lived, and run out into longer cruising on *Sugar Slalom* and *Upper Flying Mile*. *Tom Terrific* is the staple mogul course for bump skiers; *Boulder Dash* is nearly as steep and more of a fast cruising course, occasionally getting the ungroomed bump treatment. Both trails are purportedly equipped with snowmaking, but have been known to close under poor conditions, and operate only during day hours when they are open. Another option for aggressive downhillers exists off the summit on *Northridge*. The short terrain of *Northridge* features a wall on the inside of the trail that skiers and snowboarders often use for jumping.

Since many skiers seem intent on reaching the top of the mountain, Sugar's best-kept secret may be *Big Red*, off the lower summit area. It's a wide-open, secluded trail on which guests can open it up with giant slalom turns, and has its own lift to the Sugar Ski and Country Club. The resort's active racing programs are held either on *Big Red* or *Sugar Slalom*, and include U.S. Ski Association events, NASTAR on weekends, and races throughout the season.

The rest of the mountain barely qualifies as downhill—The terrain below the three-quarter lift station is a long slow ride. Wide, beginner track marks the resort's lower half, where novice skiers have several bunny hills and broad slopes for learning. Three lifts exclusively serve the lower-half terrain, which tends to be overburdened with instructional groups and developing skiers. The Sugar Bear Ski School is available for children ages five to 10.

Snowboarding

The Dead End Snowboard Park was created here at Sugar a few years ago to meet the rising tide of southern snowboarders. Built on a previously underused trail, the park isn't altogether exciting, but there's enough action to mess around in it for awhile. Some modest hits were constructed during the 1996-97 season, having featured at different points some spines, gaps, table tops, and rail slides, as well as an occasional quarterpipe. The park suffers, however, from the terrain's narrow course and meager vertical drop, which keeps freestylers from catching long hang time. To its credit, Sugar installed a poma lift for the park and added lights for night boarding.

The resort hosts the Edge of the World Snowboard Series in January, and there's also a pro race with a division for boarders, usually held the same month. More area boarders tend to hit nearby Beech Mountain, though its small halfpipe often isn't open enough to gain attention. Guests can also rent Big Foot skis and use the snowboard park. Snowmaking can be suspect in the park, so boarders should call ahead to confirm its opening.

Snowboard Rentals
• Mostly Burton boards, some with step-in bindings
• $25/day, $16/night ($20 deposit required)

Snowboard School
• Private $30
• Group $15

Lift Tickets/Rentals/Services

Since a visit to Sugar is certain to include unbearably long lift waits on weekends and holidays, skiers and snowboarders renting equipment can save time by using the private shop at the mountain's entrance. Although there's no chance of exchanging off-mountain rentals in the event of equipment failure, you'll get newer skis, cheaper rates, and possibly one or two more downhill runs by bypassing the resort's rental shop.

(continued)

Lift Tickets
- Full day: weekday $28, weekend $43
- 12:30 p.m.-4:30 p.m.: weekday $21, weekend $36
- 12:30 p.m.-close: Monday-Thursday $28, Friday $32, Saturday $43, Sunday $39
- 6 p.m.-close: Monday-Thursday $18, Friday-Saturday $22, Sunday $18
- * Reduced rates for children 11 and under (15%-25%)
- * Group rates available

Ski School
- 60 instructors: PSIA certified
- Private $40/hour
- Group $15/person
- Learn-to-Ski Package $45, midweek only (includes ticket, rental, lesson)
- Sugar Bear Ski School at the Childrens' Learning Center for ages 5-10: $55, 10a.m.-3 p.m. (includes ticket, rental, lesson, lunch, supervision)

Ski Rentals
- 2,700 sets, with step-in bindings
- Weekday $10-$12
- Weekend $10-$15
- * Discounts for ages 11 and under
- * Big Foot ski rentals available

Racing
NASTAR held on *Sugar Slalom* or *Big Red* trails, weekends at noon

Base Lodge Facilities
Ticket/rental offices, ski school, cafeterias, lounge, sports shop, repair shop, locker rooms, game room

Other Winter Sports
Cross-country skiing, weather permitting, at nearby state parks and forests; *See* the North Carolina cross-country section, *pages 248 to 253.*

Summer Activities

Mountain bikers can access over 10 miles of trails year-round, with some runs closed during the ski season. During August of 1996, the resort hosted The Showdown at Sugar—its third annual mountain bike race—on a 6.5-mile, two-track, technical course that culminated on an open ski slope. The annual Oktoberfest celebration is held each fall at the resort, with live bands, authentic German foods, and events and festivities. And a challenging par-64 golf course and six-court tennis facility are offered from mid-April through October.

Calendar of Events

* Slalom and giant slalom races held numerous weekends throughout the season

December
- Sugar Race Clinics
- Burton demo days
- USSA Holiday Slalom and Giant Slalom Races

January
- Edge of the World Snowboard Series, with races held in snowboard park
- Septuagenarian Ski Party (ages 70 and older)
- Southern Region Pro Race

February
- Stewart Smith Memorial Sugar Cup Slalom
- Snowboard demo days

Lodging/Dining/Aprés-Ski

Guests can choose from on-mountain accomodations such as condominiums, chalets, homes, and a slopeside lodge. The nearby towns of Boone and Blowing Rock offer a longer list of inns, bed and breakfasts, resorts, hotels, and motels. Guests will also find all the tourist trappings they can handle in Boone, including numerous specialty shops and attractions.

Lodging
On-site

- 32-room slopeside lodge, condominiums, chalets, and homes; Call 1-800-438-4555 for complete on-site lodging information and rates.
- Sugar Mountain Accommodations (condominiums and houses); 1-800-545-9475
- Sugar Top Resort (condominiums); (704) 898-5226

Nearby

Era Realty & Rentals, Banner Elk; 1-800-438-4555

High Country Realty, Banner Elk; 1-800-227-6521

Highlands at Sugar, Banner Elk; (704) 898-9601

See Beach Mountain, *Nearby Lodging*, for bed and breakfasts, cabins/condominiums/houses, resorts, and hotels/motels in nearby Blowing Rock and Boone, *page 164.*

Dining/Aprés-ski
On-site

- Two cafeterias, deck grill (weather permitting), the Last Run Lounge (pub grub, fireplace, music, television)

Nearby

See Beech Mountain, *Nearby Dining/Aprés-ski, page 164.*

169

NORTH CAROLINA'S **OTHER ALPINE SKI AREAS**

Appalachian Ski Mountain

Appalachian Ski Mountain

P.O. Box 106
Blowing Rock, NC

Ski Report: (704) 295-7828
Information/Reservations: 1-800-322-2373
Credit Cards: VISA, MC, AE, Discover

Operating Hours
9 a.m.-4 p.m. and 6 p.m.-10 p.m. daily

Season
Late November to late March

Getting There

- **From Asheville:** Take I-40 east to Route 221/105 north toward Boone, then pick up Route 221/321 toward Blowing Rock and follow signs for Appalachian Ski Mountain.

- **From Atlanta, GA:** Take I-85 to I-26 north to Asheville and follow directions from here.
- **From Columbia, SC:** Take I-77 north to I-40 west toward Hickory, then take Route 321 north past Blowing Rock and follow signs to Appalachian Ski Mountain.
- **From Johnson City, TN:** Take Route 321 east to Boone, then pick up Route 221/321 toward Blowing Rock and follow signs to Appalachian Ski Mountain.
- **From western Virginia:** Take I-81 south into Tennessee and turn off onto I-81 south/Route 23 to Johnson City. Follow directions above from Johnson City.

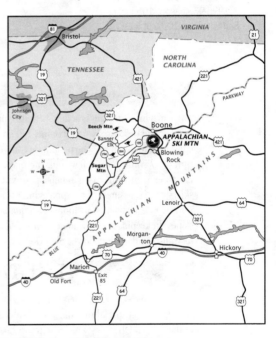

Background

A round the same time that Cataloochee Ski Area opened to mark the advent of commercial alpine skiing in North Carolina, Blowing Rock Ski Lodge followed suit in the state's western High Country region. The stockholder-owned turned family-run resort changed its name six years later in 1968 to Appalachian Ski Mountain, and has become one of the state's most highly regarded facilities for learning skiers. Guests with little or no skiing experience can expect attentive and patient instruction from the resort's acclaimed French-Swiss Ski College.

Mountain Stats

Appalachian is located a few miles from Boone and is equidistant from nearby alpine giants Beech and Sugar Mountains. The resort was designed with families and large groups in mind, and caters to all ages, even offering complete accessory and clothing rentals for the true neophyte skier.

And though there's more chance of injury by colliding with other skiers than spilling on the resort's gentle slopes, Appalachian rents junior helmets for children ages four to 12. The base lodge nursery cares for infants ages one to four daily, and the trail network is small enough that parents can spot their kids on the slopes from the balcony of the spacious Bavarian lodge. Rounding out the area is a lighted outdoor ice-skating rink that was built last year—open throughout the season and on Christmas Day from noon to 9 p.m., with rentals and instruction available.

Most of Appalachian's beginner skiers could care less about snow conditions as long as there's something to slide on, but the north-facing mountain and 4,000-foot elevation maintains reasonable conditions for skiing, with natural snow often mixed with the artificial stuff. Most southern downhillers love spring skiing on artificial oatmeal snow, so Appalachian does its best to keep its slopes open well into March.

Base Elevation: 3,635 feet
Summit Elevation: 4,000 feet
Vertical Drop: 365 feet
Longest Run: 2,700 feet
Primary Slope Direction: North
Skiable Terrain: 22 acres
Average Annual Snowfall: 60 inches
  1996-97 season: 45 inches
  1995-96 season: 105 inches
Snowmaking: 100% of area

Skier Visits
  1996-97 season: 98,000
  1995-96 season: 105,000
Slopes and Trails
  2 beginner, 4 intermediate, 3 advanced
Lifts
  2 quads, 1 double, 1 rope tow, 1 handle tow
Uphill Capacity: 5,650 skiers per hour
Night Skiing: 100% of area, nightly until 10 p.m.
Snowboarding
  Not permitted on the trail system

Trail Profiles

Appalachian's terrain is solidly beginner throughout nine short, wide trails over a gradual 365-foot vertical descent. Two tiny bunny hill areas, each serviced by its own tow lift, help ease young children into the sport. The remaining trails offer gentle, straight courses—aside from a fun elbow turn on *Orchard Run*. A few trails are marked as advanced runs but are simply a bit steeper and narrower relative to easier blue slopes, with little variation in pitch among them. What novice skiers can be assured of at Appalachian is plenty of runs minus the lift lines of bigger Carolina resorts. Five chair lifts, including two quads, just about guarantee an active day's session on the slopes. In keeping with the area's controlled atmosphere, Appalachian prohibits snowboarding on its trails but does rent slower Sled Dog snow skates, with full mountain use.

Lift Tickets/Rentals/Services

A reputable ski school offers *SKI* magazine's national SKIwee program, and additional emphasis is placed on special programs for disabled skiers, including the North Carolina Winter Games of the Special Olympics which the resort hosts each January.

Lift prices are reasonable, with major markdowns for children 12 and under and senior citizens. Guests can also bypass ticket lines through a prepaid reservation system. Look for free skiing opportunities on opening day and reduced price lift tickets during early and late seasons, in addition to vintage 1962 lift tickets in December 1997 when the resort celebrates its thirty-fifth anniversary weekend.

Lift Tickets
- 9 a.m.-4 p.m.: weekday $20, weekend $30
- 9 a.m.-4 p.m./6 p.m.-10 p.m.: weekday $26, weekend $38
- 1 p.m.-4 p.m.: Sunday $21, weekday $14
- 1 p.m.-4 p.m./6 p.m.-10 p.m.: weekday $20, weekend $30
- 6 p.m.-10 p.m.: weekday $13, weekend $16
- 9 a.m.-1:30 p.m.: $25 (Sunday only)
* Reduced rates (20%-35%) for ages 12 and under and 60+
* Early- and late-season discounts open to December 14 and from March 10 to close
* Group rates for 15 or more skiers, reduced multi-day passes, and student discounts available

Ski School
- 65 instructors: PSIA-certified
- Private $29/hour
- Group $13/hour
- Learn-to-Ski package $21 (includes group lesson, rental, beginner lift ticket)
- SKIwee program (ages 4-12): 9:30 a.m.-3:30 p.m. $43; 1 p.m.-3:30 p.m. $30

Ski Rentals
- 1,600 sets: Rossignol, Volkl
- Salomon step-in bindings, Nordica boots
- Adult: weekend $8-$15, weekday $7-$15
- Ages 12 and under and 60+: $5-$10
* Clothing Rentals: jackets, bibs, gloves, goggles $4-$5, complete set $13

Adaptive Skier Program
Lessons arranged by appointment

Child Care
Offered daily from 8 a.m.-4:30 p.m. for ages 1-4; rates: half day $16, full day $28

Base Lodge Facilities
Cafeteria/restaurant, gift shop, ski/rental shop, childrens' facility, lockers

Other Winter Sports
- 6,000-foot outdoor **ice-skating** rink, with two-hour sessions from noon-9 p.m.; Rentals and lessons available
- **Sled Dog** snow skates allowed on slopes; rentals $4/hour, $10/day

Calendar of Events
December
- 35th Anniversary Weekend—1962 prices
- Demo days

January/February
- New Year's Eve Celebration: late-night skiing and ice-skating, fireworks
- North Carolina and Southeast Region Special Olympic Games

March
- Subaru Master the Mountain Weekend

Lodging/Dining/Aprés-Ski

Guests should have no trouble accessing the base lodge, regardless of the weather: It's an easy two-mile drive off U.S. Highway 321. The vast majority of Appalachian's skier base are day-trippers, but families traveling longer distances can pull off moderately priced vacations or weekend stays in both Boone and Blowing Rock, where hotels, inns, resorts, and rental houses are complemented by a number of dining and shopping opportunities.

Lodging
On-site
- 2 fully equipped slopeside and near-slopeside houses, with fireplaces
* Call 1-800-322-2373 for information and rates on ski packages on-site and nearby

Nearby
See Beech Mountain, Nearby Lodging, *page 164,* for complete list of inns, bed and breakfasts, condominiums, houses, and resorts in Boone and Blowing Rock.

Dining/Aprés-ski
On-site
- Cafeteria in base lodge

Nearby
See Beech Mountain, Nearby Dining/Aprés-ski, *page 164,* for restaurants and pubs in Boone.

Cataloochee
Ski Area

Cataloochee Ski Area

Route 1, Box 502
Maggie Valley, NC 28751

Ski Report: 1-800-768-3588, (704) 926-3588
Information: 1-800-768-0285
Group Skiing: (704) 926-0285
Credit Cards: VISA, MC

Operating Hours
9 a.m.-4:30 p.m. daily
1 p.m.-10 p.m. Tuesday-Saturday

Season
Mid-December to mid-March

Getting There

- **From Asheville, Raleigh, and Durham:** Take I-40 west to Exit 27 and follow Route 276. At the 276/19 intersection, turn right at the stoplight and follow 12 miles to Cataloochee Ski Area (look for Ghost Town in the Sky signs).
- **From Charlotte:** Take I-77 north to I-40 west and follow directions above.
- **From Columbia, SC:** Take I-26 north to Asheville and follow directions above from there.
- **From Knoxville, TN:** Take I-40 east to Exit 20 and follow Route 19 and signs for Maggie Valley and Cataloochee Ski Area.
- **From Atlanta, GA:** Take I-85 north to Route 23 north, then pick up Route 19 and follow signs for Maggie Valley and Cataloochee Ski Area.

Background

North Carolina's oldest ski area began operating in 1961 when Cataloochee Ranch owner Tom Alexander converted his isolated, mile-high pasture-land peak into a small alpine facility on Moody Top Mountain. Alexander developed the mountain into a ski area to further the region's tourism trade and to keep his ranch hands employed through the winter months. Cataloochee sits in western Carolina's Maggie Valley, 35 miles west of Asheville, with part of the resort property bordering the Great Smoky Mountains National Park.

Mountain Stats

Base Elevation: 4,600 feet
Summit Elevation: 5,400 feet
Vertical Drop: 740 feet
Longest Run: 4,000 feet
Primary Slope Direction: North
Skiable Terrain: 15 acres
Average Annual Snowfall: 55 inches
1995-96 season: 78 inches
1994-95 season: 36 inches
Snowmaking: 100% of area

Skiable Days
1995-96 season: 89 days
1994-95 season: 84 days
Slopes and Trails
3 beginner, 4 intermediate, 2 advanced
Lifts
2 doubles, 1 rope tow
Uphill Capacity: 2,200 skiers per hour
Night Skiing: 100% of area, Tuesday-Saturday until 10 p.m.

Trail Profiles

The small network of nine slopes and trails features a nice blend of tree-lined intermediate cruisers and gentle, wide novice runs. Cataloochee's headliner trail is *Omigosh*—a fast, steep run from the summit. It features an initial steep drop-off, nicknamed "The Headwall," which flattens out to some degree on a couple of small turns, then runs to the mid-station lift with a moderately steep pitch. Intermediate *Upper* and *Lower Snowbird* is a narrow, serpentine, gradual run with three switchback opportunities. The resort's designated racing trail is *Alley Cat*—a short trail with a nice pitch and a few small turning areas.

There's wide-open bowl skiing available off the ridge in Cataloochee's *High Meadow* section, opening up another 80 acres of terrain that's suitable for all abilities when natural conditions permit. *High Meadow* is a beauty when it's open, but requires at least 14 inches of a powder base to ski.

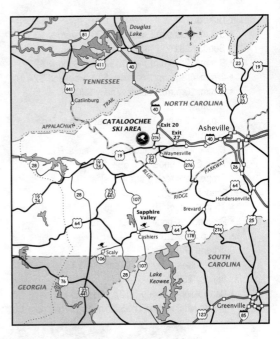

And because there's somewhat of a natural funnel on the mountain, strong winds tend to blow snow right off the meadow. A wet-consistency snowfall is typically required to keep the trail open. (It wasn't accessible at all for the 1996-97 season.) Beginner terrain is more plentiful here, with a large expanse of bunny turf and two wide slow-skiing slopes.

Snowboarding

Cataloochee gets a fair number of snowboarders, mostly of the beginner variety. No immediate plans are underway to establish more of a boarding environment, but all slopes and trails are open to carving.

Snowboard School
- Private $28/hour
- Group $13/1.5 hours

Snowboard Rentals
- 12 sets: K2
- Ski rental rates apply

Lift Tickets/Rentals/Services

The ski school is excellent, which is why many families introduce their young ones to the sport at Cataloochee. And instruction is extremely affordable, with groups lessons running just $13 per session. Families can take advantage of special midweek offers, including free lift tickets for ages 17 and under on Wednesdays after the first week in January.

As far as Carolina resorts go, Cataloochee is one of its least crowded. Weekend lift lines rarely exceed 15 minutes on peak Saturdays. Night skiing is available Tuesday to Saturday until 10 p.m., and is used mainly by local skiers and nearby high schools and colleges through programs and races.

Lift Tickets
- 9 a.m.-4:30 p.m.: weekday $20, Saturday $33, Sunday $31
- 9 a.m.-12:30 p.m.: weekday $14, Sunday $24
- 1 p.m.-4:30 p.m.: weekday $14, weekend $24
- 1 p.m.-10 p.m.: Tuesday-Friday $20, Saturday $33
- 6 p.m.-10 p.m.: Tuesday-Thursday $14, Friday-Saturday $16
- * Discount rates for students and ages 7-12; ages 6 and under and 65+ ski free
- * Group rates for 15 or more skiers

Ski School
- 75 instructors: PSIA certified
- Private $28/hour
- Group $13/1.5 hours
Childrens' Programs:
- Catt Trackers (ages 4-6): half day $35, full day $55
- Catt Explorers (ages 7-12): $45, $65
- Private kids' instruction: $28/hour, 15/half hour

Ski Rentals
- 1,300 sets: K2, Elan, with 15 sets shaped skis
- weekday $10-$13, weekend $11-$15
- * Discount rates for students and ages 12 and under

Racing
Weekly school slalom races, normally held on *Upper Omigosh* or *Lower Omigosh* trails

Base Lodge Facilities
Cafeteria/lounge, rental and gift shops, ski school

Calendar of Events
- * Weekly Interscholastic High School Slalom Race Series

December
- Early season discount days

March
- Spring Frolic: races and events

Other Winter Sports

When enough natural powder graces the region, cross-country skiers and winter hikers can access trails in the Great Smoky Mountains National Park or hit closed sections of the Blue Ridge Parkway. Aside from skiing, Cataloochee's other big draw is the Cherokee Casino, 20 miles west of Maggie Valley. The Cherokee Indians first established the facility in the mid-1980s, and Harrah's is currently building a new facility. Ghost Town in the Sky is a mountaintop amusement park built in the 1960s around a Wild West theme, open during the summer season only.

Cross-country skiing, natural snow permitting, on nearby Blue Ridge Parkway (closest access from ski area is in Maggie Valley, 3 miles west, on Route 19); **Cross-country skiing** also available nearby in the Great Smoky Mountains National Park *(see page 251 for information)*

Lodging/Dining/Aprés-Ski

Vacationing skiers have numerous resorts, inns, and motels just outside the ski area in Maggie Valley, all of which offer ski-and-stay packages. The Cataloochee Dude Ranch is one mile away, offering year-round lodging in their main ranch house and adjoining cabins.

Lodging
Nearby (Maggie Valley)
Cataloochee Ranch, 1 mile from the ski area, with 25 units in both cabins and the main ranch house; Call 1-800-868-1401 for information

Maggie Valley Resort & Country Club; 1-800-438-3861, (704) 926-1616

Best Western Maggie Valley; 1-800-528-1234, (704) 926-3962

Four Seasons Inn; (704) 926-8505/8501
Comfort Inn; (704) 926-9106
Smokey Shadows Lodge; (704) 926-0001
Meadowlark Motel; (704) 926-1717
*Most lodging includes day lift ticket

Dining/Aprés-ski
On-site
Cafeteria/lounge, open until 10 p.m.

(continues)

(continued)

Nearby (Maggie Valley)
Arf's Restaurant & Lounge; (704) 926-1566
Blast from the Past Café; (704) 926-8999
J. Arthurs Restaurant; (704) 926-1817
JB's Café & Tavern; (704) 926-3828

Maggie Valley Resort & Country Club;
(704) 926-1616
Mountaineer Buffet Restaurant; (704) 926-1730
The Copper Kettle Steak House;
(704) 926-1710

Sapphire Valley

Sapphire Valley Ski Area
4350 Highway 64 West
Sapphire, NC 28774

Ski Report: (704) 743-1162
Information: (704) 743-1163/1164
Lodging/Ski Packages: 1-800-722-3956,
1-800-533-8268
Operating Hours
1 p.m.-6 p.m. Monday-Thursday
1 p.m.-10 p.m. Friday
9 a.m.-10 p.m. weekends
Season
Mid-December to early March

Getting There
- **From Asheville, NC:** Take I-26 south to Route 64 west and follow signs to Sapphire Valley, 3 miles east of Cashiers.

- **From Atlanta, GA:** Take I-85 north to I-985 north, then take Route 23/441 north to the Georgia/North Carolina border. Pick up Route 106 toward Cashiers and follow signs for Sapphire Valley.
- **From Athens, GA:** Take Route 441 north to Route 23/441 north and follow directions above.
- **From Greenville, SC:** Take Route 123 west to 178 north into North Carolina, then follow Route 106 and signs for Sapphire Valley.

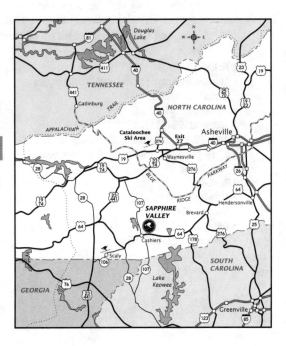

Background

Just five miles from the South Carolina and Georgia borders lies a four-seasons' retreat situated nearly one mile high in a secluded valley wedge of the Blue Ridge Mountains. Jackson County's Sapphire Valley Ski Area is but one small component of the popular resort, offering three short slopes for its property owners, resort guests, and day skiers. It's a comfortable environment for introducing the sport to new skiers, and a patient ski school welcomes anyone from young children to senior first-timers.

Mountain Stats

Base Elevation: 4,375 feet
Summit Elevation: 4,800 feet
Vertical Drop: 425 feet
Longest Run: 2,400 feet
Skiable Terrain: 16 acres
Slopes and Trails
2 beginner, 1 intermediate, 1 advanced

Lifts: 1 double, 1 rope tow
Uphill Capacity
1,800 skiers per hour
Average Annual Snowfall: 22 inches
Snowmaking: 100% of area
Night Skiing: 6 p.m.-10 p.m. Friday-Sunday

Sapphire advertises four slopes—one of which doesn't appear to exist on its trail map—possibly in an attempt to outdo rival Scaly Mountain's scant three runs. Its small novice hill has an easy pitch and extra-wide shoulders. The area is conveniently serviced by a rope tow, but most children can hike the slight uphill faster than the lift can transport them. An intermediate and advanced slope each hold 2,000-plus feet of wide cruising track over a steady 425-foot vertical drop. Snowboarding is also welcomed on the slopes.

As expected from a small ski facility, weekend guests rarely have to wait more than 10 minutes at any time for a spot on the double chair. Sapphire also offers continuous weekend skiing from 9 a.m. to 10 p.m., on the off chance that guests wish to ski the same few runs some 30 times over.

The resort is easily accessible off Highway 64, three miles east of the small town of Cashiers. Its clientele essentially comprises families looking to get away for a day, with Asheville just 50 miles away, Atlanta 135 miles away, and Athens and Chattanooga both within 90 miles. Families opting for an alternative to Christmas Day indoors can ski from 3 p.m. to 10 p.m., with 9 a.m. to 10 p.m. hours from December 23 to January 3.

Lift Tickets/Rentals/Services

Sapphire bills itself the cheapest lift ticket in North Carolina, and affordable lodging/ski packages provide full use of resort facilities. Golf, tennis, horseback riding, canoeing, fishing, swimming, and hiking round out the list of activities during the warmer seasons at the 5,700-acre resort.

Lift Tickets
- Monday-Thursday: $17/adult, $7/children/students*, $45/family
- Friday: $22, $10, $65
- Weekend: $24, $12, $70
* Ages 17 and under and students with valid I.D.
** 25% group rate discount for 6 or more people (tickets and rentals)

Ski Rentals
- Monday-Thursday: $13/adult; $8/children, students; $42/family
- Friday: $15, $8, $45
- Weekend: $17, $10, $55

Snowboard Rentals
- Weekend: $10/hour, $25/day
- Weekday: $8/hour

Ski Instruction
- Private $20/hour
- Group $10/hour
- Learn-to-Ski package: $45/adult, $25/child (includes lift ticket, rental, group lesson)

Base Lodge Facilities
- Cafeteria, ski/rental shop

Lodging/Dining/Après-Ski

The ski slopes are little more than an added amenity to the four-seasons' resort. Vacationing guests usually spend more time inside—the resort offers a restaurant and lounge, indoor pool, Jacuzzi, sauna, health club, and exercise and game rooms. Sapphire's cozy base lodge features a wood-burning fireplace, cafeteria, and a ski and rental shop.

Lodging

250-room Sapphire Valley Resort; Call 1-800-722-3956 or 1-800-533-8268 for information and rates

Dining

On-site

Restaurant/lounge

Nearby (Sapphire)

Mount Toxaway Restaurant; (704) 966-9660
Restaurant Vienna; (704) 884-9727

Scaly Mountain

Scaly Mountain

North Carolina Route 106 S
Scaly Mountain, NC 28775

Ski Report/Information: (704) 526-3737
Credit Cards: VISA, MC
Operating Hours
9 a.m.-4 p.m. and 5:30 p.m.-10 p.m. daily
Season
December to early March

Getting There

- **From Atlanta:** Take I-85 north to I-985 north, then take Route 23/441 north to the Georgia/North Carolina border. Pick up Highway 106 for 7 miles and follow signs for Scaly Mountain.
- **From Asheville:** Take I-40 west to Route 23 south, then pick up Highway 106 for 7 miles and follow signs to Scaly Mountain.

Background

Scaly Mountain is North Carolina's southernmost ski area—mere miles from the Georgia and South Carolina border on Highway 106, near the town of Highlands. It's a tiny, three-slope molehill for children and first-time skiers. The 1,800-foot beginner slope is the longest run—a gentle cruise even for neophyte skiers. An intermediate slope is slightly shorter and not much more difficult, while a 1,200-foot advanced-rated run has just enough pitch to gain a little speed over its unthreatening 225-foot vertical drop. All three trails operate under lights for full night skiing.

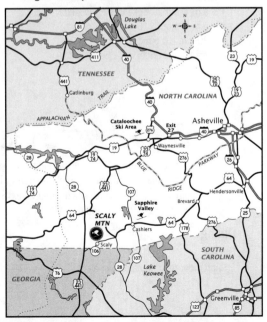

Mountain Stats

Base Elevation: 3,800 feet
Summit Elevation: 4,025 feet
Vertical Drop: 225 feet
Longest Run: 1,800 feet
Primary Slope Direction: North
Skiable Terrain: 12 acres
Average Annual Snowfall: 25 inches

Slopes and Trails
1 beginner, 1 intermediate, 1 advanced
Lifts: 1 double, 1 tow
Uphill Capacity
1,500 skiers per hour
Snowmaking: 100% of area
Night Skiing: 100% of area, nightly until 10 p.m.

Scaly Mountain's location is anything but a magnet for natural snowfall, so the resort relies almost exclusively on constant snowmaking. The mountain's southern exposure, though, induces soupy conditions on the slopes, which is perfect for slow-trudging first-time skiers. Because of the area's weather variances, calling ahead for up-to-the-minute conditions comes highly recommended before leaving. The resort tends to close up shop in poor skiable conditions.

Lift Tickets/Services

With its proximity to Atlanta (just two hours away), Scaly can develop sizable family crowds for such a small area, usually reaching its peak by noon on Saturdays. But visitors rarely stick around long enough to keep the lifts full, considering the lack of terrain. Bargain ticket and rental rates are another part of the attraction: A beginner combination package offers ticket, rental, and instruction for pennies compared to larger Carolina resorts.

Lift Tickets
- 9 a.m.-4 p.m.: weekend $25, weekday $15
- 1 p.m.-4 p.m.: $16
- 5:30 p.m.-10 p.m.: $13
* Ages 12 and under and 65+: $10-$19

Ski Lessons
- 8 instructors
- Private $20/1 1/2 hours
- Group $10/hour

Ski Rentals
Call (704) 526-3737 for equipment rates and information

Lodging/Dining/Après-Ski

Scaly's comfortable lodge and cafeteria, with an adjoining outdoor deck, are close enough to the slopes that parents can keep children in full view through the building's large windows. Purely a day area, there's no on-site lodging here, though seven nearby motels/hotels are available just in case. Call (404) 746-5348/5321 for lodging information.

Dining
On-site
Short-order restaurant/cafeteria

Nearby
Several restaurants nearby on Route 106 in Highlands

Ski Hawksnest

Hawksnest Golf & Ski Resort

1800 Skyland Drive
Seven Devils, NC 28604

Ski Report: 1-800-822-HAWK
Information: (704) 963-6561
Credit Cards: VISA, MC, Discover

Internet: http://www.hawksnest-resort.com
E-mail: hawksnest@appstate.campus.mci.net

Operating Hours
9 a.m.-10 p.m. Sunday-Thursday
9 a.m.-2 a.m. Friday-Saturday

Season
December to mid-March

Getting There

- **From Raleigh/Durham:** Take I-40 west to Route 321 north, then pick up Route 105 and follow signs for Hawksnest.
- **From Asheville:** Take I-40 east to Route 322 north and follow directions above.
- **From Atlanta:** Take I-85 north past Greenville, South Carolina, then take Route 221 north to Route 105 and follow signs to Hawksnest.
- **From Florida:** Follow I-95 north into South Carolina, then take Route 26 north toward Columbia. From Columbia, take I-77 north past Charlotte and Statesville, then pick up Route 421 west toward Boone. Pick up Route 105 and follow signs to Hawksnest.
- **From Richmond:** Take I-85 south to Durham, North Carolina, then follow I-85/40 west to Winston-Salem. Take Route 421 west to Boone and pick up Route 105, following signs to Hawksnest.

Background

Nestled 4,800 feet above sea level atop North Carolina's Blue Ridge Mountains is Hawksnest Ski Resort. Also known as the "Hawk" and Seven Devils, it's a viable alternative to the more popular and crowded Beech and Sugar Mountains. Despite a humble 669-foot vertical drop and short-lived trails, intermediate to advanced skiers will be graciously surprised with Hawksnest's terrain. Negotiating the trail network's mostly narrow track requires at least some degree of experience, and five fairly challenging black diamond runs are steep by North Carolina standards. The resort also allows skiers and snowboarders to open it up on the advanced trails with generally liberal restrictions.

Mountain Stats

Base Elevation: 4,131 feet
Summit Elevation: 4,800 feet
Vertical Drop: 669 feet
Longest Run: 2,600 feet
Skiable Terrain: 40 acres
Primary Slope Direction: North
Slopes and Trails
   3 beginner, 5 intermediates, 5 advanced

Lifts: 2 doubles, 2 surface tows
Uphill Capacity
   3,200 skiers per hour
Average Annual Snowfall: 78 inches
Snowmaking: 100% of area
Night Skiing: 100% percent of area, Sunday-Thursday until 10 p.m. and Friday-Saturday until 2 p.m.

A nearly mile-high altitude and 78-inch average annual snowfall provide strong conditions for southern skiing, while Hawksnest's snowmakers and groomers keep the entire mountain open during winter thaws. When a strong powder base blankets the region, the drive up the mountain can be a bit intimidating, though, with several hairpin curves.

Hawksnest gets just a fraction of the crowds seen at Beech and Sugar Mountains, primarily because it doesn't have their big-resort reputation and extensive on-site accommodations. But the resort compensates with better terrain and several perks, including continuous weekend skiing. Guests can enjoy the Mid-Atlantic's longest lift ticket hours with a nighttime program appropriately dubbed "Nighthawk." All 14 trails stay open until 2 a.m. on Fridays and Saturdays, while live music plays inside the festive lodge.

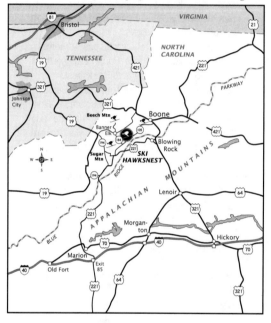

Trail Profiles

Hawksnest likely owns the state's most challenging terrain, though its vertical drop is almost half that of nearby Sugar's longer mountain. Considering that its trails are a bit steeper, more gladed, and much less crowded, the resort is the preferred destination for the area's advanced skiers and snowboarders. Its signature piece is the new *Top Gun* trail—a half-mile run with an average grade of 38 percent—one of a small selection of steep slopes in the state. The lower section of *Sock-Em-Dog* is bumped up for mogul fans, and NASTAR racing is held on selected trails each weekend.

Five intermediate trails are of moderate pitch but quite narrow. Skiers searching for longer runs with a variety of twists, bends, and steeps can hit the perimeter trails on both sides of the mountain: *Upper-Sock-Em-Dog* to *Proposed Expansion* and, on the other end, *The Right Stuff* to *8 Turns* and the straight runout of *Goshawk*.

Children and true beginners have limited territory on the mountain, but a spacious bunny hill area is set aside from the flow of skier traffic, with two surface lifts for access. The hill has just an 11 percent grade and is well suited for kids. For learning skiers and snowboarders, the resort offers a strong variety of instructional packages, as well as a good beginner Telemark ski program. Both adult and childrens' training centers are available, and guests can pick from one of nine different ability levels for private or group coaching sessions.

Snowboarding

Hawksnest is the snowboarding mecca of North Carolina, easily the most boarder-friendly environment among the state's ski areas. The Snowboard Heaven terrain park, located on the bottom run-out of the resort's *Sock-Em Dog* black diamond trail, offers freestylers a private arena of aerial energy. The Edge of the World snowboard shop and its sponsored snowboarders helped design and build the park. Last year's changing obstacles included tabletops, rail slides, big "S" turns, and a sizable gap jump. Snowboard events or races are held almost every weekend of the season, and the resort hosts the Edge of the World Snowboard Series in January, with season championships in February.

(snowboarding continues)

(snowboarding continued)

The park is equipped with lights for night boarding. Unfortunately, it doesn't have its own serviced lift, and it's a long, slow ride to the summit. Most surrounding trails are a bit narrow for wide-arcing turns. The terrain on new *Top Gun* is full of steeps, though, and *8 Turns* trail has a boulevard width and a few switchback options. Like Wolf Laurel Resort—the state's other snowboard-happy mountain—the Hawk grooms its trails out with wales and jumps to satisfy aggressive boarders and skiers.

Snowboard School
- 22 instructors: ski school rates apply

Snowboard Rentals
- 100 sets
- Weekday $15-$18, extended day $30
- Weekend $20-$25, extended day $40
- High-performance snowboards available

Lift Tickets/Rentals/Services

Hawksnest won't stretch your budget, either. Lift tickets here are substantially more affordable than at money-stashing Beech and Sugar Mountains, which price their fees above many northern Mid-Atlantic resorts. Tickets are as much as 25 percent cheaper here, and for a mere $10, skiers and snowboarders can take advantage of the resort's early and late seasons in early to-mid December and during March (excluding Saturdays). This bargain deal also attracts skiers from nearby Appalachian State University, with special midweek discount days afforded to all students with college I.D.

Lift Tickets
- 9 a.m.-4:30 p.m.: weekday $20, weekend $33
- 12 p.m.-4:30 p.m.: weekday $14, weekend $28
- 5 p.m.-10 p.m.: Sunday-Thursday $14
- 6 p.m.-2 a.m.: Friday-Saturday $20
- 9 a.m.-2 a.m.: Friday $34, Sat. $45
- 12 p.m.-2 a.m.: Friday $20, Sat. $33
* Reduced rates for ages 12 and under and 62+; ages 4 and under ski free
* $10 lift ticket, excluding Saturdays, offered during early and late seasons (open to December 22 and during month of March)
* Season pass: Sunday-Friday night $275, unlimited $375

Ski Rentals
- Over 1,000 sets, mostly step-in bindings
- Weekday $10-$17
- Weekend $10-$20
* High-performance skis available

Ski School
- Private $30
- Group $15
- Telemark ski coaching available by appointment
- Kiddy Hawk Ski School (ages 5-7), Top Gun Performance School (ages 8-12), and Kiddy Hawk Snowboard Patrol (ages 8-12); rates: $35/half day, $50/full day (includes ticket, instruction, and rental)
- Learn-to-Ski package $32, snowboard $45 (both midweek only, reduced rates available until December 22)

Adaptive Ski School
Available by appointment

Base Lodge Facilities
The Nest Bar & Grill, cafeteria, rental shop, ski/gift shop, lockers

Racing
NASTAR program offered Thursday-Sunday, clinics available Saturday mornings

Other Winter Sports

Cross-country skiing, snowfall permitting, on the Blue Ridge Parkway and nearby state parks and forests; *See Beech Mountain, Other Winter Sports, page 163.*

Calendar of Events
January
• Snowboard events and races
January-February
• Edge of the World Snowboard Series and Championship
March
• Michelob Cup pro race
• Top Gun Pro-Am Challenge and ski/snowboard events

Lodging/Dining/Aprés-Ski

A moderate selection of on-site houses and condominiums are available for rent, and there's a small inn at the base of the mountain. Most guests arrive from local regions, but overnighters have an abundance of lodging and dining opportunities in Boone and Blowing Rock, both within 15 minutes' drive. From April to November, golfers can hit the links on the resort's 72-par, mountain course.

Lodging
On-site
• Condominiums, houses, and a 15-room inn at the base of the mountain; Call 1-800-822-HAWK for lodging information and rates

High Country Realty, with slopeside and secluded houses scattered throughout the mountain, 1-800-227-6521

Nearby
* For complete listing of nearby accommodations, see Beech Mountain, *Nearby Lodging*, page 164, and Sugar Mountain, *Nearby Lodging*, page 169.

Dining/Aprés-ski
On-site
Base lodge cafeteria and The Nest restaurant/lounge with third-floor slopeside view, open until 2 a.m. weekends, with live music or entertainment most weekends
Nearby
Towns of Boone and Blowing Rock both within short drives of Hawksnest, with numerous restaurants and pubs. See Beech Mountain, *Nearby Dining/Apres-ski*, page 164.

Wolf Laurel

Wolf Laurel Ski Area

Route 3, Box 129
Mars Hill, NC 28754

Information/Reservations: 1-800-817-4111
Local: (704) 689-4111

Credit Cards: VISA, MC, Discover
Internet: http://www.ioa.com/home/wolflaurel/

Season
Late November to mid-March

Operating Hours
9 a.m.-10 p.m. daily

Getting There
- **From Atlanta:** Take I-85 north to Greenville, South Carolina, then take Route 25 north to I-26 to Asheville. Pick up Route 23 north and follow signs to Wolf Laurel.
- **From Tennessee:** Take I-40 east to Asheville, then take Route 23 north and follow signs to Wolf Laurel.
- **From Raleigh/Durham:** Take Route 40 west to Asheville, then take Route 23 north and follow signs to Wolf Laurel.
- **From Virginia and points north:** Take I-81 south into Tennessee, then pick up Route 23 south and follow signs to Wolf Laurel.

Background

Just over the eastern tip of Tennessee and directly off the Appalachian Trail lies Wolf Laurel—a mom-and-pop ski area serving nearby Asheville; Knoxville, Tennessee; and surrounding locales. The newest of Carolina's ski resorts, "The Wolf" has a prevailing free-for-all atmosphere. There's a mix of families, snowboarders, and Telemark skiers, and in early spring you might spot some good-ol'-boys flying down the slopes in T-shirts and jeans.

Mountain Stats

Base Elevation: 3,950 feet
Summit Elevation: 4,650 feet
Vertical Drop: 700 feet
Longest Run: 1 mile
Skiable Terrain: 54 acres
Primary Slope Direction: North
Average Annual Snowfall: 60 inches
Slopes and Trails
2 beginner, 10 intermediate, 2 advanced
Uphill Capacity: 2,200 skiers per hour
Snowmaking: 100% of area
Lifts: 1 quad, 1 double, 1 surface tow
Night Skiing: 100% of slopes, nightly until 10 p.m.

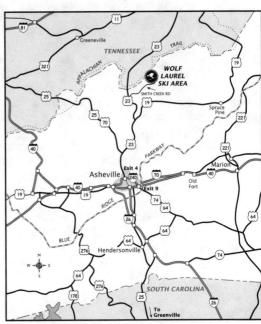

A small network of 13 slopes and trails provides ample novice and intermediate track and a few short, steeper black runs. Its 700-foot vertical drop isn't altogether shabby for southern standards. But what keeps Wolf Laurel regulars coming back time and time again is the resort's unconventional grooming methods. Rather than grooming its slopes smooth and flat, Wolf Laurel spreads its mostly man-made snow into wales and mounds to make its rolling terrain more challenging. The bumps and ruts left behind are a natural fit for challenge-seeking skiers and snowboarders, who will also discover dips, berms, and a few gladed sections on which to carve.

The resort suffers, however, from a tight base and loading area. A quad and double chair lift run skiers efficiently to two mid-stations and summit areas, but the slopes all funnel into the narrow base, which can get congested on Saturdays and peak weekends. All slopes are equipped for night skiing, though dimly lit.

Trail Profiles

There aren't a large number of trails to choose from on the mountain, but Wolf Laurel has some relatively steep terrain. The summit-flowing *Howling* trail is one of Carolina's steepest, longest runs. It has a prolonged pitch with a natural headwall at the mid-section, where skiers and snowboarders can catch some major air. Without a no-jumping policy, the resort only asks that skiers use extreme caution. Two black diamonds—*The Bowl* and *Flame Out*—drop somewhat steeply into a wide bowl area for giant slalom-turning.

Most of the remaining trails are baby blues in which novice skiers should be able to negotiate with ease. Wolf recently cut a new green run off the quad lift midway station: It's little more than a flat cat track that opens up to the wide run-out of *Broadway's* beginner section. A tiny bunny hill with its own handle tow is set aside from the lodge, but the only other learning area is in *Broadway*. Here, faster skiers are forced to negotiate their way around hordes of slow-moving beginners.

Snowboarding

Along with Hawksnest Ski Resort, Wolf Laurel is one of North Carolina's burgeoning snowboard destinations. The usual mass of boarders here is a testament to the resort's alternative style of trail grooming. When the snow guns finish firing, what's left after grooming out the track and its contours are wales, mounds, and ruts that boarders use for carving and jumping. The resort's trails are completely slopestyle, with naturally rolling terrain. Snowboarders also have some small glade sections on the trails and a mid-mountain natural bowl for big turns.

Wolf Laurel's 400-foot halfpipe, located in a slip above the *Broadway* area, doesn't get the same marks as its trail system. The resort has difficulty keeping it open in the absence of natural snowfall. And when it is open, it tends to ice up quickly. Without the benefit of a first-rate grooming apparatus, employees have to use an old machine to groom the bottom of the pipe before shaping it. Freestylers will, however, find some clean obstacles incorporated into the pipe, such as last year's series of rail and pipe slides, spools, and a gap jump.

Wolf Laurel also holds the distinction of having the first nationally certified snowboard patrol in the country. A few years ago, general manager Dave Durham assembled a group of dedicated riders and developed a snowboard demonstration project. The program is now certified through the National Ski Patrol. But that doesn't mean snowboarders can't open it up on the trails—the boarder patrol just monitors reckless behavior.

Snowboard Rentals
- 150 sets: Ride, Oxygen, Hooger, Fosfour (some with step-in bindings)

- $25/board and boots, $20/board only
Snowboard School
- 15 instructors: Ski school rates apply

Lift Tickets/Rentals/Services

The resort's operating hours sometimes seem as varied as the weather conditions, so don't pack your skis or snowboards before calling ahead first. Some skiers have been disappointed to find the area closed during unfavorable winter or spring conditions. Group skiing is the hot ticket at Wolf Laurel, with reservations guaranteeing slope time, and significant discounts on lift passes, rentals, lessons, and dining packages. Laid-back, personalized instruction ranges from the Wolf Cub Ski School (ages four to seven), adult and junior lessons, and racing and snowboarding clinics. Guests wishing to learn the Norwegian-based Telemark ski turn can take private lessons offered by the resort's Telemark-certified ski school.

Lift Tickets
- 9 a.m.-4:30 p.m.: weekday $20, weekend $30
- 1 p.m.-4:30 p.m.: weekday $15, weekend $25
- 1 p.m.-10 p.m.: weekday $20, weekend $30
- 6 p.m.-10 p.m.: weekday $15, weekend $20
* Reduced rates for ages 9-12, under 8, and ages 65-69 (over 70 ski free)
* Group rates for 16 or more skiers

Ski School
- 35 instructors: PSIA certified
- Private $30/hour
- Group $12/hour
- One-hour clinic $10

- Wolf Cub Ski School (ages 4-7): half day $35, full day $50
- Telemark ski instruction (private lessons only): $30/hour

Ski Rentals
- 1,600 sets: Dynamic, with Salomon bindings and boots
- $8-$14
* Sled Dog snow skate rentals available: $12

Racing
- Racing clinics and events held some weekends

Base Lodge Facilities
Grill/cafeteria, ski/rental shop, viewing deck

Other Winter Sports

Wolf Laurel joined the lucrative snow tubing craze last year by opening a lift-operated tubing run, equipped with lights. There's also a small sled run behind the lodge for children who don't find skiing the bunny hill to their liking.

On-site
Snow tubing park, with lights; rates: lift tickets apply, or 4:30 p.m.-6 p.m. $10
Telemark skiing permitted on all trails

Nearby
Cross-country skiing, snowfall permitting, at the top of Wolf Laurel on Big Bald Mountain, with a small network of roads and trails

Calendar of Events

January
- Winter Carnival: snowboard races and various events

February
- Edge of the World Snowboard Series: freestyle events
- Memorial Ski Race

Lodging/Dining/Aprés-Ski

Wolf Laurel's lodge was expanded recently, adding much-needed space on a second floor that overlooks the base of the slopes. There's a grill available inside the lodge, but without alcohol—Wolf Laurel sits in a dry county. Other than a few establishments in Mars Hill, the closest town with full-service dining and aprés-ski options is Asheville, which has more than its share of eateries, pubs, and entertainment. The historic town—home of the renowned Biltmore House—is a wise choice for Wolf Laurel overnighters who don't mind the 45-minute haul to the slopes. Asheville has numerous luxurious and bargain lodging opportunities and tourist attractions. Wolf Laurel's limited on-site accommodations include the new Wolf Laurel Inn and 40 rental houses and cabins throughout the mountain.

Lodging

On-site

- Wolf Laurel Inn, with motel-style rooms and dorm rooms; 1-800-541-1738
- 40 rental houses and log cabins; 1-800-541-1738

Nearby

Comfort Inn, Asheville; 1-800-836-6732
Days Inn North, Asheville; (704) 645-9191
Hampton Inn, Asheville; (704) 255-9220
Shoney's Inn, Arden; (704) 684-6688

Dining/Aprés-ski

On-site

Base lodge grill

Nearby (Asheville)

Annabelle's Restaurant & Pub; (704) 298-8082
Applebee's Neighborhood Bar & Grill; (704) 251-9194
Barley's Brew Pub; (704) 255-0504
Beaver Lake Seafood & Steak Restaurant; (704) 252-4343
Cahoots Eating & Drinking Emporium; (704) 252-2838
Angelo's Family Restaurant; (704) 628-4031

-*"Exhibition"*

Meet Thigh Master.

You've skied the rest, so this season break out of that winter rut and
experience Whitetail Ski Resort.

WHY?

It's The Place To Be: Whitetail was voted among North America's favorite day trips by
Snow Country Magazine readers.

Fast Lifts: Four Quad chairlifts including The Whitetail Express, the region's first
high-speed quad chairlift, allow you to consume more vertical feet by lunch than
you'd get in a day at most other areas.

Great Trails: Whitetail offers almost 1000 vertical feet of skiing across wide,
challenging slopes which means there's plenty of room for the family.

Lots Of Snow: Whitetail has a state-of-the-art snowmaking system with
300 snowguns designed to cover 100% of our 17 trails with blankets
of powdery snow.

AND for those of you looking for a real workout try *Exhibition,* Whitetail's
version of The Thigh Master. This is your winter to find out why
"Nothing Close Comes Close" to Whitetail.

WHITETAIL

Fun For The Whole Body.

Whitetail Ski Resort & Mountain Biking Center • Mercersburg, PA • 717.328.9400 • Internet: www.skiwhitetail.com

CROSS-COUNTRY SKIING

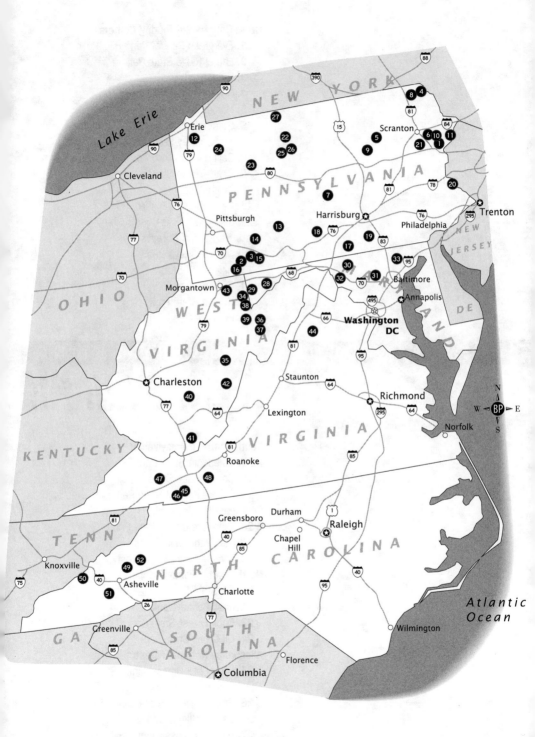

Cross-Country Ski Touring Centers
1. Evergreen Park at Penn Hills Resort
2. Laurel Ridge State Park
3. Hidden Valley
4. The Inn at Starlight Lake
5. Hanley's Happy Hill
6. Sterling Inn
7. Stone Valley Recreation Area
8. Callender's Windy Acre Farms
9. Crystal Lake Ski Center
10. Skytop Lodge
11. Camp Spears Eljabar/YMCA
12. Elk Valley Cross-Country Center

State Parks and Forests
Southwest Pennsylvania:
13. Blue Knob State Park
14. Forbes State Forest
15. Kooser State Park
16. Ohiopyle State Park

CROSS-COUNTRY SKIING:
PENNSYLVANIA

South-Central Pennsylvania:
17. Caledonia State Park
18. Cowans Gap State Park
19. Gifford Pinchot State Park

Southeast Pennsylvania:
20. Delaware Canal State Park

Northeast Pennsylvania:
21. Lackawanna State Forest

North-Central Pennsylvania:
22. Elk State Forest

Northwest Pennsylvania:
23. Cook Forest State Park
24. Oil Creek State Park

Allegheney National Forest:
25. Laurel Mill Cross-country Ski Center/Hiking Area
26. Brush Hollow Cross-country Ski Center/Hiking Area
27. Westline Cross-country Ski Center/Hiking Area

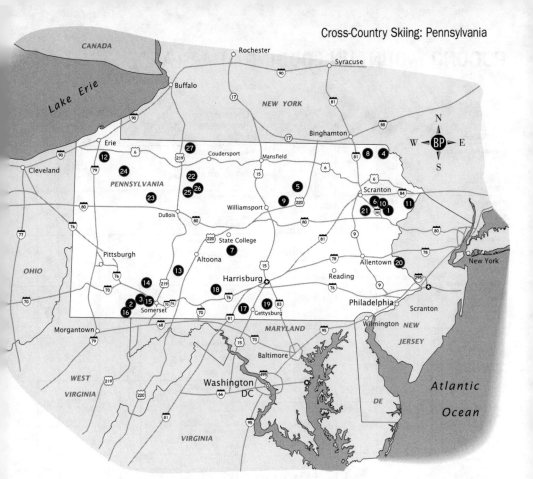

P ennsylvania's considerable size and several strong snowfall regions allow a large number of cross-country touring centers and state and national parks and forests to operate. Most Nordic touring centers are concentrated in two sections of the state: the snow-filled, high-elevation Laurel Highlands region (one hour southeast of Pittsburgh) and the Pocono and Endless Mountains in northeastern Pennsylvania, where snowfall is slightly less consistent. A few other touring facilities are scattered throughout the state, including far-western Pennsylvania's Elk Valley, near the town of Erie, and centrally located Crystal Lake and Stone Valley Recreation Area. All Pennsylvania touring centers offer equipment rentals and instruction, with the exception of Stone Valley Recreation Area, which recently closed its rental shop.

With so many state parks and forests in Pennsylvania, the areas that are most commonly used by Nordic skiers are listed herein, representing different regions in the state. Laurel Ridge State Park, which benefits from major snowfall in the region, is the only state-run facility to offer a complete touring center. A sampling of other state parks extend rental equipment on-site, including Cook Forest and Kooser State Parks.

Lodging is available at a few touring centers, some of which operate as year-round resorts, while some state parks offer fully equipped cabin rentals. Nearby lodging and dining is listed when available. *(See the at-a-glance chart on the next page for an easy-to-reference listing of lodging, amenities, and winter recreation in the **Pocono Mountain** area).*

POCONO MOUNTAIN LODGING AT A GLANCE

Bed & Breakfasts

	downhill skiing	cross-country skiing	snowmobiling	sledding	tobogganing	ice-skating	hiking	horse-drawn sleigh rides
Blueberry Mountain Inn Thomas Rd, HC 1 Box 1102 Blakeslee, PA 18610 1-800-315-BLUE (717) 646-7144		❄					❄	
Britannia Country Inn P.O. Box 8 Swiftwater, PA 18370 (717) 839-7243				❄				
Brookview Manor B&B Inn RR 1, Box 365 Canadensis, PA 18325 (717) 595-2451		❄					❄	
Bryn Mawr Conference Center & Mountain Retreat RR 5, Box 410 Honesdale, PA 18431 (717) 253-2488	❄	❄						
Country Surrey Inn Box 341 Gouldsboro, PA 18424 (717) 842-2081						❄	❄	
Double W Ranch B&B RR 2, Box 1540 Honesdale, PA 18431 (717) 226-3118			❄	❄			❄	❄
Eagle Rock Lodge & Rentals River Road, Box 265 Shawnee-on-Delaware, PA 18356 (717) 421-2139		❄		❄			❄	
The French Manor Huckleberry Road South Sterling, PA 18460 1-800-523-8200 (717) 676-3244				❄	❄		❄	❄
Holiday Glen Bush Road, Box 96 Swiftwater, PA 18370 (717) 839-7015		❄				❄	❄	
The Inn at Meadowbrook RR 7, Box 7651 East Stroudsburg, PA 18301 1-800-441-7619 (717) 629-0296		❄					❄	
Memorytown Grange Rd. Mt. Pocono, PA 18344 (717) 839-1680						❄		
Mountain Manor Inn & Golf Club P.O. Box 1067, Creek Road Marshalls Creek, PA 18335 (717) 223-8098		❄				❄	❄	
Pegasus B&B RR 2, Box 2066, Woodtown Rd. Shohola, PA 18458 (717) 296-4017		❄				❄	❄	
Stroudsmoor Country Inn Rt. 191 & Stroudsmoor Rd. Stroudsburg, PA 18360 (717) 421-6431/421-6962						❄	❄	

Couples/Honeymoon Lodging

	downhill skiing	cross-country skiing	snowmobiling	sledding	tobogganing	ice-skating	hiking	horse-drawn sleigh rides
Caesars Cove Haven Rt. 590, P.O. Box 40 Lakeville, PA 18438 1-800-233-4141 (717) 226-2101			❄			❄	❄	
Caesars Paradise Stream Rt. 940 Mt. Pocono, PA 18344 1-800-233-4141 (717) 839-8881			❄				❄	❄
Caesars Pocono Palace Rt. 209 Marshalls Creek, PA 18335 1-800-233-4141 (717) 588-6692			❄			❄	❄	❄
Penn Hills Resort Exit 52 off I-80 to Route 447 North Analomink, PA 18320 1-800-233-8240 (717) 421-6464				❄		❄	❄	❄
Pocono Gardens Lodge Paradise Valley Mount Pocono, PA 18344 1-800-441-4410 (717) 595-7431			❄			❄	❄	
Strickland's Mountain Inn Mt. Pocono, PA 18344 1-800-441-4410 (717) 839-7155	❄	❄				❄	❄	
The Summit Resort Rt. 715S (I-80, exit 45) Tannersville, PA 18372 1-800-233-8250 (717) 629-0203			❄			❄	❄	❄

Houses/Cottages

	downhill skiing	cross-country skiing	snowmobiling	sledding	tobogganing	ice-skating	hiking	horse-drawn sleigh rides
Countryside Housekeeping Cottages Bartonsville Ave. Stroudsburg, PA 18360 (717) 629-2131					❄	❄		
Mountain Springs Lake Resort Mountain Springs Drive Reeders, PA 18352 (717) 629-0251					❄	❄	❄	
Willow Run Housekeeping Cottages Rt. 715 (I-80, exit 45) Stroudsburg, PA 18360 (717) 629-0752		❄		❄	❄	❄	❄	❄

Motels

	downhill skiing	cross-country skiing	snowmobiling	sledding	tobogganing	ice-skating	hiking	horse-drawn sleigh rides
Harmony Lakeshore Inn P.O. Box 546 Lake Harmony, PA 18624 (717) 722-0522						❄		
Box 87 Kresgeville, PA 18333 (717) 722-0288	❄							
(motels continue)								

(motels continued)	downhill skiing	cross-country skiing	snow-mobiling	sledding	tobogganing	ice-skating	hiking	horse-drawn sleigh rides
Penn's Wood Motel & Cottages Rt. 611, Box 77 Tannersville, PA 18372 (717) 629-0131						❄		
Sandy Beach Motel P.O. Box 150 Hawley, PA 18428 (717) 226-3858			❄			❄		

Resorts/Hotels

	downhill skiing	cross-country skiing	snow-mobiling	sledding	tobogganing	ice-skating	hiking	horse-drawn sleigh rides
Birchwood Resort 3400 Birchwood Drive East Stroudsburg, PA 18301 1-800-233-8177 (717) 629-0222			❄	❄		❄	❄	
Caesars Brookdale Rt. 611 Scotrun, PA 18355 1-800-233-4141 (717) 839-8843			❄		❄	❄	❄	
Daniels Top-O-The-Poconos Resort Rt. 447 North Canadensis, PA 18325 (717) 595-7531		❄		❄				
Fernwood Resort & Country Club Rt. 209, Box 447 Bushkill, PA 18432 1-800-233-8103 (717) 588-9500	❄		❄	❄	❄	❄	❄	
Hillside Lodge & Resort P.O. Box 268 Canadensis, PA 18325 1-800-666-4455 (717) 595-7551			❄	❄		❄	❄	
Mount Airy Lodge Mount Pocono, PA 18344 1-800-441-4410 (717) 839-8811	❄		❄			❄	❄	
The Mountain Laurel Resort & Golf Club P.O. Box 126 White Haven, PA 18661 1-800-458-5921 (717) 443-8411		❄		❄			❄	
Penn Estates Resort Community P.O. Box 309 Analomink, PA 18320 (717) 424-8795/421-6464				❄			❄	
Pocono Manor Inn & Golf Resort Box 135 Pocono Manor, PA 18349 1-800-233-8150 (717) 839-7111		❄	❄			❄		❄
Split Rock Resort & Conference Center Lake Harmony, PA 18624 1-800-255-7625 (717) 722-9111	❄		❄				❄	
Tamiment Resort & Conference Center Tamiment, PA 18371 1-800-233-8105 (717) 588-6652	❄		❄		❄			
(resorts/hotels continue)								

(resorts/hotels continued)	downhill skiing	cross-country skiing	snow-mobiling	sledding	tobogganing	ice-skating	hiking	horse-drawn sleigh rides
Woodloch Pines Resort, Inc. RR 1, Box 280 Hawley, PA 18428 1-800-572-6658 (717) 685-7121			❄		❄	❄	❄	

Vacation Home Rentals

	downhill skiing	cross-country skiing	snow-mobiling	sledding	tobogganing	ice-skating	hiking	horse-drawn sleigh rides
Big Bass Lake Rt. 507 Gouldsboro, PA 18424 1-800-762-6669 (717) 842-7600				❄	❄	❄		
Penn Estates Resort Community I-80, exit 52, Rt. 447 North to Cherry Lane Analomink, PA 18320 (717) 424-8795/421-6464				❄			❄	

CROSS-COUNTRY SKI TOURING CENTERS

1

Evergreen Park at Penn Hills Resort

Evergreen Park at Penn Hills Resort
P.O. Box 309
Cherry Lane Road
Analomink, PA 18320

Information: (717) 421-7721
Operating Hours: 8 a.m.-5 p.m.
Elevation: 1,000 feet
Average Annual Snowfall: 50 inches

Getting There
- **From I-80:** Take Exit 52 (Marshall's Creek), then follow Route 447 north, traveling roughly 8 miles to Analomink, then turn left onto Cherry Lane; Evergreen Park is just down the road.
- **From the Northeast Extension of the Pennsylvania Turnpike:** *See directions from Alpine Mountain Ski Area,* Getting There, *page 16.*

ach winter this Pocono Mountain nine-hole golf course is transformed into a pleasant cross-country ski touring area. With 25 acres of primarily flat terrain, it's is an ideal place for families and learning skiers when enough of a snow base develops on the low-lying area. Located just miles from Alpine Mountain Ski Area, Evergreen offers a full fleet of late-model touring skis, private and group instruction, and a restaurant at its base concession.

Seasoned cross-country skiers won't find many challenges here, but the entire grounds are free to roam amidst a backdrop of tall pines, around a lake, and by a stream that runs parallel to the property. A few small hilly sections are scattered throughout the course, which is fully marked by trail name and relative difficulty rating. Other nearby winter activities include snowmobiling at Alpine Mountain Ski Resort (rentals available) and ice-skating at Penn Hills.

Information

Trail Fee: $6; With rental: $11
Instruction
- Private $35/hour
- Group $15/1.5 hours

Lodging/Dining
See Alpine Mountain Ski Area, Lodging and Dining/Après-ski, page 16.

2

Laurel Ridge State Park

Laurel Ridge State Park
RR 3, Box 246
Rockwood, PA 15557-8703

Park Office: (412) 455-3744
Ski Report/Concessionaire: (412) 455-7303
Operating Hours: Thursday-Sunday 10 a.m.-4:30 p.m.

Elevation: 2,700 feet
Average Annual Snowfall: 100 inches

Getting There
- **From the Pennsylvania Turnpike (70/76):** Take Exit 9 (Donegal), then follow Route 711 south to Normalville; Pick up Route 653 east for 6 miles and follow signs to Laurel Ridge State Park.

erched high atop Laurel Mountain in southwest Pennsylvania, Laurel Ridge State Park offers excellent backcountry skiing throughout 20 miles of marked, groomed, set track on a single loop system. Laurel Ridge is Pennsylvania's only state park to operate a cross-country ski touring center, and therefore charges a nominal trail fee. The park hosts some outstanding terrain for daring Nordic skiers, with some trails actually too steep for the park service to groom.

And Laurel's high elevation and north-facing mountain help hold the region's typically abundant amounts of snowfall for long periods of winter.

The terrain is tremendously varied, suitable for the neophyte skier to the expert. Three miles of novice track are even lit for night skiing. There's a small beginner loop, intermediate trails, and an expert run filled with steep ascents and descents. Sections of the 70-mile Laurel Highlands Hiking Trail, which runs from Ohiopyle State Park to Johnstown, Pennsylvania, are open to skiing without a trail fee, but should only be attempted by experts. Log erosion barriers, stone stairways, and a multitude of switchbacks make for difficult skiing on the trail's narrow singletrack.

A warming hut and snack bar are available at the touring center, in addition to a rental fleet featuring both skating and touring skis. Nordic instruction is available by appointment. Guests have ample parking at the base, and primitive winter camping is permitted on the Highlands Hiking Trail. Call the park for a free trail map and current snow conditions.

Information

Trail Fee
- $4-$6; $13-$15 with ski rental (cross-country skating and touring skis)
- Half price for ages 6-12

Instruction: Arranged by appointment with River Sports; (814) 395-5744

Lodging
- Primitive winter camping on Laurel Highlands hiking trail by reservation, with well water available via pump; Call park office for information.
- For nearby lodging and dining, see Hidden Valley Ski Resort, page 48, and Seven Springs Resort, page 57.

Hidden Valley

3

Hidden Valley
1 Craighead Drive
Hidden Valley, PA 15502

Ski Report: 1-800-443-SKII, ext. 473
Information: (814) 443-2600
Operating Hours: 9 a.m.-5 p.m.

Elevation: 2,300-2,900 feet
Average Annual Snowfall: 150 inches

Lodging/Dining/Getting There
- See Hidden Valley Ski Area, page 48.

Western Pennsylvania's Laurel Highlands is the home of Hidden Valley—one of the Mid-Atlantic's premiere cross-country touring centers for the last 23 years. Eighteen trails over 33 miles are available altogether, including access to endless track on adjacent Kooser State Park and Forbes State Forest. Hidden Valley has been selected as a host site for Ski Fest '97—a national celebration of cross-country skiing at various touring centers across the nation. Events, races, and clinics will be held for cross-country skiers of all ages and abilities; Call the touring center for information and dates.

Hidden Valley's touring trails surround its popular family alpine ski area (see page 48): The more advanced Valley View and Gardner's Nordic trails connect with Hidden Valley Ski Resort's summit and base locations. Several trails wind over the mountaintop golf course, offering views of the Laurel Highlands, while other runs follow old logging and tram roads built in the late 1800s. Most runs can be finished in under one hour. For experts, four secluded trails combine open, rolling terrain with several steep drops. The four-mile Mountain View trail is a staple among seasoned gliders with its varying pitches, and there's a warming hut at the trail's midway point. *Kooser* trail is a beginner's favorite—a four-mile flat trek that winds past old rustic cabins and a scenic lake. Expansion is planned off the *Greenbrier* trail to provide additional terrain.

Located one hour southeast of Pittsburgh, the Laurel Highlands region is a virtual snow magnet (the touring center averages 40 to 65 skiable days per year). Hidden Valley also machine grooms most of its terrain, packing it when necessary with snowmobiles, and will also set track periodically on connecting Kooser State Park and Forbes State Forest trails when conditions permit. Hidden Valley's trails are marked by blue triangles, while red triangles indicate Kooser and Forbes trails.

Hidden Valley's cross-country center is well equipped, offering instruction, full ski rentals, and child care. The neighboring four-seasons resort has deluxe accommodations and amenities.

Information

Trail Fee
- Adult: $10/full day, $6/half day (1 p.m.)
- Ages 6-12: $8/full day, $5/half day

Rentals
- Touring skis and new Fisher Control shorter skis (147s and 167s); no skating or telemark ski rentals

- Adult: $12/full day, $7/half day
- Ages 6-12: $10/full day; $5/half day

Instruction (weekends only)
- Private $20/hour; Group $12/hour
- Beginner weekend package $25 (includes lesson, rental, trail fee)

4

The Inn at Starlight Lake Touring Center

The Inn At Starlight Lake Touring Center
P.O. Box 27
Starlight, PA 18461

Ski Report/Reservations/Information:
1-800-248-2519

Operating Hours: 9 a.m.-dark (daily), conditions permitting

Elevation: 1,500 feet-1,800 feet

Average Annual Snowfall: 100 inches

Getting There
- **From points east in New York/New Jersey:** Take Route 17 west to Hancock, New York (at the northeastern tip of Pennsylvania and the Delaware River), then take Exit 87, Pennsylvania Route 191, to Route 370 and follow signs to Starlight.
- **From points south:** Take I-81 north to Exit 62, then take Route 107 east to Route 247 north; Follow Route 171 northeast to Route 370 east, and turn left on Route 370 at the sign for Starlight Inn.
- * Shortline Bus service available from Port Authority Terminal in New York City to Hancock, New York, with Starlight shuttle (by reservation).

Located one hour northeast of Scranton and just a few miles from the New York state border sits the stately Starlight Lake—a 90-year-old, five-star country inn and Nordic touring center set in the Lake District of northeastern Pennsylvania's Appalachian Mountains. Starlight offers 9 miles of marked, groomed track, 6 miles of which are set on abandoned logging roads, rolling hills and meadows, and through hardwood forest. Its diverse landscape includes ridges, stone quarries, fern banks, moss-covered boulders, and clear spring-water lakes.

Situated at the foothills of the Moosic range of the Appalachian Trail, Starlight is a closed-loop system of varied difficulty with several turnaround points for novice skiers. *Yes-You-Can* trail winds steeply uphill before opening to a wide field that's ideal for Telemark turns. The most challenging trail is *Uranus*, which features two difficult turns toward its finish.

Abundant amounts of light, fluffy snow grace this neck of the woods most winters: Starlight averages 35 to 50 skiable days per year. From the 1,800-foot peak, guests can catch views as far as the New York Catskills on clear days, and summit vistas are available on both sides of the trail system.

Guests can return from their backcountry excursions to the inn's wood-burning fireplace and stovepipe lounge, with homemade meals served in the turn-of-the-century lakeside dining room. Equipment rentals and instruction are available, and guided tours can be arranged by appointment. Starlight also extends free ice-skating privileges on its front-yard lake and sled rentals on its surrounding hills. Alpine enthusiasts have solid downhill skiing at Elk Mountain, 30 minutes away, and beginner terrain at Mount Tone within 15 minutes.

Information

Trail Fees
- Adult: $10/day; $5/half day
- Ages 12 and under ski free

Rentals
- Track and Fisher touring skis
- Adult: $8-$15
- Ages 12 and under: $4-$8

Instruction
- Private $18/hour; Group $10/hour
- * Reservations recommended

Lodging/Dining:
Inn at Starlight Lake
- 26-room inn, most with private baths
- one suite available
- Rates range from $127/night (midweek, double occupancy) to $140/night on weekends
- Restaurant and fireplace lounge

Nearby
The Nethercott Inn/Bed & Breakfast, Starruca; (717) 727-2211
- *See* Elk Mountain Ski Resort, *page 43, for more lodging and dining information.*

Hanley's Happy Hill

Hanley's Happy Hill
Route 42, Laporte and Ridge Avenue
Eaglesmere, PA 17731

Information: (717) 525-3461
Operating Hours: 9 a.m.-4:30 p.m. weekends, Friday noon-dusk, and occasional Wednesdays
Elevation: 2,100 feet
Average Annual Snowfall: 85 inches

Getting There
- **From the Northeast Extension of the Pennsylvania Turnpike:** Follow the turnpike to I-80 west, then take Exit 34 (Buckhorn), heading north on Route 42 from the Exit ramp; Follow through town 1.5 miles and look for signs to Hanley's Happy Hill.
- **From points east and west:** Take I-80 and follow signs above.
- **From points north:** Take I-81 south to I-80 west and follow signs above.

Hanley's Happy Hill began in 1957 as an alpine ski center, ceasing operations in 1986. The area's acreage was later developed throughout scenic Eaglesmere for cross-country touring terrain, opening up in 1972. The atmosphere at Hanley's Happy Hill is as pleasant as its name implies. An honor system even applies for signs-ins and trail fees.

The expansive 31-mile trail system in northeastern Pennsylvania's Endless Mountains is a series of loops beginning from the trailhead. Hanley's grooms and maintains 25 miles of its terrain, setting track on flats and hills of varying sizes, elevations, and difficulty. There's also a designated section for ski skating and an additional six miles of ungroomed, unmarked wilderness trails for more advanced skinny skiers. Because of the remoteness of its east wilderness section, Hanley's closes its advanced *Big Run Trail*—a three-mile backcountry run that culminates down a steep hill—at 2:30 p.m. Intermediate *Rooker* and *Scenic Trails* also offer some steep sections and access the backcountry, staying open until dusk.

Beginners can use a half-hour-long warm-up jaunt that loops or leads to several intermediate trails. Hanley's easier terrain meanders past bogs, meadows, and a beaver pond, while views of North Mountain and Eaglesmere across the valley are afforded from surrounding trails.

Heaps of snowfall blanket the region most winters, allowing 50 skiable days per year on average. Over 90 days of touring were available during the blizzard season of 1995-96. Powder sticks around a lot longer at this elevation, and it often snows here when it's dry elsewhere in the region.

Hanley's trails are marked by letters, and there's a warming hut, with microwave, at the trailhead. The lodge offers rentals, instruction, and guided tours, and a restaurant sits nearby. Other winter activities include a community-operated ice toboggan slide in town, several nearby snowmobile trails on state-run land, and two miles of easy ski touring at nearby World's End State Park, which also offers cabin rentals. Two miles away in Eaglesmere there are several beautiful but pricey Bed & Breakfasts, a few quaint country inns, and more reasonable rates at the Sonestown Hotel, eight miles out of town.

Information

Trail Fees
- Weekend $10/day; $23/day with rental
- Weekday $7/day
- rentals by reservation

Rentals (trail fee included)
- 300 sets: Karhu skis, Solomon step-in bindings (touring skis only)
- Full day $21; Half day $17; Friday-Sunday $35

Instruction (with advanced notice)
- Private $18; Group $10

Lodging/Dining
Nearby in Eaglesmere:
The Flora Villa Bed & Breakfast: old Victorian house; (717) 525-3245
Shady Lane Bed & Breakfast; (717) 525-3394
The Crestmont Inn, with lounge; (717) 525-3519
The Eaglesmere Inn, with lounge; (717) 525-3273
Sonestown Hotel: moderately priced, 8 miles from Eaglesmere; (717) 482-3000
The Lodge in Eaglesmere: large dormitory with 9 rooms, hot tub, excellent for large groups; (717) 525-3169
- Cottage rentals available in Eaglesmere (call Hanley's Happy Hill)

Sterling Inn

Sterling Inn

South Sterling, PA 18460

Information/Reservations: 1-800-523-8200
Local: (717) 676-3311
Operating Hours: 9 a.m.-5 p.m.
Elevation: 1,900 feet
Average Annual Snowfall: 60 inches

Getting There

- **From New York/New Jersey:** Take I-84 or I-80 west. From I-84, take Exit 6 and follow Route 507 south, then take Route 191 south in Newfoundland, and follow 4 miles to the inn. From I-80, bypass Stroudsburg, then bear right on I-380 north to Route 423 north (Tobyhanna). Turn left on Route 191 and follow to Sterling Inn.
- **From points south:** Follow the Northeast Extension of the Pennsylvania Turnpike to Exit 35, then follow Routes 940 east, 423, and 191 north to the inn.

Cross-country skiing at the Sterling Inn, located in the heart of the Pocono Mountains, is just a small feature of this posh country inn and resort. The moderate, five-mile touring system offers varied landscapes and is snowmobile tracked. Unfortunately, it's available only to guests of the inn, and inconsistent snowfall limits skiable days.

Most of the skiing here is easy, punctuated by a scenic beginner trail that skirts Sterling's lake. Six connecting trails meander through open fields and woodlands. Slightly more challenging terrain can be found on upper hiking trails that lead up the ridge of the Pocono Mountains. Trails are nameless but are well marked by color blazes.

Sterling recently erected a new ski shop and purchased a new line of rental equipment after its previous building succumbed to fire. The inn also offers its guests ice-skating on its lake, snow tubing, and nearby horse-drawn sleigh rides and an ice toboggan slide. The historic lakeside town of Eaglesmere sits two miles from Sterling, where inn guests can explore the Gas Light Village specialty shops and Cheney's Gallery and Craft Shop.

More novice ski touring trails can be found at nearby Tobyhanna State Park (four miles away), and Promised Land and Gouldsboro State Parks. Additionally, four Pocono Mountain downhill ski resorts are within 20 miles of Sterling.

Information

Trail Fees: Free to inn guests
Rentals
- 60 sets: Alpina touring skis
- $11/day, $7/half-day

Instruction
- Free beginner lesson for inn guests

Lodging/Dining
- 54 rooms at the inn, including standard suites and a few Victorian fireplace suites
- Indoor pool and Jacuzzi; fine dining in the Hearthstone Dining Room
- Midweek discount ski packages available

Stone Valley Recreation Area

Stone Valley Recreation Area
108 Business Services Building
University Park, PA 16802

Ski Report/Information: (814) 863-0762
Internet: http://www.psu.edu/Stone_Valley
Operating Hours: sunrise to sunset
Elevation: 1,000 feet
Average Annual Snowfall: 48 inches

Getting There
- **From I-80:** Take the Boalsburg Exit onto Route 45, which turns into Route 26, then follow signs from Route 26 to Stone Valley Recreation Area/Shaver's Creek Environmental Center.
- **From Baltimore/Washington, DC:** Take I-695 to I-83 north past Harrisburg, then pick up Route 15 north to I-80 west and follow directions above.

Part of and operated by Pennsylvania State University, Stone Valley's 25-mile multi-use trail network winds through a wooded backdrop of tall pine and parallels several streams. It's a big-time destination for intermediate to expert skiers, with little in the way of novice terrain. Regrettably, natural conditions vary: Skiing opportunities can be few and far between when Mother Nature doesn't cooperate. Just nine skiable days were available during the warm 1996-97 season. During normal winters, Stone Valley averages 25 days.

When conditions permit, the recreation area grooms roughly 11 miles of track, including the popular 1.25-mile circular-loop *Lake Trail.* Twelve other trails feature mainly rolling, hilly terrain, with steeply pitched downhill runs and long uphill climbs. *Iron Stone* and *Mid-State* trails are long, difficult runs that, on occasion, are tracked by snowmobiles, though other skiers tend to pack the narrow trails down sufficiently themselves. All trails are marked by color blazes and numbered intersection markers.

The concession holds private and group Nordic instruction, but gave up renting equipment last year. On-site winter lodging is available in 11 cabins, while nearby State College (15 miles) hosts several bed & breakfasts and hotels/motels. Families bringing the kids can use the sledding hills off the Civil Engineering Lodge's west entrance. Additionally, ice-skating (with rentals) and ice fishing are offered on the Lawrence J. Perez Lake, near the east entrance. Stone Valley's Lake Winter Extended Fishing program runs until the end of February.

Information

Trail Fees/Rentals: None
Instruction
- Private $18/hour
- Group $12/hour

Lodging/Dining
On-site
- Year-round cabins, $11/night

Nearby (State College)
Bed & Breakfasts:
Fairmount B&B; (814) 237-1101
Ginther's B&B; (814) 234-0772

Brewmeister's B&B; (814) 238-0015
Cooke Tavern B&B; (814) 422-8787
Windswept Farm B&B; (814) 355-1233
Hotels/Motels:
Days Inn at Penn State; 1-800-258-DAYS
Hampton Inn, State College; 1-800-HAMPTON
Ramada Inn, State College; (814) 238-3001

Callender's Windy Acre Farms

Callender's Windy Acre Farms

RD #2, Box 174
Thompson, PA 18465

Ski Report/Information: (717) 727-2982
Operating Hours: 10 a.m.-sunset Friday-Monday;
Tuesday-Thursday by appointment
Elevation: 1,989 feet
Average Annual Snowfall: 40 inches

Getting There

- **From New York/New Jersey:** Take I-80 west to I-380 north and follow to I-81 north, then take Exit 64 (Lennox). Bear left on Exit 106 south for 500 yards, then turn right on Route 92 north for 8 miles. Turn right off Route 92 at the sign in Thompson and follow for 7 miles. Turn left on Route 171 north, traveling 1 mile through Thompson, and make a right turn at the firehouse. Follow 2.5 miles and turn right into the driveway at Callender's.
- **From Philadelphia and points south:** Take the Northeast Extension of the Pennsylvania Turnpike to its end at Clarks Summit, then pick up I-81 north to Exit 64 (Lennox) and follow directions above.

Located in Pennsylvania's northeast corridor in Susquehanna County, Callender's is a dairy farm that turns into a cross-country touring center during the winter. Skiers have nearly 10 miles of marked trails through meadows, pastures, open fields, and logging and maple-sap roads, all flanked by scores of maple trees that are tapped each spring to make syrup. With the farm's overwhelmingly easy grade and snowmobile-groomed track, Callender's makes for a leisurely Nordic skiing excursion.

The novice *Maple Trail* is a flat trek through maple woods—an ideal first run. The longer and more intermediate *Blackbear Trail* winds outside the perimeter of Callender's network over steady, rolling hills. The *Windy Meadows* trail is aptly named: It's a wide, open jaunt through an exposed windy tip of Callender's meadow area. There's also a scenic run past an evergreen swamp area on the novice *Evergreen Trail*.

The farm has managed over 200 skiable days over the last three years, including 90 during 1995-96. Callender's also draws a growing number of snowshoers, and rents eight sets of snowshoes from its concession. Outstanding alpine skiing is within 20 miles at Elk Mountain, and a section of the state's northeastern Rails-to-Trails project is just a few miles away for winter hiking and ski touring.

Information

Trail Fees
- $10.50/day with rentals; $7/half day
- $5/day without rentals
- * Reduced rates for children under 12

Rentals
- 100 sets of touring skis: Fisher, Trak, Asnes, Voltenen childrens' skis
- 8 sets of snowshoes

Instruction: By appointment only
Lodging/Dining
Within 5 miles
- **Nethercott Inn/B&B**, Starrucca; (717) 727-2211
- **Jefferson Inn/B&B**, Thompson; (717) 727-2625
- * For more nearby lodging/dining information, see Elk Mountain, page 43.

Crystal Lake
Ski Center

Crystal Lake Ski Center

RR 1, Box 308
Hughesville, PA 17737

Ski Report: (717) 584-4209
Information/Reservations: (717) 584-2698
E-mail: clcamps@aol.com
Operating Hours: 9 a.m.-5 p.m. weekends/holidays
Elevation: 1,500 feet-2,100 feet
Average Annual Snowfall: 50 inches
Getting There

• **From I-80:** Take Exit 31 (Interstate 180), following 180 west to Route 220 north to Hughesville.

Continue on Route 220 for 5 miles to Tivoli, then turn left at the sign for Crystal Lake Camp/Ski Center, and follow 7 miles to the area.

• **From Washington, DC:** Take I-495 to I-270. Follow I-270/Route 15 through Frederick, Gettysburg, and Harrisburg all the way to I-80. Turn east on I-80 for 1 mile across the Susquehanna River, then take Exit 31 (Interstate 180), and follow directions above.

• **From Philadelphia:** Take the Northeast Extension of the Pennsylvania Turnpike, then take I-80 west from the turnpike to Exit 31 (Interstate 180), and follow directions above.

Crystal Lake is one of the state's first cross-country touring centers—and arguably its best. Before opening in 1971, the area was known as Highlands Ski Center. It was moved from its former valley location to its present 2,100-foot elevation, where the cross-country operation benefited from a surge in skinny skiing's popularity during the mid-1970s. Crystal Lake is a member of the Cross-Country Ski Areas of North America, and was chosen as a host site of Ski Fest '96. The center used to hold numerous cross-country races, but ended the practice after complaints that competitions tarnished the laid-back atmosphere of the resort.

With 960 acres of mountain woodlands in a remote section of northern Pennsylvania, cross-country skiers have 24 miles of trails, 18 miles of which are machine groomed and track-set. There's an even mix of beginner to expert terrain, and an easy, two-mile stretch is equipped with snowmaking when lean natural conditions plague the area. Trails leading from the plateau's 2,100-foot summit drop 600 feet through forest-sheltered trails that hold snowfall longer than nearby valley locations. Crystal Lake doesn't lie in the state's major snow belt, but most winters allow between 30 and 60 days of skiing per year from mid-December through March.

When the snow arrives in full force, getting to the area can be a hairy task. Road conditions get very slippery during sudden temperature dips, freezing rain, or sudden snow squalls, so bring your tire chains along for the ride if you don't have a four-wheel-drive vehicle. The steep mountain doesn't get plowed regularly in snow-filled conditions, making access quite difficult.

The network is expertly maintained over a maze of short, winding, intersecting trails that roll past three lakes and several streams. Crystal Lake's Nordic terrain surrounds its small downhill ski area, which welcomes guests on any type of skis. Some of the steeper cross-country trails travel down to the alpine area, and skiers often use the lifts to get back up to their backwoods trails. Crystal Lake charges $1 per trip to reach the *Mountain* and *Laurel* trails.

Beginner-level terrain is in the slight majority, but 12 advanced trails offer numerous steeps and plenty of serpentine track. At the *Grand Central Station* intersection, skiers will find fast downhills and modest climbs, dips, and bumps. *Hungry Bear* trail is the expert's choice, featuring steep drops and tight switchbacks between *Whipple Mill* and *YoYo* trails. *Bear Creek* trail is a pleasant, long intermediate run with a steady pitch that breaks into sharper steeps and over a bridge toward the bottom.

There's a day lodge at the base that offers lunches in its restaurant, and Crystal Lake guests can reserve one of a limited number of partially equipped or primitive cabins accommodating up to 180 visitors. The cabins go quickly: Your best bet is to reserve them a full year in advance. Otherwise, the closest lodging to the isolated area is 30 minutes away in either Eaglesmere or Williamsport. The wealthy lakeside cabin community of Eaglesmere offers several well-appointed bed & breakfasts. Williamsport has a larger variety of accommodations, and skiers may wish to stay in the town's old lumbering community, where large frame houses built by lumber barons of yesteryear have since been converted into inns and restaurants.

Downhill Skiing

With just three open slopes and two tree-lined trails, Crystal Lake's alpine ski area simply doesn't measure up to its Nordic counterpart. A 250-foot vertical drop is 350 feet less than what the cross-country ski terrain offers, and a strong powder base virtually guarantees more skinny skiers on the backcountry trails. The area does get its fair share of use, though. It's an ideal place to learn the sport, and Telemark and Nordic skiers love the wide, open terrain. The center makes snow on four of its five slopes and features two surface lifts for uphill transport. It also offers a three-lane, lift-serviced snow tubing park, ice-skating, and ice fishing.

Other Winter Sports

On-site
Three-lane **snow tubing** area, with tow lift; rates: $10/day, $7/half day
Telemark, cross-country skiers, and **snowshoers** welcome on alpine slopes
Ice-skating, with rentals, and **ice fishing** offered on the lake near the rental shop

Information

Cross-Country Trail Fees
- $10 weekend
- $7 weekdays

Downhill Area Lift Tickets
- 9 a.m.-5 p.m.: weekday $15; weekends $20
- 6 p.m.-10 p.m.: weekday $10
  (*Call ahead to confirm weeknight opening)

Cross-Country Ski School
- Nordic, skating, and Telemark lessons
- Private $35/hour; semi-private $20/hour; group $10/hour

Downhill Area Ski School: 3-4 instructors: PSIA certified; Nordic rates apply

Cross-Country Ski Rentals
- Touring and Telemark skis and snowshoes
- $7/weekday, $10/weekend; Telemark skis: $15

Downhill Ski Rentals: $7-$15

Lodging: On-site
- 12 cabins (2 with kitchens) sleeping 6-50 people
- 2 primitive cabins without electricity, running water, or bedding (*Cabins by reservation only, often a full year in advance)

Nearby
See Hanley's Happy Hill Touring Center, *page 199, for more lodging information in Eaglesmere*

Williamsport area (28 miles away)
The Reighard House Bed & Breakfast: beautifully restored inn; (717) 326-3593
Snyder House Victorian Bed & Breakfast, set in the downtown restored lumbering community; (717) 326-0411
Holiday Inn; (717) 326-1981
Econo Lodge; (717) 326-1501

Dining/Après-ski: On-site
- Restaurant at base area

Nearby
- **Herdic House Restaurant**, next-door to **Snyder House Victorian B&B** in Williamsport; (717) 322-0165
See Hanley's Happy Hill Touring Center, *page 199, for more dining information in Eaglesmere*

10

Skytop Lodge

Skytop Lodge

One Skytop Rd
Skytop, PA 18357

Ski Report/Information: (717) 595-7401
Operating Hours: 9:30 a.m.-12:30 p.m./1:30 p.m.-
4:30 p.m. Friday-Monday
Elevation: 1,700 feet
Average Annual Snowfall: 50 inches

Getting There

- **From New York/New Jersey:** Take I-80 west through the Delaware Water Gap toll booth, then turn right at Exit 52. Stay in the inner lane and bear left on Route 447 north for 25 minutes. Then travel through the village of Canadensis, turn right onto Route 390, and follow signs 3 miles to Skytop.
- **From the Northeast Extension of the Pennsylvania Turnpike:** Take Exit 35, then take Route 940 east. Follow 940 to Route 390 north and look for Skytop signs.

Skytop Lodge is a sprawling estate and lavish resort with unlimited year-round activities on its 5,500 acres. The lodge offers both cross-country and alpine skiing free to guests only, closing the trails to outsiders. The Nordic trail network covers 12 miles on sections of the lodge's golf course and, to a larger degree, through forest and wetlands surrounded by pine, birch, and oak. Skiers will find a mix of rolling and flat terrain past scenic waterfalls, trout streams, and beaver ponds, with spectacular summit vistas of Pocono valleys. Without the benefit of major snowfall in the area, the cross-country operation is open sporadically, at best, as conditions permit. But with enough natural powder, a small portion of the trail system is groomed by snowmobile track. The flat, beginner loop on the golf course offers the option of doubling back or accessing the more expansive but relatively flat backcountry.

The lodge's small downhill ski area sits next to Skytop Lake. Six trails over a 295-foot vertical drop are served by two poma lifts and 100 percent snowmaking. Skytop's alpine trails generally get more action than the Nordic trails, catering mainly to families and children. Instruction and rentals are available for downhill skiing, while instruction, but no rentals, is offered for cross-country skiing. The lodge also has an outdoor ice-skating pavilion (with rentals), snowshoe rentals for the golf course trail, guided tours of the backcountry, and a toboggan slide over the lake that's open under freezing temperatures. Inn guests often use the Pocono Mountains' Camelback (*page 35*) and Alpine Mountain (*page 16*) ski areas, both within 20 miles.

Information

Trail Fee: Included in lodging packages
Rentals
- 60 sets of touring skis: mostly Atomic
- 100 sets of alpine skis: Head, Atomic
- $15/full day, $10/half day

Instruction
- Alpine ski school on weekends by appointment

- Nordic lessons by appointment only
- Private $35/hour; Group $12-$16/hour

Lodging/Dining
- Skytop Lodge offers mini, family, and VIP suites (meals provided with rates) and several bed & breakfast rooms

Camp Spears Eljabar/YMCA

11

Camp Spears Eljabar/YMCA

RD 1, Dingmans Ferry, PA
Ski Report/Information: (717) 828-2329

Operating Hours: 9 a.m.-4 p.m. weekends/holidays
Elevation: 1,800 feet
Average Annual Snowfall: 50 inches

Getting There
- **From I-84 west (New York):** Follow I-84 west to Exit 9 (Lord's Valley/Dingman's Ferry). Then turn left after Exit to Route 739 south. Follow Route 739 for approximately 8 miles, and look for Camp Spears signs on the right.
- **From I-84 east:** Take Exit 9 (Lord's Valley/Dingman's Ferry), turn right, and follow directions above.
- **From New Jersey:** Take I-80 west to Route 15 north, which turns into Route 206 north, and follow to Route 560 north. Then turn right at the blinking light, follow over Dingman's Ferry Bridge to Route 739 north, and look for Camp Spears signs.

Camp Spears is a YMCA-operated cross-country ski center set in the Pocono Mountains, with 9.5 miles of machine-groomed novice trails. Located just miles from the Delaware River and the Delaware Water Gap National Recreation Area, Camp Spears is a loop system of interconnecting trails through woodlands and meadows, and around several wetland bogs and private 42-acre lake. The center is a big draw for conference groups and families, offering a variety of near-flat, easily negotiable trails marked by signposts and arrows. Its only advanced trail is the *Grand Loop*, which holds moderately steep ascents and drops on slightly more narrow track, but is still suitable for beginners. Sporadic snowfall and weekend-only hours provide just 10 to 20 skiable days per season on average.

Information

Trail Fee
- Free to YMCA members
- $5/all others

Rentals
- Adult $15/day
- Ages 11 and under $10/day

Instruction: Group lesson $6
Lodging/Dining
Motels/hotels 8 miles away in Milford; Call (717) 828-2329 for information

Elk Valley Cross-Country Touring Center

12

Elk Valley Cross-Country Touring Center

7085 Van Camp Rd
Girard, PA

Ski Report/Information: (814) 474-2356
Operating Hours: 9 a.m.-9 p.m. daily
Elevation: 200 feet
Average Annual Snowfall: 82 inches

Getting There
- **From Ohio and New York State:** Follow I-90 into Pennsylvania and take Exit 4 (Fairview) onto Route 98, heading south for roughly 2 miles, and follow signs to Elk Valley.
- **From I-79 in western Pennsylvania:** Follow I-79 north to I-90 west and follow directions above.

T ucked away in the northwestern slip of Pennsylvania, 15 miles from Lake Erie, is Elk Valley Touring Center. Though it sits just north of a major Great Lakes snow belt, Elk manages enough residual effect to provide over 70 skiable days per year on average. Its woodland loop system, at an altitude of only 200 feet, begins and ends at the lodge and golf course area, with 18 miles of snowmobile-groomed track. The touring center hosts eight serpentine trails of varying degrees of difficulty, marked by tree signposts. Advanced gliders can practice turning on several wide areas with changing pitches. Crowd favorite *2J* trail flows two miles on steadier track, with a hilltop view of Lake Erie that's afforded on clear days. The east-end *Eurica* trail once held a bridge over its track, but a recent storm washed it out, leaving skiers with the option of hightailing it back or connecting with one of three adjoining trails. The golf course cart path is straight and wide, and well groomed to accommodate beginner skiers.

Cross-country enthusiasts can also enjoy Presque Isle State Park—a 3,200-acre peninsula that juts seven miles out into Lake Erie. Seven miles of groomed track and open areas are offered throughout the park, replete with remarkably scenic terrain and varied wildlife. There's an inviting fireplace at the trailhead cabin, and ski equipment is rented here as well. Call the park office at 814-833-7424 for more information.

Elk is a short drive from Erie—Pennsylvania's third-largest city—which has a thriving downtown area and an abundance of restaurants, bed & breakfasts, inns, and hotels. Guests new to the area will discover an assortment of urban trappings, including museums, specialty shops, and events and activities at the Presque Isle Bay downtown area.

Information

Trail Fee
- $6.50/day
- Season pass $50

Rentals
- 70 sets of touring skis
- $6/day

Instruction: By appointment only

Nearby Lodging

Riverside Inn, Erie: historic, luxurious inn and Concord Dining Room; 1-800-964-5173

Best Western Motel, 2 miles from Elk; (814) 838-7647

Raspberry House Bed & Breakfast, Erie; (814) 734-8997

Rooster Ridge Bed & Breakfast, Erie; (814) 756-5135

Spencer House Bed & Breakfast, Erie; (814) 454-5984

Dining

On-site
- Short-order restaurant/bar in fireplace lodge

Nearby

Plymouth Tavern, Erie; (814) 452-6210

Sullivan's Pub & Eatery, Erie; (814) 452-3446

The Waterfront Seafood & Steakhouse, Erie; (814) 459-0606

STATE PARKS AND FORESTS

All Pennsylvania state parks and forests, excluding the full touring center at Laurel Ridge State Park *(see page 196)*, offer free use of their trail systems for cross-country skiing and/or hiking. A small number of state parks offer equipment rentals and instruction. Call the park offices for trail maps (usually no charge), information, and current snow conditions. Pennsylvania state park office hours are 8 a.m. to 4 p.m., Monday through Friday. Keep in mind that some of the following addresses listed for state parks are for their park headquarters, and are not necessarily the location of their trail systems.

Southwest Pennsylvania

Blue Knob
State Park

13

Blue Knob State Park

RR 1, Box 449
Imler, PA 16655-9407

Ski Report: (814) 239-5111
Information/State Park Office: (814) 276-3576
Operating Hours: 8 a.m.-dusk daily
Elevation: 2,100 feet-2,500 feet
Average Annual Snowfall: over 100 inches

Highly regarded as Pennsylvania's most challenging alpine ski area, Blue Knob's surrounding state park land also has an enormous expanse of terrain for cross-country skiing. With an elevation that ranks among the highest in the state, the extensive, forested Nordic network provides excellent scenery on the foothills of the Appalachian plateau and beautiful vistas of the topography below. Bountiful snowfall graces Blue Knob's mountaintops, providing over three months of ski touring during strong winters. Its north-facing mountain and high altitude help keep powder stashes around long after the last snowfall.

Most visitors are of the beginner variety, and want nothing more than a field to try the sport. Others wish to explore some of the unmarked, rugged trails available throughout the mountain. Skiers have 5,600-plus acres of ungroomed, blaze-marked, terrain, with a huge trail system inside park boundaries that has numerous loop trails. Some trails are marked for Nordic skiing, while others are designated for hiking. Skiers are permitted on hiking trails, which are extremely narrow, more rugged, and quite challenging—even by expert standards. Skiers should use extreme caution on all park trails: Expect some incredibly steep drops, arduous climbs, varying trail widths, and a multitude of natural obstacles.

A popular touring run is offered on a designated seven-mile loop trail that makes use of four hiking trails. It has several steep grades, most of which are on roadways closed off to vehicles. The trail takes skiers from the start at the campground down the mountain toward the park office, then back across the Chappels Field unloading area. One of the problems, though, with skiing the terrain down to the state park office is that it's difficult to get back to your car from there. Trails are also marked somewhat poorly here with small red tags. The Chappels Field area near the campground (closed during winter) is good beginner turf, with several open areas for skiing. Most skiers, though, tend to stick near Blue Knob's summit golf course area, where they can traverse easy, open fields and not steer far from their vehicles.

Blue Knob's downhill ski area *(page 26)*, which lies primarily on state property, rents cross-country ski equipment at its summit lodge, and also features a cafeteria and lounge. Cross-country and Telemark skiers are welcome on its alpine trails as well.

Information

Rentals: Call Blue Knob Ski Resort for current rates; (814) 239-5111/1-800-458-3403

Lodging/Dining/Getting There
See Blue Knob Ski Resort, *pages 26*

14

Forbes State Forest

Forbes State Forest
P.O. Box 519
Laughlintown, PA 15655

Information: (412) 238-9533
Operating Hours: Dusk to dawn
Elevation: 2,500 feet-2,900 feet
Average Annual Snowfall: 110 inches

Getting There
• **Laurel Highlands Ski Touring Area:** From Pittsburgh (heading east), follow Route 30, which parallels the Pennsylvania Turnpike (70/76), to the top of Laurel Mountain. Then turn right onto Laurel Summit Road, and follow roughly 2 miles to

the state forest entrance. *From Route 30 heading west, follow to the top of the mountain and turn left onto Laurel Summit Road, then travel 2 miles to the state forest entrance.
• **North Woods Ski Touring Area:** From the Pennsylvania Turnpike (70/76), take Exit 9 (Donegal), then follow Route 31 east, passing Firetower Road. Drive down the road and turn left onto Tunnel Road (opposite the entrance to the stone quarry), then continue a half-mile to the small lot on the left and access trails from there.
• **Roaring Run Natural Area:** Take Exit 9 (Donegal) from the Pennsylvania Turnpike, following Route 31 east. Then turn right onto Firetower Road at the top of the mountain, which leads into Roaring Run.

High atop Pennsylvania's Laurel Highlands sits Forbes State Forest. Over 50 miles of well-marked backcountry trails is available in three separate areas: Laurel Highlands Ski Touring Area, North Woods Ski Touring Area, and Roaring Run Natural Area. Laurel Highlands is the most popular cross-country destination of the three areas, combining mostly flat track with a few rolling hills. The North Woods area features the steepest trails and is also widely used, while Roaring Run is rarely skied, though suitable for touring. Easily negotiable *Spruce Run* and *Summit Trails* are the Laurel Highlands' signature runs.

Another way to access the state forest (either North Woods or Roaring Run) is from Hidden Valley *(page 197)*. Its Nordic trail system utilizes much of Forbes' territory, though it surely doesn't advertise it. You'll have to pay a trail fee if you park at Hidden Valley, and if you park in the state forest and enter Hidden Valley's trails, they'll knock you up for a fee as well. There's plenty of parking at Forbes' three separate area lots, but little winter maintenance on the roads. When snow hits the area hard, as it's apt to do, it's wise to park at Hidden Valley and suck up its trail fee. Calling the state forest office also comes highly recommended before making the trip out here; They'll give you a snow, trail, and road report.

All state forest cross-country trails are marked by red rectangles. Hiking trails, which also accommodate skiing, are designated by blue marks. Snowmobilers have 80 miles of trail in surrounding areas, and are restricted from using any Nordic trails. Occasionally, skiers will encounter illegal snowmobilers, so keep your ears open for the sound of motors.

Information

Lodging/Dining
See Hidden Valley Ski Resort Nearby Lodging and Dining/Aprés-ski, *page 51, and* Seven Springs Resort, *page 57.*

Kooser State Park

15

Kooser State Park

RR 4, Box 256
Somerset, PA 15501-8509

Information: (814) 445-8673
Operating Hours: dusk to dawn
Elevation: 2,600 feet
Average Annual Snowfall: 130 inches

Getting There
- **From Pittsburgh:** Take the Pennsylvania Turnpike (70/76) and pick up Exit 9 (Donegal) onto Route 31, then follow signs for Kooser State Park.
- **From eastern points:** Take the Pennsylvania Turnpike (70/76) and pick up Exit 10 (Somerset). Then get on Route 31 west for roughly 12 miles, and follow signs for Kooser State Park.

Just across the highway from Forbes State Forest lies Kooser State Park—a popular cross-country skiing destination. The mountainous region receives heaps of snowfall each year, and Kooser gets a more-than-healthy portion of it at its high altitude, lingering long into spring. Located on the eastern foothills of the Laurel Mountain summit, Kooser offers a 1.5-mile groomed and marked trail that's suitable for novice skiers. The level trail crosses six bridges over Kooser Run and circles Kooser Lake, using an old railroad bed and park roads for easy skiing. The trail connects with other state park trails as well as Hidden Valley Touring Center's trails and its varied terrain. The 70-mile Laurel Ridge Hiking Trail also accommodates skiers, and can be accessed by the Kooser Tower.

Skiers can shack up in Kooser's rustic cabins, open year-round, with affordable Sunday through Thursday lodging rates. The park also rents a full line of equipment, by reservation only. Send a self-addressed, stamped envelope for maps and information of the area, or call the park office.

Information

Rentals: Ski rentals available inside the park at Winter Cabin Rentals; (814) 359-2893
Lodging/Dining:
On-site:
- 9 cabins for 4, 6, 7, or 9 persons; rates from $100-$150/weekend

Nearby: See Hidden Valley Ski Resort, On-site and Nearby Lodging and Dining/Aprés-ski, *page 51, and* Seven Springs Resort, *page 57.*

16

Ohiopyle State Park

Ohiopyle State Park
P.O. Box 105
Ohiopyle, PA 15470-0105

Information: (412) 329-8591
Elevation: 2,600 feet
Average Annual Snowfall: 90 inches
Getting There
• **From western points along the Pennsylvania Turnpike (70/76):** Take Exit 9 (Donegal) and turn

left onto Route 31. Then travel 2 miles and turn right onto Route 381. Follow Route 381 for 25 miles heading south into Ohiopyle State Park.
• **From eastern points (Washington, DC, Harrisburg, New York):** Take the Pennsylvania Turnpike (70/76) to Exit 10 (Somerset), and turn right into Somerset. Then take Route 281 south and follow for 25 miles to Confluence. Continue 3 miles uphill, turn right at the church onto Sugarloaf Road, and follow 9 miles to Ohiopyle.

Located five miles from West Virginia and Maryland on Pennsylvania's southern tip, Ohiopyle's 30-mile, marked, ungroomed trail system holds some challenging terrain for advanced skiers. Steep drops, long climbs, and near-singletrack width mark many of its trails. There's also a bike trail alongside the river that can be used for ski touring. But it's the striking scenery that makes Ohiopyle a destination not to be passed up. Skiers can traverse pristine trails along the Youghiogheny River Gorge and spot waterfalls along Jonathan and Cucumber Runs. Other trails offer views of river rapids and connect with nearly 200 acres of open land. There is one trail available for snowmobilers, so be on the lookout. Ohiopyle's parking lot offers plenty of spaces. Get a trail map from the park office and access the trails directly from there.

Information

Nearby Lodging
Stone House Bed & Breakfast, Farmington; (412) 329-8876
Laurel Highlands River Tours (guest house), Ohiopyle; 1-800-472-3846

The Lodge at Chalk Hill, on Route 40; 1-800-833-4283
National Trails Motel, Markleysburg; (412) 329-5531

In Addition: Pennsylvania's Laurel Highlands Region

The towering-elevation region of southwestern Pennsylvania's Laurel Highlands hosts an array of winter recreation that extends beyond its outstanding alpine and cross-country skiing. The following is a list of winter activities offered at selected state parks and forests.

• **Blue Knob State Park**; (814) 276-3576: 8 miles of **snowmobile trails, ice-skating**
• **Forbes State Forest**; (412) 238-9533: 80 miles of **snowmobile trails**
• **Keystone State Park**; (412) 668-2939: 5 miles of **snowmobile trails, ice-skating, ice fishing, sledding**
• **Laurel Hill State Park**; (814) 445-7725: 10 miles of **snowmobile trails, ice-skating, ice fishing**
• **Laurel Ridge State Park**; (412) 455-3744: 2 miles of **snowmobile trails**
• **Ohiopyle State Park**; (412) 329-8591: 19 miles of **snowmobile trails, sledding**
• **Prince Gallitzin State Park**; (814) 674-1000: 20 miles of **snowmobile trails, ice-skating, ice fishing, ice boating, sledding**

For more information on recreation and lodging/dining in the Laurel Highlands, contact:
Laurel Highlands Visitors Bureau, 120 E. Main Street, Ligonier, PA 15658; (412) 238-5661

South-Central Pennsylvania:

Caledonia State Park

17

Caledonia State Park

40 Rocky Mountain Road
Fayetteville, PA 17222-9610

Information: (717) 352-2161
Elevation: 1,000 feet to 1,200 feet
Average Annual Snowfall: 38 inches

Getting There
- **From Washington, DC:** Take I-495 to I-270 and follow to Route 15 north to Gettysburg. Then take Route 30 west and follow signs for Caledonia.
- **From the Pennsylvania Turnpike (70/76):** Take the Carlisle Exit (near Harrisburg) and get on I-81 south. Then take Exit 8 (Scotland) and turn south on Route 997. Follow 6-8 miles and take Route 30 east, then travel 2 miles to the intersection of Routes 30 and 233. Turn left here, take the first road to the left, and follow to the park office.

Caledonia doesn't get the snowfall numbers necessary for consistent skiing opportunities, but when the powder falls in excess it can be a worthwhile venture. Ten miles of marked track over seven trails is available, including two difficult miles of the rugged Appalachian Trail. Remaining runs are mainly flat, intersecting with several streams. Visitors can use any skiing/hiking trails that are suitable for them, though many aren't recommended, including *Charcoal Harth*, *Ramble*, and *Whispering Pine* trails. *Charcoal Harth* is quite steep, traveling up one side to the mountain's summit and back down on a difficult loop trail. *Ramble* is set partially near a swampy area and also has steep areas that are too difficult to negotiate on skis.

The most appropriate skiing trail is *Thaddeus Stevens*—a fairly flat meander that's about a mile long. Guest will also find *Midland* trail to their liking. It's a nice, level jaunt that runs roughly three-quarters of one mile. Most beginners who use Ohiopyle take advantage of its baseball field, which opens up 20 acres of wide-open skiing.

None of the terrain is groomed or maintained for skiers, and bridges are a particular problem because they're designed for flood planes. Skiers have to step up to some of the bridges rather than glide over them.

Located 10 miles east of Interstate 81, near Chambersburg and Gettysburg, Caledonia offers two large, modern cabins that stay open during winter months.

Information

Lodging/Dining
On-site
- 2 modern cabins, up to 10 persons each; Call the state park office for information

Nearby
- *See* Ski Liberty, *page 71*

18

Cowans Gap
State Park

Cowans Gap State Park

HC 17266
Fort Loudon, PA 17224-9801

Information: (717) 485-3948
Elevation: 2,000 feet
Average Annual Snowfall: 80 inches

Getting There

- **From Pittsburgh:** Take Route 30 and follow to the top of Tuscarora Mountain. Turn left at the signs for Cowans Gap State Park onto Augwick Road and follow roughly 5 miles into the park.
- **From Route 30 heading west:** Follow Route 30 onto Route 75 north at Fort Loudon. Then travel approximately 4 miles, turn left on Richmond Furnace Road, and follow 3 miles to Cowans Gap State Park.

Located smack in the middle of Buchanan State Forest, Cowans Gap has a wide variety of terrain throughout its 10 miles for cross-country skiers. *Ski Trail* is only a half-mile long, but it's not necessarily for beginners. The terrain is rather rocky and generally unsuitable for skiing. Plenty of other trails are available, including the *Lakeside Trail*—a novice, 1.25-mile run that circles the lake over primarily level track. *Overlook Trail* climbs 1.5 miles on steady terrain to a mountain summit vista. From there skiers can access state forest game land trails. This section is tricky and rather steep, though, and should be reserved for strong intermediates and experts. The trail also features a fire road off to the left, which leads back to the valley over eight or nine miles of track. Unfortunately, it dead ends on an unskiable road, so skiers have to turn around.

Advanced skiers can also access part of the 220-mile *Tuscarora Trail* that cuts through parts of Cowans Gap on a considerably steep area. Its narrow singletrack has many rocky sections, and closes down when strong storms force tree limbs and debris onto its course. The *Tuscarora Trail* winds through a large section of central Pennsylvania, and dead ends on the Appalachian Trail.

Most guests prefer to roam unplowed parking lots, the campground area, and park roads, in addition to logging and fire roads that run throughout the mountain. All roads are skiable: The park plows one lane for car access.

Information

Lodging
- 10 rustic cabins for up to 4 persons, with adjacent showers/toilets

19

Gifford Pinchot
State Park

Gifford Pinchot State Park

2200 Rosstown Road
Lewisberry, PA 17339-9787

Information: (717) 432-5011
Elevation: 470 feet
Average Annual Snowfall: 35 inches

Getting There

- **From Baltimore/Washington, DC:** Take I-95 north to I-695 west to I-83 north. Then pick up Exit 13, heading west on Route 382. Take Route 177 west from there and follow signs to the state park office.
- **From I-83 south:** Take Exit 15, pick up Route 177 west, and follow signs to the park office.
- **From the Pennsylvania Turnpike (70/76):** Take Exit 18 onto I-83 south and follow directions above.

Located a few miles from Ski Roundtop—a popular alpine ski area for Baltimore and southern Pennsylvania residents *(page 75)*—Gifford Pinchot affords eight miles of marked, ungroomed cross-country/hiking trails through pine and evergreen countryside. Its 12 trails form a series of interconnecting loops. Skiers can choose from short trips under one mile or longer, more undulating loop trails. Most runs are plenty wide for beginner skiers, with just a few small downhill sections on the network's 150-foot vertical drop. Two general areas are most served by skiers: state park trails, which join some flat beach and grassy turf areas, and the campground, which provides level, open skiing.

As Ski Roundtop downhillers can attest, the area isn't subject to great amounts of snowfall, so Nordic skiers have to be opportunists. The park plows the parking lots during snow storms, but only a limited number of spaces are available. There are, however, portable bathrooms open during winter months.

Information

Lodging/Dining
On-site
- 10 year-round modern cabins, sleeping 6-8 persons; Call park office for fees

Nearby
- *See* Ski Roundtop, Nearby Lodging and Dining/Aprés-ski, *page 78.*

Southeast Pennsylvania:

Delaware Canal State Park

20

Delaware Canal State Park
RR 1, Box 615 A
Upper Black Eddy, PA 18972-9540

Information: (610) 982-5560
Elevation: 700 feet
Average Annual Snowfall: 35 inches

Getting There
- **From Philadelphia and Allentown:** Follow Route 32/611, which parallels the 60-mile course and the Delaware River. Park anywhere in public areas, including county parks and public roads. Park-and-ski access can be found in the city of Easton; the towns of Robbsville, Rieglesville, and New Hope; Tinicum County Park; and the Virginia Forrest Recreation Area.
- **From eastern and western points**: Take I-80 or I-78 toward the Delaware River, exit onto Route 32/611, and follow directions above.

This Philadelphia and Allentown Nordic-skier attraction is a 60-mile-long tow path that runs parallel to old Delaware Canal. Over a century ago, mules would pull canal boats along the tow path. The trail starts in Easton and runs south to Bristol, just north of Philadelphia. Hundreds of roads intersect the path, including eight public recreation areas along the way. Many skiers prefer to park along River Road, north of Washington's Crossing. Route 32/611, which parallels the 60-mile course and the Delaware River that separates Pennsylvania and New Jersey, covers 40 miles of the path.

Its level terrain crosses some roads and other light obstructions, and is open to hiking, biking, horseback, and cross-country skiing. No side trails exist off the tow path, but there are several bridges connecting with points in New Jersey.

The area doesn't get enough snow to allow many skiable days per year, so waste no time getting out on the trails after a good snowfall—it's often gone in a few days. And the trail is so close to the Delaware River that its water effect often turns the snow into ice crystals quickly.

Northeast Pennsylvania:

21

Lackawanna State Forest

Lackawanna State Forest

401 Samters Bldg.
101 Penn Ave.
Scranton, PA 18503

Information: (717) 963-4561
Elevation: 1,000 feet
Average Annual Snowfall: 52 inches

Getting There
• **From the Northeast Extension of the Pennsylvania Turnpike:** Take Exit 35 (White Haven) onto Route 940 east, then turn left onto Route 115 toward Wilkes-Barre, crossing the Lehigh River. Then follow 1.25 miles to LR40042, turn right toward Thornhurst, then turn left onto LR 2016. Follow 4 miles to the trailhead on the right.
• **From I-81:** Take Exit 49 to Route 315 one mile to Dupont. At the second light in Dupont, turn left onto Suscon Road (southeast), which follows to Lackawanna State Forest after 10 miles. The trailhead is on the left, one mile east of the Luzerne/Lackawanna county line.

Near most major Pocono ski areas, Lackawanna State Forest offers 24 miles of cross-country touring on a multi-use and snowmobile trail system. There's a mix of flat and rolling terrain through woodlands and around small streams. Trails are marked by signposts and machine groomed by the park whenever possible. The winding, level terrain suits mostly novice skiers. The northern section's *Pinehill Vista* area is the major intersection, with several connecting trails.

Lackawanna sits in the village of Thornhurst, and skiers can access the forest from two parking lots along SR 2016, northwest of Thornhurst. The closest Pocono alpine ski area is Montage. Lodging isn't available at the state park, but winter camping is allowed anywhere within the park. Lackawanna keeps a map box and trail register a short distance from the trailhead.

Information

Lodging/Dining
See Montage Mountain Ski Area, Nearby Lodging and Dining/Après-ski, *page 56*.

North-Central Pennsylvania:

Elk
State Forest

22

Elk State Forest

RR 1, Route 155, Box 327
Emporium, PA 15834

Information: (814) 486-3354
Elevation: 1,500 feet
Average Annual Snowfall: 90 inches

Getting There
- **From eastern points off I-80:** Take Exit 22 heading north (Snowshoe) and take Route 144 to Moshannon. Then take Route 879 to Karthaus, and follow the Quehanna Highway to the trail system. There are several parking points here with access to the trail system.
- **From western points off I-80:** Take Exit 17 (Route 255 north) to Penfield and turn right at Penfield. Then travel south on Route 153 for roughly 4 miles, and turn left onto the state forest road to Parker Dam State Park.

The Quehanna Wild Area of Cameron County is the site of Elk State Forest, and its 25 miles of trails marked by blue paint blazes. Its remote location and snow-filled, extreme winters offer diverse topography and wildlife, including white-tailed deer and turkeys. Abandoned logging roads and railroad grades make up most of the system, with a host of switchbacks, steeps, and climbs to satisfy advanced skiers. The forest is so isolated and primitive, with occasionally brutal weather, that skiing is recommended only for experienced intermediates and experts. Local volunteer groups partially maintain the network of hiking and ski touring trails, though the terrain is mostly ungroomed.

There's no park office here, so call ahead to receive your trail map, available by calling 814-486-3354. The forest is located about 30 miles southwest of Ski Denton *(alpine skiing on page 66)*, where ample lodging and dining facilities are available.

Skiers can also use Sizerville State Park, which lies north of Emporium, and has a rental shop (closed last season, but likely re-opening). The park offers additional ski touring on snowmobile trails and blocked roads. Parking is available at the Sizerville State Park trailhead.

Information

Lodging/Dining
- *See* Ski Denton, Nearby Lodging and Dining/Aprés-ski, *page 70.*

Northwest Pennsylvania: Cook Forest State Park

Cook Forest State Park

P.O. Box 120
Cooksburg, PA 16217-0120

Information: (814) 744-8407
Operating Hours: 8 a.m. to dusk
Elevation: 1,520 feet
Average Annual Snowfall: 100 inches

Getting There
- **From eastern points:** Take I-80 to Exit 13, then follow Route 36 north to the state park.
- **From western points:** Take I-80 to Exit 8, then take Route 66 north to Leeper. Follow Route 36 south for 7 miles to the state park.

This 6,668-acre state park sits just outside the southern tip of the expansive Allegheny National Forest in one of Pennsylvania's heaviest snow belts. Skiers are afforded numerous winter days to wander through Cook's nine miles of marked trails. Virgin white pine and hemlock timber form the backdrop of the state park, designated by the National Park Service as a registered National Natural Landmark. The trail leading from the park concession drops off to an abandoned fire tower: Its stairs can be climbed to provide glimpses of surrounding vistas. Nearby Seneca Point Overlook also provides scenic photo opportunities of the Clarion River Valley.

Most skiers use the two beginner/intermediate trails, which consist mostly of steady terrain with a few sizable hills. Several side trails are available, as well as three dirt roads open in the winter months for ski touring and snowmobiling. Cook's trails, closed to snowmobilers, are sign-marked and machine groomed. The state park runs a rental concession at the entrance to Ridge Campground off Route 36, open mainly on weekends during agreeable weather and weekdays by appointment. For skiers who can do without amenities, there are 24 rustic cabins open year-round and 12 additional river cabins. Nearby deluxe accommodations can be found at Gateway Lodge—the four-seasons resort at the foothills of Cook Forest State Park on Route 36 in Cooksburg. The lodge has a fine-dining restaurant and offers ski rentals.

The North Country National Scenic Trail (NST) flows through part of Cook's network. The NST is one of the country's emerging trail systems, estimated to be 4,400 miles long, with over 1,400 miles open to the public in seven northern states.

Information

Rentals: 50 sets of touring skis; $8.50/day

Nearby Lodging: Gateway Lodge; (814) 744-8017

Oil Creek State Park

Oil Creek State Park

RD 1, Box 207
Oil City, PA 16301

Information: (814) 676-5915
Elevation: 1,200-1,300 feet
Average Annual Snowfall: 85 inches

Getting There
- **From I-80:** Take Exit 3 (Route 8 north), then turn right on Route 227 in Rouseville. Travel 2.8 miles and follow signs for Oil Creek State Park and directional arrows to cross-country skiing parking area. Numerous access points for skiing can be found along Route 8, with directional signs posted.

W estern Pennsylvania's snow belt provides enough powder in this region that it often lasts well into spring, and Oil Creek State Park provides the turf on which to cross-country ski. One of five state parks created through the Western Pennsylvania Conservancy, Oil Creek's 7,000-plus acres includes a 10-mile Nordic trail system (three marked trails) with groomed track on the plateau of its historic gorge's east rim. There's a one-mile connector road—and a 500-foot elevation difference—between the flood plain and the higher-lying rim of the gorge. The park also features a level, 9.7-mile bike path, which also serves winter ski tourists and hikers. It occupies an old railroad grade with a general width of about 8 feet.

Experts also have access to a 36-mile hiking trail that features lots of steeps and turns on narrow terrain, but it's considered too rugged for good skiing.

A warming hut is available, open weekends from 9 a.m. to 5 p.m., in which skiers can pick up trail maps and information and rest before a wood-burning fire. A reasonable number of parking spaces can be found at the beginner/intermediate trailhead near Plumer, as well as at the trail junction at the Drake Well Park and Oil Creek Park office. Maps are also offered at the park office, which lies about one mile from the ski trails, and a few shops rent equipment in nearby Oil City.

Information

Nearby Lodging

The Lamberton House Bed & Breakfast, Franklin; (814) 432-7908

McMullen House Bed & Breakfast, Titusville; (814) 827-1592

Oil Creek Lodge Bed & Breakfast, Titusville; (814) 677-4684

The Inn at Franklin; 1-800-535-4052

Corbett Inn, Oil City; (814) 676-0803

Holiday Inn, Oil City; (814) 677-1221

Nearby Dining

Hoss's Steak & Sea House, Oil City; (814) 677-3002

Famoore's Family Restaurant, Oil City; (814) 676-4789

Badland's Barbecue, Franklin; (814) 437-7427

Allegheny National Forest:
U.S. Department of Agriculture Forest Service

T he national forest encompasses 500,000 acres of woodlands, and several districts have trails equipped for cross-country skiing. Lodging is few and far between in the region, with a few inns and bed & breakfasts available, but winter camping is allowed anywhere within the forest.

Laurel Mill Cross-Country Ski/Hiking Area

25

Laurel Mill Cross-Country Ski/Hiking Area

Ridgway Ranger Station
Box 28A
Ridgway, PA 15853

Information: (814) 776-6172
TTY: (814) 726-2710

Elevation: 1,200 feet to 1,800 feet
Average Annual Snowfall: 80 inches

Getting There
• **From I-80:** Take Route 219 north at DuBois, then take Township Road 307 (Spring Creek Road) and follow signs for Laurel Mill Cross-Country Ski Area (located 3 miles west of Ridgway).

L aurel Mill is the most popular Nordic skiing site among national forest trail networks in Pennsylvania. The forest service grooms most trails, and cross-country ski races are held yearly. Roughly 10 miles of terrain includes seven trails ranging from under one mile to 3.2 miles. The terrain is mostly level, and not extremely difficult to negotiate, though a few steep downhill sections do exist.

Parking is plentiful, and there's a warming hut available at the trailhead. The area receives a fair shake of snow, allowing many ski opportunities each winter.

Information

Nearby Lodging
  Faircroft Bed & Breakfast, Ridgway;
  (814) 776-2539

The Post House Bed & Breakfast, Ridgway

---

26 | Brush Hollow Cross-Country Ski/Hiking Area

Brush Hollow Cross-Country Ski/Hiking Area
Ridgway Ranger District
Box 28A
Ridgway, PA 15853
Information: (814) 776-6172
TTY: (814) 726-2710

Elevation: 1,200 feet-1,800 feet
Average Annual Snowfall: 80 inches

Getting There
From I-80: Take Route 219 north at DuBois to Ridgway, then take Route 948 north for roughly 10 miles. Follow signs for Brush Hollow Cross-Country Ski Area.

B rush Hollow is another widely used cross-country ski area, but unlike Laurel Mill, its trails get no grooming. The terrain is much steeper, though, and attracts many expert Nordic skiers, particularly Telemarkers. Three major loop trails are available, two of which have solid vertical drops and climbs. *Challenger Loop* is suitable only for the advanced skier. The trail requires a bit more snow than other runs, considering its many changes in elevation and numerous nooks and crannies that get frequent sun exposure.

An overlook on Brush Hollow is breathtaking, and wildlife is abundant. Skiers will likely meet up with white-tailed deer and turkey, and may spot a black bear on rare occurrences. Adequate parking is available for 20 to 25 cars.

Information

Nearby Lodging
  The Kane Manor Country Inn/Bed & Breakfast;
  (814) 837-6522

Kane Motel, Kane; (814) 837-6161
Kane View Motel, Kane; (814) 837-8600
Reazley Hotel; (814) 837-9111

Westline Cross-Country Ski/Hiking Area

Westline Cross-Country Ski/Hiking Area
Bradford Ranger District
Bradford, PA 16701

Information: (814) 362-4613
Elevation: 1,464 feet to 2,611 feet
Average Annual Snowfall: 85 inches

Getting There
• **From I-80:** Take Route 219 north at DuBois and follow roughly 45 minutes past Ridgway. Then take Route 59 west and follow signs for Westline Cross-Country Ski Area.

When adequate snowfall permits, Westline is an ideal setting for cross-country skiing. Nearly 10 miles of track is available over five trails. Four trails are under 1.5 miles, while *Thundershower* provides four miles of steeper, more rugged terrain. The trail also holds a splendid view of Thundershower River, which flows into the old milling village of Westline. Parking is abundant off Route 59. Overnight accomodations and restaurants are in short supply in the area. Call the national forest office for further information.

Information

Nearby Lodging
  Westline Inn, 4 miles to the south

In Addition: Pennsylvania's Northern Alleghenies

There's a winter wonderland in the Northern Allegheny mountain range that offers an assortment of outdoor activities. **Snowmobilers** can explore over 300 miles of designated groomed trails throughout Allegheny wilderness. Many of the trails have taverns, restaurants, and services directly on their paths. For **cross-country skiers**, numerous groomed trail networks are available in prime snow country in the Allegheny National Forest, with warming huts on many of them. *(See page 219 for Allegheny National Forest cross-country skiing information.)* The Allegheny River Reservoir and surrounding lakes—stocked with walleye, perch, and bass—provide outstanding **ice fishing** opportunities. Call the Allegheny Fishing Hotline ((814) 726-0164) for updated information. And **dog sled racing** is another popular pastime in the Northern Alleghenies. The Bell Atlantic Classic is held each January at the national forest's Westline area and the Pennsylvania Dog Sled Classic runs each February at Chapman Dam State Park.

For more information on any of the following, call the Northern Alleghenies Vacation Region at **1-800-624-7802** or **(814) 726-1222**. Inquirers can also write to **P.O. Box 608, Tionesta, Pennsylvania 16353**, or E-mail: **TNA@PENN.COM**

Maryland:
   28. New Germany State Park
   29. Herrington Manor State Park
Other State Parks and Forests
   30. Cunningham Falls State Park
   31. Patapsco Valley State Park
   32. Greenbrier State Park
   33. Gunpowder Falls State Park

CROSS-COUNTRY SKIING:
MARYLAND/WEST VIRGINIA

West Virginia:
Cross-Country Ski Touring Centers
   34. Alpine Lake Resort Nordic Center
   35. Elk River Touring Center
   36. White Grass Ski Touring Center
   37. Canaan Valley Resort State Park
State Parks and Forests
   38. Cathedral State Park
   39. Blackwater Falls State Park
   40. Babcock State Park
   41. Pipestem Resort State Park
   42. Watoga State Park
   43. Coopers Rock State Forest

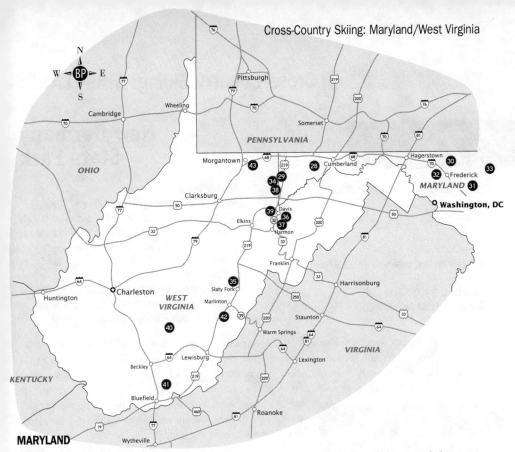

MARYLAND

Like its alpine ski scene, Maryland's cross-country terrain is limited, but nonetheless quite exceptional. New Germany and Herrington Manor State Parks form the backbone of Nordic skiing in Maryland, both of which benefit from Garrett County's strong, powder-packed winters and offer designated, groomed ski trails. Cabin rentals are available year-round at both parks, while ample accommodations can be found nearby. In January of 1997, the state incorporated a 1-800 reservation system for cabin rentals (1-800-432-CAMP). It's recommended that reservations be made one year in advance, since cabins go quickly.

WEST VIRGINIA

With the Mid-Atlantic's most abundant snowfall, it's no surprise that West Virginia hosts some of its best cross-country trail networks. White Grass and Elk River make up two of the state's three privately run Nordic touring centers. Each offers groomed, on-site trails and access to surrounding backcountry terrain. Several state parks hold touring centers or rental facilities on their trail networks, including Canaan Valley, Blackwater Falls, and Pipestem. Remaining state and national parks and forests offer ungroomed hiking/cross-country skiing systems—many of which provide more difficult, rugged terrain, without trail fees. Trail maps are available free of charge from park and forest headquarters, by mail or in person.

To facilitate cross-country skiing in the state, the West Virginia Department of Tourism offers a toll-free telephone number for many state parks and forests (1-800-CALL-WVA), from which guests can get free ski reports and information and reserve lodging at various state parks. The line is available weekdays from 8:30 a.m. to 4:30 p.m., and is listed herein at state parks/forests that it services.

Skiers will find on-site accommodations at many of West Virginia's touring centers and state parks, including lodges, houses, condominiums, chalets, townhomes, cabins, and campsites. State park cabins are equipped with electricity, modern kitchens and appliances, and bathrooms with showers, and can be rented by the day, for weekends, or for the week. Reservations here are strongly recommended, as these cabins—like the ones in Maryland—are very popular.

Cross-Country Skiing: MARYLAND:

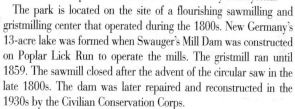

28

New Germany State Park

New Germany State Park

349 Headquarters Lane
Grantsville, MD 21536

Information: (301) 895-5453
TTY (for hearing impaired): (410) 974-3683

Elevation: 2,400-2,700 feet
Average Annual Snowfall: 110 inches

Getting There
- **From Washington/Baltimore:** Take I-70 west through Maryland to I-68 west. Follow I-68 to Exit 22, and turn left on Chestnut Ridge Road. Travel roughly 3.5 miles and turn left on New Germany Road, then follow 2 miles to New Germany State Park.
- **From Pittsburgh/Morgantown:** Take I-79 to I-68 east, then take Exit 22. Turn right on Chestnut Ridge Road and follow directions above.

Savage River State Forest's 52,812 acres includes New Germany State Park—a popular cross-country trail network in Garrett County. Heavy snowfall provides the perfect setting for ski touring on 12 miles of marked, groomed track on New Germany's nine-trail system. Some advanced terrain is available, but the trail system more realistically suits novice to intermediate skiers. Most runs are in the half-mile to 1.5-mile range, winding past streams, over bridges, and through Western Maryland forestland. Snowmobiles are prohibited from the cross-country trail system.

The park is located on the site of a flourishing sawmilling and gristmilling center that operated during the 1800s. New Germany's 13-acre lake was formed when Swauger's Mill Dam was constructed on Poplar Lick Run to operate the mills. The gristmill ran until 1859. The sawmill closed after the advent of the circular saw in the late 1800s. The dam was later repaired and reconstructed in the 1930s by the Civilian Conservation Corps.

Surrounding New Germany are miles and miles of state forest hiking trails on which advanced skiers can test their mettle. The six-mile *Poplar Lick* trail begins at New Germany, crossing four streams before ending at Savage River. Five other trails ranging from 1.5 miles to 24 miles are extremely narrow and rough. The state doesn't advertise Nordic skiing on these hiking trails because of their rugged nature: Skiers will encounter log barriers, steps, and other obstacles along the difficult terrain.

Visitors are charged a $2 park entrance fee on weekends and holidays, but have the parking lots completely plowed. Skiers can also wind down in the park's recreation hall and its fireplace and wood stove. Hot drinks and snacks can be found at New Germany's weekend-running concession, and nearby Meadow Mountain Ski Rental (301-689-8515) offers Nordic rentals, instruction, and backcountry tours.

Eleven year-round cabins offering two- to eight-person occupancy come fully equipped, including fireplaces, heat, electric stoves, water heaters, refrigerators, shower/bathrooms, cooking utensils, and full bedding.

Information

Lodging/Dining

On-site

- 11 log cabins (sleeping 2-8) from $65-$95/night to $325-$475/week; call (301) 895-5453 for more information
- Winter camping, with bathhouse; rates $10/night

Nearby

Carmel Cove Inn, Deep Creek; (301) 387-0067

Savage River Inn Bed & Breakfast, McHenry; (301) 245-4440

Country Inn Bed & Breakfast, McHenry; (301) 387-6694

Lake Point Inn Bed & Breakfast, McHenry; 1-800-523-LAKE, (301) 387-0111

Oak & Apple Bed & Breakfast, Oakland; (301) 334-9265

Deer Park Inn/Bed & Breakfast, Oakland; (301) 334-2308

Board Room Motel, with restaurant, Oakland; (301) 334-2126

* See Wisp Resort, *Nearby Lodging and Dining*, page 113, for further lodging and dining information.

Herrington Manor State Park

Herrington Manor State Park

222 Herrington Lane
Oakland, Maryland 21550

Information: (301) 334-9180
TTY (for hearing impaired): (301) 974-3683

Elevation: 2,400-2,700 feet
Average Annual Snowfall: 110 inches

Getting There

- **From Washington/Baltimore:** Follow I-70 west to I-68 west, passing Cumberland. Then exit off I-68 onto 14A south (Route 219 south), and travel roughly 19 miles before turning right on Mayhew Inn Road. Follow 4.5 miles, and turn left at the stop sign onto Oakland Sang Run Road. Then turn right on Swallow Falls Road and follow 5 miles to Herrington Manor State Park.
- **From Pittsburgh/Morgantown:** Take I-79 to I-68 east and follow directions above.

The 365-acre state park was originally part of a 2,000-acre tract donated to the state in 1906 by the Garrett brothers—of B&O Railroad fame—with the stipulation that the land be used for the protection of wildlife and advancement of forestry. Herrington Manor's name derives from Sgt. Abijah Herrington, who patrolled the surrounding forestland during the Revolutionary War.

Plentiful snowfall graces this picturesque section of the Alleghenies, with over 200 inches posted during the 1995-96 season. The park's loop trail system includes six miles of essentially flat, easily negotiable terrain around Herrington Lake. Its four wooded trails range from one to 2.5 miles, and are well marked by color names and blazes. Herrington Manor track sets the trail system when conditions permit, and another six miles of primitive trails are available for more experienced cross-country enthusiasts. Each January, Herrington Manor hosts a cross-country ski race on its groomed course.

In addition, there's a 5.5-mile trail that extends from the parking lot into Swallow Falls State Park, which also holds hiking trails suitable for Nordic skiing. The trail leading to Swallow Falls boasts several stream crossings before finishing with some scenic overlooks.

Skiers can base themselves in one of the park's 20 fully equipped log cabins situated in a pine-hemlock setting. The park also rents cross-country skis at its concession on weekends.

Information

Ski Rentals
- $13/day, $11/half day
- $22/two days

Lodging/Dining
On-site
- 20 fully furnished log cabins (with fireplaces), sleeping 2-6 persons; call (301) 334-9180 for rates and information

* Snack bar open on weekends at the concession

Nearby
- *See* New Germany State Park, *page 224,* and Wisp Resort, *page 109,* for more lodging and dining information

Other Maryland State Parks and Forests

Several of Maryland's 50 state parks and forests feature ungroomed hiking trails and open tracts of land that Nordic skiers are welcome to use. Outside of Garrett County, though, snowfall is much less prevalent, so skiers have to be opportunity-driven. Hiking trails are narrow enough to demand some experience on the part of skiers, but many novices use the parks' lots and any campgrounds and open fields available. The following is an abbreviated listing of state parks offering trail systems and/or available land for ski touring. Call the park offices for updated weather and trail conditions before departing.

30. Cunningham Falls State Park
14039 Catoctin Hollow Road
Thurmont, MD 21788
(301) 271-7574

This Frederick County park in the scenic Catoctin Mountains features a winding trail system that meanders past mountain streams and a 43-acre lake. Cunningham Falls is a 78-foot cascading waterfall inside a rocky gorge.

31. Patapsco Valley State Park
8020 Baltimore National Pike
Ellicott City, MD 21043
(410) 461-5005

Patapsco's 12,699 acres spans Baltimore, Howard, Carroll and Anne Arundel Counties, with five separate recreation areas.

32. Greenbrier State Park
21843 National Pike
Boonsboro, MD 21713
(301) 791-4767

Just 10 miles east of Hagerstown, Greenbrier's multi-use park permits cross-country skiing on its campground area and around its 42-acre man-made lake.

In Addition: Maryland's Ice Fishing

The state's best ice fishing can be found at Western Maryland's Deep Creek Lake and Savage River Reservoir, typically during January and February. The most abundant species are yellow perch and walleye, with smaller numbers of northern pike, trout, pickerel, crappie, and bass. The following rules should be observed for ice fishing.
- Only emergency vehicles are permitted on the ice of Deep Creek Lake.
- Fishermen should exercise extreme caution when ice conditions are unsafe from weather conditions or lake level fluctuations.
- Swimming and diving are restricted on any area of Deep Creek Lake where waters are covered by ice.

33. Gunpowder Falls State Park
10815 Harford Road
P.O. Box 5032
Glen Arm, MD 21057
(410) 592-2897

With 13,000 acres in Baltimore and Harford Counties, over 100 miles of hiking trails are available for Nordic skiers in the Gunpowder River Valley, including the gently pitched Northern Central Rail Trail.

WEST VIRGINIA:
Cross-Country Ski Touring Centers

Alpine Lake Resort Nordic Center

34

Alpine Lake Resort Nordic Center
Route 2, Box 99-D2
Terra Alta, WV 26764

Information: 1-800-752-7179, (304) 789-2481
Operating Hours: 9 a.m.-4:30 p.m. weekends

Elevation: 3,000 feet
Average Annual Snowfall: 150 inches

Lodging/Dining/Getting There
See Alpine Lake's *downhill area, page 114, and* Wisp Ski Resort, On-site and Nearby Lodging and Dining, *page 113.*

Surrounding Alpine Lake's small downhill ski area is a 15-mile cross-country trail network, also known as the Terra Alta Touring Center, that rambles through open rolling meadows, lakeside track, and backcountry woodlands. The full Nordic center lies in a prime snow area, with an extraordinary 300 inches having dropped during the stormy season of 1995-96 and over 150 inches last year. Its 3,000-foot elevation and north-facing tip of the Alleghenies doesn't hurt either. Ski seasons generally begin in December and extend into early April.

There's a nice mix of easy to difficult terrain over four trails that range from 2.8 miles to 7 miles, and about two-thirds of the track is machine groomed by the resort. The *Seven Bridges/Lakeside Loop* trail is the designated beginner loop that winds nearly three miles around Alpine Lake on extra-wide terrain. Six miles of ungroomed backcountry pine-woodland trails are available for more adventurous skinny skiers—most notably *Camp Rock* trail. It's a side run off the *Castle Rock* trail that leads to a West Virginia/Maryland historical boundary marker, and features several steep drops and natural barriers such as rocky outcroppings.

The Alpine Lake touring center offers cross-country rentals, instruction, guided tours, and a warming hut. Overnight guests can base themselves in one of 42 units and suites at the resort, which features an indoor heated pool, hot tub, sauna, and fitness center. And Maryland's Wisp Ski Resort is a short drive from Alpine Lake, with numerous on-site and nearby lodging options.

Information

Trail Fees
- $6.50/full day, $4.50/half day (combination alpine, Nordic, and sledding passes available)

Rentals
- $16/day, $11/half day
- Junior rates: $13/day, $9/half day

- Snowshoe rentals available (call resort for rates)

Instruction
(both classical and skating techniques)
- Private $20/hour
- Group $10/hour
- Free beginner lesson available with rental

35

Elk River
Touring Center

Elk River Touring Center

Highway 219
Slatyfork, WV 26291

Information/Ski Report: (304) 572-3771
Internet: http://www.ertc.com

Operating Hours: 8:30 a.m.-4:30 p.m. daily
Elevation: 2,700 feet to 4,400 feet
Average Annual Snowfall: 180 inches

Getting There

- **From I-81 in Virginia:** Take the 250 exit to Route 254 west through Stanton to Buffalo Gap, then take Route 42 south to Goshen. Follow Route 39 west to Marlinton, West Virginia, then take Route 219 north 15.5 miles to the sign for Elk River and turn left.
- **From northern West Virginia:** Take Route 219 south, travel 4 miles south of Snowshoe Road, and turn right at the sign for Elk River (1 mile past Slatyfork Post Office).

Elk River, along with nearby White Grass, make up two of the most prominent cross-country touring centers in the Mid-Atlantic. Situated on a 100-year-old sheep farm on the headwaters of the Elk River—10 miles from Snowshoe Resort—the center's extensive and varied terrain includes nine miles on-site and another 31 miles in the adjoining Monongahela National Forest, off Scenic Highway. Skiers can plow through a mixed backdrop of fields and meadows, dense hardwood forest, logging roads, and railroad grades. A nominal trail fee is charged for use of Elk's trails, while stronger skiers can explore trails in the Monongahela with free access. Elk River's Nordic Specialty Shop offers full rentals and instruction, and full-moon tours are available during agreeable conditions.

The Blizzard of '95-'96 overwhelmed Elk, dumping an incredible 300 inches of snow on the mountain and providing 85 days of skiing, despite somewhat difficult access by car. Typical ski seasons run from mid-December to mid-March. The touring center is increasing its terrain for the 1996-97 season with a few new trails, including a two-mile upper loop for experts only. Snowshoeing is another big part of the equation at Elk River, with four designated trails that total six miles in length.

All six of the touring center's base trails are machine-groomed and marked by triangle blazes and ability. There's an even mix of beginner, intermediate, and advanced trails, which generally run at car's width. Novice skiers tend to occupy the flat meadow sections—the site of Elk's Nordic ski school—while considerably steeper trails are available for the true expert. *Minnie's Loop Trail*, named after the woman who previously ran the farm, has been expanded to include longer terrain and a few small climbs. *Gay Sharp Knob* is another well traveled run, located across from Scenic Highway, offering excellent ski touring and scenic vistas from its windy tip.

The 10 backcountry trails off Scenic Highway are fully marked by cross-country poles. Like Elk's base runs, these trails are evenly distributed between ability levels, but include a wider variety of terrain, including difficult singletrack sections, relatively flat jeep roads with picturesque views, and some challenging downhill runs. Many skiers park at Elk and warm up on its trails before roaming into the national forest area. Another option is to park at the beginning of Scenic Highway (Route 150) and hit the side trails that feed from that point. Forest trails, some of which are extremely long, are routinely groomed by Elk River when conditions permit. The forest service closes Scenic Highway at the hint of snowfall and usually doesn't plow the road, which leaves wide track available on the highway itself. Access without four-wheel-drive can be quite tricky, so exercise caution under such conditions.

At the end of Scenic Highway—about 23 miles from its starting point—lies the Cranberry Glades, which provides additional ski trails for the more advanced skier. Strong winters practically negate any vehicle's ability to get here, but those who dare can take Route 219 south to Highway 39 west, following to the Cranberry Glades.

Regrettably, those who like to mix up the alpine and Nordic style can't access Snowshoe Resort from any of these trails. For children, though, there's a sledding hill five minutes from Elk's lodge on a forest service road. No rentals are available, so just bring your sled and they'll show you the way.

Visitors to the Restaurant at Elk River will dine in a charming but casual atmosphere, with a selection of dishes such as fresh Elk River trout, sworfish specialties, and hearty steaks. Choose from locally brewed beers and fine wine to drink, and don't miss out on their delicious apple cranberry dessert, granola, and chocolate dressing—all of which is homemade.

Information

Trail Fees
- Weekdays $5
- Weekends $7
- * Free backcountry access

Guided Tours
- All-day or half-day tours available for intermediate to advanced skiers; $40–$90 fee includes transportation, equipment, and lunch (reservations required)
- Moonlight Madness Tours offered during full-moon periods with proper conditions ($25/person, includes rentals)

Instruction
- Private (cross-country/Telemark) $30/hour
- Group $15/person

Rentals
- 60 sets of touring skis: mostly Karhu and Trak
- 10 snowshoe rentals
- Adult $15/day
- Children $8/day

- 20 sets Telemark/backcountry rentals: $25-$30/day

Lodging/Dining
On-site
- **Five-room farmhouse** ($40/single, $45/double, $55/triple), 3 two-bedroom cabins, and a five-room inn, with private baths; outdoor hut tub available for guests, and full breakfast included at farmhouse and inn (rates from $40-$95)
- **Restaurant at Elk River** serves dinner from 5-9 p.m. nightly except Wednesdays; lunches on weekends when weather permits

Nearby
- **Slatyfork Farm Bed & Breakfast**, 2 miles north of Elk River, with 5 rooms, outdoor hot tub; (304) 572-3900
- **Seneca Trail Inn & Restaurant**, 6 miles from Elk River, with 12 rooms; (304) 572-2800
- * *See Snowshoe Mountain Resort, page 126,* for on-site lodging and nearby bed & breakfasts, cabins, chalets, and motels.

White Grass Ski Touring Center

36

White Grass Ski Touring Center
Route 1, Box 299
Davis, WV 26260

Information/Ski Report: (304) 866-4114
Local Lodging Information: 1-800-782-2775
Cross-Country Trail Conditions: 1-800-CALL-WVA

Operating Hours: 9 a.m.-dark daily
Elevation: 3,240-4,436 feet
Average Annual Snowfall: 150 inches

Getting There
- **From points north:** Take Route 79 south to Route 33 west. In Harman, take Route 32 north to

Canaan Valley. White Grass is located off Freeland Road (2 miles north of Canaan Valley State Park).
- **From points south:** Take I-77 north to Charleston and I-79 north to Weston. Then take Route 33 east to Harman and Route 32 to Canaan Valley, following signs for White Grass.
- **From Washington, DC:** Take I-495 to Route 66 west to Strasburg, following Route 55 west. In Harman, take Route 32 north to Canaan Valley, and follow signs to White Grass.
- **From Pittsburgh:** Take I-79 south past Clarksburg, then pick up Route 33/55 east past Elkins. Go north on Route 32 to Canaan Valley and follow signs for White Grass.

White Grass is one of the Mid-Atlantic's favorite cross-country destinations, and the hub of Nordic skiing in West Virginia. Located just a few miles from Timberline and Canaan Valley Ski Resorts, it lies on 1,800 acres of private land within the Cabin Mountain range of the Alleghenies. The touring center occupies the old lodge of the defunct Weiss Knob Ski Area—the South's first ski resort—whose heyday was during the 1960s. White Grass retains the same classic skiing flare of that genre, and was featured by *The Washington Post* as one of its Top Ten Nordic Ski Areas in the nation in 1994.

When strong northwesterly winds drop out of Canada over the Great Lakes, West Virginia's arctic Canaan Valley region benefits from large dumps of snowfall that stick around in its high elevations. The touring center is afforded ideal skiable conditions, with an average annual snowfall

of 150 inches. The best skiing is typically offered from January to early March.

A complete Nordic skier's haven, White Grass offers a full fleet of cross-country and Telemark rental equipment, expert PSIA-certified instruction, guided daytime and moonlight tours, special events and races, sleigh rides, a unique natural foods cafe, inn-to-inn skiing, and even a 1.3-mile beginner trail that's lit for night skiing and equipped with snow farming. Over 30 miles of well-marked terrain is available, half of which is machine groomed by White Grass. And unlike most Mid-Atlantic cross-country areas, trails are maintained entirely for Nordic skiing.

Guests can choose from 41 trails, most of which are under three miles, including nine beginner, 18 intermediate, and 14 advanced runs. Novice skiers occupy White Grass's on-site trails, but what attracts many advanced skinny skiers is the Nordic center's access to unlimited backcountry terrain in Monongahela National Forest land, Canaan and Blackwater Falls State Parks, and Dolly Sods Wilderness Areas. Guests can ski back and forth to Canaan Valley's downhill ski area and their Nordic trails via the *Springer Orchard* trail, as well as Timberline Resort, where skiers can traverse its alpine trails, via the *Timberline* trail. Access to rugged backcountry trails include the Dolly Sods Wilderness Area—part of the Monongahela National Forest.

Telemark skiing is also a staple here at White Grass, which provides designated glades. The touring center cleans out the glades, nipping trees and bushes to open the woods and to facilitate Telemarking.

White Grass trails feature a mix of wide and narrow track, depending on ability rating, with an alpine-like 1,196-foot vertical drop that begins at its 4,436-foot summit. *Double Trouble* trail will thrill the experts. It's a fast run offering over 600 feet of vertical on several steep drops and curves. The trail was cut on one of the access roads used by the former Weiss Knob Ski Area. The heavily traveled *Three Mile* trail is a novice's dream, with level, serpentine terrain that also winds to the 4,308-foot elevation of Bald Knob, offering scenic vistas of the surrounding valleys. It serves as the determination point for looping back or accessing more difficult trails.

Another White Grass specialty includes backcountry and Telemark adventures and lessons, with reduced group rates. Guided backcountry tours extend to the deeper snow and cooler conditions of its highest north-facing mountains, the lunar landscape of the Dolly Sods Wilderness, and Weiss Knob. Call the center for can't-miss full-moon tours, offered on select nights each season.

Counterculture is revisited at the funky Natural Foods Cafe, punctuated by its potbellied stove and earthy atmosphere. Even when the area is without snow, the cafe and lodge remain open for meals, videos, and reading. The menu features home-cooked lunches, baked goods, gourmet soups, and a selection of organic and fish cuisine. Dinners are by reservation only, accompanied by live acoustic music on weekends. An abundance of lodging can be found within miles of White Grass as well, including lodges, chalets, cabins, and houses at Timberline and Canaan Valley resorts, and numerous surrounding rental units and bed & breakfasts.

Information

Trail Fee
- Adult $7, junior $3

Rentals
- Weekday: adult $10, child $5
- Weekend/holiday: $15, $5
- Telemark rentals: $18 (adult only)

Instruction
- Group $10
- Mini-lesson $5
- Telemark $15

Calendar of Events

January
- Backcountry Telemark Slalom
- Snowshoe/Telemark workshops

February
- Nordic Track & Skate Clinics
- Mountain State 25 km (15-mile) Cross-country Ski Marathon

March
- West Virginia Telemark Race Series
- Womens Winter Weekends

Dining
White Grass Natural Foods Café serves lunches and Friday and Saturday night dinners (by reservation). Natural foods café complete with a unique coffeehouse atmosphere. Hearty home-made soups, chili, and baked goods complimented by herbal teas, spiced cider, and micro-brewery ales and lagers. Saturday evenings enjoy a specialty in international fare.
- Lunch: 11:30 a.m. – 4:00 p.m. daily
- Dinner: Saturday night: 6:00 p.m. – 8:00 p.m. reservations. (Groups of 10 or more may request dinners on other nights of the week.)

Nearby Lodging/Dining
See Canaan Valley Ski Resort, page 116, and Timberline Resort, page 135.

Canaan Valley State Park and Cross-Country Touring Center

37

Canaan Valley Resort State Park and Cross-Country Touring Center
Route 1, Box 330
Davis, WV 26260

Ski Report: 1-800-CALL-WVA

Information: 1-800-622-4121
Operating Hours: 9 a.m.-4 p.m. daily
Average Annual Snowfall: 150 inches

Getting There
See Canaan Valley Ski Resort, page 116.

This Allegheny Mountain state park lies in one of the highest valleys east of the Mississippi, in the heart of West Virginia snow country. Located just off the Canaan Valley Ski Area and a few miles from White Grass Touring Center, the 6,000-acre park has 18 miles of marked, generally ungroomed terrain, along with access to several trails surrounding the area. Skiing and snowshoeing are permitted on nine trails, ranging from one to three miles, while three narrow runs are reserved for hiking.

With some challenging climbs and descents and a long vertical drop, the 2.5-mile *Bald Knob* run offers access to the trail system at White Grass, and the 4,308 elevation at the Bald Knob summit reveals a 360-degree panoramic view of the valley. Skiers can enter the Knob, marked by green circles, from the downhill ski area summit chair lift or the parking lot. Canaan's remaining eight trails represent beginner to intermediate ability, including the *Loop* trail's gentle, one-mile trek through a meadow section that starts from the Nature Center/parking lot. The intermediate *Railroad Grade* trail, on an abandoned logging rail bed, winds along the base of Canaan Mountain on mixed terrain with several elevation changes. Northern hardwoods, including American beech trees, form the backdrop of the trail. Don't be surprised to catch a distant glimpse of bobcat, black bear, and other unique wildlife. Another option for the more experienced can be found on the *Canaan/Blackwater* trail, joining Canaan Valley and Blackwater Falls State Parks to form an eight-mile traverse across Canaan Mountain.

The park is well maintained by the state to preserve its natural resources. Its diverse landscape features northern bog, heath barren plants, and the country's second-largest inland wetland. Canaan doesn't charge a trail fee or groom its trail system, though the terrain is used often enough by skiers that snow is self-packed. Rentals, lessons, and a retail ski store are offered at the Ski Touring Center, inside the Nature Center Building near the park headquarters. Guided tours are also available.

■ Information

Rentals
$13/day, $11/half day

Instruction
• Private $30/hour
• Group $12/hour

Lodging/Dining
See Canaan Valley Ski Resort, *page 116.*

▮ State Parks and Forests: WEST VIRGINIA

38

Cathedral State Park

Cathedral State Park
Route 1, Box 370
Aurora, West Virginia 26705

Ski Report: 1-800-CALL-WVA
Information: (304) 735-3771

Elevation: 2,460-2,620 feet
Average Annual Snowfall: 100 inches

Getting There
• **From Baltimore/Washington:** Follow I-70 or I-270 to I-68 west, then take Route 220 south at Cumberland. Take Route 50 west to Aurora, and follow signs to Cathedral State Park.
• **From Pittsburgh:** Take I-79 south to Route 50 east to Aurora, and follow signs to the state park.
• **From West Virginia points south:** Take I-79 north to Route 50 east to Aurora, and follow signs to the state park.

Northeastern West Virginia's Cathedral State Park is a good option for novice Nordic skiers, but is better known for its pristine landscape. Registered by the Society of American Foresters, the 133-acre state park is a natural community unhindered by ax or saw. It's the only stand of mixed virgin timber left in West Virginia, and one of the last of the Appalachian Highlands region. The woods were preserved by local ownership until the state purchased the area, maintaining its mix of cherry, maple, beech, and birch hardwoods, as well as mountain laurel evergreens that are beautiful in winter. Ninety-foot-tall trees form cloisters in the park, with hemlock as the climax species.

An abundance of touring centers and state parks lie to its north and south, so Cathedral sees relatively few skiers. Five miles of terrain on six well-marked, ungroomed trails are available, providing opportune beginner skiing with easy road access from Route 50 in Preston County. All trails stem from the park entrance and lower parking lot, conveniently looping back to the same area. There aren't any steeps or climbs to suit advanced skiers, and the only degree of difficulty lies in some sections where the trails become narrow. Guests will encounter several rustic bridges crossing Rhine Creek, which winds through the park's property. *Cathedral Trail* follows the creek on both sides.

The area normally gets a lot of snow cover—enough to ski until the first of March most winters. Cathedral's primitive nature also means few amenities: no lodging, winter bathrooms, or even ice fishing, for that matter. There is, however, plenty of lodging and dining within a short drive, including accommodations and restaurants in nearby Oakland, Maryland, and West Virginia's Alpine Lake Resort and Blackwater Falls State Park.

Information

Nearby Lodging/Dining
Oakland, MD (12 miles away):
- **Oak & Apple Bed & Breakfast**; (301) 334-9265
- **Deer Park Inn Bed & Breakfast**; (301) 334-2308

- **Board Room Motel**, with restaurant; (301) 334-2126
* For more nearby lodging and dining information, see Alpine Lake Resort, *page 114, and* Maryland's Wisp Ski Resort, *page 109.*

In Addition: Canaan Valley—Winter Paradise of the Allegheny

In skiing terms, a "face plant" is any unplanned contact between your kisser and the snow below you. It is an effective technique in stopping especially when zipping along on cross-country skis. "There are better ways to do that, but that way will cool you down," says Matt Marcus as he swishes to a halt beside me.

I have arrived in Canaan Valley, much like discovering the last glacier of the Ice Age, alive and well in a high plateau near Davis, WV. This is snow country, "a bit of Canada gone astray," as it is promoted. If you like evergreen mountains, rivers that float through postcard-pretty valleys, and lots of snow, a visit here can overheat a body.

For the growing numbers of cross-country fans, Canaan Valley has provided a bastion of sport during winter months when nature is exceedingly stingy elsewhere. Lake effect snows spill into the lofty Allegheny plateau here, yielding over ten feet annually, more akin to Vermont-like weather.

Steep, winding roads separate Canaan from much of the world, and as a result, the valley has remained largely undeveloped. For cross-country skiers, the reward for this long, winding drive is a small, cozy resort called White Grass, nestled in an area of stunning wilderness. This is what New England must have been 30 years ago.

Cross-country is attracting a variety of people; Those interested in fitness sports, extending the hiking season, those who have become disillusioned with lift skiing, and those who simply enjoy the beauty and solitude of a snowscape.

In Canaan there are many miles of prepared ski trails criss-crossing through its four neighboring Nordic centers. Many tours begin atop either of the two downhill slopes, where the deeper snows hug the wind-shaped spruce. Cross-country showcases the wide, remote plains of the Dolly Sods after Jack Frost has done his painting here. Snow covers frozen bogs and stacks high on cranberry bushes, an untracked world seldom seen by others on the outside.

This canoe-shaped valley, highest east of the Dakotas at 3,200 feet, has more to recommend than skiing alone. The trout fishing is said to be spectacular. The cross-country trails become paths for hiking, horseback riding, mountain biking, and access to legendary whitewater runs in the warmer months of the year. Snow typically starts melting in April, but returns again in late November, to the delight of all those eager Mid-Atlantic skiers.

— *Chip Chase*

Blackwater Falls State Park

Blackwater Falls State Park

Drawer 490
Davis, WV 26260

Information: (304) 259-5216
Concession/Touring Center: (304) 259-5117
  (Blackwater Outdoor Center)
Ski Report: 1-800-CALL-WVA

Elevation: 3,100-3,300 feet
Average Annual Snowfall: 150 inches

- **From Baltimore/Washington:** Take I-270/I-70 to I-68 heading west, then follow Route 219 south to Route 32 south toward Davis. Follow signs for Blackwater Falls State Park onto Route 29 and the park entrance.
- **From Pittsburgh:** Take I-79 south into West Virginia, then pick up Route 50 east to Route 219 south and follow directions above.
- **From Charlottesville, Richmond, and Virginia Beach:** Take I-64 west into West Virginia, then pick up Route 219 north past Elkins, and follow signs to the state park.

Two miles north of the old logging town of Davis sits one of the state's most reliably maintained state-run ski touring centers at Blackwater Falls State Park. Its name derives from the river's 65-foot-high waterfalls that run out through an eight-mile gorge. The water's amber color is caused by leached tannic acids from hemlock, rhododendron, red spruce needles, and peat bogs. The canyon's south rim is home to the Blackwater Lodge, where views of the massive gorge combine with the waterfalls to provide ideal photo opportunities. As part of West Virginia's strongest snow region, favorable conditions allow continuous skiing that often lasts into March.

Blackwater offers 21 miles of marked hiking/skiing trails, nine miles of which are groomed, and connects with nearby Canaan Valley State Park on eight miles of the *Blackwater/ Canaan Trail* (*B/C*). To access the popular *B/C* from the state park, skiers can pick up the *Davis* trail, which follows into the dense woodlands of the Monongahela National Forest before becoming the *B/C*. It's a fairly long trek to Canaan, and part of the trip is fairly difficult. The first section is flat, then drops over a gradual 200 feet of vertical, with one steep downhill on the way to Canaan. Technically speaking, the *B/C Trail* is part of the 248-mile *Allegheny Trail*, which stretches from the southern end of the state all the way to Pennsylvania. A good bet for skiing the *B/C* trail is to check in at the park office around 10 a.m., which allows an average return time of 2-3 p.m. for the 16-mile round trip.

The small differences in elevation on the state park trails seem less than threatening, but advanced skiers should find enough to challenge them. Some of the terrain tumbles over old railroad tracks and skirts past canyons. Experts will enjoy the changing widths and pitches of *Elakayla* trail, as well as views of a waterfall and the Blackwater Canyon. Beginners tend to stick to either the wide-open picnic area or the *Red Spruce* trail—a wide, two-mile horse trail ideal for skiers practicing gliding and turning.

Blackwater is a year-round vacation retreat, keeping its Blackwater Lodge/Restaurant and numerous cabins open during winter. Nearby Bright Morning Bed & Breakfast—a restored boarding house fashioned in a Victorian mold—is another popular overnight destination for Blackwater visitors. Families can use the sledding and tobogganing hills adjacent to Blackwater's ski center, with a rope tow operating on weekends. The concession offers rentals, solid instruction, and free trail use.

Information

Rentals
- Classical touring skis:
- Weekend: $18/day
- Weekday: $15/day
- Ages 12 and under: $7.50/all times
- * Snowshoe rentals available (call touring center for rates)

Instruction
- Private $25/hour
- Group $10/hour

Lodging/Dining
On-site
- 54-room **Blackwater Lodge**, with private baths, reservations required
- 25 cabin units, one mile from lodge, with baths and fireplaces
- Restaurant overlooking the canyon, serving regional dishes, open year-round

Nearby
- **Bright Morning B&B,** Davis; (304) 259-5119
- * For a complete list of nearby lodging and dining information, *see Canaan Valley State Park, page 231.*

Babcock State Park

40

Babcock State Park
HC 35, Box 150
Clifftop, WV 25831

Information: (304) 438-3004
Cabin Reservations: (304) 438-3003

Elevation: 3,000 feet
Average Annual Snowfall: 85 inches

- **From Pittsburgh and northern West Virginia:** Take I-79 south to Route 19 south, then pick up Route 41 south and follow signs to Babcock State Park.
- **From points east in Virginia:** take I-81 south to I-64 west into West Virginia, then follow Route 60 north/west to Route 41 south to the park entrance.
- **From North Carolina:** Take I-77 north into West Virginia to Beckley, then pick up Route 41 north and follow signs to Babcock.

Babcock State Park in south central West Virginia has 4,127 acres replete with open meadows, mountain woodlands, waterfalls, trout streams, and boulder-strewn canyons. Located near the New River Gorge National River, where whitewater rafting rules the warm seasons, Babcock is less of a cross-country destination than the Monongahela National Forest's numerous touring centers and state parks to the east. Most of Babcock's 20 miles of trails are equipped for hiking only, though experienced skiers sometimes test its narrow, tumbling pathways when snowy conditions prevail. Not recommended for skiing, the *Island in the Sky* trail makes for an excellent quarter-mile winter hike over rocky, steep terrain, offering scenic views of Manns Creek Gorge from the 3,000-foot summit.

Skiers most often use wide park roads for easy gliding when a six-inch or more powder base blankets the area. Visitors also take advantage of the trail's short distances to capture several scenic points on film, including the Glade Creek Gristmill across from the parking lot, which is especially beautiful under fresh snowfall. Skiing in this neck of the woods is opportunity-driven, since the area doesn't receive or retain the same amount of snow usually found in the state's eastern snow-belt region.

Information

Nearby Lodging/Dining

- **Garvey Bed & Breakfast**, Winona, 9 miles from Babcock, with 5 rooms, private baths, scenic views, and a mountain pond; 1-800-767-3235
- **Historic Morris Harvey House**, 25 minutes south of Babcock in Fayetteville (Route 19):

Queen Ann Victorian home, circa 1902, near New River Gorge Bridge; (304) 574-1179
- **White Horse Bed & Breakfast**, Fayettesville, 18 rooms; (304) 574-1400

41

Pipestem Resort State Park

Pipestem Resort State Park

P.O. Box 150
Pipestem, West Virginia 25979

Ski Report: 1-800-CALL-WVA
Information: (304) 466-1800

Elevation: 1,500-3,000 feet
Average Annual Snowfall: 90 inches

Getting There

- **From I-77 in West Virginia and Ohio:** Take I-77 south to the Athens Road exit and follow signs for 14 miles to Pipestem Resort State Park.

- **From Pittsburgh and Morgantown:** Take I-79 south to Route 19 south, then pick up I-64/77 heading south. Take the Athens Road exit and follow signs to Pipestem.
- **From Washington:** Take I-66 west to I-81 south, then follow I-64 west into West Virginia. Take the Sandstone exit and follow 22 miles south on Route 20 to Pipestem.
- **From Richmond and Virginia Beach:** Take I-64 west into West Virginia and follow directions above.

Southern West Virginia's Pipestem Resort State Park has operated for 27 years as one of the state's most versatile year-round recreation areas. Its name is taken from the native pipestem bush (*spirea alba*). Centuries ago several Native American tribes used its hollow, woody stems to make clay and corncob pipes.

The park sits on a windswept plateau on the canyon rim of the Bluestone River Gorge, combining a diverse trail system with amazing landscapes and scenic vistas. Sixteen trails and a small fleet of Nordic rentals are available to skiers, most of whom prefer to traverse the golf course area. Just three inches of snow is needed to ski the course's primarily flat terrain, mixed in with some small dips and hills on the back side. Guests can also tour the color-blazed, ungroomed hiking/cross-country network, which features 11 trails under one mile long and five under three miles.

The majority of Pipestem's trails are ideal for novices and intermediates, most notably *County Line* trail—an exceptionally scenic two-mile run accessible from the Nature Center parking lot. It travels over a level-graded horseback trail before descending through a backdrop of hardwoods and hemlock. Rocky cliffs and a large waterfall can be viewed off Indian Branch, where skiers will encounter steeper and more rugged track on the way to the *River* trail. Another option for beginners is the Long Branch Lake area near McKeever Lodge, on *Den Tree* and *Law Hollow* trails. Pipestem also runs a sledding area near the amphitheater, offering rentals and a rope tow lift.

Two advanced trails should satisfy experts: 1.7-mile *Canyon Rim* boasts a 500-foot descent to Heritage Point and views of the Bluestone River Gorge. *Farley Ridge* trail, starting behind

Mountain Creek Lodge, is considered the network's most difficult run, with tight switchback turns, rocky climbs, and several steeps over nearly one mile of terrain. Its midway point is Raven Rock Overlook—a sandstone outcropping that affords visitors a peak of the 1,000-foot-deep Bluestone Canyon. The canyon is accessible only by aerial tramway (open from April to fall) at Mountain Creek Lodge.

Most of the state park's various facilities are closed for the winter, including the Mountain Creek Lodge at the base of Bluestone Canyon. McKeever Lodge and its Bluestone Dining Room operate year-round, as do numerous cottages and camp sites. Spring and summer seasons at Pipestem feature two lodges and restaurants, mountain biking, hiking, two golf courses, swimming pools, and an arboretum.

Information

Rentals
- Classical touring skis only
- $15/day
- $5/first hour, $2/each additional

Lodging/Dining
On-site
- **McKeever Lodge** (main lodge): 113 rooms and suites, the **Bluestone Dining Room**, indoor pool, game room, snack bar; rates from $46/single to $52/double, with group rates available
- 25 fully equipped cabins with fireplaces (call state park for rates)

Nearby
See New Winterplace Ski Resort, *Lodging and Dining*, page 125.

Watoga State Park/ Greenbrier River Trail

42

Watoga State Park/ Greenbrier River Trail

HC-82, Box 252
Marlinton, West Virginia 24954

Ski Report: 1-800-CALL-WVA
Information: (304) 799-4087

Elevation: 3,200-3,400 feet
Greenbrier Trail: 2,200 feet
Average Annual Snowfall: 65-75 inches

Getting There
- **From Virginia points east:** Take I-81 south to I-64 west into West Virginia, then follow Route 219 north toward Hillsboro. Turn right on Seebert Lane and follow through the town of Seebert. Parking is available after crossing the bridge at Greenbrier River in the state park.
- **From points south:** Take I-77 from North Carolina and southern Virginia to I-64 east in West Virginia, and follow directions above.

Seventeen miles south of Marlinton lies Watoga—West Virginia's first and largest state park, with over 10,000 acres of sprawling, high-altitude woodlands in Pocahontas County and the Monongahela National Forest. Watoga's name is derived from the Cherokee term "Watauga," or the "river of islands," referring to the Greenbrier River that borders the park. Cross-country skiing is available on 16 miles of marked, ungroomed hiking trails through Watoga's deep forests and around its 11-acre lake.

In addition to the trail system inside Watoga, the state maintains the 76-mile Greenbrier River Trail, with the park serving as its near-midway point. Greenbrier is an abandoned linear tract from the Chesapeake and Ohio Railroad, developed into a multi-use trail that skirts the park's boundary and extends almost as far north as Cass Scenic Railroad State Park (near Snowshoe Mountain Resort). The last three miles of the trail, following south toward Lewisburg, often close from flooding, but the remaining track is used for slow ski touring, with numerous access points along the way. The entire trail is as flat as a board, offering barely a one-percent grade. There is striking scenery on its path, though, as well as some tunnels and bridges. The trail requires a lot of snowfall, which typically falls heavier on its northward points. Skiers can access the Greenbrier River Trail by parking on either side of the river, directly before entering the state park. The trail link begins just in front of the river.

The state park doesn't offer a rental concession, but lodging is available in eight year-round, fully equipped cabins. The Greenbrier Trail is used for other recreation in warmer weather, including backpacking, bicycling, and horseback riding.

Information

Lodging/Dining
On-site
- 8 deluxe cabins, with fireplaces, kitchens, and baths; Call state parks for rates
* 25 standard cabins and two campgrounds closed from November to mid-April

Nearby
- **The Carriage House Bed & Breakfast**, Huntersville, 8 miles from Watoga on Route 39, with 5 rooms/private baths; (304) 799-6706

- **The Current Bed & Breakfast**, Hillsborough, 20 minutes from Watoga, with 4 rooms/3 baths, one suite with private bath, outdoor hot tub; (304) 653-4722
- **The River Place Restaurant**, Marlinton (15 miles); (304) 799-7233
- **The Frontier Restaurant**, Marlinton; (304) 799-4134

43

Coopers Rock State Forest

Coopers Rock State Forest
Route 1, Box 270
Bruceton Mills, WVA 26525

Information: (304) 594-1561

Elevation: 1,000-2,200 feet
Average Annual Snowfall: 90 inches

Getting There
- **From Washington/Baltimore:** Take I-70/I-270 to I-68 west. Then take the Coopers Rock exit and follow three miles to the state forest.
- **From Pittsburgh:** Take I-79 south to I-68 east and follow directions above.
- **From West Virginia points south:** Take I-79 north to I-68 and follow directions above.

The largest of West Virginia's state forests with over 12,700 acres, Coopers Rock is located on the state's northern end, 15 miles from Morgantown and West Virginia University. Scenic overlooks and unique rock formations form Coopers' setting, and over 50 miles of ungroomed hiking trails and additional state forest roads are suitable for Nordic skiing. Federal dollars used to be available to maintain cross-country trails at Coopers Rock and most state parks and forests, but when the funds ended, so too did the practice of track setting terrain with snowmobiles.

Unfortunately for Nordic enthusiasts, skiing at Coopers Rock has recently taken a back seat to mountain biking. If snowfall is deep enough, skiers usually have the trails all to themselves. But with a base of under six inches, mountain bikers arrive in droves to plow through the trails, turning the track into mush. For this reason, most skiers use wide, level state roads that surround the area and are closed to motor vehicles during snowfall.

Of Coopers' 50 miles of hiking/skiing terrain, three designated loop trails and two additional runs are available. The half-mile *Beginner's Loop* trail winds past ore pits and sassafras trees on an easy ascent and culminates along the road back to the parking lot. Starting at the first intersection of the beginner loop is the 2.2-mile *Intermediate* trail—an out-and-back run featuring streams, footbridges, a 200-foot climb, and a long, steep drop. The 5.2-mile *Advanced Loop* trail also begins from the outer parking area, following the *Intermediate* trail before reaching the historic Henry Clay Iron Furnace, which was used in the early 1800s to make various iron products. From this point, the narrow path runs steadily uphill, past power lines, and over a stream, before turning back to the parking lot. The 7.2-mile *Outer Ski* trail offers more challenging terrain, but it's seldomly skied because of its narrow width, arduous climbs, and sharp drops.

The Young Adult Conservation Corps cut Coopers' trails in 1974, marking them with blue squares and signposts. To access the trails, skiers should park in the outer lot near I-68 or on the roadsides prior to the state forest entrance, as the state forest gate also closes during winter.

Information

Nearby Lodging/Dining
- **Lakeview Resort at Cheat Lake**, 5 miles from Coopers Rock off I-68, with 187 guest rooms and a restaurant; 1-800-624-8300

Morgantown (15 miles away):
- **Applewood Bed & Breakfast**, with sauna, hot tub, fitness center; (304) 296-2607

- **Acacia House Bed & Breakfast**, with antique furnishings; (304) 367-1000
- **Comfort Inn**; 1-800-221-2222
- **Days Inn**; 1-800-325-2525
- **Ramada Inn/Lounge**; (304) 296-3431

In Addition: Snowshoeing Can Be Fun

An easier way to climb the mountains seeking recreation as well as fitness is with a trek on the all new snowshoes of today. High-tech materials and updated designs give great flotation, high performance, and ease of operation. You notice the smaller, more quiet things about nature, and everyone travels along at the same skill level.

It's a different experience than skiing. Many ski operators now offer snowshoe rentals, sales, special events, and even separate trail systems. Snowboarders are climbing the back bowls with the aid of lightweight snowshoes as well. Snowshoeing is a great way for the family to explore winter wonderlands, and it's now happening in record numbers in some of the world's oldest mountains within West Virginia.

— *Chip Chase*

CROSS-COUNTRY SKIING:
VIRGINIA

44. Shenandoah National Park
45. Mount Rogers National Recreation
Area
46. Grayson Highlands State Park
47. Hungry Mother State Park
48. New River Trail State Park

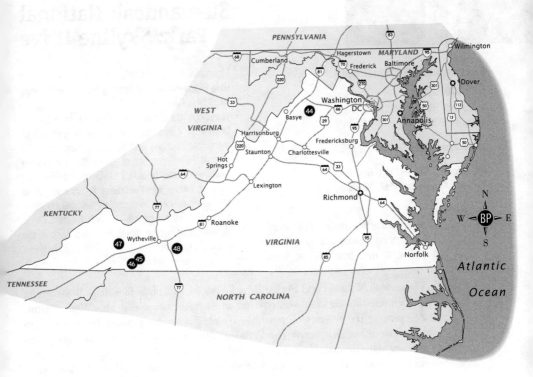

M ost of Virginia's 43 state parks have hiking or multi-use trails, but just a few parks average enough snowfall to allow ski touring opportunities on a fairly consistent basis. Though
remotely located for metropolitan Mid-Atlantic skiers, the southwest tip of Virginia hosts
some wildly scenic and rugged backcountry terrain at its 5,000-foot Allegheny Mountain
High Country elevations, including trail networks at Mount Rogers National Recreation
Area and several nearby state parks. Trails are completely ungroomed and unmaintained
for Nordic skiing, and snowfall is most heavily concentrated in the higher elevations, often getting a late start
and extending into March. Several days of skiing are typically allotted after heavy dumps, while smaller
amounts tend to blow off the crest zones. Skiers can also use all points along the Appalachian Trail—the
world's second-longest footpath—which connects with several of the Nordic skiing areas listed in this section. The region is somewhat of a well-kept secret among cross-country skiers, who have all trails free of
snowmobiles.

Old Dominion and Washington, DC-area residents can also strap on their skinny skis after a heavy snowfall and traverse the road shoulders of Shenandoah National Park's scenic Skyline Drive. In addition, the
105-mile stretch of Skyline Drive has over 15 hiking trails at different mileposts—many of which are quite
challenging and should be reserved for experts.

Regrettably, cabins and campsites are available only through December 2 and after March 1 each year, so
skiers planning trips usually settle for nearby towns with lodging. Marion, just off Interstate 81, is within
reasonable driving distance of Mount Rogers as well as each of the state parks mentioned below. This quaint
mountain town offers a few inns, motels, and restaurants.

Shenandoah National Park: Skyline Drive

Shenandoah National Park: Skyline Drive

3655 U.S. Highway 211 East
Luray, VA 22835

Information: (540) 999-3500/3283

Elevation: 1,900 feet to 3,500 feet
Average Annual Snowfall: 20-35 inches

Getting There

• Skyline Drive runs parallel to Interstate 81 in northwest Virginia, beginning at mile post 0 in Front Royal and ending at mile post 105 at Afton Mountain (Rockfish Gap), where it turns into the Blue Ridge Parkway, extending another 365 miles into North Carolina.

• Cross-country skiers can either get onto Skyline Drive after it has been plowed, or park at one of many intersections and access it from there. To park at the intersection of Route 211 and Skyline Drive near Luray, take I-81 to Route 211 east and park at either the Panorama Restaurant or at Shenandoah's entrance station. Another option— a little further south—is off Route 33 in Harrisonburg, where skiers can also park at the entrance station.

Shenandoah National Park's Skyline Drive follows the crest of the Blue Ridge Mountains for 105 miles, allowing cross-country skiers an enormous playground when Mother Nature cooperates. The low-snowfall region doesn't allow many opportunities, but Nordic skiers come out in droves after strong powder dumps. Operated by the U.S. Park Service and Department of the Interior, ski touring is available on unplowed sections of Skyline Drive and on marked, ungroomed connecting trails, most of which are suitable only for hikers and more accomplished cross-country enthusiasts.

The trick to actually skiing Skyline Drive is getting there. The park service closes sections (especially the northern half) when snowfall begins, re-opening it after it's been plowed. Skiers can park at specific mile posts if they can get onto Skyline Drive, but often have to settle for access from one of the many intersecting highways and roads. When a thick base blankets the region, most skiers use the shoulders of Skyline Drive, which carry heaps of powder stashes pushed onto the sides from the park's snow removal equipment. The road changes elevations slowly and almost unnoticeably, making for an easy excursion. Recreational skiers also tend to use the Big Meadows Area—a 12-acre flat-basin section located at milepost 50.

More daring Nordic tourists can venture off onto numerous hiking/cross-country trails in the park's North and Central Districts. All trails are marked by color blazes, including the Appalachian Trail (AT) that intersects and runs parallel to the park. Blue blazes represent hiking trails, yellow marks the park's horse trails and fire roads, and white indicates the AT. At least a foot of snowfall is required to ski the AT, which generally isn't recommended because of its narrow track and rugged terrain. A better bet is on the yellow-marked fire roads and their extra width and gentle pitches.

The North District holds largely beginner to intermediate terrain on five trails ranging from 1.5 to 5 miles, with additional track on two administrative roads and the Mount Marshall Trail. *Dickey Ridge* trail is an easy and accessible 1.3-mile jaunt beginning at the north entrance to Skyline Drive at milepost 0 (Front Royal). At milepost 10.4, skiers can park at Compton Gap on the east side of Skyline Drive—or at Indian Run Overlook (mile 10.8)—to traverse the *Compton Gap-Fort Windham Rocks* trail. Weather permitting, the novice 1.5-mile trip also affords views of the Virginia Piedmont and ice formations from the overlook's rock ledges. If Skyline Drive is closed, enter the park from the east off Route 610.

The more challenging Central District holds a mix of terrain for all levels, including several difficult climbs and exhilarating downhills. Expert-only *Whiteoak Fire Road* trail begins on the sharp curve at milepost 45. An easy first mile precedes a steep, 2,500-foot downhill run that culminates at a stream. Skiers should return via the same path, but can walk a short distance from the stream to the scenic Whiteoak Canyon Falls. A few other trails offer shorter, more leisurely terrain, while others access more difficult stretches of the AT off Skyline Drive.

For free trail maps and information, call the Byrd Visitor Center at (540) 999-3283, or visit them at milepost 51, where rangers will be glad to assist with any questions.

Mount Rogers National Recreation Area

45

Mount Roger National Recreation Area

Route 1, Box 303
Marion, VA 24354

Information: (540) 783-5196

Elevation: 4,450-5,729 feet
Average Annual Snowfall: 60-80 inches

Getting There

• *Virginia Highlands Horse Trail*: Take I-81 to Exit 35 (Chilhowie), then follow Route 762, which turns into Route 600. Stay on 600 until Konnarock and follow to Elk Garden parking area. Trail access is available from the parking lot, and the Appalachian Trail can also be reached within a short walk.

• *Virginia Creeper Trail*: Take I-81 to Exit 20 (the second of the three Abingdon Exits), then turn right off the ramp. Take the first road on the right and follow one-half mile to the parking area on the right. The parking area is just beyond the train tracks, with trail access available from there.

One of Virginia's best cross-country skiing circuits, Mount Rogers (Virginia's highest peak at 5,729 feet) lies in a remote region of southwest Virginia, inside the expansive Jefferson National Forest. Revered as the "Rooftop of Virginia," Mount Rogers National Recreation Area is run by the Forest Service of the U.S. Department of Agriculture, with over 140,000 acres of pristine woodlands that include huge wildfire balds and red spruce and fraser fir forests. The area borders Grayson Highlands, Virginia's highest state park and another focal point in the state's limited scheme of Nordic skiing.

Although inaccessible from any metropolitan centers, Mount Rogers offers the state's largest expanse of high-country wilderness skiing on its scenic, snow-filled crest zones, generally drawing a limited number of experienced visitors. A surprising amount of snowfall is concentrated at the higher elevations, where an abundance of trails are available. The terrain isn't terribly steep, but includes numerous skiable basin areas. The popular *Virginia Highlands Horse Trail* begins on a roadbed at Elk Garden Gap on Route 600, where ample parking is provided. Skiers have several choices on the trail's open meadows and woodlands, including access to the Appalachian Trail

(AT). The AT is the preferred ski route to Virginia's highest peak at Mount Rogers—the 5,729-foot elevation of Lewis Fork Wilderness. The *Virginia Highlands Trail* is broken into six sections over 67 miles and is marked by orange blazes and plastic diamonds. Most skiers are content with the two-mile trek to Deep Gap, which features a roadbed, downhill bowl run, and a culminating wooded ascent. More determined visitors can continue past Deep Gap, climbing steeply to the open meadows at Briar Ridge. (Turning around here marks a six-mile trip.) Continuing further, the trail leads to the balds of Wilbur Ridge and access to bordering Grayson Highlands State Park.

Over 400 miles of trail are available within Mount Rogers, including the 33-mile *Virginia Creeper Trail*—a multi-use path connecting Abingdon with the Virginia/North Carolina line. The trail began as a Native American footpath, later used by Daniel Boone and many European pioneers. The 15.9 miles of trail between Iron Bridge (mile 17.5) and the state line represents the Mount Rogers National Recreation Area of the Jefferson National Forest. Aside from a small stretch through Taylor's Valley, the property is open to the public for ski touring and hiking.

Skiers are advised to check in with the park office before hitting the trails. Track may be difficult to find in extreme wintry conditions, so bring extra copies of trail maps and a compass. The National Park Area prohibits snowmobiling on its trails.

Information

Nearby Lodging

- **Mount Rogers Inn**, Chilhowie (off I-81 and Route 16); (540) 646-8981
- **Best Western**, Marion; (540) 783-3193
- **Fox Hill Inn Bed & Breakfast**, Troutdale; 1-800-874-3313

Nearby Dining

- **Mountainside Restaurant at Mount Rogers Inn**, Chilhowie; (540) 646-3086
- **Happy's Restaurant**, Marion; (540) 783-5515

46

Grayson Highlands State Park

Grayson Highlands State Park

Route 2, Box 141
Mouth of Wilson, VA 24363

Information: (540) 579-7092

Elevation: 4,600-5,700 feet
Average Annual Snowfall: 60-80 inches

Getting There

Take I-81 to Exit 45 in Marion, then take Route 16 to Volney and follow west on Route 58. The entrance to Grayson Highlands is along Route 58. After paying the parking fee, drive to the Massie Gap parking area and obtain trail maps from the kiosk station.

L ocated near Virginia's highest point, Grayson Highlands State Park borders the southcentral end of Mount Rogers National Recreation Area. The park's landscape includes scenic waterfalls and spectacular mile-high peaks of surrounding open balds and woodlands. During winters, considerable amounts of snow grace the high elevations of the state park, providing many opportunities for cross-country skiing on eight marked, ungroomed trails that range in length from a half-mile to two miles. As is the case with nearby Mount Rogers, wind tends to blow a lot of the snow away, so expect a combination of skiing and walking in some areas. For this reason, snowshoes are a good bet for your backpack.

Novice and intermediate skiers have the benefit of short trail lengths and relatively moderate terrain over wide-open meadows and woodlands. Only a few steep sections exist on the trail system, but more advanced skiers have a few options beyond the state park. They can connect with rugged sections of the Appalachian Trail (AT) that lead to trails and roads inside Mount Rogers. The AT can be reached by following the *Rhododendron Trail* one-half mile from the Massie Gap parking area, though it's recommended for hiking only.

Few skiers actually make their way out to this isolated neck of the woods. Access, though, is one factor in its favor. For a nominal trail fee, skiers can drive paved roads all the way to Massie Gap, where trail access is available. Because of constantly changing conditions, do call ahead to the park office for trail updates and maps. It's often difficult to plan a trip here in light of the varying weather patterns, but skiers have been known to find snow lasting into late spring some years.

Information

Lodging/Dining
* See Mount Rogers National Recreation Area, page 243.

Hungry Mother State Park

47

Hungry Mother State Park
Route 5, Box 109
Marion, Virginia 24354

Information: (540) 783-3422

Elevation: 3,500 feet

Average Annual Snowfall: 35-45 inches

Getting There
Take I-81 to the town of Marion in southwest Virginia, and follow Route 16 north to Hungry Mother State Park.

The story of Hungry Mother dates back a few hundred years. After Native Americans raided and destroyed several settlements along the New River, two prisoners managed to escape their clutches—Molly Marley and her young child. Virginia legend holds that Molly collapsed in the surrounding wilderness after eating wild berries, leaving her small child wandering along a creek and muttering the words "hungry mother." A search party arrived at the foot of the mountain, only to find Molly passed away. Today the state park sits on Molly's Knob Mountain and includes the 108-acre Hungry Mother Lake, which was dammed from the storied creek when the park opened in the 1930s.

Situated between the Appalachian Trail and Mount Rogers, the 2,000-acre state park offers nine miles of marked, ungroomed woodland trails for hiking and Nordic skiing. Its trail system features a backdrop of oak, maple, pine, and hemlock trees inside the Brushy Mountain range. When conditions permit, the 2.7-mile *Lake Trail* serves as an easy loop for novice skiers. The trail has a level grade, as well as convenient parking at the trailhead. Beginners can also use asphalt pathways that network through the activities and recreation areas. The park's remaining six trails are short but fairly narrow, demanding a higher level of experience.

Cabins and bathhouses are available until December, but there's often not enough snowfall by that time to welcome skiers. The town of Marion is just two miles away from the park entrance, with several options for lodging and dining.

Information

Lodging/Dining
See Mount Rogers National Recreation Area, page 243.

New River Trail State Park

New River Trail State Park
Route 2, Box 126 F
Foster Falls, VA 24360

Information: (540) 699-6778

Elevation: 1,800-2,100 feet
Average Annual Snowfall: 30-50 inches

Getting There
The trail can be accessed from Ivanhoe, Fries, Galax, Draper, Pulaski, and Shot Tower State Park.

- **To reach the office headquarters and trailhead access at Foster Falls:** Take I-81 to I-77 south (or follow I-77 north from North Carolina), then take Exit 24 (Popler Camp), and follow signs to Foster Falls and New River Trail State Park.
- **To reach the northernmost entrance to the trail:** Take I-81 to Exit 94 north (Route 99) into downtown Pulaski. Then turn onto Xaloy Drive, and look for parking there.

Virginia's New River is the world's second-oldest river—surpassed in age only by the great Nile. It's also the rarest of rivers that flow from south to north. The state park gets better use out of the other seasons, but occasional strong Virginia winters allow leisurely cross-country skiing on its 54-mile linear pathway. The trail follows an abandoned railroad right-of-way and parallels the scenic New River for 39 miles. A three-mile stretch at mile 17-19 (Barren Springs at the Route 100 bridge) is closed and under development, but when the park is completed it should stretch to a total of 57 miles. The park winds through four different southwest Virginia counties: Carroll, Grayson, Pulaski, and Wythe.

Norfolk Southern Corporation donated the 57-mile tract to the state in 1986 to be maintained as a state park. Its cinder roadbed required little grading because of the prior rail track, and the park opened just one year later with four miles of completed trail, set mostly by volunteer groups. The trail features two long tunnels, three major bridges (Hiwassee, Ivanhoe, and Fries Junction), and roughly 30 smaller bridges and trestles. With enough snowfall at its 2,000-foot elevation, the trail is actively pursued by ski tourists, who have an easy four-percent grade and a width that averages 80 feet.

The park also links with Mount Rogers National Recreation Area, two Department of Game and Inland Fisheries boat launches, and Shot Tower State Historical Park, and borders Grayson Highlands and Clayton Lake State Parks.

The park's new administrative headquarters is at Foster Falls, and bathrooms are available at five or six points along the 57-mile track. Skiers can park and access the trail from six different points between Pulaski/Xaloy and Galax.

Information

Lodging/Dining
Restaurants and motels in the town of Galax, located at the intersection of Routes 58 and 89

57. Blue Ridge Parkway, NC
58. Great Smoky Mountains National Park
59. Pisgah National Forest
60. Mount Mitchell State Park

CROSS-COUNTRY SKIING:
NORTH CAROLINA

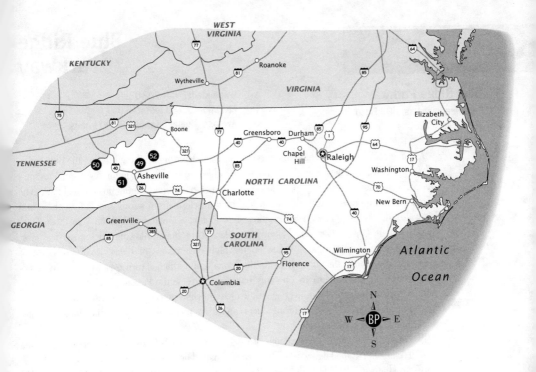

N ordic skiing opportunities do exist in North Carolina—but on an extremely limited basis. A select number of western Carolina state and national parks and forests serves cross-country ski tourists on hiking trails and roads. The region's towering, mile-high elevations afford fairly consistent snowfall, though conditions are often patchy—Wind tends to blow powder off skiers' paths, while sunlight exposure also does its damage. Skiers must therefore be opportunists. But even then, access to trails and roads can be quite difficult, as many park and forest roads either close down in winter or remain unplowed.

Like Virginia, North Carolina has no designated Nordic touring centers, and none of its downhill resorts offers on-site cross-country skiing. Most ski areas are, however, within a short commute of the parks and forests listed herein, including Roan Mountain State Park, which lies inside Pisgah National Forest. At Wolf Laurel Ski Area, a small network of roads and trails sits near it on Big Bald Mountain. And several ski shops in the town of Banner Elk, near Beech and Sugar Mountains, offer cross-country equipment rentals.

Cross-country skiers can also enjoy the wide roadways of the scenic Blue Ridge Parkway when snowfall permits. All points of the Parkway, from Carolina to Virginia, are open to skiers, but most snowfall is concentrated on the high altitudes of North Carolina's western mountainous regions. For this reason, Virginia sections of the Parkway are not listed in the book. Skyline Drive, which culminates at the northern end of the Parkway, is listed under Virginia's cross-country skiing section.

Blue Ridge Parkway

Blue Ridge Parkway

Park Headquarters: 400 BB&T Building
Asheville, NC 28801

Voice Mail: (704) 298-0398
Elevation: 2,780 feet to 6,047 feet
Average Annual Snowfall: 35-80 inches

An agency of the National Park Service and U.S. Department of the Interior, the Blue Ridge Parkway stretches 469 miles over the Southern Appalachian Mountains, from Virginia's Shenandoah National Park to North Carolina's Great Smoky Mountain National Park. The Parkway permits cross-country skiing when the road closes from strong snowfall, with several high-altitude access points on intersecting state highways, including Balsam Gap, Soco Gap, Mount Pisgah, Craggy Gardens, Mount Mitchell, and the Boone-Blowing Rock area. The most abundant snow, on average, is found on the higher elevations of Black Mountain, north of Asheville, and around the Boone-Blowing Rock and Mount Mitchell turn-offs. After a hefty snowfall, visitors can park their cars on state roads and traverse the Parkway's 20-foot-wide, easy-rolling roadway, which has an average grade of six to eight percent. For updates on road conditions during periods of snow, inquiring skiers can leave a message on Parkway headquarters voice mail and expect a returned call.

Two of the most widely used sections of the road are Balsam Gap—milepost 443.1 (40 miles west of Asheville) at the Highway 23/74 intersection, and nearby 5,200-foot Soco Gap—mile post 455.7, at Highway 19. Mile-high Mount Pisgah is accessible near the crossroads of Highways 215 and 276, Craggy Gardens and Mount Mitchell are near Highway 80, and Boone-Blowing Rock is near the Route 321 and 221 intersection. Parking isn't allowed by closed gates, so skiers have to park on state roads and walk to Parkway points they wish to ski.

Creation of the Blue Ridge Parkway stemmed from an idea brokered by President Roosevelt and members of his cabinet, who suggested that a scenic mountain route be built to connect the Shenandoah and Great Smoky Mountains National Park. Road construction began in 1935 in North Carolina, and in 1959, the National Association of Travel Organizations declared the Parkway "America's most scenic highway."

The Parkway is an extension of Virginia's Skyline Drive, beginning near Waynesboro at Rockfish Gap and the intersection of Interstate 64. The road contours the peaks of the Blue Ridge Mountains for 355 miles, skirting the southern end of the mammoth Black Mountains before winding down in the Great Smokies. More snowfall is concentrated in western North Carolina regions than in lower-lying Virginia locations. Elevations range from 649 feet at Virginia's Otter Creek to 6,047 feet at milepost 432, near North Carolina's Richland Balsam and the town of Waynesville. The Historic Appalachian Trail winds through the Parkway at several points as well.

Great Smoky Mountains National Park

50

Great Smoky Mountains National Park

107 Park Headquarters Road
Gatlinburg, Tennessee 37738

Information: (423) 436-1200

Elevation: 6,643 feet (peak altitude)
Average Annual Snowfall: 80 inches

Getting There

- **From Asheville and southern points:** Take Route 19 north into Cherokee, then follow Route 441 north toward Gatlinburg. From there, travel 17 miles to the Newfound Gap parking area.
- **From I-40:** Take I-40 to Exit 407 (Great Smoky Mountains, Gatlinburg exit), follow signs to the state park for 18 miles, then travel 15 miles from the park boundary to the Newfound Gap parking area.

Over 520,000 acres make up the massive Great Smoky Mountains National Park in North Carolina and Tennessee. The park headquarters is in Tennessee, but more than half of the park's acreage lies in North Carolina. And while Nordic skiing is allowed throughout the park, the best site is at the state border on Clingmans Dome Road, which is closed to vehicular traffic from December 1 to April 1 and remains unplowed during winter storms. Visitors can park at the intersection of the state line at Newfound Gap Overlook. In the right conditions, the road makes for excellent ski touring over gradual climbs and some steeper stretches. The altitude here is 5,400 feet, rising to 6,643 feet at the Clingmans Dome parking area and observation tower (the second-highest peak east of the Mississippi). The 1,200-foot vertical rise is spread out over seven miles, and skiers who make the gradual, uniform climb to Clingmans Dome can catch incredible views before skiing back down. Without an abundance of trees to break up views of North Carolina valleys, skiers can see the Snowbird Mountains and Fontana Lake—a 60-mile reservoir along the Tennessee River. The bordering state of Tennessee, however, isn't visible over top the ridges.

Snow conditions are tremendously varied here, but the highest elevations often get over 90 inches of powder during hardy winters. The road follows the southern edge of a ridge, with unshaded snow typically melting from exposure, then refreezing. Opportunistic skiers should therefore move quickly. Regrettably, lack of access takes away from the skiing equation. Guests need to have precise timing to ski here since Newfound Gap Road also closes in heavy snow. The environmentally conscious national park doesn't fill the roads with salt when plowing, and it's often a few days before the roads re-open. Unfortunately still, the best skiing usually exists when Route 441 is closed. The road is subject to short-term closures in heavy snow and ice, and there's no alternate route outside of Route 441.

Clingmans Dome Road sits off Newfound Gap Road—the main artery between Gatlinburg, Tennessee and Cherokee, North Carolina. The area can be reached from Highway 441, which leads to abundant parking on Newfound Gap Road at the state border intersection. Signs will direct you from there to Clingmans Dome.

51

Pisgah National Forest

Pisgah National Forest

Forest Headquarters:
U.S. Forest Service
P.O. Box 2750
Asheville, NC 28802

Information: (704) 257-4200/257-4202

Elevation: 6,285 feet
Average Annual Snowfall: 90 inches

Getting There

- **From I-40:** Take Route 221 north at Marion, then take Route 226 to Spruce Pine. Stay on 226 to Bakersville, then take Route 261 and follow signs for Carver's Gap and parking.
- **From Asheville:** Take Route 19 east to Spruce Pine, then follow Route 226 north to Bakersville. Turn right on Route 261 and follow signs to Carver's Gap and parking.

Like Great Smoky to the north, Pisgah National Forest permits ski touring throughout its Blue Ridge Mountain acreage. The destination of choice during optimal wintry conditions is Roan Mountain on the North Carolina/Tennessee border, roughly 20 miles southeast of Johnson City.

Closed roads off Carver's Gap make up the skiable terrain, with parking available at the gated road at the mountaintop. The towering elevation accounts for large doses of snowfall, though smaller dumps frequently blow away quickly, leaving patchy conditions. Stronger winters see blizzards that last well into March and April. When the snow falls in abundance, cross-country skiers and snowshoers head to Roan Mountain's 6,285-foot altitude to traverse park roads, trails, and open meadows and mountain balds surrounded by strands of spruce fir forest. The roads are mostly level but can get pretty steep and winding in some areas, particularly in the open mountain balds that lie immediately north of Carver's Gap, providing truly opportune Nordic skiing. One thing skiers should look out for is freezing rain and road ice, which can also make access quite difficult by car.

Experienced skiers can also head off on the Appalachian Trail's rugged hiking terrain that winds through the national forest, connecting at one point close to the parking area at Carver's Gap.

52

Mount Mitchell State Park

Mount Mitchell State Park

Route 5, Box 700
Burnsville, NC 28714

Information: (704) 675-4611
E-mail: jsharpe@yancey.main.nc.us

Elevation: 6,684 feet
Average Annual Snowfall: 90 inches

Getting There

The only road access is via the Blue Ridge Parkway. Follow the Parkway to milepost 355 and signs to Mount Mitchell State Park. Skiers can take Route 80 from Burnsville or Marion, then head south on this frequently plowed section of the Blue Ridge Parkway to Mount Mitchell. The state park is approximately one hour from Asheville, Burnsville, Marion and Spruce Pine.

Mount Mitchell's 6,684-foot summit crest lies on Black Mountain—the highest point east of the Mississippi River. Trails are available during strong snowfall for cross-country skiers, who may feel the mist of low-lying clouds at the park's lofty elevation. Mount Mitchell's altitude also affords striking, mile-high views of surrounding ridges and valleys. The park borders Pisgah National Forest, with many connecting trails. The *Commissary Shelter* trail is the primary ski run. It's an old railroad bed, requiring deep snow, and offers a steady grade with very little change in elevation. Surrounding park roads usually get plowed, so they're not a good option for ski touring. The observation tower at the east coast's highest peak can be reached via the *Mount Mitchell, Camp Alice,* or *Old Mount Mitchell* trails, but they're not equipped for skiing. Many points of the trails are only 18 inches wide, demanding a hike to get to the observation tower.

The area averages nearly 100 inches of snowfall per year, but is plagued by frequent rains that melt powder within days. Another problem stifling ski opportunities at Mount Mitchell is road access. The only means of getting there is on the Blue Ridge Parkway, which quickly closes—specifically from Asheville and northern points—if it's snowing badly or major ice sets in. The state does plow the Parkway from Mount Mitchell to Route 80, and drivers can usually make it there via the Parkway, which is typically accessible within two to three days of major snowfall for administrative access and ski tourists. Call the park office for updated skiable conditions and to find out which sections of the Parkway are open to driving.

APPENDIX

GLOSSARY OF TERMS

GLOSSARY OF RESORT STATISTICS:

Base Elevation: The altitude, in feet, of a ski resort's lowest-lying (base) area.

Summit Elevation: A resort's highest skiable point, in elevation.

Vertical Drop: A measure of the drop in feet from a ski area's highest point to its base, or summit elevation minus base elevation.

Longest Run: The longest, continuous trail on a ski area's network, measured in feet or miles.

Primary Slope Direction: The bearing of a resort's mountain, facing either north, south, east, or west. North-facing slopes hold snowfall longer, while southern-facing mountains leave trails exposed to sunlight.

Skiable Terrain: The acreage of land available for skiing.

Average Annual Snowfall: A statistic based on a mountain's 10-year, average per-season snowfall.

Snowmaking: The percentage of slopes and trails a ski area equips with manmade snow.

Skier Visits: The number of lift tickets sold at a ski area during a given year. Some resorts keep skier visit counts private.

Skiable Days: The number of days, per season, open for skiing at a resort.

Slopes and Trails: A total count of individual runs offered at a ski area. Slopes and trails are broken down by the number of beginner, intermediate, and advanced runs available.

Night Skiing: The percentage of slopes and trails equipped with lights.

Lifts: The number of chairs or surface tows available for uphill transport. Lifts are broken down by number and type, including quads, triples, doubles, handle bar tows, or rope tows.

Uphill Capacity: The number of skiers a resort's combined lifts can transport per hour.

GLOSSARY OF SKI TERMS:

Alpine: The term used to define a downhill ski area.

Après-ski: post-skiing entertainment, including dining, drinking, and clubbing.

Backcountry skiing: A term most often used to describe cross-country, or Nordic, skiing on ungroomed terrain, usually outside a ski area's boundaries.

Big air: A snowboarding term used by freestylers for flight off a jump or obstacle.

Binding: A device used to fasten feet to skis and snowboards.

Black diamond: An advanced or expert trail, relative to a ski area's other slopes.

Bowl: A term used to describe any wide-open, basin-shaped run at a ski area.

Bump run: Technically known as a mogul run, bumps are formed when terrain is left ungroomed, leaving mounds of snow shaped by continuous turning made in the same spot.

Bunny slope: A gentle, low-grade slope used by beginner skiers and a resort's ski school.

Carve: A term used to describe the correct method of making and finishing a turn.

Cat track: A flat, fairly narrow connector slope (also known as a traverse) between trails or mountains, often marketed as trails by resorts to boost total run counts.

Corduroy: A term used to describe snow texture furnished by fresh grooming of trails.

Corn snow: Loose granules of machine-made snow, shaped like corn kernels.

Cruiser: A smooth, groomed slope or trail, unlike mogul or bump runs.

Diagonal stride: A cross-country skiing term describing the classic kick and glide technique, in which skiers kick with one ski and pole, using the opposite pole for propulsion.

Freestyle: A skiing and snowboarding term, but more often used for boarders, in which aerial maneuvers are performed.

Fun box: A snowboard obstacle, sometimes known as a mailbox, made of different types of objects. Boarders can jump, stall, or slide on the object.

Gap jump: A large snowboard obstacle, constructed of snow, with a space in the middle over which boarders can catch varying degrees of air time. Some ski areas are beginning to shy away from building gap jumps, as not-ready-for-prime-time snowboarders sometimes injure themselves jumping or landing.

Glade skiing: A trail in which skiers can wind through stands of trees, as opposed to a wide-open slope.

Goofy-foot: A term indicating a right-foot-forward stance on a snowboard.

Granular snow: Powder granules identified as hard (near-frozen), loose, or wet.

Grooming: A ski area's practice of using equipment—usually snowcats—to smoothen trail surfaces.

Halfpipe: A concave, cylindrical, snow-filled ditch with hard-packed walls, fashioned like skateboard ramps, that snowboarders use to perform aerial maneuvers. Halfpipes are generally several hundred feet long, over 20 feet wide, and more than 10 feet deep (depending on snowfall).

Hit: Another term for a snowboard obstacle; Any snow mound or object used by boarders to jump, slide, or grind.

Mono-ski: A single, wide ski featuring two bindings that face forward.

Mogul: See "bump run."

NASTAR: Short for National Standardized Racing, NASTAR is an event run at ski areas to simulate slalom racing around a series of gates. Skiers and snowboarders use NASTAR to compare their timed runs with a national standard and other downhillers during the day's events.

Nordic: A Scandinavian-based term for cross-country skiing or touring.

Out-of-bounds skiing (also known as off-piste): Skiing beyond a ski area's designated boundaries on ungroomed, uncut terrain—to be performed by experts only, at their own risk.

Packed snow: Loose powder compressed by grooming machines or skier traffic.

Poma lift: A surface tow lift that uses a disk attached to a cable, to transport skiers.

Quarterpipe: Similar to a snowboarding halfpipe, but with only one sidewall.

Rail slide: A snowboard tabletop with a flat, steel rail on which boarders slide. Rail slides can be found in a variety of places, including snowboard parks, halfpipes, or quarterpipes.

Regular-foot: A term indicating a left-foot-forward stance on a snowboard.

Rope tow: The first form of uphill transport employed by ski areas, still in use today. Skiers are pulled up the mountain via a continuous loop of moving rope.

Serpentine: An adjective used to describe a trail that twists and undulates, shaped somewhat like a snake.

Shred: A snowboarding term equivalent to "carving."

Skating: A variation of cross-country in which skiers move by pushing off at an angle; Skating skis are usually shorter than classic Nordic skis.

Skinny skiers/skaters: Another term for Nordic skiers, based on cross-country's thin equipment.

Slalom: Competitive racing around a series of gates; Giant slalom requires extreme precision around more narrowly placed gates.

Snow base: The depth of snow on a ski area's track, not including freshly fallen powder.

Snowboard Park: Also known as a terrain park, a tract of downhill terrain with built-in obstacles or hits (made of either snow or objects) that snowboarders use to catch air, ride, slide, or perform maneuvers.

Snowcat: A vehicle used by ski areas to spread man-made snow over slopes and trails.

Snow gun: Equipment used by ski areas to produce man-made snow. Snow guns spray atomized water that falls and freezes on slopes and trails.

Snowmaking: Machine-made snow crystals produced by snow guns in the absence of natural snowfall.

Spine: A snowboard park obstacle in which two quarterpipe-like snow mounds meet. Snowboarders grind on the top, middle section or rail—known as the spine.

Surface lift: Means of uphill transport in which skiers are pulled on the snow itself. Surface lifts include poma, rope tow, or T-bar.

Switchback: Terrain that turns at an angle, requiring a quick carve by skiers.

Tabletop: A snowboard park obstacle with a launch ramp, a flat area in the middle, and a landing ramp. Boarders work the level middle section.

T-bar: A surface tow lift that uses a pole with a crossbar attached to a moving cable, for uphill transport.

Telemark: An early form of skiing, the Telemark ski has a detachable heel for uphill climbing, while its sturdy frame allows skiers to carve turns downhill.

Yard Sale: The unfortunate event of crashing, whereby skis and poles are left littered on the slopes.

SKI AND SNOWBOARD ORGANIZATIONS

NASTAR
National Standard Races—amateur races for skiers and snowboarders at participating resorts (P.O. Box 4850, Aspen, Colorado 81611).

PSIA
Professional Ski Instructors of America—professional organization that sanctions teaching and certification programs for skiing and snowboarding (133 South Van Gordon, Suite 240, Lakewood, Colorado 80228).

CCSAA
Cross Country Ski Areas Association—professional trade association dedicated to promoting cross-country skiing in North America. Membership includes publications, annual conferences, marketing/industry trends, and discounts on equipment and apparel.

MID-ATLANTIC SKI CLUBS

PENNSYLVANIA

Western Pennsylvania Ski Council
(13 ski clubs representing northwest, southwest, and central
Pennsylvania and northwestern
Maryland)
Internet:http://www.merlink.
org/organize/wpsc/index.htm

Steel on Ice Ski Club
P.O. Box 99652
Pittsburgh, PA 15233

Flying Dutchmen Ski Club
Box 14233
Reading, PA 19612
Hotline: (610) 370-2760
Internet: http://www.fdsc.org/presi-
dent.html
E-mail: publicity@fdsc.org OR
trips@fdsc.org

Snowmasters Ski Club
P.O. Box 3625
Harrisburg, PA 17105-3625

Shenango Valley Ski Club
P.O. Box 945
Sharon, PA 16146
Internet:http://www.merlink.
org/organize/wpsc/svsc.htm

Alphorn Ski Association
P.O. Box 356
Lahaska, PA 18931

Blazers Ski Club
(Philadelphia chapter of the
National Brotherhood of Skiers,
Inc.)
P.O. Box 13052
Philadelphia, PA 19104
Hotline: (215) 829-8100
Internet: http://www.nbs.org
/clubs/blazers.html
E-mail: thompso7@mailgate.navss-
es.navy.mil

Black Diamond Ski Club
1000 Market Street
Ste. 41-230
Bloomsburg, PA 17815

Philadelphia Handicapped Ski Club
4318 Spruce Street
Philadelphia, PA 19115

New Hope Nordics
P.O. Box 52688
Philadelphia, PA 19115

King of Prussia Ski Club
P.O. Box 60146
King of Prussia, PA 19406
Hotline: (610) 26-KOPSC

Philadelphia Ski Club
1325 O'Reilly Drive
Festerville, PA 19053

Main Line Ski Club
9245 Eagle View Drive
Lafayette Hill, PA 19444

Brandywine Valley Ski Association
113 W. Chestnut Street
West Chester, PA 19380

Bucks Ridge Ski Club
P.O. Box 179
Bala Cynwyd, PA 19004

Bucks County Ski Club
P.O. Box 763
Doylestown, PA 18901

Bucks Mount Ski Club
P.O. Box 424
Levittown, PA 19058-0424
Hotline: (215) 364-4790

NADC Ski Club
675 E. State Road #1610
Warminster, PA 18974

Lancaster Ski Club
E-mail:
clohr@marauder.millersv.edu

DELAWARE

Wilmington Ski Club
P.O. Box 1331
Wilmington, DE 19899

Dewey Beach Ski Club
306 Euclid Avenue
Wilmington, DE 19809

DuPont Ski Association
38 Yorktown Road
New Castle, DE 19720

MARYLAND

Columbia Ski Club
P.O. Box 204
Columbia, MD 21045
Hotline: (410) 730-SNOW
Internet:
http://www.cen.com/ski/
E-mail: ksall@cen.com

Baltimore Ski Club
Hotline: (410) 825-7669

Frederick Ski Club
P.O. Box 3226
Frederick, MD 21705

Harford Ski Club, Inc.
(Harford County)
Internet: http://pages.prodigy.
com/skiing/harford.htm
E-mail: Meckelnburg@prodigy.net

Southern Maryland Ski Club
P.O. Box 1044
Waldorf, MD 20604
E-mail: cbms@erols.com

WASHINGTON, DC
(including metro-area Maryland and Virginia)

Pentagon Ski Club
Hotline: (301) 587-2073
E-mail: peter_porton@hq.dla.mil
OR porton.psc@worldnet.att.net

Capitol Ski Club
P.O. Box 50441
Washington, DC 20091
E-mail: afuller@gpo.gov

Flash Ski Club
P.O. Box 46539
Washington, DC 20050-6539

Ski Club of Washington, DC
Hotline: (703) 532-7776

Black Ski Club, Inc.
Hotline: (301) 231-3900

Fagowees Ski Club (pronounced "Fugauweez")
Hotline: (301) 441-8585

VIRGINIA

Virginia Ski Club
(headquartered in Richmond, includes entire state)
Hotline: (804) 262-3275
E-mail: bada@erols.com

Richmond Black Diamond
P.O. Box 25913
Richmond, VA 23260

Roanoke Ski Club
P.O. Box 371
Roanoke, VA 24003
E-mail: wkelley@internetmci.com

Ski Breeze of Hampton Road
P.O. Box 12190
Norfolk, VA 23502

WEST VIRGINIA

Kanawha Ski Club
P.O. Box 1775
Charleston, WV
Hotline: (304) 346-4427
Internet:
http://www.newwave.net/~pamela/
E-mail: mnmjones@aol.com

NORTH CAROLINA

Carolina Ski Trek Association
P.O. Box 2424
Chapel Hill, NC 27525-3271

Raleigh Ski and Outing Club
E-mail: rscott@eos.ncsu.edu

Greensboro Ski & Outing Club
E-mail: lscott@nr.infi.net

Triad Diamond Ski Club
P.O. Box 24217
Winston-Salem, NC 27104-4217
E-mail: mellis5364@aol.com

Winston-Salem Ski & Outing Club
Internet: http://www.ols.net/~rummy/index.htm

A

A&A Realty,   113
Acacia House Bed & Breakfast, 239
Adaptive Skier Program,   6
AJ's Fireplace family restaurant,103
Ale House (Ye Old), 79
Allegheny National Forest,   218, 219
Allegheny River Reservoir,   221
Allen's Eatery,   79
Allentown Comfort Suites,   35
Allentown Hilton,   34
Almost Heaven,   125
Alphorn Ski Association,   258
Alpine Lake Resort Nordic Center, WV,   227
Alpine Lake Resort, WV,   114-116
Alpine Mountain Ski Area, PA, 16-20
Alpine Resorts,   4
Alpine Village,   113
Alpine Village,   19
Alter Ego Sports,   119
Amelia's Restaurant/Yeager's Bar at the
   Windwood-Fly Inn,   121
American Teaching System,   5
Antlers' Inn,   70
Appalachian Highlands,   232
Appalachian Resort Inn,   125
Appalachian Ski Mountain, NC,   171-173
Appalachian State University,   183
Appalachian Trail,   185
Appalachian Trail,   154, 241, 250, 252
Applewood Bed & Breakfast,   239
Aprés-ski,   6
Ararat Lodge,   47
Arcaro & Genell's,   56
Archers Mountain Inn,   164
Auntie Pasta's Ristorante,   134

B

Babcock State Park, WV   235-236
Badland's Barbecue, 219
Bailey's Steakhouse, 39
Bally Hotel,   43
Balsam Gap,   250

Baltimore Ski Club, 258
Banana Belt, 1, 15
Banner Elk Café, 164
Banner Elk, NC 163,165
Banner Elk/Beech Mountain Rentals, 164
Barley Creek Brewery/Restaurant, 19
Barley Creek Brewing Co., 39
Barley's Brew Pub, 188
Barn House Village, 34
Bavarian Room restaurant, 113
Bayberry Inn B&B, 51
BC's Family Restaurant, 79
Beaver Lake Seafood & Steak Restaurant,
Beckley, 125
Bed & Breakfast of Valley Forge, 100
Beech Alpen Inn, 164
Beech Alpen Restaurant, 164
Beech Haus Restaurant, 164
Beech Mountain Chalet Rentals, 164
Beech Mountain Realty and Rentals, 164
Beech Mountain Ski Resort, NC, 160-164
Beech Tree Restaurant & Pub, 164
Beechwood Realty, Inc., 164
Beford's Covered Bridge Inn B&B, 30
Belle Hearth B&B, 157
Bert Brothers Family Restaurant, 79
Bert's Steakhouse & Restaurant, 35
Betty's Restaurant, 96
Big Bass Lake, 56, 195
Big Boulder/Jack Frost Mountains, PA, 20-26
Birchwood Resort, 195
Black Bear Resort/Condos, 121
Black Diamond Ski Club, 258
Black Ski Club, Inc., 259
Blackberry Inn B&B, 70
Blackwater Falls State Park, WV, 234-235
Blackwater Lodge Restaurant/Lounge, 122
Blackwater Lodge, 234
Blackwater/Canaan trail, 120
Blazers Ski Club, 258
Blowing Rock, 169
Blowing Rock, NC, 171
Blue Heron Grille, 26
Blue Knob slopeside condominiums, 30
Blue Knob State Park, 212, 209-210
Blue Knob, PA, 26-31
Blue Marsh, PA, 86-88

Blue Mountain, PA, 31-35
Blue Ridge Parkway, NC, 250
Blue Ridge Terrace, 157
Blue Stone Inn & Restaurant, 149
Blueberry Mountain Inn, 194
Bluestone Dining Room, 237
Bluestone River Gorge, 236
Boalsburg, 104
Board Room Motel, 225, 233
Body and Soul Cafe, 121
Boone-Blowing Rock, NC, 250
Boston Beanery Restaurant & Tavern, 149
Boyce Park, PA, 88-90
Brandi's, 134
Brandywine Valley Ski Association, 258
Breezee Hill Farm, 83
Brewmeister's B&B, 202
Brickhouse Inn B&B, 75
Brigham, Thomas, Dr., 127
Bright Morning Bed & Breakfast,121, 234, 235
Britannia Country Inn, 39, 194
Broad Street Inn, 157
Brookview Manor B&B Inn, 19, 194
Brush Hollow Cross-Country Ski/Hiking Area,
    PA, 220
Bryce Four Seasons Resort, VA, 142-
    145
Bryn Mawr Conference Center & Mountain
    Retreat, 194
Buchanan State Forest, 214
Buchanan's Beech Mountain Rentals, 164
Buckeye Tavern, 43
Bucks County Ski Club, 258
Bucks Mount Ski Club, 258
Bucks Ridge Ski Club, 258
Budget Motel, 19
Buffalo Run B&B, 134
Burkey's Restaurant, 88

C

Cab Frye's Motel, 43
Cabin Creekwood, 157
Cabin Mountain, 117
Caesars Brookdale, 195
Caesars Cove Haven, 194

Caesars Paradise Stream,   194, 39
Caesars Pocono Palace,   194
Cafe Fratelli,   52
Cahoots Eating & Drinking Emporium,   188
Caledonia State Park, PA,   213
Calendar of Events,   6
Callender's WindyAcre Farms, PA,   203
Cambridge Family Restaurant, 96
Camelback, PA,   35-39
Cameltop,   39
Camp 4 condominiums,   133
Camp SpearsEljabar/YMCA, PA,   207
Canaan Realty,   121
Canaan Valley Resort State Park,   120
Canaan Valley Resort, WV,   116-122
Canaan Valley State Park and Cross-Country
     Touring Center, WV,   231-232
Canaan Valley State Park, WV, 234
Canaan Valley, WV, 230, 233
Canyon Motel,   97
Capitol Ski Club,   259
Cappuccinos Ristorante,   19
Carmel Cove Inn B&B,   113
Carmel Cove Inn,   225
Carolina Ski Trek Association, 259
Carousel B&B,   47
Carriage House B&B,   134
Carriage House Bed & Breakfast,   238
Carroll Valley Resort Hotel   75
Cascades,   1
Cashtown Inn,   75
Cass Inn,   134
Cass Scenic Railroad State Park,   238
Cataloochee Ranch,   176
Cataloochee Ski Area, NC,   174-177
Cathedral State Park, WV,   232-233
Catoctin Mountains,   226
Cellar Nightclub,   26
Central Asia,   2
Chapman Dam State Park,   221
Charnita Ski Area,   71
Checkerberry Cabin,   157
Cheney's Gallery and Craft Shop,   201
Chet's,   47
China Buffet,   19
Christmas Chalet,   113
Christmas Shop,   120

Chuck Barfoot,   3
Ciro's Pizza,   157
Clarion River Valley,   218
Classy Sassy's,   19
Clayton Lake State Parks,   246
Clingmans Dome,   251
Clock Tower Restaurant,   52
Close Quarters Restaurant,   26
Cloverleaf Motel, Allentown,   43
Clubhouse, The   31
Coach Stop Inn,   70
Coleman's Basye Bistro,   145
Columbia Ski Club, 258
Comedy Cellar, The, 134
Comfort Inn,   34, 39, 125
Comfort Inn, Allentown,   43
Comfort Suites, Allentown,   43
Comfy Camping Cabins,   134
Connection Nightclub, The,   134
Construction,   250
Cook Forest State Park, PA,   218
Cooke Tavern B&B,   202
Cooper's Vantage Restaurant & Pub,   157
Coopers Rock State Forest, WV 238-239
Copper Kettle Lounge,   145
Copper Mine, The,   157
Corbett Inn,   219
Cornish Manor Victorian restaurant,   113
Country Cabins,   125
Country Café,   152
Country Inn Bed & Breakfast, The,   113,
     225
Country Kitchen Restaurant,   113
Country Surrey Inn, 194
Countryside Cottages,   39
Countryside Housekeeping Cottages,   194
Covered Bridge Inn, 35
Cowans Gap State Park, PA,   214
Craggy Gardens,   250
Cranberry Glades,   228
Crestmont Inn, The, 200
Critters Restaurant, 103
Cross-country ski touring centers,   7
Cross-Country Skiing,   2
Crystal Lake Ski Center, PA,   204-205
Cunningham Falls State Park, MD,   226
Current Bed & Breakfast, The, 238

D

Dane Anthony's Restaurant,   31
Daniels Top-O-The-Poconos Resort,   195
Day Care, 6
Days Inn, 34, 157
Dead End Snowboard Park,   167
Deep Creek Lake,   109, 226
Deer Park Inn Bed & Breakfast, 225, 233
Deerfield Village Resort and Restaurant,   121
Delaware Canal State Park, PA, 215-216
Delaware Water Gap National Recreation Area,
    25, 65
Denton Hill State Park,   67
Devil's Arena,   111
Dewey Beach Ski Club,   258
Dining,   6
Dobbin House,   75
Doe Mountain Ski Area, PA,   40-43
Dogwood Ridge B&B,   125
Dolly Sods Wilderness Area,   120
Dolly Sods Wilderness Areas,   230
Dominick's New York Style Italian Pizzeria,
    113
Double W Ranch B&B,   194
Dough Company, The,   56
Downs, David,   135
Duffy's Boalsburg Tavern,   105
Dulaney's Steak & Seafood,   157
DuPont Ski Association,   258

E

E-2000 Bar/Lounge,   26
Eagle Rock Lodge & Rentals,   194
Eagles Nest,   120
Eaglesmere Inn, The,   200
Eastern ice,   2
Easy Bumps Saloon, 66
Edinboro Ski Association, Inc., 95
Ehrhardt's Lakeside Restaurant,   103
Elk Mountain Ski Area, PA,   43-47
Elk River Inn B&B, 134
Elk River Restaurant,   134

Elk River Touring Center, WV,   228-229
Elk State Forest, PA, 217
Elk Valley Cross-CountryTouring Center, PA,
    207-208, 228
Encounter's Lounge, 149
Endless Mountains,   200
Era Realty & Rentals,   169
Erehwon Cabins,   134
Evergreen Lodge,   70
Evergreen Park at Penn Hills Resort, PA, 196

F

Fagowees Ski Club,   259
Faircroft Bed & Breakfast,   220
Fairmount B&B,   202
Famoore's Family Restaurant, 219
Fanucci's,   39
Fareways Restaurant & Lounge,   149
Farmhouse B&B, Mt. Pocono, 39
Farnsworth House B&B/Restaurant,   75
Fernwood Resort & Country Club,   195
Fireline Inn,   35
Flash Ski Club,   259
Flora Villa Bed & Breakfast, The,   200
Flying Dutchmen Ski Club,   258
Foggy Goggle,   61
Foot of the Mountain Restaurant,   84
Forbes State Forest,   197, 210-211,
    212
Four Seasons Dining Room, The,   113
Four Seasons Inn,
Fox Hill Inn Bed & Breakfast, 244
Fox Run Inn,   83
Fox's Pizza Den,   84
French Manor, The, 194
French's Diner,   134
Front Porch, The, 122
Frontier Restaurant, The,   238

G

Gabello's Pizza,   56
Gap jumps,   4
Garden Terrace Restaurant/Lounge,   157

Garish, John   2, 21
Garvey Bed & Breakfast,   236
Gary's Place Restaurant & Tavern,   97
Gas Light Village,   201
Gathering, The,   113
Gettysburg Hotel/Restaurant,   75
Gettysburg,   74
Gifford Pinchot State Park, PA,   214-215
Ginther's B&B,   202
Giuseppe's Italian Restaurant,   149
Glaciers Pub,   52
Glade Springs Resort,   125
Glade Springs,   125
Glades Pike Inn B&B,   51
Glass House Bar/Lounge,   26
Glen Lodge,   39
Globe Inn, East Greenville,   43
Godfather's Pizza,   134
Golden Anchor & Portside Pub, 121
Golden Trout restaurant,   93
Goode, Thomas, Dr.,   150
Goodtime Bobby's,   134
Gouldsboro State Parks,   201
Grass skiing,   144
Grassy Hill B&B,   34
Grayson Highlands State Park, VA,   244-245
Great Lakes,   1
Great Smoky Mountains National Park, NC,   251
Great Smoky Mountains,   159
Green Mountains,   1
Greenbrier River Trail,   237
Greenbrier State Park, MD,   226
Greensboro Ski & Outing Club,   259
Gristmill, The,   157
Guest Quarters,   100
Gulf Coast,   1
Gunpowder Falls State Park, MD,   227
Gunpowder River Valley,   227

Hampton Inn, Allentown,   43
Hanley'sHappy Hill, PA,   199-200
Happy's Restaurant,   244
Harford Ski Club, Inc.,   258
Harley Farm B&B,   113
Harmony Lakeshore Inn,   194
Harper's Old Country Store,   120
Harrisonburg, VA,   145
Hawksnest Golf & Ski Resort, NC,   181-184
He Hill at Bryce,   145
Hearthside Restaurant,   52
Herdic House Restaurant,   205
Herr Tavern B&B/Restaurant, The,   75
Herrington Manor State Park, MD,   225-226
Herzwoods and Northwoods,   139
Hibernia,   157
Hickory Hollow Farm B&B,   30
Hickory Lick's Restaurant and Bar,   66
Hidden Valley Resort, PA   48-52
HiddenValley, PA,   197-198
High Country Realty,   169, 184
Highlands at Sugar,   169
Hill House B&B,   121
Hill Motor Lodge,   39
Hillside Lodge & Resort,   195
Hillside Lodge,   19
Hillside Lodge,   66
Historic Hinton Manor B&B,   125
Historic Morris Harvey House,   236
Hojo Inn,   39
Holiday Glen,   194
Holiday Glen,   39
Holiday Inn Express,   157
Holiday Inn,   39
Holiday Inn, Allentown,   43
Hoot's Pub,   134
Hoss's Steak & Sea House,   219
Howard Johnsons Plaza Hotel,   19
Hunan House Chinese Restaurant,   35
Hungry Mother Lake,   245
Hungry Mother State Park, VA, 245-246

H

I

Halfpipes,   4
Hampton Inn,   34

Inglenook Gift & Craft Shop,   113
Inn 287,   97

Inn at Afton, The,   157
Inn at Franklin, The, 219
Inn at Georgian Place, The,   51
Inn at Jim Thorpe B&B, The,   34
Inn at Maple Grove, 43
Inn at Meadowbrook, The,   194
Inn at Snowshoe, The,   133
Inn at Tannersville, The,   39
International Sled Dog Racing Association, 51
Intrawest Corporation,   127
Iris Inn B&B, The,   157
Italiano Delite,   43

J

Jake Burton,   3
James Buchanan Pub & Restaurant,   84
James Madison University,   146
Jefferson Drive-in, 88
Jefferson Inn/B&B, 203
Jefferson National Forest,   244
Jerico B&B,   134
JG's Pub, 113
Jocko's Restaurant/Pizzeria,   88
Joe's Italian Supper Club & Lounge,   122
JR's Greenscene Restaurant,   66

K

Kaltenbach's B&B,   70
Kanawha Ski Club, 259
Kane Manor Country Inn/Bed & Breakfast, The,
    220
Kane Motel,   220
Kane View Motel,   220
Kaufman House,   100
KD Sports, Inc.,   165
Keley's Inn The Poconos,   103
Kelley's Inn, Gouldsboro,   56
Keystone State Park,   212
Keystone Winter Games Winter Sports Festival,
    55
King of Prussia Ski Club,   258
Knights Inn, Bartonsville,   39
Kooser State Park,   197, 211

L

Lackawanna State Forest, PA,   216
Lake Breeze Motel,   113
Lake Harmony Lodge Sports Bar Cafe,   26
Lake Point Inn B&B,   113
Lake Point Inn Bed & Breakfast,   225
Lakeside Motor Court,   113
Lakeside Resort, Greentown,   103
Lakeview Lodge B&B,   34
Lakeview Resort at Cheat Lake,   239
Lamberton House Bed & Breakfast, The,   219
Lancaster Ski Club,   258
Landis Store Bed & Breakfast,   43
Last Run Lounge,   169
Laurel Grove Inn & Resort,   19
Laurel Highlands Region,   212
Laurel Highlands River Tours, 212
Laurel Highlands,   15
Laurel Hill State Park,   212
Laurel Mill Cross-Country Ski/Hiking Area, PA,
    219-220
Laurel Mountain Inn,   52
Laurel Mountain,   2, 15, 98
Laurel Ridge State Park, PA,   212
Laurel Ridge,   7
Laurelwood Inn,   70
Le French Cafe,   113
Lee's Japanese Restaurant,   39
Lewis Fork Wilderness,   244
Lift Tickets,   5
Lobster Trap, The, 56
Locher, Horst,   142
Lodge at Chalk Hill, The,   212
Lodge at Newton Lake,   47
Lodge in Eaglesmere, The,   200
Lodging, 6
Log Cabin Barbecue,   149
Luray Caverns,   149
Lush Victorian B&B, The,   70

M

M.E. Ingalls,   150
Maggie Valley Resort & Country Club,   176

Maggie Valley, 176
Mahoning Court Motel, 35
Main Line Ski Club, 258
Manning House Inn, 164
Manns Creek Gorge, 235
Mansion House, 84
Maplewood Inn B&B, 75
Marco Polo's Restaurant & Lounge, 39
Martinville Streamside Cottages, 19
Marvelous Muggs Restaurant & Pub, 56
Massanutten Intergalactic Race of Champions (MIROC), 147
Massanutten Resort, VA, 145-149
Massanutten Tour Company, The, 149
Massanutten Village, 146
Mattox, William, 153
McClive's Lakeside Restaurant & Lounge, 113
McHenry Highland Festival, 112
McKeever Lodge, 237
McMullen House Bed & Breakfast, 219
Meadow Mountain Ski Rental, 224
Meadowlark Motel, 176
Mellon family, 98
Memorytown B&B, 39
Memorytown, 194
Mercersburg Inn (& Restaurant), The, 83
Metcalfe's B&B, 83
Meyer House B&B, 121
Michigan, 15
Mimi's Streamside Café, 66
MINIrider, 5
Monongahela National Forest, 1, 108, 230, 228
Montage Mountain, PA, 52-56
Montwood Motor Inn, 121
Moore's Mountain Inn B&B, 79
Mosch's Tavern & Country Inn, 70
Mother Tucker's, 47
Mount Airy Lodge, 195
Mount Mitchell, NC, 252-253, 250
Mount Pisgah, 250
Mount Rogers Inn, 244
Mount Rogers National Recreation Area, VA, 241, 243-244
Mount Tone, PA, 90-92
Mount Toxaway Restaurant, 179
Mountain Aire Lodge, 121
Mountain House, The, 125

Mountain Laurel Resort & Golf Club, The, 195
Mountain Mama's, 125
Mountain Manor Inn & Golf Club, 194
Mountain Manor Inn, 39
Mountain Manor Inn, 66
Mountain Momma Pizzeria, 145
Mountain Springs Lake Resort, 194
Mountain Top Rentals, 121
Mountain View at Edinboro, PA, 94-96
Mountain View Motel, 47
Mountain View Restaurant/Lounge, 47
Mountainside Restaurant at Mount Rogers Inn, 244
Mt. Davis, 27
Mulligan's Pub, 157
Myron's Restaurant at Ramada Inn, 52
Mystic Mountain, PA, 92-94

N

NADC Ski Club, 258
Nakiska Chalets, 134
NASTAR, 6
National Trails Motel, 212
Nemacolin Woodlands Resort, 93
Nethercott Inn/B&B, 203
Nethercott Inn/Bed & Breakfast, The, 199
New Germany State Park, MD, 224-225
New Hope Nordics, 258
New Market, 149
New River Gorge National River, 235
New River Trail State Park, VA, 246-247
New Winterplace Ski Resort, WV, 122-125
New York, 15
Newfound Gap Overlook, 251
Nick's Restaurant & Pub, 164
Nittany Lion Inn, 105
Nordic, 2
North Carolina, 159
North Country National Scenic Trail, 218
North Woods Ski Touring Area, 210
Northern Alleghenies, 221
Northern Russia, 2
Northpoint, 121
Northridge Condominiums, 39
Norway, 2

O

Oak & Apple Bed & Breakfast, 225
Oak & Apple Bed & Breakfast, 233
Oakland's Grand Central Station,   113
Ohiopyle State Park, PA,   212
Oil Creek State Park, PA,   218-219
Old 22 Inn,   88
Old Appleford Inn,   75
Old Spruce Realty,   134
Olde Millside Inn,   43
Oliveri's Crystal Lake Hotel,   47
Oliveri's,   47
Orazzi's Blue Ridge Inn,   47
Original Italian Pizza, The,   70
Oriskany Inn Restaurant/Lounge,   122
Other Winter Sports,   6
Overlook Village,   134

P

Papa Joe's Raw Bar & Grill,   134
Paradise Cafe,   134
Paramount Motel,   19
Patapsco Valley State Park, MD,   226
Pegasus B&B,   194
Peggy's Diner,   31
Penguins, 125
Penn Estates Resort Community,   195
Penn Estates Resort, 19
Penn Hills Resort,   19
Penn Hills Resort,   194
Penn Skiers Motel,   19
Penn State's University Park,   104
Penn Wells Hotel,   70
Penn's Wood Motel & Cottages, 195
Penn-Wells Hotel,   97
Pennsylvania State University,   202
Pentagon Ski Club,   259
Philadelphia Handicapped Ski Club,   258
Philadelphia Ski Club,   258
Pine Knob Inn,   19
Pine Log Motel & Cabin Run,   70
Pink Floyd,   118

Pinnacle Inn Resort,   164
Pipe Dragon,   37
Pipestem Resort State Park, WV,   236-237
Pisgah National Forest, NC,   252
Pittsburgh,   15
Pizzeria Uno,   113
Plymouth Tavern,   208
Pocono Blues Festival,   26
Pocono Gardens Lodge,   194
Pocono Manor Inn & Golf Resort,   195
Pocono Mountain,   15
Pocono,   194
Poconos,   15
Poet's Walk B&B, The,   70
Ponda-Rowland Inn (B&B) at Rowland Farm,
   56
Post House Bed & Breakfast, The,   220
Potato City Motor Inn,   70
Pour Victoria B&B,   121
Powder Monkey,   133
Powderidge,   133
Prince Gallitzin State Park,   212
Princeton, 125
Professional Ski Instructors of America,   5
Promised Land,   201
Pryor's Cafeteria,   157

Q

Quarterpipes,   4
Quehanna Wild Area,   217

R

Racing,   6
Raleigh Ski and Outing Club,   259
Ramada Inn, Clarks Summit,   47
Ramps,   4
Ranch House Family Restaurant,   31
Rascals Bar-B-Que & Pub,   164
Raspberry House B&B,   96
Raspberry House Bed & Breakfast,   208
Reazley Hotel,   220
Red Lion Inn,   43
Red Run Lodge B&B,   113

Rederick Ski Club, 258
Redwood Lodge B&B, 157
Reflections Night Club, 19
Reighard House Bed & Breakfast, The, 205
Restaurant at Elk River, 229
Restaurant Vienna, 179
Ribs & More, 39
Richard's Country Inn, 134
Richmond Black Diamond, 259
Ridgeview Chalet Rentals, 164
River Place Restaurant, The, 238
Riverside Inn, 208
Riverside Inn, 96
Roan Mountain State Park, 249
Roan Mountain, 252
Roanoke Ski Club, 259
Roaring Run Natural Area, 210
Rockies, 1
Rolling Rock Brewery, 98
Romano's Pizzeria, 39
Rooster Ridge Bed & Breakfast, 208
Royal Oaks, 157
Ruby, J.W., 114

S

Salvatore's Pizzeria, 43
Sandy Beach Motel 195
Sapphire Valley Ski Area, NC, 177-179
Savage River Inn Bed & Breakfast, 225
Savage River Reservoir, 226
Savage River State Forest, 224
Sawmill Restaurant at Best Western, The, 122
Scaly Mountain, NC, 179-180
Scandinavia, 2
Scotto's Italian Restaurant, 157
Seneca Caverns, 120
Seneca Point Overlook, 218
Seneca Rocks-Spruce Knob National Recreation Area, 120
Seneca State Forest, 134
Seneca Trail Inn & Restaurant, 229
Seneca Trail Inn, 134
Sepp Kober, 150
Seven Devils, 181

Seven Springs Mountain Resort, PA, 57-61
Shady Lane Bed & Breakfast, 200
Shamrock, 133
Shannon Inn & Pub, 39
Shannon Inn, 66
Shawnee Inn, 66
Shawnee Mountain, PA, 62-66
Shawnee Valley, 66
Shawnee Village & Valley View, 66
Shenandoah National Park: Skyline Drive, VA, 242-243
Shenango Valley Ski Club, 258
Shenanigan's of Lake Harmony, 26
Shenanigans Lounge, 113
Sheraton Inn Jetport, 34, 43
Sherman Poppen, 3
Sherwood Motel, 97
Shot Tower State Historical Park, 246
Siberia, 2
Sierra Nevada mountains, 2
Sierras, 1
Silver Creek Lodge Condominiums, 134
Silver Lake Inn, 79
Silver Tree Inn, The, 113
Sirianni's Cafe, 122
Sizerville State Park, 217
Ski Barn, The, 119
Ski Breeze of Hampton Road, 259
Ski Club of Washington, DC, 259
Ski Denton, PA, 66-70
Ski Fest, 3
Ski Hawksnest, (see Hawksnest Golf & Ski Resort)
Ski Liberty Tavern/Restaurant, 75
Ski Liberty, PA, 71-75
Ski Roundtop, PA, 75-79
Ski Sawmill, PA, 96-97
Ski School, 5
Ski Windham, 71
SKIwee, 5
Skyline Drive, 242
Skytop Lodge, PA, 206
Slatyfork Farm Bed & Breakfast, 229
Slatyfork Farm, 134
Sleep Inn, 125
Slides, 4
Slopeside Lucio's Restaurant, 145

Smith's Restaurant,   56
Smoke Hole,   120
Smoketree Lodge & Restaurant,164
Smokey Shadows Lodge,   176
Smuggler's Cove,   39
Sneads Tavern,   152
Snow Ridge Village,   25
Snowboarding,   3
Snowcrest Village,   133
Snowdrift Lounge,   125
Snowmasters Ski Club,   258
Snowshoe Lounge,   52
Snowshoe Mountain Resort, WV,   126-134
Snowshoeing,   239
Snurfer,   3
Snyder House Victorian B&B,   205
Snyder House Victorian Bed & Breakfast,   205
Soco Gap,   250
Somerset Country Inn,   51
Sonestown Hotel,   200
Southern Maryland Ski Club,   259
Spencer House Bed & Breakfast,   208
Spines,   4
Splatter paintball,   25
Split Rock Resort & Conference Center,   195
Spring Mountain, PA,   99-100
Spruce Lodge,   133
Squires Table Restaurant,   152
Station Inn B&B, Cresson,   30
Steel on Ice Ski Club,   258
Steiger House, The,   83
Stemwinder,   133
Sterling Inn, PA,   201
Stewart Smith Memorial Sugar Cup,   168
Stone Bridge Inn/Restaurant,   47
Stone House Bed & Breakfast,   212
Stone Valley Recreation Area, PA,   202
Stony Court at Bryce Resort,   145
Stratton Mountain,   3
Strickland's Mountain Inn,   194
Stroudsmoor Country Inn,   194
Sugar Bear Ski School,   167
Sugar Mountain Resort, NC,   165-169
Sullivan's Pub & Eatery,   208
Summit Condominiums,   134
Summit Resort, The, 194
Sun Valley,   2

Sunbowl Complex,   39
Sundown Hutches,   133
Susque Homestead & Chalet,   70
Suzanne & Company,   157
Suzie's Chic Inn Restaurant,   134
Swallow Falls State Park,   225
Sweden Valley Inn,   70

T

Tabletops,   4
Tahoe Lodge,   61
Tamiment Resort & Conference Center,   195
Tanglwood Ski Area, 101
Tanglwood, PA,   101-103
Tannery B&B, The,   75
Tar Heel, 159
Taylor's Pub at Colony Village, 19
Telemark Skiing   3
Terra Alta Touring Center,   115
The Homestead Dining Room,   152
The Homestead Hotel,   152
The Homestead Ski Area, VA,   150-152
The Inn at Starlight Lake Touring Center, PA,
   198-199
The Pub, 75
The Red Fox   134
The Red Oak Lounge,   134
Timber Hill Ski Area,   16
Timberhaus Cafeteria,   139
Timberlake Rentals, 113
Timberline Four Seasons Resort, WV   135-139
Timberline Lodge,   133
Timbers Pub,   139
Tobyhanna State Park,   201
Tom & Jerry's,   56
Tom Sims,   3
Tony's Pizzeria,   35
Top of the World,   134
Topton House Restaurant,   43
Treetop, 133
Triad Diamond Ski Club,   259
Trillium House B&B, 157
Tucker Country Inn, 121
Tussey Mountain Ski Area, PA, 103-105

U

UCI/Grundig Mountain Bike Downhill World Cup
   Circuit, 149

V

Vasarelys Fine Dining Restaurant,
Victoria Inns/Jad's Place dining,   56
View Haus,   164
Village Court Motel & Cottages, 19
Village Eating House, The,   105
Village Inn Restaurant,   31
Village Inn,   121
Village Inn, The,   149
Villages, The,   25
Virginia Creeper Trail,   243
Virginia Highlands Horse Trail, 243
Virginia Ski Club,   259

W

Wabasso, 134
Wales,   4
Walker, Thomas, Dr.,   150
Warrington Farm B&B,   79
Water Gap Trolley, 25
Waterfront Seafood & Steakhouse, The,   208
Watoga State Park/Greenbrier River Trail, WV,
   237-238
Wayside Colony Saloon,   19
Webb, Del   146
Weiss Knob Ski Area,   108
Weiss Knob Ski Area,   230
West Virginia Department of Tourism,   223
West Virginia University,   238
Western Pennsylvania Ski Council,   258
Westgate Inn,   70
Westline Cross-Country Ski/Hiking Area, PA,
   221
WHFS Ski Festival, 74
Whistlepunk Condominiums,   134
Whistlepunk Inn,   133

White Grass Natural Foods Café, 231, 121
White Grass Ski Touring Center, WV,   229-231
White Horse Bed & Breakfast,   236
White Oak B&B,   121
Whitetail, PA,   79-84
Wilderness Recreations,   16
Will O'the Wisp,   109
Willow Run Housekeeping Cottages,   194
Wilmington Ski Club,   258
Wilson World Hotel, 88
Windborne Farm B&B, The,   75
Windsor Inn, The,   47
Windswept Farm B&B,   202
Windwood-Fly Inn, 121
Winston-Salem Ski & Outing Club,   259
Wintergarden Lounge,   47
Wintergreen Resort, VA,   153-157
Winterhaven Condos, 125
Wisp Ski Resort, MD,   109-113
Wolf Laurel Inn, 188
Wolf Laurel Ski Area, NC,   185-188
Woodlands Inn & Resort,   56
Woodloch PinesResort, Inc.,   195

Y

Yodeler's Pub,   134
Yokum's Vacationland,   121
Youghiogheny River Gorge,   212

ABOUT THE AUTHOR

John Phillips, a 1992 graduate of the University of Delaware with a degree in English, is currently the Public Relations Director for a nonprofit association in the Washington, DC area. John also serves as author and series editor for Beachway Press' *Winter Sports Guidebook Series*™. In his spare time, he is a frequent guest at snowboard parks and halfpipes throughout the Mid-Atlantic.